MW01295267

The GM's Handbook

Marketing, Promotions & Business Principles Set in the Fun World of Minor League Baseball

Edited By
Troy Kirby
Chris LaReau

Kirby Publishing, LLC
Lacey, WA 98503

ISBN 978-1-947863-00-2 (Paperback Form)

ISBN 978-1-947863-01-9 (E-Book Form)

Library of Congress Control Number 2018907324

The Official MiLB logo is trademark and copyright of MiLB, including those of every MiLB affiliated team logo and photograph, were provided to the publisher with the expressed written permission by MiLB.

Edited by Troy Kirby and Chris LaReau.

Front cover image & book design by Troy Kirby.

All graphs, charts, tables, illustrations, contributions, strategies and concepts listed in this book are copyright of Troy Kirby.

Printed and bound in the United States of America.

First printing July 2018.

Published by Kirby Publishing, LLC

Lacey, WA 98503

Visit www.gmshandbook.com for more information.

Editors' Note:

No book collection of this size is formed without the help of several people working together toward the common goal of getting it conceived, produced, and published. This means hours, days, weeks, months, and years of thankless e-mails, phone calls, time away from family, friends and their own livelihoods at their actual jobs to drive this initiative forward until its final completion.

Each of the contributors to this text got the concept without having anything more than trust in the editors and, as Jenna Byrnes phrases it "batshit passion" toward getting the job done. Doing so means putting aside egos or personal gain, resisting the urge to give up because something needs to be added or clarified in a chapter when you've put way too much time in it already while in-season with your day job.

The point of this passage is to recognize the valued effort and time taken away from things that actually make everyone listed below an income, instead focusing on how to better the industry as a whole by developing a collection of personal perspectives for the improved acumen of the reader. It has been mentioned by several of the chapter contributors, as well as sample readers, that this effort has never been achieved before, which means that truly remarkable people had to come forth to be a part of something greater than themselves, for not only the good of the industry, but each with a shared vision of how to make the industry better for the future as a whole.

In no particular order, these are the people who helped get this vision off of the ground and toward the formation of a solid text that hopefully will help readers understand, engage and grow for the art of revenue generation at the minor league baseball level: Michael Abramson, Chris Asa, Jason Behenna, Mike Birling, Kyle Bostwick, Kathy Burrows, Jenna Byrnes, Greg Coleman, Brent Conkel, David Crawford, John Dittrich, Jeff Eiseman, Derek Franks, Joe Hudson, Chris LaReau, David Lorenz, Josh Olerud, D. Scott Poley, Augusto Rojas, C. Ryan Shelton, Brad Taylor, and Amy Venuto.

Table of Contents

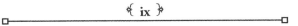

Table of Contents

Table of Contents

Table of Contents

There is nothing minor about the business of Minor League Baseball (MiLB).

Over 44 million fans are welcomed into the ballparks of 160 affiliated MiLB franchises annually, generating close to $850 million dollars in revenue.

Discovering Your Baseball "Why"

Jenna Byrnes
Senior Vice President
Oklahoma City Dodgers
Pacific Coast League, Triple-A Baseball

About The Author

Jenna Byrnes has served as Senior Vice President of the Oklahoma City Dodgers since September 2010, managing a team of 20 focused on ticket packages, group events, hospitality sales and direct mail campaigns. During her tenure with the Dodgers, attendance has increased by 24 percent, leading the franchise with five consecutive years of attendance growth, one of two Triple-A teams to achieve this mark in ticketing metrics. Byrnes was recognized as the 2013 Pacific Coast League Female Executive of the Year. Prior to her arrival in Oklahoma City, Byrnes served as Senior Director of Ticket Sales for the Frisco RoughRiders, which led Double-A baseball in attendance during each of her seven seasons with the franchise.

"The person who knows 'how' will always have a job. The person who knows 'why' will always be his boss."
- **Diane Ravitch**[1]

"I want to get into management"

Such a short, simple phrase that seems innocent enough. It is often the answer a recent college graduate gives me when I ask about their professional goals. But management is not a word with only one meaning. It should unleash a multitude of thoughts and feelings on anyone who dares to venture down the path. The gravity of the responsibility that comes with managing others is greater than most anything else in business.

It is not just getting to make all the decisions and getting to do whatever you want, or telling others to do whatever you want. In order to be a successful manager, you absolutely have to shift your priorities to focusing on the best interest of the organization, then your team, then yourself. To be clear, most people view management and leadership as separate ideas, those two words are interchangeable to me even though they have two different meanings.

My expectation is anyone who is a manager is also a leader. A manager must passionately lead others, build their value, simultaneously draw inspiration from them and inspire them at all times to drive the overall business value. When I was young, I thought being in management meant getting to make decisions that other people had to listen to and follow.

It all sounded so great, compared to the stark reality. Management means having to make hard decisions, instead of merely easy ones. There are decisions that will haunt you at night because they have repercussions on people's income, living status and employment.

My professional work existence has transitioned into constantly thinking about and making decisions to create an environment of success for the team members that work for us. A frequent question we get asked during an interview is what type of work environment we have. This answer has evolved over the recent years as I've identified some of the most important things about our culture and our principles.

In the organizations that I've led, we believe strongly in providing continuous and direct feedback. We start all team members with a strong foundation of training and then find ways to revisit the training and grow upon it. My career and many others on our leadership team has benefitted from a promotion from within mentality, identifying top performers and seeking new ways to challenge them, even if at times that challenge will stretch them before they are ready. And finally, a work hard, play hard mentality from our team members.

At the Oklahoma Dodgers, we find that people who are competitive and fun gravitate toward working in sports, which is great because we spend a lot of time together, so fun is better than not fun, right? But more than just fun, we want teammates that go the extra mile and take pride in providing unsurpassed internal and external customer service. Some people are built for that, some aren't. Many people who work with us are not from Oklahoma, we have around 50 full-time employees and they are from all over the country. What has become apparent in my time recruiting new team members to Oklahoma is that our staff don't want to relocate simply for a job, they are looking for and evaluating a lifestyle.

It comes back to that management comment that I hear from a lot of recent graduates over the past few years. It's a common reply uttered as a long-term goal answer. Because it sounds good to them. However, when I follow up by asking what department or process they want to manage, the answers diminish to a variation of *"I don't know, anything is fine."* It is concerning that college graduates have serious misconceptions about what goes into a managing dynamic, especially when it comes to people that they will supervise. If they do not have a clear understanding of the impact of a good manager, it means that they do not know the difference that a positive or negative management style can have on an organization or its people.

The ability to communicate can effect whether someone possesses a positive or negative management style. Communication used to be an afterthought, something that fell into the *'nice but not necessary'* category. Now communication is a must. Providing employees with transparent and fast communication is an expectation. We live in a world where information is at your fingertips all day, every day. The typical social media user sees 285 pieces of content daily which is about 54,000 words.[2]

I just Googled that and adweek.com provided this staggering statistic in less than 15 seconds. Employees don't separate wanting the latest, real-time information in other aspects of their life from their work life. There is an expectation that leaders communicate and keep teammates as up to date as CNN news alerts. We've been challenged in our style for communicating to employees in recent years.

Not that long ago, our senior leadership believed strongly that we needed to have all the details, potential outcomes, and questions we'd be asked thought through completely before sharing information with our team members. It wasn't a power play, or a need to keep information from them, it was an intent to have all of our ducks in a row to reinforce to the team that we were prepared.

Now, and don't get me wrong, our intent is always to be thorough and have looked at a topic through every angle, but we are more likely to introduce a concept to the team members along the way, with more information to come. Seek some feedback, be nimble and adapt as we go. It's a reflection of the 'on demand' world and it matches up to how our team members are receiving communication in all other areas of their lives.

In addition to this, we have created five unique methods for our team members to provide feedback that range in their formality. We emphasize once they join the team that we expect them to provide feedback, but to do it in a constructive manner, using one of the various communication channels. This has created a meaningful difference in the conversations we are having with our team members now versus just three years ago.

The Role Isn't For Everyone

There was a newly promoted manager I worked with in Frisco who was certain he could manage people based on only being positive and telling people what they did right. This person was an excellent group sales rep who was a super nice guy, he just didn't like to not be super nice and didn't appreciate the firmness of my management style. So, as everyone does, when they get the opportunity to do things their way, they overcorrect the areas they never liked as the person being managed. This new manager wouldn't have conversations to correct what reps were doing wrong and only focused on the positive. Don't get me wrong, I like seeing the good in people but as a manager, my priority is working with people on the areas that need improvement, and that requires some challenging conversations.

It came down to his inability to communicate effectively that made his management style a negative for the organization. He was a great person, super nice, but could not communicate in a way that created a positive environment for those who he supervised. His direct reporting employees were often times frustrated because they didn't get the direction and guidance they were looking for. After a few months, the manager and I had enough weekly meetings that the main topic was how frustrated he was with people not doing their job well and me just asking how he as holding them accountable. It was a rocky time and although he got more comfortable communicating expectations and bringing up shortfalls, management in this way wasn't for him.

Mentoring isn't simply about putting your time in. It is a war of attrition on your mindset. Everything that you believe today may not be what you believe tomorrow. Experience changes that. So do mentors who help guide you into becoming a great manager of other people. I did not become a better supervisor without the help of others guiding me. That's not how it works. You need to be challenged by those supervising you, in order to help those who report to you later on.

My first manager kept me focused. Because she stayed focused. It was about an *"earned perspective"* of knowing and concentrating on the things I needed to do every day in order to be a great sales representative, along with understanding the sales process. Without her early input, I wouldn't have developed the key asset of how to focus on my work and conveying that later on to those sales representatives that I ended up managing.

We learn different things from different mentors. Some don't even act with the knowledge that they are our mentors, yet they end up shaping us continually. I had one mentor who drove home the value of employees and doing right by them, as well as their paycheck, early on in my career. And now when I am managing others, I challenge myself to continue to do what is right by them, concerning myself with their paycheck, to live up to the standard that mentor set for me. The advice provided to me by him was that when you are having a difficult conversation, you have to be the most comfortable person in the room, value treating people the right way, hiring people with respect, and firing people with respect.

Another piece of advice was seeing the big picture to drive team results. What gets measured ends up being what gets done. That means that you have to know what to determine as success for your team. It will be what incentivizes everyone and will push them toward that set goal. The worst thing that any manager can do is worry about uncontrollable business factors. It confuses the goals of both you and the employees who report to you.

Many of us found ourselves in management positions because we were the best at the original job we were hired to do. For example, the best salesperson gets promoted to lead their sales team. I think we can all agree, just because you are good at a job doesn't mean you are cut out to manage others doing that same job. The best salespeople know how to work their book of business, they understand the sales cycle and know the grind.

And they don't get bogged down in what others are doing. They get a rush from the close and can't wait to do it again. This is not the same type of person who wants to be responsible for other people and genuinely care about their growth personally and professionally. For a manager, the source of that rush is different, it comes at you at a different pace and what led to success is less likely to work the same way twice (*that would be too easy, wouldn't it?*). The list of unsuccessful top salespeople turned sales managers is extensive and if they are smart, they go back to selling because that is what they are best at. I have enjoyed my fair share of cocktails with sales managers who have exclaimed, "*I wish I could just go back to selling again, be in control of my own destiny and only worry about myself.*"

Many people who get promoted into a management role have an idea of the strategy and process related to making their department run. They've been exposed to that part to some frequency along the way in their career and are often fooled into thinking that's primarily what the job of managing the department is about. What they aren't yet equipped to manage is the people part of the job. In the 10 years I have been managing people in MiLB, I can say without a doubt that the best thing you can provide for an employee is perspective.

Information about how you got to a decision, key factors others may not be aware of that build into direction are so vital in helping them see the big picture and to trust the process and that you have made an educated and thoughtful decision. Then repeat it…again, and again. We can't only tell an employee something once and expect it to have a lasting result. For things to become second nature, repetition is critical.

We take a different approach to some of the typical '*promotions*' associated with MiLB. These aren't preferences, they have become so ingrained in our standard operating that it would dramatically impact the foundation of our business if we were to change course. For many years, when a new team member or fan would suggest we add some of those promotions to our schedule it usually elicited a thoughtful response, but it was quick and meant to move along.

But at some point this thought of '*perspective*' clicked with me. Now whenever those topics come up, it captures a part of my brain that sends signals to my voice to share layers of perspective, to repeat messages that have been shared and to drive home the concept that everything we do stems from a very thoughtful decision. I enjoy these conversations now, because there is a teaching component, one that develops a deeper connection to our team members. See, there's that rush.

Each interaction with an employee should teach you how to be better in the future. Unfortunately, it is something that you can't be good at immediately. Even now, there are new situations that come up that are new to me. I remember the first time I had to address a female employee's unprofessional attire, I was not prepared. So I knew I needed to talk with her because there was a lot of chatter on the sales floor about her low cut top and I am big on minimizing distractions.

I am a personal branding advocate. Back then, I didn't realize that's what it was but now that is a key speaking point with staff members. You show people who you are with every interaction both verbally and non-verbally. So when I say how unprepared I was for the conversation that I built up in my head, I wasn't prepared for how easy it was. I have learned that most times, people know when they are wearing something inappropriate, so they aren't surprised. Also, when you take the stance during the conversation of wanting this to be a learning experience for them because one day they could be in your seat, the conversation tends to go better.

Embrace the Journey

The importance of why is something that can take years for managers to understand. In many cases, when you finally find yourself in a leadership position, you just want to jump in and get started. And then you take a step back and think '*what the hell do I do first?*' Even back as part of my internships, there were training periods to establish my management skills. Every component of what you do before you are a manager sets the stage for how you will end up managing later on. With my first internship, I was responsible for in-game promotions so scheduling National Anthems, coordinating the run of show and scripting the in-game experience were my responsibility. I was 19 years old and had no clue about anything.

Before a home game, I got a call from the person scheduled to sing the National Anthem and they bailed. I told our Marketing Director about the situation and he asked what I was going to do and I said I didn't know, and asked if we just play a recording of the anthem. He shared with me that not having a live performance was not an option. He told me he didn't care if someone played the skin flute *(it is too relevant, I couldn't clean this up)* to start the game, we would have a live anthem.

So I started calling anyone I could think of and found a season ticket holder (STH) who could step in. That was my quick lesson in just figuring it out.

My first full time position in sports was with the Frisco RoughRiders as a Group Sales Coordinator in the fall of 2004. This came after three internships that ranged from unaffiliated Minor League baseball to affiliated baseball to the MLS. Paid and unpaid. In New Jersey, the most memorable experience was living in a campground along with 10 other interns but my best takeaway related to work was learning the best way to find new opportunities in the same organization. I was the last intern to arrive in New Jersey because my college was on quarters so while most interns got there in May, I arrived in June.

I knew I was going to get the worst roommate and the worst job at the stadium. I was an operations intern to start the season so the benefits were, I could wear what I wanted and I got a great tan. I learned how to operate the bucket lift so that was cool, but not exactly what I was hoping to build my resume off of. As the season progressed I knew if I did my best at my current role, I would be able to ask for increased responsibility along the way. So while pulling trash from the parking lot barrels almost made me vomit, I did it and with as best of an attitude as I could muster. By the time I finished the season, I was managing the gameday staff and was able to get some great bullet points on my resume.

That separated from the stack resume landed me in Frisco, Texas. My time with the RoughRiders was an incredible learning experience. I got to learn from the best and my colleagues were phenomenal sales professionals. I was exposed to the most creative sports marketers of that time and the experience and perspective I gained was invaluable. When I was in Frisco, I had been in my role for a few seasons and we had been successful. Each year we increased our revenue and hit goal. All good, right? Nope. I was burnt out and I was bored. I loved the people there but I was getting close to being done, I needed a new challenge. Be careful what you wish for, a few months later, I learned about an opportunity in OKC and my life got flipped upside down, but it energized me and taught me so many new lessons. The biggest likely being that not everything can be a 10.

There were times I let small problems get me riled up, when there are many issues to handle prioritizing the big stuff helps put the small stuff in perspective. My first manager in Frisco was female and she was awesome. The thing I appreciated about her was she didn't manage me any differently than the males on our team. I try to do the same now with the people I manage, I am equal opportunity in that I have high expectations from everyone, no matter their gender. What separated me from everyone else was that I stuck it out. I would love to say that I was the smartest and most savvy sales rep but I wasn't. I did however, work hard and allow myself to work the process of learning and getting better. So many reps exhibit the talent for being great but jump to their next thing before they are ready or into a situation that isn't a good fit just because they got anxious for something new.

After being a Group Sales Representative for two seasons, I was promoted to a manager position then as the director of the group sales team. I followed a path of being the best rep in that department to being promoted without much training on how to manage it. During that time, I started in a similar way as many others by thinking you have to be tough and abrasive to get results. I should mention that my personality tends to skew tough and abrasive anyway so that wasn't much of a stretch for me, but it isn't usually the best way to go.

Because I was early in my career, I viewed asking for help as a sign that I didn't know what I was doing. I wasn't confident, so I thought the best fix was to '*fake it until you make it.*' I made a ton of mistakes in those years and let's be real, I still make a lot of them. But at least now, I am not coming from a place of insecurity. Over the next few seasons, I had an opportunity to learn from some great (*and not so great*) leaders. Seeing those leaders in action and learning from their decision making, communication techniques and team management made an enormous difference in my style. Repetition gave me confidence, but the most important growth came from a better understanding of what I needed to accomplish and why it was important.

When I was in Frisco, our food and beverage provider was a separate company, as you will find with most sports teams. It was a relatively combative relationship as our organizational goals did not align. There was a lack of proactive communication with our hospitality customers who had been sold one experience in contrast to the one our catering under-delivered for them. Because of this, I was in constant communication with our catering manager during the season. They were '*beat your head against the wall*' conversations that showed the disconnect of customer service expectations between each organization.

Instead of working to lessen the issues, our catering manager started *comp'ing* a dessert for the hospitality clients whose orders were messed up and she called it her '*apology pie.*' We got a quarter of the way into the season when I learned her term for this make good and I was in complete disbelief. I caught up with her during the next game to let her know the apology pie was officially off the menu and instead of using this as a way to smooth over a poor experience, we needed to come up with a plan to ensure these issues didn't keep reappearing. This comes back to the issue of communication while managing. Communication and management skills aren't simply for those employees that report to you, it is also a skill set for those third-party vendors and other community contacts that you are in touch with. I am happy to say that was the last *apology pie* of that season and while there were still some mistakes, they were much less than earlier in the season.

Being in management means seeing through the nonsense when employees aren't doing their job and addressing it. But it also means owning up to your mistakes, when you call employees out incorrectly. When I was a Group Sales Manager in Frisco we had a call minimum of 100 calls each day, no exceptions. Honestly, it breaks down to 12 calls an hour so it isn't that crazy. We had a call tracking software for accountability and we pulled numbers every week. One week, the numbers pulled showed three reps with weird repeating numbers that registered a call but no talk time. Our VP of Ticket Sales was beside himself. He was newer to the organization and felt like reps were taking advantage of him so he wanted to pull them in his office and let them know he didn't appreciate it.

I didn't feel great about it, mostly because I knew these guys and it didn't seem like something they would do. I shared that with our VP and he let me know that the evidence showed I was wrong. I was pretty new to management and went along with this. So the three reps came in, were presented with the evidence and told that they were cheating the system. We quickly learned they were each calling a new list that wasn't being recognized by the tracking system and these reps were pissed, and I didn't blame them.

So I learned: *Trust your gut, if it doesn't seem right, it probably isn't. Each of us has the responsibility to stop something they think is wrong. Ask questions to understand, don't jump to a conclusion without learning what is going on.*

MiLB is a wonderful place to work. There is no dynamic like it in the world. Even in the world of sports. We are really able to get to know our fans because of the scale of what we do. There was a premium season ticket holder in Frisco who would occasionally have one too many and need a ride home, so his account rep would drive him. We have had season ticket holders that we watch their kids grow up in front of us. One just graduated college and got his first full-time job in baseball, they are great people and it is such a unique relationship we have. At another team, a member of the operations department used to let an older fan pull her car to the front gate and he would park it for her to help minimize her walking. We didn't learn about this until he left the organization. Minor League Baseball will always be about creating an experience for fans to enjoy with friends and family, for those who work in the front office, sometimes we become part of that experience too.

You Will Never Be Fully Prepared

After being in Frisco for six seasons, it was time for a change. At that time, our ownership group had been going through the process of buying the Oklahoma City RedHawks and I had the opportunity to make the move three hours north and oversee my own sales department. I was pumped. This is what you say to yourself right, '*when I am in charge, I'll do it this way*' or that way or whatever way you think made the most sense before it was all on you. All of it. Everything. That's what we want, being in charge of all of it.

You quickly learn that some decisions are thought through in a meaningful way and others must happen so fast just to keep your head above water. The thing is, those that you lead judge your decisions that same way no matter the circumstances in which the decisions were made. You don't get the benefit of the doubt, because you are in charge. They want to know if those decisions are being made in the best interest of them no matter how challenging the environment is in which you are sorting through the details of making those decisions. Studied the details for hours, or passing comment in the hallway, your decisions are your decisions.

My first week in OKC was all observation. I was coming into a situation where there were already three sales reps and a manager who had been held to much different standards than I was used to. Not their fault, attitude reflects leadership (*Remember the Titans*). This was like nothing I had seen before. I watched a young sales rep paint her nails in the middle of the sales day and another walk around the office wearing Crocs. There was minimal sales effort going on during renewal season and my head was exploding.

I found myself in a situation where there were so many things to do - set sales direction and strategy, hire more reps (*and train them!*), develop relationships with season ticket holders, suite holders, vendors, key stakeholders in the community, learn the historical information on accounts and initiatives. Oh, and learn about the actual city that I was living in only part time at the hotel just beyond centerfield.

One of the many things I love are quotes. Inspirational, funny, whatever. If I can glean anything of value from it, I am in. With that, the saying - *how do you eat an elephant? One bite at a time.* It seemed like an insurmountable project but if I didn't start somewhere, I wouldn't get anywhere.

In my first 30 days we hired 17 new sales reps with 10 of them starting the Monday after Thanksgiving. It was a wild ride and the phrase drinking from a fire hydrant could not be any truer. Even though it was a huge undertaking, we felt like it was important that all new reps went through the same training at the same time to ensure a level playing field and consistent messaging. Plus, we were working to maximize our time and this was the best use of time for those training. This is where having support from an involved ownership group was a lifesaver.

We needed so many people in a short amount of time that we enlisted the help of *Teamwork Online* to do the recruiting and initial screening calls. I would clear my schedule for blocks of time and I would do phone and *Skype* calls with the candidates. I did these during the workday, after hours (*Note: the latest Skype was at 9 p.m.*) and over the weekend.

I am big on in-person interaction when making hiring decisions, so this was difficult but I tried to learn as much as I could while on the call, including observing the person's surroundings. I had one candidate do the interview in his parent's house in what was likely his childhood room based on the videogame posters on the walls. Although the situation was different in this practice of interviewing, the constant of trusting my gut remained. I ended up making a few hires that were not the best, but I needed to get people on the ground. Those were the ones that didn't stick. Always trust your gut.

This was a project that we tackled together and in some cases learned as we went. As much as you try to think through every detail and plan every interaction, there are some instances that are good reminders that you can't plan everything. On the first day of having increased our sales staff by 6x, we planned a lunch for everyone on staff to begin to meet the new reps. We worked to be inclusive and not have everyone in the same department sit together so a new outside sales rep sat at a table and made small talk with the person next to him. After a few minutes the rep asked, '*so what do you do for the team?*' the answer was, '*well, I'm the team president.*' That's right, in all the work we were doing to get everyone trained and up to speed, we didn't introduce them to the team president. We certainly made a note to do things differently moving forward.

This is a situation many have found themselves in, there is so much to do that we all revert back to our upbringing in the industry of just putting your head down and getting to work. The trouble with that is, when you are a leader of the organization, you can't put your head down, you have to keep it up so you can look ahead. When you get your blinders on and only focus on a task in front of you, you aren't setting the vision and you aren't teaching. Most importantly, when you are stuck inside your own head you don't ask questions.

I'm certainly an inquisitive person and feel that I have been all my life, so asking questions doesn't seem odd to me. I can't emphasize enough the value of doing this. It could be to get two or three more layers of information to make a better decision. It could be in an effort to clarify information that's been presented. Or, my favorite is asking questions, with no malice behind them, that suddenly makes the answer quickly appear to the person who brought a decision to you to make.

If you are in the thick of transition right now, you might be Googling my address and carving out time you don't have to drive to OKC and punch me in the face. I get that. This is easier for me to reflect on now after being here for seven seasons and having a more structured environment.

Create Future Leaders

The way I started this chapter was with the quote – '*Those who know how will always have a job and those who know why will always be their boss.*' We use this frequently to drive direction on providing perspective for employees. I have had many conversations that start with a basic question and end 12 minutes later with that person having raised eyebrows and an expression that confirms they didn't know what they were in for.

As leaders, we should be wanting to create more bosses, every day. That means your team is growing professionally and probably personally, they are getting it. Telling the story of your business philosophies are a difference maker to creating an engaged and empowered staff. No opportunity is too small to do this as it's how you develop a belief system in our shared success.

A friend and mentor of mine, Bob Murphy, is the team president for the Dayton Dragons. They are an incredible organization that has sold every ticket to every game since they opened a new downtown ballpark in the year 2000. This is an amazing feat, for any of us who know what goes into selling a baseball game, it isn't as easy as just running a few promotions and opening the gates. Seriously, I went to a game in Dayton on a Monday night and saw a packed house, it was crazy.

Bob has a key phrase – '*Every conversation in business serves a purpose.*' We have adopted that here and use it often. It is such a great reminder that you should never sidestep an opportunity to build into what we do. When a staff member asks a question, help them understand the why behind it. Grow their perspective.

Outside your organization, when a community stakeholder asks how things are going in the off-season, don't just tell them you're fine or busy. Give them more.

Share great successes or off-season initiatives, arm yourself with the information in advance to always be prepared. The more you do that, the fewer times someone will ask you if working for the team is a full-time job or just something you do during the season.

Share Belief In Your Brand

Off-season ballpark improvement talking points:

✓ We believe in keeping the ballpark fresh.

✓ We have an incredible relationship with the City who also believes in the purpose we serve of impacting the quality of life for citizens in our community, they coordinate with us to find funding.

✓ Offering premium products is important to the experience we want for our fans.

✓ We pay attention to the habits of our fans and listen when we ask them what improvements they would like to see.

✓ Our ownership is passionate about providing the tools for our team to succeed and for us to continue to impact the quality of life in our community.

✓ Exciting partnership opportunities in the works.

✓ Engaging in key partnerships in our community reinforces that we are an organization that is impactful to do business with.

✓ Our partnerships drive community altering initiatives using the strength of our brand to add value to motivating outcomes important to our partners.

✓ Ways to keep the ballpark active in the off-season.

✓ We host the *LifeShare WinterFest* from November through the New Year. This is an event that features a manmade snow slide that begins on our second level seating bowl, goes down a 25-30 foot decline and ends around second base. We also host around 20 High School Baseball games in the month of March leading into the season to give student athletes a big-league experience by playing a game on our field. Along with those large initiatives, we also have numerous events for partners and businesses in our community to help them achieve their goals and use our venue in a unique way.

✓   Baseball talent that will likely be at your team's disposal to use for public relations events. Or you can use the stats available talking about what the team has been up to on the field. (*If you don't know this, have someone on staff give you some general speaking points, our broadcaster served as an excellent resource in this area*).

Culture Creators

As much as storytelling is an important part of what you do, execution and follow through need to accompany it, or else you are just full of shit. Always look for opportunities to deliver a message, let me give you a snapshot of our hiring and onboarding processes. We work in sports, so we are always looking for talent. That said, this is a point of emphasis throughout the year and in many cases, something that sets us apart from other organizations. We have a corporate culture of growth from within the organization. Ideally, someone joins our team and travels through the ranks, learning the whys and telling our story along the way. It is my background, and the same for many in our team leadership. If we want people to stay here and continue to grow, we must start with recruiting great talent and then making a solid first impression.

Our interview process usually begins through a few channels. I would bet most of us use *Teamwork online* to post our jobs and we also work our networks, both in sports and locally. We filter candidates through the same process, so someone is responsible for screening and then another person does a phone interview before it gets to the hiring manager. If all three like the candidate, we will set up an in-person or *Skype* interview to make sure we get a good feel from them. During the interview process we try to learn as much about the candidate as humanly (*and legally*) possible. We are intentional about multiple team leaders outside their department meeting with them, as well as peers that they will work with and all of our senior leadership. We spend a ton of time with our employees, so someone needs to be as much of a character and culture fit as they are a professional fit. We also invest a great deal of resources in those on our staff so making smart hiring decisions is a must.

After someone completes the interview process and accepts an offer, we want to welcome them and make them feel great about their decision to work with us. It would be similar to the way you treat a season ticket holder. After you sell them, you are now in the renewal business to keep them engaged with the team, and happy with their decision. Employees should be your biggest fans.

Upon accepting a position with us, we will overnight a welcome package. This includes information about the team and a stakeholder's report to show the prior year's community contribution. It will also have information about Oklahoma City and a relocation guide provided by our Chamber. There is a letter included that gives them the information about their start date and when they should arrive along with dress code and other details. We do the best we can to over communicate and remove any concern or hesitation on their decision. Over the next couple of days, the new employee will receive welcome emails from all members of our leadership team sharing their enthusiasm for the impact the new team member will have on the organization.

On the employee's first day, we will present to them their first week scheduled out for them – tour, first day lunch, meetings with every department head to learn how they will work together, a sit down with our team president, a full presentation about our core business philosophies and what makes us different. We work to minimize the uncertainty that accompanies change. Our onboarding begins as soon as someone accepts the position. We send them a package of information about the team and Oklahoma City so they can become familiar with everything before their first day. We also have every department head send them a welcome email to share the excitement of them joining our team. On the employees first day, we start with a tour and someone who has been with the team for a while, but isn't in a leadership position, introduces them to everyone.

On their first day they will meet with our Team President and also learn "*What Makes Us Different*" a presentation that every new hire gets. In their first week, they will meet with every department head to learn about their department and how it fits in the overall mission of the team. This process has certainly evolved over the past three or four years and we take it very seriously. You never get a second chance to make a first impression, and that goes for joining a new organization too. All of this is meant to equip new hires to start telling our story and learning the why's behind our what's. We will also ensure their workspace is set up. This might sound obvious but many of our employees are floored when they arrive, and their business cards are already at their desk along with their laptop, pad folio and office supplies. We never want someone to arrive and they wonder if we were expecting them. We also have them arrive on their first day at 10 a.m. to make sure we are prepared. Despite the frequency of hiring in our business, it is easy for the process to feel like it's in addition to our '*day job*' and not give it the attention it deserves. By starting the employee off right with our organization, it begins to define what their story is about working for us.

Week two starts the real work for these employees. So, when you work so hard to start off on the right foot, you can't under deliver from that time until they leave the company, right? I love the idea that with every interaction with your employees you are either adding to your equity account or making a withdrawal. The more you add, the more your people will trust you and trust that you have their best interest in mind. Most of us have experience with a manager we trusted vs. one we didn't. The manager I trusted could provide feedback to me that I took and acted on to improve, they could ask me to do something outside my job responsibilities that I saw as an opportunity to contribute more and learn. On the flip side, if I didn't trust them I would become defensive with feedback and additional asks were frustrating.

The best way to add into this account is by genuinely caring about your people and their career trajectory. When you care, you take extra time to show it. So, when you have an idea or feedback to help them improve, you add context and information. You don't just tell them what they are doing is wrong. You take time to learn about them as people. Where they are from, what their interests are, what matters to them, significant others, pets, goals, etc. Know your people. The idea that people don't stay or leave an organization, they stay or leave because of their manager is so true. Connect by telling a personal story that is relatable, show them you have tackled a similar challenge.

We do two formal meetings with employees each year in addition to their regular one on one's that are either weekly or bi-weekly. These formal meetings are mid-season and end of year. The purpose of the mid-season review is to get as much feedback as possible while planning for the following year. If someone isn't happy or planning to leave, you usually find out during this time and you can either help correct it if you want that person to stay, or you can plan for their exit. It might sound harsh, as much as I love our people and want them to be happy and successful, if we have someone who doesn't share that same vision, they need to find it someplace else. Experience has taught me that the effort put in to change someone's perspective is better served driving success for those that are engaged and want to be there.

We send out question sets to start the conversation for each of these meetings and the employee needs to complete this and send it back, so the manager can prepare. You should go into these interactions with performance feedback and ideas to help them grow. In most of these meetings, your employee will share that they want more of something. Responsibility, money, recognition, leads, etc. never feel like you need to make a decision during that meeting. But you absolutely must ask questions.

Learn more about their intentions. Are they wanting more money because they are considering starting a family? Do they want more responsibility or an increased role because their best friend from college just got a promotion? If you have a better understanding about the reason why someone thinks they want more, you will truly know how to help them and in some cases, be able to over-deliver for them.

Work-Life Balance

Being a female in this industry definitely has its challenges, especially with perception from those around you. When I was pregnant, the first question I got was boy or girl, the second question was always asking if I was going back to work after my maternity leave. In some cases, this could have been our first conversation, it was amazing how many people felt like this was their business. I have asked my husband if anyone was curious if he was going back to work and, a surprise to no one, this was not a question he was asked.

Finding a balance in family and work is challenging but it is not impossible. Balance is about prioritizing, and I have gotten pretty good at it. I will always do my best to prioritize the parts of motherhood that are important vs. those that aren't. Example, I won't miss an event that is important to my daughters, but I will sign up to bring paper plates to the class party instead of baking something. My husband is awesome, for many reasons but especially because he is the first person to point out that our daughters are ours, not mine, not his and we are a team. No one should be expected to do all this alone, I ask for help frequently and have a whole tribe of people to help us manage it all. If I am ever treated differently because I am a woman, I don't really pay much attention, because I don't have time for that shit.

Having children changed my perspective as a manager. Before I had kids, I used to get so irritated when it seemed like my co-workers with kids time was seen as more valuable than mine. Now that I have kids, I get it but you don't until you have them. My two girls go to daycare and it closes at 6 p.m. so I need to leave by 5:40 p.m. to get them, if you total up the hours in the office, I work one full business day less now. Unfortunately, the things I need to don't lessen, so after dinner and bedtimes, the laptop comes back out and my workday continues.

Being a manager means receiving constant feedback. You have to want to listen. Even when you think the organization is running smoothly, it may have troubled waters ahead. In one instance, we had an entire department that provided feedback that they felt disconnected from the mission of the team. They each took very firm and opposite stances to the way we operate and shared frustration and distrust. It was not at all what we wanted to hear, but I would much rather learn it then than in an exit interview.

Upon peeling back more layers of the onion, we realized that this was a team tasked with creating collateral for our organization and they weren't getting the direct feedback from their manager that was being shared by other department heads on the projects they were producing. So, the feedback they were hearing was that their work wasn't good or right, but they weren't getting the big picture of why it needed to change. They weren't hearing about the other parts of the project that were creative and thoughtful or could be used in another way.

As you can imagine, that rushed and short feedback will make someone question their role and contribution and lead to dissent within a team. We all spend a lot of time together so when grumbling starts, things can escalate quickly. It leads to a narrative created by these employees that is likely much worse than the actual situation. Once we learned about this, changes were made fast.

We realized the manager wasn't providing the full scope of information and that was a direct result of them being stretched too thin and was always rushing from project to project. We reviewed time management strategies and took a few things off his plate to allow better interaction. We also ramped up the information provided with feedback and in many cases asked department heads to speak directly to the person submitting the work for feedback on projects. Another important outcome was that we made some organizational structure changes and moved this manager into a new role that allowed him to use his creative strengths to focus on our brand and have oversight of all creative but managing the people in the department has shifted to the overall department head.

I am sure everyone is familiar with the saying about getting the right people on the bus and how important that is, and it certainly is. However, after you get the right people on the bus, you have to make sure they are sitting in the right seat and the one that will be the best for the team. If you have built into that equity account and have built trust, then you can work quickly and without conflict with the right person on the bus to find a better seat.

Transition in and out of organizations is part of life and it is most certainly part of sports. As much as an employee leaving the organization can be frustrating, it can also be a learning experience. Anytime an employee moves on, they do an exit interview. This is a set of questions compiled by our leadership team that is intended to help us get better as an organization. These questions are meant to encourage honest thoughts and are submitted to HR and sealed for 30 days.

When the 30 days are up, the feedback is given to our team president then myself to review then finally passed to the manager. We used to learn so much in these and it was frustrating that employees didn't give us the feedback when it could have made a difference. We can fix most things, but not if we don't know there is a problem. This was one of those exercises that made the *'perspective'* light bulb go off a few years back. From this, we created opportunities for teammates to submit ideas on ways we can improve. It is also helpful because it can remove the 'they' employees have a tendency to talk about. It empowers all employees to make a difference and not rely on team leadership to see everything.

All of this – recruiting, hiring, onboarding, training, formal and informal meetings, exit interviews, etc. – takes time. So much time. But this time allows you to shape and guide your team. It gives you the undivided focus to share your vision and communicate your *'why'*. It is your time to continue to invest in your employees, your best brand ambassadors. As we all know, the value of your brand is only as great as its people.

The Negatives Of The GM Role

Working in sports is a choice. There are a million people who will do more work for less money in order to have the perception of your job in sports. Not the reality, but the perception. They see what they want to see, not the long nights making calls, but hanging out with players or standing on the field. That's the perception which clouds how people entering the industry feel about what someone does in sports.

Let me first say, I hate firing people. Some people are more affixed to the idea of the perception of what working in sports is, so much that it ends up not working out for either them or the organization. If we get to the point that we are considering the termination path, I think you need to reflect on yourself as a leader and either you made a bad hiring decision or the person wasn't trained and managed effectively. Or they didn't understand the reality, compared to the perception, of the position that they were hired for. Also, if you fire someone and they are surprised, you likely didn't provide the right feedback to help them improve.

Now that I have established those things, the first time I had to fire someone, I was sick to my stomach. He had been with the team in OKC for a few years prior to my arrival and he was not interested in adapting to our new processes. You can't have a turnaround with only some of the people buying in so he needed to find another opportunity. I called our head legal executive to *"fire"* him over the phone and after I had gotten a few in, he thought I was ready.

His parting words to me were – *"Jenna, it is never as bad as you think it's going to be"* and right when I was breathing a sign or relief he added *'except, sometimes, people really lose their shit."* I definitely didn't laugh then but I do every time I think about it now. As far as firings go, it was pretty uneventful and while it wasn't fun, it was the right thing for the organization to progress and set the right tone moving into the next chapter for growth. Some people fire themselves. Or they aren't happy in the first place, and as a leader, you are helping them realize that it isn't working out to stay there. The majority of employee terminations are simply the organization helping the fired party come to that conclusion faster than they would themselves.

Become A Pipeline Of Success

A common phrase around our office is that employees are always interviewing for their next job. Our best-case scenario is that when we have an open position, we want to fill it with someone who has been with our organization and understands our culture and has been over delivering in their current role. We have a track record of adjusting our organizational chart to fit the people we have. To continue to evolve and progress, we can't get stuck in doing what we have always done.

I mentioned when I started overseeing the sales team in OKC, we hired 17 new sales reps. In that time, each of them reported to me. A general rule of thumb is you should allow 30 minutes in your day for each person you directly manage. In that instance I needed 8.5 hours only for the people, not for anything else.

We operated in that way for three seasons and by that time, we had three sales reps who had separated themselves from the others. We knew that in order to continue to grow our people and promote from within, and also grow revenue from having more focused management, we needed to make a change. After some internal discussion with team leadership, which at the time was our team president and myself, we presented the idea to ownership and were able to have the very unexpected conversation.

These three sales reps became managers of each area of our sales team – outside sales, group sales and inside sales. We never posted or recruited these positions, we had immense talent here who had spent the previous seasons over-delivering in their roles and learning the why's of our company. There were countless examples of these team members providing additional value to our organization and it was time to recognize them and put them in a position to grow professionally.

Be Batshit Passionate

What are your organization's common phrases? Shared beliefs? Aspirations? Spend some time to put into words what makes your business succeed and stand out from others. Then you'll have your messages that you'll be ready to communicate, reinforce, recruit towards and live. Spend the time to know your organization's why and then be so passionate about it that you never get tired of repeating it.

Some people confuse passion with crazy. Let me be clear, I am *batshit passionate*.

As I mentioned earlier, when I became a first-time manager, I wasn't ready. I made a ton of mistakes and wasn't always sure how it would get better. One thing is for certain, first time managers are scary. They have an abundance of know how in their current role but lack the overall perspective and empathy to translate that into the teaching and growth of others. And they are now responsible for the success of their employees. As a team leader, you understand how scary that is. They also have built up years of thinking, well, when I am in change, I won't do things this way, or that way. That is scary. I often times will work with new managers in our organization on some of the basics and importance of recruiting, hiring, training, onboarding, etc.

Investing in one another will always be something I am passionate about. We have a culture of training and working with our team to get them better, faster. One piece of this is to openly share areas that I have made mistakes or had less than stellar results for an initiative. The idea is not to completely discredit myself but to hopefully allow people to learn from my mistakes, so they don't have to make their own. If they can bypass that junk and come to a better solution, then I have done my job. Along with that comes additional training for our first-time managers. These will be the ones who have the most direct and constant interaction with most of your employees. If they aren't successful in their management, you will see it in every area of your business.

We went through a transitional period at our team in 2014 where we were introducing several new managers into our company. We had just restructured a great deal and created new opportunities for several people. With that, we wanted to ensure preparedness. My past experience of fumbling through my first few years became an inspiration for our syllabus. The biggest challenge I encountered was time. Time to put something like this in action was something I didn't have, but it was important, and I always think people make time for what is important to them.

With this, I proposed a leadership book club of sorts and we assembled and began a weekly meeting to review *The 21 Irrefutable Laws of Leadership*.[3] It took the heavy lifting of curriculum development off the table and allowed us to use each chapter as a guide for discussion in our sessions. The main outcome of this was to carve out time to give people a chance to learn from one another, to share their concerns or successes or frustrations. Last week, I had someone on our leadership team talk about how important that was to him when he was getting started and how it helped him get a grasp on what was bigger than managing process but managing people.

Get Staff Buy-In

As leaders, we should all be curious. Asking questions will do so much for you to learn what is important for your people, how to grow the organization and to continue to invest in success. In the sales process you ask questions to learn what the prospect would find value in and commit to. Employees are no different and each person will show you how they can contribute on a larger scale, you just have to look for it. Spend some time with them to draw on employee's expertise from other organizations, it shows you value their feedback and experience.

If something isn't working, ask why. A few years ago, we instituted a peer recognition program called '*Shout-Outs.*' The basic idea was for recognition to not only live with department heads but to empower those in other departments to share appreciation for another teammate going above and beyond for a customer or the organization. These would be shared during our monthly staff meetings and could be submitted in advance or done on the spot. These worked for a few months then we noticed a drop off in the quality of shout-outs. People started submitting them to check a box, not because they truly meant them. When an initiative is no longer genuine, it misses the mark. It was clearly time for a change. We asked employees for ideas on other programs, they are the ones this is intended for, right? What we learned was "*X*." So instead of just scrapping something that was intended to serve a purpose, we asked questions to find a way to make it fit.

Questions allow for us to be purposeful and strategic in the way we run our business. They allow us to be continuous learners and find ways to progress in our business. The answers will also show us where we need to improve to ensure our '*why*' is being communicated.

Common Q&As

Whenever I speak to any audience, my favorite part is the Q&A at the end. Since this format obviously doesn't allow for that, I thought I'd add in some of the questions I get asked the most:

What's It Like To Be A Female In Sports?

This is the question I get asked the most. I recently saw a quote from Sarah Silverman that really resonated with me:

"Don't tell girls they can be anything they want they grow up. Because it would have never occurred to them that they couldn't."[4]

I get asked a lot what it is like to work in a male dominated industry and every time it catches me off guard, I don't have a great answer because, I only think about it when someone asks, I don't know any different.

I don't know any different than being female in this industry and I think the best thing I have going for me is like Sarah Silverman's thought, it never occurs to me that me being a woman is the reason I am treated one way or another.

Sure, I am sometimes talked to differently than my male co-workers and I get interrupted in professional settings. I never stop and think that it must be because I am a woman, I usually just think it is because the interrupter is an asshole.

Having a thick skin could be from many things, I like to think it is likely from my dad's basic response to any perceived hardship or unfair situation was, and still is, *"them's the breaks."* So, for 36 years, I have been hearing a mantra that tells me to get over it and move on. So, I do.

I can't approach every day like a victim or overanalyzing ways that someone is treating me badly, it would be an exhausting way to live. The main point I tell other women is no one should treat you as less than an equal, if they do, it isn't about you any longer. It has nothing to do with you and everything to do with them.

I have two daughters, one is 3.5 and one is six months. I am really careful, even now with my toddler, to not overplay the girl power sentiment… Solely because I never want the idea that maybe she shouldn't be doing something to creep into her mind.

Is A MiLB Career Worth It?

There are so many things I love about Minor League Baseball. First, I love cultivating an experience that allows people to create memories. I just don't think we can overlook that honor to be a part of peoples' stories. Second, I can't tell you how great it is to only focus on what we can control. I will never be in a position that directly impacts team performance, that isn't what I am passionate about. Our success doesn't hinge on team performance and most of our fans leave the ballpark knowing they had a great time, not knowing the final score. And lastly, it will never be lost on me that I have been exposed to so much more in our organization than I would have at one of the Big Four. More importantly, because we operate like any small business, we have a lot of say in our direction and strategy.

Is Work-Life Balance Achievable In Sports?

Work-life balance seems to be the million-dollar question right now. I have mixed feelings about this concept. My first thought is if you are looking for a traditional 9 a.m. - 5 p.m. job, sports just isn't for you. We are the ultimate hosts and have to love having people to our 'house' at the times they want to be entertained. Basically, we work while others play, and I am good with that. If you aren't, you might want to consider season tickets instead. I should also say I am not the poster child for balance, but here is my experience. As I previously stated, you make time for things that are important to you. Whenever you say yes to one thing, you must say no to another so consider this when presented an opportunity. Kris Kristofferson has given me the best line that I have on repeat daily: "*If you can't get out of something, get into it*"[4] It reminds me that if something is important that I need to be present, and if it isn't, I shouldn't be spending time on it.

What's The Hardest Skill You've Had To Learn?

Prioritizing is the hardest skill that I had to learn. I find it challenging to say no to immediate things, especially when it is a person asking for help. If I am getting ready to leave for a meeting that starts in a few minutes and someone stands in my doorway to ask a question, I will help them first then show up to the meeting 5 minutes late. Not a good look. So, I try to communicate with that person that they are important, and I will help them as soon as I return. Seems easy but I have to remind myself often.

I also have a tendency to get caught up in the small stuff – I am a recovering micro-manager and I struggle with it daily. I love details and those can really separate you when it matters. The trick is to know when it matters and when it doesn't. I have tried to get better at what battles I fight. I have learned over the years that I don't have the bandwidth for everything to be a 10. I only have so many opportunities for 10's each day. At this point, my team knows my classifications for what I do and don't need to weigh in on. And I trust them to make great decisions. I realized that as much as I love teaching people, I had to also love letting them apply that knowledge and grow into their own.

How Do You Identify Future Leaders?

Identifying future leaders is the area that I enjoy the most. It starts in the interview process, someone who is a highly regarded headhunter in the sports industry once told me that you need to look for someone who either gets it, or is predisposed to getting it. I think of this often when hiring someone and looking for high performers. Once they are on your team, it starts slow and increases by observing and asking questions. When you see someone in an entry level role, it is easy to evaluate them based on their contribution only in that department. When an employee starts looking outside their basic job responsibilities to find more ways to contribute, they peak my interest. I like to ask them more about themselves and use casual interactions to find out their goals and ideas. Attitude is something that can't be taught and finding people who are positive and self-aware is so important, these interactions tend to show what you need to know about someone in addition to their overall performance in their role.

What Are Your Most Successful Interview Questions?

I view interviews as a time that you need to learn absolutely as much as you can about someone in a short amount of time. In most cases, I am not looking at what their work experience has been, I want more. I want to know how they handle adversity, are they flexible, do they have a can-do spirit, if put in a challenging situation do they act in an appropriate way. I often times make the joke that I would like to start interviewing candidate's parents to really learn about them and their family dynamic that likely shapes their view of interactions. And by joke, I mean I would definitely do this if it was at all acceptable.

As far as questions go, I usually ask different questions depending on the role and spend some time to think about what that particular role needs in order to be successful. So, if I am interviewing a sales rep and I know that enthusiasm over the phone is crucial to success, I will ask them what hobbies they have. Not at all related to what they would actually be doing daily, but a person's hobby is something they choose to spend time on, so it must be important to them. In order to be successful in sales over the phone, you have to get your prospect leaning forward and you can do this through painting the picture of excitement at our games.

There is likely a group of people I have interviewed that walked away wondering why I asked so many questions about them learning to play the guitar. One of the best examples of this is someone I interviewed early in my career who was a little reserved until I asked about his hobbies and he went on to share why he loved following the weather in such great detail. I thought if anyone can get this fired up about a snowstorm, he can surely translate this to baseball. I hired him, and he was a great producer. This question is not the only one that gets people hired but in an effort to get to know someone in depth, I think you have to mix in questions to learn someone's character in addition to their work product.

Best Piece of Advice For Someone In Your Role?

In order to be effective, you need to be comfortable with crucial conversations (*if you aren't, there is a book about it called – Crucial Conversations*[6]). Our leadership team talks so much about them and the importance of clear and direct communication. This is a place that can be very uncomfortable, as a general rule, most people want to be liked and telling someone a place they are falling short and need to show improvement doesn't lend itself to the warm fuzzies… The biggest piece of advice I give people is *they have to be more concerned with that person's overall development than the discomfort of getting them there.* You can see the difference in someone who has had a strong coach in their life to get them where they want to be, no matter the challenges along the way. As a manager, you owe it to your employees to make the commitment to make them better. If you manage people, this is your job. If you are looking for opportunities, you should be looking for someone to manage you that will make that commitment to you.

5 Keys To Becoming A General Manager

1. Remembering that not everyone is like you.

This took me more time to realize than I care to admit but as a manager you need to appreciate that you are there for your team and you need to craft your training, messaging and style to their needs.

2. Perspective is key.

You are always providing information to your team to learn the why behind the what.

3. If your employees aren't doing their job, it is your fault.

You are responsible for the hiring and training of your team so if they aren't performing well, you either hired the wrong person or you haven't trained them effectively.

4. Your performance directly impacts the overall goals of the organization.

In every area of our business, one team underperforming can negatively reflect on the rest of the teams. This can be from a revenue or reputation (internal or external) shortfall. When departments view what they do in a silo, they tend to not see the bigger picture and where they fit. The responsibility of a manager is to show their employees where they fit and their importance to the overall goals.

5. Never ask someone to do something you wouldn't.

This one is pretty basic but very important. Whether it is pulling tarp or picking up trash or moving boxes or making customer service follow up calls, your employees want to see you do the hard stuff. Show them you are a real person and it will reinforce to them that no task is too small to be important.

Create Your
Opportunities

Augusto "Cookie" Rojas
Senior Vice President / General Manager
New Orleans Baby Cakes
Pacific Coast League, Triple-A Baseball

About The Author

Augusto "Cookie" Rojas, Jr. JD, a United States Marine & Persian Gulf War Veteran, has worked in professional sports since 2007, serving as General Sales Manager of the Pawtucket Red Sox for 7 years, General Manager at Learfield Sports, Brown Bears Sports Properties (2014–15), and is currently serving as the New Orleans Zephyrs' Senior Vice President/General Manager, relaunching the brand as the New Orleans Baby Cakes in the Fall of 2016.

Networking saved my life.

If it hadn't been for networking, I would have had a legal career as an unhappy lawyer, stressed and worried about billable hours, angry that I didn't pursue my true dream of working in sports. Behind a desk in an office tower law firm with a mountain of paperwork, I would have questioned why I didn't take a leap of faith in myself, pursuing my passion. It would have been a miserable life.

The art of networking, coupled with the act of being able to relate to complete strangers in face-to-face interactions, along with the courage to speak, actively listen and learn, created a dynamic that I am continuing to reap the rewards from to this day. The skill of networking created the situation that I am in today. Had I not taken that first awkward, uncomfortable step toward reaching out to someone, I would not be living the life that I dreamed about.

I drive to the stadium every day, realizing that my office is inside. It is an amazing feeling, years in the making, that I can walk out onto the field, stand at home plate, look out at the stands and outfield walls, realizing the epic goal has been accomplished. Being a C-Suite level executive in minor league baseball, general manager of the New Orleans Baby Cakes as a Triple-A affiliate of the Miami Marlins, is a dream come true. And it was fashioned by networking.

Laughable as it may sound, I skipped a contracts class at Suffolk University Law School, in order to attend a sports and entertainment association meeting on campus. I asked a fellow classmate to do me a favor, take notes for me. Insignificant as it sounds, the decision launched my career into the sports world. It changed my life from being on a path headed toward being a lawyer to where I am today. Choices are what make a person's life, both bad and good, and whether they seize the opportunities in front of them when presented.

Everything in my family's life has been about taking chances. My parents are from Colombia, South America, who took a chance on the *American Dream* when they immigrated here with their children. It still drives me crazy when people misspell Colombia as "*Columbia*," same as when they confuse me for "*Cookie*" Rojas, the former Major League Baseball player. My nickname is something that I share with the famous Cuban, and I actually watched him play with the Kansas City Royals, had his baseball cards, and swore that I would eventually meet him personally. And everyone who meets me believes that I earned the *"Cookie"* nickname in the same way that he did. Not even close to being accurate.

Everyone always asks me how I earned the nickname, *"Cookie."* Growing up in Central Falls, Rhode Island as the only Latino family in a neighborhood block surrounded by French Canadians, it was a rather urban setting that I experienced. Central Falls is a blue collar, mill worker city sitting north of Providence, the state's capital. We lived in a triple-decker home, two aunts sandwiched between the floors that my family used. My immigrant parents worked multiple shifts to pay rent and exist, while my aunts took care of me as well as my cousins. My eldest cousin would give me dinner nightly, and I wouldn't eat unless the Cookie Monster was on TV. Thus, she called me *"galleta,"* Spanish for cookie.

Playing in the streets with the neighborhood kids, my cousin would call for me, using the *"galleta"* nickname. The kids would question what it meant, and when I told them that she was calling me *"cookie,"* well, the nickname stuck. They figured that it was easier to call me *"Cookie"* rather than *"Augusto"* and I've been unable to shake the moniker since. Throughout grade school, middle school and high school, I kept having people refer to me as *"Cookie."* When I enlisted in the U.S. Marine Corps, I figured no one would know my nickname, but that didn't last long either. I had a girlfriend whose friends sent me a letter with *"Cookie"* on the back envelope, and my drill instructors never let that nickname go.

When I graduated from college and was hired as a paralegal, I entered the position at the firm as Augusto Rojas, Jr. That was until a fraternity brother who served as a fellow intern at the firm saw me, called out *"Hey, Cookie!"* and the nickname spread like wildfire through the office. At that point, I chose to embrace the moniker, put it on my business cards, and I've never left it off since. The *"Cookie"* nickname is also a great one to have when working in professional baseball. So many people think that I am the son of *THE* Cookie Rojas.

The nickname has become a bit of currency for me. I've walked into the offices of several company presidents or CEOs, who each thought that they were going to meet *THE* Cookie Rojas, only to be disappointed that I am not an 80-year-old former Major League Baseball player from Cuba. Even when this situation occurs, I defuse it by still asking for five minutes of their time. I did finally have the opportunity to meet *THE* Cookie Rojas at a Marlins Spring Training, which shows that as long as you continue to network, you will end up reaching your goals eventually.

Whose Dream Are You Living?

An important lesson that I've learned over my life: *Not every dream that your parents have for your career is shared by you.*

My parents wanted me to become a lawyer. They saw the *American Dream*, projected that on me, and were convinced that I would be successful as an attorney. The secret to life is that you will zig and zag even more than anyone will ever be able to convince you of.

I zigged after graduating from a prestigious All Boys Catholic High School in Providence, enlisting in the U.S. Marine Corps instead of attending a four-year university. Everything happens for a reason is a theme that I've adopted, simply because I've witnessed the zig and zag of my life and career in a continuous, unexplained pattern that wound up working in sports today.

I also didn't quit when I made a decision. Even if it was a zig instead of a zag. I went through the Marine Corps Recruit Depot on Parris Island, served eight years and was stationed in 29 Palms, California in San Bernardino. I was 17-years-old, living over 3,000 miles away from Rhode Island, and learned how to grow up. When my time came up to go to my reservist station in New England, I elected to use the GI Bill, enroll at the University of Rhode Island, and managed to make some childish decisions, such as believing that my radio tech position with the U.S. Marine Corps would make an Electrical Engineering major easy to pass. Big mistake on that one, as I also joined a fraternity, nearly flunked out and by the second semester, had changed to a Political Science major.

My mother has always served as a bigger influence on my life, especially when I made the switch from Electrical Engineering to Political Science. Her vision of being successful in the United States was either to become a doctor, an architect or a lawyer. Well, I cannot stand the sight of blood, while I can doodle it doesn't translate well when letters are incorporated into mathematical equations, thus leaving my gift of gab as the sole option at the time. I believe my mother's exact words were: '*Augustico, usted hablas demasiado mierda debes debes ser un abogado*' which loosely translated to '*Augustico, you talk so much sh*t you should be a lawyer!*'

The conclusion that I arrived at when examining my political science classes was that there were no right or wrong answers. Justify your position or theory, argue both sides of the coin, and you earned a higher grade as a result. I excelled immediately in this academic format, moving from academic probation during the second semester of my freshman year to graduating on the Dean's List. It got noticed by each Law School that I applied to, each one accepting me, putting me on the path to becoming an attorney.

Despite the fact that my future wife was attending University of Rhode Island at the same period that I was, we didn't actually meet until we were in Cancun, Mexico during Spring Break. Kristin Cicilline was very popular on campus, held a leadership role in the Panhellic Council, was an academic committed to pursuing a Psychology Degree with a minor in English, and a tremendous worker.

She paid her way through college by waitressing every weekend in Newport, Rhode Island at one of the fanciest hotel and resorts in the city by the sea. Unlike my family, she came from one of the well-known families in the state. When we met, I fell for her right away, told her that I was going to become a lawyer, also told her parents that I was going to become a lawyer, and that I was going to take care of her. Life zagged as we were married in 1993, with a honeymoon cut short so I could take the LSATs. I then chose to work during the day while attending Law School at night.

At the start of our marriage, Kristin worked full-time in the mental health field, while I worked for the Rhode Island Attorney General's Office as a paralegal. We had two children before we realized that we were really working to pay for day care. Kristin wanted to stay home to raise our children, which was realized when my parents offered us financial assistance to cover the cost of an apartment, making it both utility and rent free. We relocated to my hometown of Pawtucket, Rhode Island so Kristin could be a stay at home mother while I started law school.

My Law School Schedule

In order to make our financial ends meet, I also did a paper route every morning.

✓ Wake up at 4 a.m. Get papers by 4:30 a.m. Deliver papers by 6:30 a.m.

✓ Be in court by 9 a.m. Get out of court by 3:30 p.m.

✓ Get home by 4 p.m. Get to the Commuter Lot by 4:45 p.m. Drive to Boston, during rush hour, and get to class by 6 p.m.

✓ Stay in class, then drive home around 10 p.m. Get home around 11 p.m.

✓ Sleep by midnight, starting the process all over again.

The Day It Happened

When you attend law school at night, it is not a three-year process. It is four. It becomes a grind. Not dissimilar to working in minor league baseball, where you have 70-72 home baseball games and can work 14-21 days in a row without a day off. It is a mental preparation that everyone has to go through to process and undertake the grind. And in the regular business world, there are no games to attend.

I survived my first year in law school, but was miserable. Not as bad as one of my fellow commuters who dropped out of law school entirely, but still, I wasn't happy. I was on the wrong path, attending law school for the wrong reasons, and it wasn't my dream nor was it my passion. I am not a person who quits easily, therefore I continued to move forward without any real substantial reason than that I wasn't a quitter.

It was during my second year at Suffolk University Law School, as I was walking to my contracts class, that my eyes caught a cadre of Suffolk alumni and current students discussing careers in sports. Seeing *The Sports and Entertainment Legal Society* gathering together made me want to learn more.

It was an instant connection that spoke as much to the heart as it did to the head. I found myself determined to work in sports. I was a former athlete, short and fat, getting zero sleep and attending law school while working through the day, and supporting a wife and two children.

But I kept thinking about how I used to be an athlete who specialized in football, baseball, wrestling, track & field, and was an amateur all-natural body builder during my high school years. I loved sports, was a native New Englander whose blood ran Red, White, Blue, Green, Black and Gold, all of the colors of my favorite area sports teams.

I had only one question: *How was I going to achieve this new goal of working in sports and what was I going to do once I was employed in sports?*

The Suffolk alumni in the room were members of sports commissions for local municipal sports authorities. Some of them were agent representatives of athletes. And one person served as legal counsel for a professional sports franchise. None of those roles that those alumni served in got me excited to mirror their careers, but they were working in sports, so it was a start.

The S.M.A.R.T. Strategy Forward

I elected to employ the **S.M.A.R.T.** business strategy[1] to achieve my goal of working in the sports industry: *S*pecific, *M*easurable, *A*ttainable, *R*ealistic, & *T*ime bound goals. The primary issue at that point was actually creating a goal, then initiating the creation of a plan in order to achieve it. I went to the Providence Library, searching for books focused on careers in sports and discovered "*The 50 Coolest Jobs In Sports*" by David Fisher.[2]

It was an incredible find, and I highly recommend anyone interested in working in the sports industry make the attempt to locate a copy. Within that book, the author found 50 people working in sports, across various fields throughout the country, and they provided what their duties were on a daily basis, in-depth. The book provided me helpful insight into the plethora of job opportunities that existed with teams, leagues, collegiate sports, and government entities. The 50 contributors selected provided insight into their careers as well as day-to-day responsibilities. In particular, one position focused on community relations opportunities in sports.

Having grown up in an urban community, it was the local Boys & Girls Club which saved my life, and allowed me to be introduced to a variety of adults from different career fields. As a child, I was exposed to athletes through this process including Jim Rice and Butch Hobson of The Boston Red Sox, and it made a lasting impression on my life. The community relations position in the book resonated with me and set a specific goal for me to focus on a career objective: I was going to be the Vice President of Community Relations for a professional football team located somewhere on the East Coast. By having a career goal, as well as a career destination, in mind, I knew that I would have to flesh out a plan in order to execute toward achieving that goal. That required making some drastic life-altering decisions on how to initiate that plan forward.

If I remained working at the Rhode Island Attorney General's Office, I would end up becoming an assistant attorney general, stuck in that role for the next few decades. That would be my career. Pursuing my chosen sports career, I would need to leave the confines of state employment; the trappings of having a decent salary with guaranteed time off and pay increases. I would be trading the safety net to embark on the unknown. I decided to go for my dreams, meaning that I needed to leave my role with the state as soon as I possibly could and I needed to do some informational research interviews, broadening my professional network with people who were currently working in the sports industry.

The Conversation

I knew that I wanted to pursue a sports career, which meant attacking opportunities with everything that I had in order for the goal to be achieved. The concern was the risk involved. I had promised my mother that I would earn my law degree, and I didn't want to let her down. I sat with her over a cup of coffee, a grown man who was still his mother's son, and was afraid of her response when I told her that I no longer wanted to become a lawyer. I didn't want to break her heart. I revealed to her my plans to pursue my passion by working in sports.

She offered me a puzzled look as a reply. I don't think she understood what I was saying. I let her know that I was still intent on finishing my law degree, but that I no longer wanted to pursue a traditional legal career. She told me that what I wanted to do with my life was my business. All she ever wanted was for me to be a good man, husband, and father. She still believed that if I completed my law degree, it would be very important and something that I could always fall back on. She was thankful that I wasn't quitting law school, and gave her blessing on me moving forward with a career in sports.

My mother's faith freed me from an emotional weight. I had my mother's support, as well as my wife's. But in order to move forward, achieving my dream, I had to begin by leaving state employment. We had two sons at the time, and my wife Kristin was pregnant with our third. That meant not quitting my job yet.

Thus, I had to resort to networking, embarking on informational interviews. I didn't know anyone who worked in sports, was personally making $17,000 as a salary against Kristin's $18,000 annual take-home, and we both had college degrees. The financial struggle was real. We had the bills that everyone else has; rent, car payment, utilities, groceries and other emotional stresses.

The market conditions told me that I should play it safe. I had a job with a salary and benefits. I didn't need to rock the boat and leave. It terrified me to walk into a chosen uncertainty. But if I continued to work for the state and not get out of my comfort zone, I would be miserable while paying the bills. It actually provided some clarity to think that way. Why settle for a life in order to simply pay the bills? My life was worth much more than that. I couldn't possibly preach to my children that they should pursue their dreams if I never had the guts to pursue my own.

133 Information Interviews

If you truly have the desire to work in sports, you have to create a strategic plan. That requires research, coupled with the concept of meeting sports industry connectors through informational interviews. There is no better avenue to gain accurate information on working in the sports industry than by meeting and interviewing those points of contact who have careers in the field. My first informational interview was over lunch, when a fellow paralegal who also worked as a high school wrestling referee and football coach, sat down with me to chat.

We talked about how he got into the position of being a referee, the environment of the Interscholastic League, the makeup of Rhode Island's governing body for high school sports, the demands of being a head coach, scheduling referee assignments, the expected income earned from serving in these sports positions. At the end of the interview, I asked him if he knew of anyone else working in sports, and he referred me to his high school's athletic director.

I asked for an introduction to the athletic director, which he granted, and that's how my networking with those contacts working in the sports industry began. Because none of these contacts had any pressure to hire me for an actual position, I was able to meet with high school and college administrators, sports information directors, agents, radio personalities, league officials, conference commissioners, professional team staff of local franchises and sales representatives for sporting goods manufacturers. This was during my second and third summers of Suffolk University Law School, on top of continuing my newspaper route each morning, working as a full-time paralegal, and becoming the father of a third boy.

I ended up taking a position as a sales associate for a sporting good store, *MVP Sports* which would later become *Decathlon Sports*, and spoke to each sales representative who came into our store while they were educating me on equipment. I was relentless at speaking and trying to meet with every sports contact available. My determination allowed me the opportunity to meet with so many people because at the end of each informational interview, I would ask them for names of anyone else who they knew working currently in sports.

An early mistake that I made in asking for a sports industry referral is that I asked if each of my contacts knew "*a person*" working in sports. Big mistake. When I asked for one person, I only received one contact referred back to me. I transformed myself by becoming a quick learner. At the end of every information interview, I started to ask, "*Do you know of five people who work in sports?*" That was an explosive, game-changing moment. Instead of gaining the referral to one person, I ended up getting at least three people referred to me. It led me down the path of gaining over 133 informational interviews in a three-year period.

Though the change sounds simple, it helped. I began speaking to multiple points of contact within the same sports organization. It offered me several different perspectives, people of varying backgrounds, and broadened my overall network. By having a bigger network, it would help me eventually get a job in the sports industry.

Lessons Learned Thus Far

Know what your passion is: As you read this, I envision that you may be a student in a university sports management program who is pursuing an industry that you want to work in. Or you are someone who has been either eager to gain employment in the sports industry, but currently employed within another industry without any clue as to how to get into the sports industry. I had pursued a political science degree while chasing my mother's desire for me to become a lawyer. There is a breaking point of clarity for all people, where they should ask themselves, "*Why I am pursuing this goal?*" or "*What am I in this university program?*"

Hopefully, those two questions are being asked of you now as a part of an internal retrospective:

✓ What did you answer back with?

✓ Are you studying sports management because you thought it sounded interesting or easy?

✓ Are you pursuing this degree at a university with the desire of being around athletes?

✓ Are you attempting to enter into this industry for perceived glory through your affiliation with a professional league, franchise or athlete?

If any of those reasons are why you are pursuing a sports management degree, you will discover that you are pursuing a career in an industry based on perception, not reality. And you will be very disappointed with the result. The sports industry is unlike any other career that you could pursue in the world. But it should not be one that you attempt to attain based on a desire to hang around or meet athletes. Too quickly we are all surprised at how little we are ever around athletes while working in sports. They are also just like us, and they have a job to do as well.

When you examine what your goals are for attaining employment in the sports industry, it allows you to discover what you are truly passionate about:

✓　Are you passionate about business and possess an entrepreneurial spirit?

✓　Do you love the art of writing and want to improve local communities with a creative, artistic flair?

✓　Do you welcome the challenge of sales as well as achieving goals?

✓　Are you good with coordinating systems?

If you answered *yes* to any of these questions then you can work in any field, but the beautiful thing is you can take these passions and skills and bring them to the sports industry. These are just some of the ways I could see you helping a team excel while you apply your passion.

Specifically, here's why we need people in the sports industry who answer these questions with a yes:

✓　We need business leaders to see opportunities and help our teams reach overall business objectives.

✓　We need public relations staff, to be the creative force behind our websites, souvenir programs and to get our message out to the press.

✓　We need people to help take our mascot, players and staff out to the community and create programs that positively impact our communities.

✓　We want to have the most *creative/artistic* minds in our marketing and social media departments.

✓　We always need people who love to sell and want to reach goals and fill the stadium with people.

✓　We need highly organized, detailed oriented individuals in our finance departments to ensure we pay our bills, forecast our revenue and expenses, data analysis and of course to ensure our staff is paid.

Then it becomes a matter of where you see yourself in any of the segments that the sports industry has to offer. Where do you see yourself specifically adding value for a franchise, league or vendor?

Find A Supportive Network

Once you have that, begin the research and ***Create a Plan to Achieve it***: do your homework, research the career field, the education needed for that particular role.

Explain to your family members what you want to do, some will respect you for chasing your passion and some will try to pull you back into the "*herd*" the land of the non-dreamers those that do what they are told to do, you will know who your champions are, those that want you to succeed and you will find out who the haters are, those that love you but may not want you to succeed because it will expose that they themselves either didn't have any dreams or they found reasons not to pursue them.

By providing your family with an explanation of what your goals are, the networking can become easier. Ask your parents, in-laws, family and friends about who they know that work in the sports industry. You will be amazed at the amount of warm connections that come from this conversation, and who specifically they can connect you to. This is about utilizing the power of the warm market. If you ask people you know to reach out to someone within their inner circle, networking becomes 10-times easier, and it will guarantee you an introduction to that individual.

My wife's great uncle was once the State of Rhode Island's Attorney General. He had a significant professional network. At a family wedding, we ended up chatting about law school, and my career aspirations. I shared with him my desire to work in the sports industry. Though surprised, he became one of my instant champions for pursuing my passion. He listed names of colleagues, friends and other professional contacts throughout the years who had worked in professional or collegiate sports, especially those serving as sports agents in the Boston area. Because of the movie, *Jerry Maguire*[3], for a brief period, I almost pursued a sports agent career.

After the wedding, my wife's great uncle said that he would reach out to his contacts, see if they would meet up with me, and ended up opening the doors to hundreds of people within his network. The next few weeks, I was receiving countless phone calls from my wife's great uncle, who was referring me to a whole new world of sports professionals that I was to now call and speak with.

One Floor Up

One of my best contacts actually worked on the floor above mine at the Rhode Island Attorney General's Office, the Public Relations Director Jim Martin. Literally working one floor above mine and I would have had zero idea without continuing to network constantly toward my goal. It turned out that he was the public address announcer for two professional sports franchises, the National Hockey League's Boston Bruins, and the Triple-A baseball team, the Pawtucket Red Sox. The PawSox were my hometown team. On a cold, raw and rainy April in the 1970s, I had attended my first game with my father off of a free ticket to McCoy Stadium as a kindergartener. Now, almost 25 years later, I ended up working for the PawSox as their General Sales Manager.

I met Jim Martin in his third floor office in 2000, marveling that my networking had stretched hundreds of miles, only for opportunity to reside one floor above my original place of employment when I first set out on my goal to work in sports. I explained my passion to work in sports, that I was about to graduate from Suffolk University Law School, and I was at a personal crossroads. Either I would take the bar, accepting an offer to become a Special Assistant Attorney General for the State of Rhode Island, or I would leave the Attorney General's office altogether while pursuing private practice, in order to focus on a career in the sports industry. I explained that I had zero desire to become a sports agent, that I wanted to be a Vice President of Community Relations for a National Football League team.

Jim Martin listened to me voice my goal, then indicated that he did not have any solid contacts at the New England Patriots. But he did know the PawSox general manager. I thanked him, asked for an introduction to the PawSox general manager, Lou Schwechheimer. Martin said that he would call him immediately after we completed our meeting. Interestingly enough, I had already performed a cardinal sin of eager prospective sports employees. I sent my resume to every sports team along the East Coast, but with my law degree listed. I received several rejection letters, stating that I was *"over-qualified"* which was code for *"your law degree makes you too expensive to hire."* One of those teams who had rejected me and sent me a letter was the PawSox, signed by then-assistant general manager, Daryl Jasper.

Approximately five minutes after my meeting with Jim Martin, I returned to my cubicle on the second floor, and discovered that my phone's red light was blinking, meaning that I had a voicemail waiting. I clicked the button, listened to my voicemail and played it: *'It's Lou Schwechheimer of the PawSox, Jim Martin called me and said that you may be looking for an informational interview. If you want to come to the stadium, I can set aside 15 minutes to speak with you.'* I learned early on that if you can do something face-to-face, then you should do it face-to-face rather than over the phone, by e-mail or by text.

I leapt out of my cubicle, gave the office administrative assistant a generic reason for stepping out of the office, ran down to my car, drove over 100 miles per hour and got to McCoy Stadium, home of the PawSox, in record time. Lou Schwechheimer became informational interview 133. He met me in the lobby, asked if I wanted to talk a walk onto the field, and I blurted out *"yes"* as we then began walking on the hallowed grounds of McCoy Stadium's infield. Lou's 15 minutes turned into two hours. We spoke about everything during that period, and at the end of two hours, he asked if I would like a job with the PawSox.

Without knowing the job duties, I accepted the job immediately. Schwechheimer walked me over to meet PawSox Assistant General Manager Daryl Jasper, who had rejected my resume only a few months earlier. It was then that I learned that I had been hired as an usher for the remainder of the 2000 season. Lou turned me over to Daryl, welcomed me to the team, and wanted to see me later after that night's game. Within a two hour stretch, I was a Pawtucket Red Sox employee.

I was working in sports. Sure, I had a retail sales job for *MVP Sports*, but this was a totally different feel to it. Moving forward, I could honestly say that I was working for a minor league baseball team, and in fact, I felt that I was working in a very important role, as an usher for the franchise. Ushers are the front lines of any sports franchise. They are a true reflection of your organization. There are times when fans may only speak to the usher, and that experience or interaction could determine what your fan thinks or feels toward the organization as a whole. Never underestimate who you have working in those roles or devalue the importance of customer service for your franchise.

I called my wife, thrilled that I finally earned a job in sports. She was excited for me, asked what I was going to do, and when I revealed that it was an usher position, she almost dropped the baby in her arms when she dropped the phone, stunned. My wife was under the impression that I was leaving my full-time assistant attorney general's position, with benefits, for a part-time usher position with the PawSox. When I arrived home later that night, she was happy and supportive, knowing that this was my proverbial foot in the door. It was meeting the goal of working in sports, after 133 informational interviews. She knew that I would work my hardest at getting to the next level and only needed an opportunity in order to achieve that goal. She also requested that I not quit my day job just yet.

The Greatest Usher Ever

During that entire summer of 2000, I worked my tail off as a PawSox usher. I greeted fans at the main gate, directed them throughout McCoy Stadium to their seat locations, collected trash during the PawSox's fifth inning "*HI-HO*" segment where the video board showed the seven dwarves from Disney's animated classic "*Snow White*" singing while the ushers did garbage duties throughout the stands. Over the PA, Jim Martin would direct fans to hand their trash to the usher, who each carried a large garbage bag. Ushering is about doing the little things, picking up the waste left in the concourse when no one is looking or helping a fan reach their seat whose hands are full of concessions.

Those little things matter because they are gestures which assist in growing the sense of belonging in your fan base, creating a sense of community in your ballpark and building the reputation of your franchise overall. If you ever gain an opportunity to work for a franchise, as an intern, unpaid volunteer or seasonal employee, I highly encourage you to accept it. And when you do sign-on, do so by putting your best effort forward, every single time that you put on that hat or shirt with the team's logo embossed on the front. The little things not only help you get toward your ultimate goal of working in this industry, but also help the franchise propel forward in fan experience with the effort that you put in.

There are specific sacrifices that I learned while making the choice to work in sports, especially during the remainder of that home game baseball season. I worked nearly every single home game, including those played during the day. I elected to take vacation days from my full-time assistant attorney general's job in order to work day games at McCoy Stadium. I missed Sundays at the beach so I could work Sunday afternoon games which started at 1 p.m. All of these sacrifices took away from spending time with my wife and three young children.

I relinquished coaching my oldest two sons in tee-ball, because my availability to be there for practices and games was no longer a guarantee. I had to be at McCoy Stadium around 4:30 p.m. for a 7 p.m. game, as the PawSox opened the gates two hours before game time for patrons. If you truly want to work in sports, realize that the sacrifices are larger than yourself. You are taking away time from your family, days at the beach, and your full-time job commitments if you cannot pay the bills working solely in sports. It may seem trivial at what you are giving up, such as vacation, but it all adds up and are sacrifices nonetheless.

When I accepted the usher position, I chose to seize the opportunity because I wanted to break into the business. I was willing to do whatever it took to get my foot in the door. Being presented with the opportunity to work with one of the premiere teams in all of minor league baseball, I didn't feel any duty was beneath me. My father always asked me: *'When opportunity knocks, will you be ready to open the door or will you be too afraid of what's on the other side?'*

Opportunity Knocks

A man is trapped in his home during a flood and prays to be saved. His neighbor offers to help him and to take him to safety but he is waiting to be saved by God…so the neighbor drives away in his pick-up truck and the water continues to rise and he is forced to get on his roof. While on the roof a man in a boat comes by and asked him to come in the boat and be taken to safety, he yells that he is waiting to be saved by God and then the boat leaves him. The water is surrounding him while on the roof and he is clinging to a small dry patch, suddenly a voice from above in a helicopter, bellows to him, 'Grab the ladder & we can take you to safety'…he declines the help because he is waiting to be saved by God. Sadly the man drowns. When he gets to heaven he tells God that he believed in him with all his heart, and asks God 'Why didn't you save me? Why did you let me drown?' God looked at him and replied, 'I sent you a pick-up truck, a boat and a helicopter and you refused them all. What else could I possibly do?' - "The Drowning Man" parable[4]

The position with the PawSox may have been as an usher. But it was a job with a professional sports team. I would have been stupid to turn it down. The trouble with opportunity is that it often only knocks once, and if you do not take that chance to open the door, opportunity likely won't knock on the door again, ever.

This goes back to "The Drowning Man" parable: *How many times have you let opportunity, in the form of a pick-up truck, boat or helicopter, leave you behind?*

The chance to become an usher, volunteer, intern or seasonal employee with a sports team is the universe throwing a soft-toss underhand baseball to you over home plate. If you crush the ball, hit it over the fence, the position can become a greater opportunity down the road. The choice is whether you choose to swing at the ball entirely by saying yes, or watch that opportunity go by you, hit the catcher's mitt, mainly because you are too focused on expecting an over-hand fastball pitched to you in the form of a full-time, perfect-employment position with the team. Take what you are given and make more out of it than expected.

During this same period, I also made a job change from the Rhode Island Attorney General's Office to the United Way of Rhode Island as Senior Vice

President. It stayed in line with my goal of working in sports. I knew that if I wanted to become a Vice President of Community Relations with a National Football League team, I would need to have prior experience working for a community-centric non-profit, as well as the No. 1 charity of the NFL. This was all about putting my plan into action. It was a pay cut, but an opportunity, which I swung at when it came over the plate.

My First Promotion

Near the end of the minor league baseball season of 2000, the PawSox Assistant General Manager Daryl Jasper and Chief Financial Officer Matt White asked me to lunch. They both knew based on conversations with me that I was interested in working in sports full-time. During lunch at a small family restaurant a few blocks from McCoy Stadium, the discussion focused on my future sports career. Over the course of the PawSox season, I realized how much I loved working the games, being a part of the franchise, taking care of fans and the thrill of working in minor league sports business. And I didn't stop networking when I was hired as an usher.

During the season, I networked any opportunity available, getting to know the box office manager, the community relations director, the team store manager and the interns. Everyone knew what my goals were and quickly became supportive. By the end of the season, Jasper and White wanted to survey how my first season with the PawSox had gone and whether they could help me further. By the end of lunch, they offered me a season position working in the box office, learning everything that I could about selling and distributing tickets.

Within half a season, I was promoted from usher to box office based on my goals and positive attitude. I hustled. I was now working, part-time, in the box office of a Triple-A baseball team, working side-by-side with the box office manager, who was a full-time staff member. That meant working games when PawSox President and International League Hall of Famer Mike Tamburro would walk into the box office. Lou Schwechheimer, Daryl Jasper and Matt White would also enter the box office, inquiring about tickets for guests, how the sell-out was being managed and status of our will call seats.

The conversation would extend to how the game management was going from the view of the box office or getting tickets out to *xyz* school for a ticketing campaign in order to bolster a lightly attended game night later on in the season. It grew my network by upgrading my position within the team to the meeting place where the PawSox brain trust converged each night. I was also working in the front office of a Triple-A baseball team and loved every minute of it.

My duties in the box office included fulfilling phone or online orders and selling tickets to fans arriving at game time as well as trying to upgrade fans to box seats whenever they asked to purchase general admission. The latter of the two is a must for every team's box office to do when there isn't a massive line to get into the ballpark:

✓ I also answered any questions that fans had as best as I could, and if I couldn't provide them with an adequate answer, I would investigate enough to try and provide them with an answer that was satisfactory.

✓ I helped operate the Will Call window, distributing and receiving tickets left by players for family and friends, along with handling tickets ordered online or over the phone that fans would pick up later.

✓ I worked as many games as I possibly could during the 2001 season.

✓ I took sick or vacation days to work weekday day games, choosing to miss birthdays, little league games, days at the beach, Memorial Day and the Fourth of July. To me, those things took a back seat and a lower priority if there was a PawSox home game.

✓ I needed to be available in the McCoy Stadium box office. When the box office manager would offer to send home employees early on low attended nights, I never raised my hand.

✓ I was always willing to "*print out the batch*" of tickets for the next home stand that needed to be mailed out to fans.

✓ Whatever the box office manager or assistant general manager required of me, I was willing to do and perform the task with a smile. And if we were overrun by fans due to a massive walk-up, requiring front gate help, I left the box office to help tear tickets and greet fans. Being promoted from an usher to box office position did not mean that I was unwilling to return to the former when required.

Cookie's Lesson: *No job is beneath you. Do the best job that you can at every task that you are assigned.*

Six Years As A Part-Timer

Nothing that I did came cheap. Or quick. I wasn't promoted at the end of my first part-time season with the PawSox in the box office. I worked seasonally there for the next six years. I left the United Way of Rhode Island after being offered a newly created Assistant Vice President of Community Relations position with the Pawtucket Credit Union. It was the largest financial institution in the state with $1 billion in its coffers. By taking this position, I was gaining traction in the realm of community relations, with the ultimate goal of working for a National Football League team in the same type of role.

I did not rest with the PawSox box office manager position. I continued to perform Internet searches on jobs in sports and became a member of *TeamworkOnline*. Due to my PawSox box office experience on my resume, I did get interviews. I attended the Baseball Winter Meetings when they were in Boston, and with the aid of PawSox front office staff, I got into the meetings, was introduced to contacts at the Fresno Grizzlies, and even met a headhunter who specialized in the sports industry. By the end of the Winter Meetings, I had a job offer from the Grizzlies and an excited headhunter who wanted to help me find a full-time job in sports.

Cookie's Lesson: *You need to make your own luck.*

Sometimes, saying no is a good thing. I turned down the Fresno Grizzlies offer for a variety of reasons and less than a year later, they had an ownership change which would have eliminated the position offered to me anyway. The headhunter got me interviews with the Detroit Pistons and Miami Dolphins. The Pistons flew me out to Detroit twice for a corporate sales position, but we were unable to agree on salary and benefits, meaning that I turned down that offer as well. Saying "*no*" is the hardest self-examination that you will take, questioning whether it is the right or wrong decision that you are making.

I had some doubt at this period in my life about whether I would find a full-time job in sports. I was working for the Pawtucket Credit Union and every season for the PawSox in their box office. For the credit union, I was working directly with their sponsorships of the PawSox and American Hockey League's Providence Bruins, the minor league affiliate of the National Hockey League's Boston Bruins. Incidentally, one of my 133 informational interviews was with the Providence Bruins, and I had almost quit my assistant attorney general's position to take a commission-only, inside sales job with the Bruins. I said "*no*" to that opportunity as well, mainly because it did not allow me to take care of my family in the process.

The Offer

This part of my life is where I figured perhaps, being the part-time box office manager for the PawSox and working at the Pawtucket Credit Union, was the best that I could do. While I was happy, I strived to want more. I was working in community relations, running the department, working for the PawSox each season, and was content. It was a shock to me that I received a phone call from Matt White at the PawSox, informing me that Daryl Jasper had accepted a general manager's role with another minor league franchise in New Hampshire. White said that the PawSox president, Mike Tamburro, was going to be looking for someone to fill Jasper's vacant role as assistant general manager and that Tamburro was potentially going to contact me.

I was at one of my son's middle school wrestling matches the next day when Mike Tamburro called me, asking if we could meet in his office. I cancelled whatever was on my calendar for the following day and set the meeting with Tamburro. Immediately, I got on the phone with Matt White, inquiring for tips on how to negotiate with Tamburro if he made me an offer.

Cookie's Lesson: *You never know when opportunity is going to knock on your door, so you had better be ready to open the door and meet opportunity head-on when it arrives.*

Matt's comments during our second conversation were very brief. There was zero negotiating with Mike Tamburro. He was old-school. If he wanted you to work for him, he would make the offer, then take a legal pad, writing down the financial terms of the deal. You either accepted or rejected it. Accept it and you were in, reject it and that was the final offer he would ever make. After explaining the potential scenario to my wife, we wrestled with what to do. Unless the position financially supported us, I couldn't accept it and would wait for another opportunity. I couldn't sleep that night while my mind examined the various possibilities of the unknown.

I arrived in a suit and tie, resume in hand, for the 10 a.m. meeting. Waited in the lobby like everyone else because I was only a seasonal employee without credentials. The receptionist escorted me back to Mike Tamburro's office through a maze of front office cubicles and desks. I had interviewed with several teams and organizations, but this was different, it was my hometown franchise and the opportunity felt like the right one if offered.

Tamburro's expansive office was adorned with mementos of his decades in the business of baseball. There were framed photographs of Red Sox baseball legends as they made their way through the farm system; including one with Roger Clemens and the late owner of the PawSox, Ben Mondor. I had never been in Mike's office before. My eyes were fixated on trinkets and keepsakes on his bookshelves. Despite it being a raw, cold day in January, I started to sweat, nervous.

He asked if I was still looking for full-time employment in sports. I blinked and said, "*Mike, I've been working for you and the team for six full seasons. I have forgone little league games, missed family barbeques, and trips to the beach. Missed my daughter's July birthday, used up all of my sick or vacation days to work day games at the stadium, rearranged family summer vacations to coincide when the PawSox were on a 10-game road trip to avoid missing games at the stadium. Mike, I wouldn't have done any of those things if I didn't want to work full-time for you or any other sports team.*"

Tamburro sat, listened and smiled. "*That's what I wanted to hear. We are looking to replace Daryl, and I believe you are the guy to do it.*" He reached for the legal pad on the table, jotted down notes, tore the sheet and folded it, then slid the piece of paper across the table in the manner that Matt said he would. "*This is the offer. We want a General Sales Manager, not an assistant general manager. We need someone to help our sales team, take on all of Daryl's duties, sell corporate and groups, oversee the interns, ushers and all of his other duties.*"

I liked what I was hearing as my eyes went to the financial offer. It was a *BIG* pay cut of $20,000 less per year with a five percent commission across the board, new or renewal, corporate or groups, but the team would pay for medical and dental. There was a line of demarcation between what I had promised my wife that I wouldn't accept and what Matt White told me about Tamburro's offer, either I took it or left it, because there was zero opportunity to negotiate. I calculated quickly that in order to generate back the $20,000 pay gap in commission, I would need to sell about $400,000 more in inventory. I have always believed in my ability to sell, even back in college when I sold *Cutco Knives* and cleared a lot of that inventory. It's a confidence issue of knowing that you are representing a good product and people are trusting you, as much as they are the product, when they buy.

I offered my hand to shake Tamburro's and accepted the position. After eight years of making the decision to work in sports, 133 informational interviews, three declined official job offers from sports teams, I had finally accepted a full-time position offer with the Pawtucket Red Sox. It served as an additional bonus that there was no need to move my family. I was working for my hometown team, the place where I went with my father in the 1970s, the place where I took my girlfriend and future wife to her first baseball game in 1990, the place where I took my eldest son to his first game as a baby during a Roger Clemens rehab start. I had finally accomplished my goal of earning full-time employment in sports. Now, all I had to do was leave Tamburro's office and explain it to my wife.

I am blessed that I married my best friend, she understands me and knew that I would accept the position, regardless of the salary, but she knew that I would do everything in my power to take care of our family.

Cookie's Lesson: *If you want to work in sports, you will need your family's support and they need to believe in you.*

After looking over the state of our finances, my wife decided that she would need to contribute by re-entering the workforce full-time. She had been working at a local private all-boys school part-time, but our children were older and she wanted to do something that could help me achieve my dream, while avoiding any family hardships. A month later, while leaving the Pawtucket Credit Union, my wife suggested that she could do my job there. I added her name to the list of potential candidates to replace me, she was contacted for an interview and ended up being offered my former position. Everything happens for a reason.

My Sales Slump

I wish that I could say that I started out as a sales champ for the PawSox, selling tickets and corporate sponsorships with ease. I was a sales chump. I was unable to get some sales going and had my hands full. I was focused on getting interns lined up, season staff and ushers squared away and trying to figure out my sales team. Thus, I sold nearly nothing. I started in late February after all of Daryl Jasper's accounts had been divvyed up, meaning that all of his accounts required having contacts to ensure that their sponsorships/partnerships would be fulfilled. I was at ground zero with a zero sales book.

In March, less than a month on the job, I was asked to meet with Lou Schwechheimer in his office. We had a *"come to Jesus"* meeting. One of the many that I would have with Lou over the years about the importance of sales. I agree with him, to this day, that sales is the number one thing that everyone in minor league baseball should be thinking about. The bottom line fact of minor league baseball is that we are a business, and if we don't sell, we won't be in business very long. Without sales, there is no minor league baseball, there is only a team of men playing a child's game, searching for their break into the big leagues, but people won't be attending to see the dream chasers. Those seats need to be sold.

Sports sales is unlike anything else. Once a game comes and goes, it's entirely gone. You can never recoup the loss of an empty seat. If you are the general manager of a clothing store, you can sell your inventory today, tomorrow or two months from now. There is a larger availability of time to sell in regular retail, as stores are open 365 days out of the year, even on Christmas, in order to clear their clothing inventory. That's not the case in sports. Once a game is played, and if you didn't have a sell-out, you lost out on every potential revenue gained from a sold seat, and it can never be recouped. A Triple-A baseball season has only 70 home games now, meaning only 70 dates in which you can make revenue for your business. That means 70 windows of time to sell seats, concessions, and merchandise. Only 70 days in which your corporate clients can be in front of a crowd.

Sales is hard. And sports sales is even harder, bottom line. In sales, there is an understanding that you are an independent business person. You own your personal franchise, per se. Fortunately, I had a base salary plus commissions, meaning the ability to earn unlimited income as part of an uncapped commission structure. If you work your tail off and are smarter than your competition, if you are willing to hustle every day, then you can make a great living off of sales. I know I sound like an old man, but you have to be a hustler to win at sales. Every thought has to be geared toward: *"how am I going to make my business a success?"* For me, my focus was: *"How am I going to make up the salary difference from my old position to this new one?"* or *"How am I going to pay the mortgage next month?"* or *"How am I going to pay the bills?"* or *"How am I going to make my next car payment?"* The answer was simplistic, but realistic. I would have to out-hustle the next guy.

Instead of complaining about not having enough time, I realized that I had the same 24 hours as everyone else. No different than anyone else on the planet. Managing your time is what separates you from the competition. I knew that I had to drop my children off at school, that my youngest kid wouldn't be dropped off until 8:30 a.m., meaning that I was unable to arrive at work earlier than others in the office. But I also knew that my wife could pick up our children at 3 p.m., allowing me to work later. You would be amazed at the volume of phone calls that I could make after normal business hours. Thousands. I addressed my administrative duties during normal work hours, then from 4:30 p.m. to 6:30 p.m., I could make as many calls as humanly possible with a smile and dial attitude. The beauty of making phone calls after business hours was that generally there was no gate-keeper, meaning that I could get through to the decision-maker unobstructed. I would catch them off-guard, then provide them information on group or corporate sales opportunities. It was a very effective practice for me.

If you examine the job duties from what I did as a PawSox General Sales Manager to what I do now as the General Manager/Vice President of the New Orleans Baby Cakes, there are similarities and differences. But it all comes down to the hustle, attitude and dedication that I am willing to place in both roles that made my tenure at both franchises successful.

Personal Sales

First and foremost, I needed to start selling tickets, I started off by getting as many lists as I could from the ticket office, these lists were of former ticket buyers, former season ticket holders, former FLEX ticket holders, former hospitality customers, former corporate partners, etc., etc. and I just started making calls. I would make 50-70 calls a day, with no customer relations management system (CRM), just a ticketing system the PawSox had created. I had a sheet of paper and there I listed who I called and when and just called, left voicemail messages, mailed information out, emailed information out, invited people to come to the stadium to see our stadium for seats, or to see our hospitality options or to see our signage options for corporate partnership opportunities. I attended chamber events, as many as I could, wherever I could, whenever I could. I would travel far north into territory that was closer to Fenway Park than it was to McCoy Stadium.

My logic was that maybe these chamber folks, comprised of all types of companies, Big Business, small business owners, etc., would be looking for a more affordable alternative to the Big League prices. I networked at all of them and I will tell you right now, it's not easy, I am really an introvert who has worked in roles that require an extrovert, but I knew what I needed to do and that was simple. Find prospects, prospects, prospects. In baseball, in sports, everyone is a prospect, anyone can use what we offer: customer hospitality options, employee appreciation options, branding opportunities, you name it we offer it.

Sales requires planning. Knowing every day, that I needed to make a certain number of calls to prospects, a certain number of calls to the folks that were now moving through my sales pipeline, to stay connected with them, to build a relationship with them, to earn their trust and eventually earn their business. Once I had their business it was time to under-promise and over-deliver. It sounds cliché, but it's very simple. Find a need that you can fill, build relationships. The worse thing we can do is a money grab. Do you want a customer once, or do you want a friend that will buy from you annually?

I read and have a lot of sales books, listened to a lot of tapes, CDs, and now podcasts, all with their various tactics and techniques, and I have been in various sales trainings over the years that have taught various *"openings"* & *"closes."* However, it's really very simple, out-work the competition, build a solid base of repeating business, help your clients fill their needs and continue to find prospects that match your existing clients. That has been my secret to sales success.

Team Sales

I also needed to get our sales team on the same page, we didn't have any sales goals when I got there. Let me explain, the team was so successful over the course of the last six years that when I got there, the sales team I inherited were more *"order takers"* than we were *"sales people,"* something that would affect many on our sales staff who didn't heed my warning that we constantly need to find new prospects, constantly need to fill the pipeline.

I had to lead by example and demonstrate that I was hitting my weekly sales calls that I was sending out information that I was following up with folks, that I was crafting *sponsorship/partnership* packages that make sense to the client. Bottom line I had to show them that I was doing exactly what I was asking them to do. Leadership by example.

When I was in the Corps, I respected the Lieutenant or Captain that was *"in the muck"* with *his/her* troops more than the desk jockey, who sent orders or directives from a distance. I wasn't going to make you do anything that I wasn't willing to do. It's something that I did then and continue to do now. If you get an opportunity to lead, you have to learn that you are no longer their friend, you are now their boss. You can't talk about management over lunch because you are management. Most importantly you had better not forget that people want to be led. They are especially willing to be led by someone *"who does what he says,"* not someone who *"says what to do."* There is a difference.

Therefore, we had to create a strategy and implement it. Priority number one was to craft group sales goals for everyone and the team as a whole. When crafting these goals you should get buy in for the goals by the sales person. Once they buy in and craft a goal that they create, that challenges them, they are going to try to go for it. If you craft goals for staff without their buy in, you are not going to get the buy in you need and you may not reach goal.

On the leadership front there was some animosity, as some of my team, who didn't like a former usher, a former seasonal person who worked in the box office, suddenly coming in and becoming their boss. They were not too happy that they suddenly had sales goals to reach and be judged on. They did not like the fact that they had to make and track the calls made during the day and report them at the end of the week. Consequently, when the recession hit, those that had filled their pipeline, through the expectations we set with them, survived, those that were more accustomed to being "*order takers*" fell to the way side. ***It is a business***.

If you are just happy having a business card that says you work for a sports team, that's all you may have at the end of the day… is a business card. If you aren't hustling, if you don't view yourself as an independent business person, then there are hundreds if not thousands of people that would give their right arm to come and take your desk and phone and take over your business.

I am happy to report that through the implementation of some simple tactics, such as; having sales folks join their local chambers of commerce, having sales folks go to networking events, by having sales folks have meaningful contacts with prospects, by listening to their prospects and clients, having sales folks track their calls, increase the volume of calls made, all those that followed the plan, they were able to withstand the recession and we actually reached sales highs every year. A great effort from those that wanted to be coached.

These folks were able to realize that if you follow effective and sound sales techniques and hustled, you could make money even during a global recession. In fact you had to hustle even more to find any sales. Those big 100, 200, 300 person outings may not have been there due to company layoffs, budget cuts, etc. therefore, you needed to fill that pipeline with 25, 50, 75 person outings. Its simple math, more prospects were going to be needed in order to make your goals or to even surpass them.

Administrative Duties

I wanted to build upon what we had in terms of internships but I also wanted to ensure that we had more students, more diversity, and find interns that we could possibly groom for full-time opportunities with us or with another team. I began by posting our position everywhere I could, our website, local newspaper sites, teamwork online, local colleges and universities.

The results were tremendous:

✓ We had students from Ivy League schools, public 4 year and 2 year schools.

✓ We had pre-med students, business, and pre-law, finance alongside sports management majors.

✓ We also had students of color and exchange students applying for internships.

✓ We had expanded our net and we had a plethora of candidates from different backgrounds and perspectives which makes for a richer work environment.

✓ We also elected to have interns do group sales, a skill they could take with them to any team or organization.

✓ We had our interns doing group outings and community service projects that would help them build a strong bond and what the marines refer to as a "*espirit de corps*" – a feeling of pride, fellowship, and common loyalty shared by members of a particular group. I am proud to say many of the interns we hired went on to work for other professional franchises, including the Red Sox, Celtics, Bruins and in college sports as well.

As far as our sales team, we had to make some changes, I had to *let* some folks go, and we decided to bring in new people including some seasonal employees and former interns who knew our culture and were eager to be a part of what we were building. As I mentioned previously, these folks wanted to be coached and they survived and thrived during the great recession.

In terms of our ushers, I relied heavily on my colleague the director of security, Rick Medeiros. I met Rick while working on the box office, he was a seasonal employee I believe who also came on board full-time.

He did everything, security, oversaw the ushers and he could sell too, that's what I loved about him most is that he was a great example of being able to do it all and not complain. He oversaw those who we should hire and I trusted him because he knew the value of having staff that were our front line, all needed to be cognizant of their role in interacting with our fans. Exceptional customer service was a must for Rick and he asked all his ushers to do the same.

Special Event Marketing

I thrived here. While I wasn't given free reign, I was able to come to Mike and or Lou and provide ideas that would help us increase ticket sales and potentially help us sell corporate partnerships. Here is a list of some of the events I helped to create and allowed us to sell more tickets, very few if any of these ideas are new and they are copied in several places, but what we were allowed to do was find ways to enhance the fan experience at the game.

We realized that no longer were fans interested in just coming to games and seeing baseball, the fan was evolving, they wanted an experience when they came to games. Now, more than ever, the game at times is secondary.

Once again, here is the list:

Star Wars Day – evolved over several seasons, from increasing a Sunday afternoon game with 2,500 to 5,000 fans to a Saturday game with post-game Star Wars-themed fireworks and a standing room only crowd of over 10,000 fans.

Ladies Night – taking a Thursday night and making it bigger, it evolved to a simple tabling night with tables being sold between $500 - $1500 per table, with about 10 – 15 vendors. It also led to a multi-year billboard sponsorship in the $15,000 range per season.

BIE DAYS - With the advent of the *NO CHILD LEFT BEHIND ACT*, we had to find creative ways of taking day baseball games during the school year and making them educational. This led to a partnership with Rhode Island College, the state's primary teaching school, they were able to assist us by crafting a *Baseball In Education* curriculum that we could market to schools.

Their student teachers helped us teach kids simple baseball centric lesson plans spread out throughout the stadium and an adjacent field next to the stadium with learning stations. These stations had lessons in math, science, history, social studies, physical education, etc. Schools could once again bring students by the bus load to the stadium.

Bicycle Day – through a chamber networking event I met a financial planner whose parent company believed in the health and wellness of children. We were able to create a feel good event and garner a very good corporate sponsorship of a day late in the season. The company would use their foundation to buy 100 bicycles and helmets for children at risk.

We would contact local non-profits that would bring kids to the stadium to get the bicycles before a busy Sunday Day game. The catch was the children couldn't know they were coming to the game to get a bicycle. The reactions from the children were incredible, to see their faces and really wonder if the bicycle was truly theirs, is a feeling I will never forget.

Back to School - Back Pack Celebration – during the season, the days leading up to school can be very slow, parents are prepping for school, parents with kids in private schools have to pay tuition and may not have expendable income, therefore this is an opportunity for creativity.

On the winds of success with the *Hispanic Heritage Night*, we were able to build a relationship with this group that donates thousands of backpacks to at risk children in our community. They needed a secondary distribution point and I was given the OK to offer our stadium. We just asked that each backpack have a ticket to a game before the season ended. Credit to Lou for teaching me this opportunity to get a ticket in a child's hand. We were able to do it and we have many children and their parents who may never have come to our stadium, at our ball park for the back-pack give-away and then those kids coming back in the future with their parents in tow.

PawSox 5K – Again, there are certain times during the season when you try to find a way to fill the park and we were able to host a 5K at the ball park and made it a great success, hosting walkers and runners and offering prize money for the top finishers, often getting runners to come from all over for the top prizes. Each participant would get a ticket to a game and it offered our stadium exposure, augmented our charitable efforts and helped bring people to the park who may not have come before.

One of the best events I was able to have and grow was *Hispanic Heritage Night*.

Ben Mondor, PawSox Savior

Here's some simple history. The Pawsox are a key part of Pawtucket, Rhode Island. When the stadium was built in the 1940s, the city was comprised of mostly Irish, French Canadians. They had tried to have professional baseball there and they did but eventually the teams would go bankrupt. Finally, they had a Triple-A team there. The Rhode Island Red Sox, would eventually become the Pawtucket Red Sox. Sadly, it too couldn't survive and it filed for bankruptcy. It was saved from that fate by a French Canadian businessman named Ben Mondor.

He bought the team in the late 70s. At this point the city was still, Irish and French Canadian, with some small pockets of Hispanics (*my family was one of those small pockets in neighboring Central Falls, RI*). By the time I started working for the team in the 2000s the demographics surrounding the stadium had completely changed. It was now predominantly, Hispanic. We recognized that with the growth of more *Latino/Hispanic* players on MLB rosters, we weren't seeing an increase in the Hispanic population in our fan attendance. In response we recognized that there may be an opportunity to tap into an underserved market. We started off slowly, having a particular night that had Latino music. There was some push back by the non-Latino community, but our leadership felt it was important that we continue to reach out to the community.

We knew we had to reach out to the community and the leaders of that community to learn from them as to what we needed to up the game. We reached out to the Latino community organizers, Spanish speaking Radio DJs, journalist from Latino Newspapers, Business leaders of Latino Heritage. We were able to take our simple night and blow it up into a huge event.

We leveraged our advertising with Telemundo to bring national telenovela actors to the stadium. Advertising on Latino TV/Radio helped to increase our attendance. But it wasn't enough, we decided that we would need to do more for the community, eventually we brought one of the biggest celebrities on their network to the stadium, *la Dra. Pola*, from their famous TV show **Caso Cerrado**, the event was a massive success and helped us have credibility with the Latino community. Our Latino nights were augmented with celebrity appearances, Latino food, Latino beverages, on field performances by cultural groups. It was a huge success.

That's just a short list of opportunities I had when I was with the Pawtucket Red Sox, I was truly blessed. In my time there, eight total seasons of full-time employment with the organization, I was able to reach that threshold that I needed to make the difference in the base salary. Furthermore, our owner, Ben Mondor, was extremely generous and if we had a good season, he rewarded us with bonuses. It was an honor and a privilege to work for Ben, Mike and Lou.

The End of The Beginning

Alas, all good things must come to an end. Ben passed away after a long battle with an illness. I was honored to be a pall bearer at his funeral, which was incredible, the number of people and lives that Ben touched was incredible. It was a true testament to the power of a minor league baseball team, the impact you can make in your community. A few years before Ben's passing I knew I no longer wanted to work in the NFL, I wanted to work in minor league baseball. I wanted to be a general manager of a minor league team and I wanted to eventually own a team. In the years I was the General Sales Manager for the Pawtucket Red Sox, I was courted by several franchises and ownership groups to consider being their general manager. I refused some offers and some I didn't interview with because I didn't want to relocate my children who by now where in high school and established in our community. That all changed when Ben passed.

When Ben passed away, we were all worried as to what would happen with the team, would Mrs. Mondor keep the team or sell it. At the end of the day, she elected to sell the club to Larry Lucchino and a group of investors. I knew I had to get out, most new ownership groups tend to come in and implement a *"scorched earth policy,"* in essence terminating everyone who was employed by the previous ownership group. With kids now in college, and others preparing to go, I knew I had to leave.

I received a call from Daryl Jasper, the former assistant general manager of the team who indicated that there was a general manager opportunity with the company he was working for, Learfield Sports, marketing specialists in the collegiate world. He asked if I was interested, I mentioned that I was. A few weeks later, I was offered the general manager role with *Brown Bears Sports Properties*, the marketing arm for Brown University. It was a very sad day. I felt I had to leave in order to advance my career and without any certainty of the composition of the front office under the new ownership there was no certainty I would have a job.

Mike asked me to stay until the end of the season, I checked with Learfield, and with the college football season upon us in early August, they asked if I could leave as soon as possible, before the baseball season concluded over Labor Day weekend. It was unprecedented to leave in the middle of the season, my last day was the

Friday after The Fourth of July. My time with my hometown team had come to an end, we had accomplished so much. I hadn't forgotten that I modified my career goals that I wanted to be a general manager for a minor league baseball team, that I would like to one day own a team, it was a strategic move.

I started with Brown University in July and it was a crash course in collegiate athletics, the do's and don'ts, compliance, new place to work, new office, new colleagues, new everything it was exciting and new. At the end of the day my duties were as follows: *sell, sell, sell, sell*. I was the only employee, I shared a staff person with Providence College, another Learfield School and our regional boss was Daryl, who was the general manager at the University of Rhode Island, yet another Learfield School.

In terms of technology, Learfield was light years ahead of where I was in baseball. I had so much technology and marketing information at my fingertips, it was great and I immediately got to work renewing partnerships that were about to expire, and trying to find new partners as quickly as possible for this Ivy League school's athletic department. Learfield did a tremendous job at training sales staff and I was held to the highest expectations in sales. Constantly filling my pipeline, always engaged in sales contests, focusing on competition amongst all the schools across the country.

Getting The Band Back Together

I worked for two years for Learfield at Brown, and I learned rather quickly that I missed working in minor league baseball. I missed the opportunity to be as creative as I could be, but I continued to do my best for Brown. I was in Dallas, in December, at the airport coming back from a Learfield sales training when I got a call from Lou. He and I had not spoken in the time since I left the Pawsox. He indicated that he was going to be buying a Single-A team in Port Charlotte, FL and possibly a Triple-A team in New Orleans, LA. He asked me which team would I want to be the general manager for. I thought about it and having been to both places, I knew that I really liked New Orleans. Being a history buff, I knew there was a charm, a history to New Orleans that was unlike anywhere else I had been. We decided to table our conversation until after the holidays.

On January 2, 2015, we met at a *Café on Wickenden Street*, on the East Side of Providence RI, just down the road from Brown University and near where Lou's daughter went to high school. We met and chatted and he told me he was a long way away from buying the team but that he wanted me to be the general manager in New Orleans. We agreed and decided to keep in touch and that I would work my butt off for Brown until and when it was time. The day after Thanksgiving, 2015, I got a call that the deal had been consummated and that Lou would be the owner of the New Orleans Zephyrs.

It was time to give my notice to Brown and to Learfield. I gave them a month in order to finalize some deals and on the 31st of December, I closed two big sales, one with *Moe's Southwest Grill* and the other with the *National Guard*, that was my last day with Learfield. I scanned both contracts, sent them to my bosses, cleared out my desk and on January 2, 2016, I landed in New Orleans to start in my new role as the general manager for the Zephyrs. I had realized my dream. It doesn't end there, there was, there is a lot of work to do. I was a first time general manager in MiLB. I had worked in minor league baseball for 14 seasons. I had worked in collegiate athletics as a general manager for two years, but being the general manager of a Triple-A team, that is a challenge.

We elected not to do a "*scorched earth*" policy, but I can understand why some teams do it, it's a way to completely reboot, to have everyone on the same page. Coming in January, we elected to keep folks who were part of the organization and give everyone some time to prove themselves and the value they bring to the organization. What we often forget when we are looking for a job or a career in sports, is that this is a business. If you are not in sales what are you doing to help the sales team?

Over the course of the past two seasons we have made some staff changes and as of today, we still have half of our full-time staff comprised of members of the Zephyrs and the other half is comprised of people we brought in from outside, some were employed by other teams, some employed in collegiate sports, some I am proud to say were interns and seasonal employees that we were able to groom and bring in to be a part of our staff.

Being the general manager has been everything I thought it would be and more; it's been sales, community relations, administrator, league representative, stadium operations, concessions, promotions, merchandise, game day decisions, etc. The great thing about working as the general manager, for a minor league team is that you are a small business owner because every issue comes across your desk and you hope to surround yourself with quality people in each department to help you make these decisions once all the facts have been reviewed, but at the end of the day, you have to make the final decision(s).

Music, Football & Logos, Oh My!

It has been a great two seasons, here are some accomplishments we have made over the past two years:

✓ In April 2016, we hosted the first major concert in the history of the stadium, hosting Grammy Award-winning artists *Mumford and Sons*, having the largest crowd in the history of the stadium, with over 16,000 fans in attendance.

✓ In the Fall of 2016, we hosted high school football at the stadium for the first time, hosting 8 regular season games and three playoff games. The games featured the Catholic League of New Orleans and our first game was carried nationally on ESPN.

✓ We had one of the greatest New Name/Logo unveils in MiLB history, changing the team name from the Zephyrs (*the name of the team when it was in Denver*) to the Baby Cakes. The logo pays homage to the plastic baby found in the famous King Cakes during *Mardi Gras* season throughout the region. We gave the community a team name that is reflective of the region and its culture and not a name or logo taken from Denver, Colorado.

The New Orleans Baby Cakes Are Born

Let me talk about this name change before we go on with the list. It wasn't easy. Many in our community felt the name Zephyrs came from the Roller Coaster called the Zephyr at Pontchartrain Beach. It actually came from the Denver Zephyrs. We felt that we should give the team a name that reflected the rich culture of the region.

When I got to New Orleans in January 2016, we started to get a King Cake[5] at the stadium every day. What's a king cake?

It's the small plastic baby inside the cake that inspired the name baby cakes.

You see if you get the slice of King Cake with the Baby in it, (*yes a small plastic item is placed inside an edible pastry, totally ok here in New Orleans so long as you have a warning outside the box.*) you have to buy the next slice.

King Cakes bring people together to enjoy a slice, have some coffee, some conversations. You find that baby in your slice you have to get the next one and everyone comes back together again. That's what we do in minor league baseball, we bring people together, they have a good time and we hope they come back together again.

What was created was something that is unique to a region that has *Mardi Gras* Krewes, Jambalaya, Gumbo, beignets, café au lait, snow balls not snow cones, where the east bank is west and the west bank is east sometimes. We wanted something that captured the essence that makes this region incredible.

I believe we did it, but change isn't easy. Having a team name that has about 20 years of history and suddenly after a year, this new ownership group from the north is changing it, is very hard. There was significant push back. I had several negative emails that came into my outlook inbox, some were very "*colorful.*"

The Baby Cakes Earn Their Place

After all the dust had settled, we are happy to say that the region has embraced the logo. The image of a Baby breaking out of the King Cake with a determined look, the look of the strong and resilient people of the region:

On November 15, 2016, we had the unveil at the stadium. We had over 500 guests in attendance, great New Orleans food from our Concessions partner, CenterPlate, a great video of New Orleans/Louisiana Celebrities including Baseball Coaching Hall of Famer, Ron Maestri, former MLB star and Louisiana native Will Clark, NBA Legend and Hall of Famer Shaquille O'Neill all claimed that they were Baby Cakes. Our Facebook Live was seen by thousands locally and nationally, our new name was discussed on local sports talk radio the same week as the LSU vs Alabama, and the Saints vs Panthers Football games, and it was discussed on ESPN by Barry Melrose who said he loved the name and the courage to change it.

We weathered a barrage of criticism for the name change, but we withstood the storm and thrived in the controversy. Our new logo won the best logo in *Baseball America's Logo Mania Contest*[6] beating the Vermont Lake Monsters in the final championship matchup, the fans voted on the their favorite logo. Merchandise sales for our new logo(s) were more than what we expected and helped to elevate our logo nationally and we have seen our logo in pictures sent from all over the world.

Our team was nominated in back to back seasons for the Best Community Relations Promotion in all of Minor League Baseball. In 2016 we worked with a local mission to help people get back on their feet through employment opportunities at the ball park. In 2017 we were nominated again and won for Baby Cake Nation, where any baby born in 2017 would get a life-time pass to Baby Cakes Games and one child would get a scholarship to any 4 year state school when they turn 18. It was the first *Golden Bobblehead Award* for the organization. There is hardly any chatter regarding our name, the uniforms are classy, the merchandise is truly reflective of our community. I relish when I am on a plane or in an airport somewhere and see our logo.

I am very proud of our organization, we have come a long way and we have a long way to go but we get this tremendous opportunity to make something happen here in New Orleans.

Looking Back To See Forward

As the general manager/senior vice president, my days are always different, no two days are the same and that is what I enjoy. I am glad that I still use my law degree in a variety of ways, contract interpretations and negotiations, public speaking and critical thinking. I would never change a single thing that I did to get to my current role. Everything that has happened, happened for a reason and helped me get to where I am today. Moving forward I would like to continue my work with the LSED, the Louisiana Stadium and Exposition District, the government agency that oversees our stadium, to find ways to make necessary improvements to the facility that would enhance the fan experience and help our players achieve their goals.

I think my life would be a great book, heck I may even take this chapter and really go into some serious detail to make the book a reality. I am the *American Dream*. Think about it, my parents are immigrants that came to America so that their children could live the life of their dreams and I am. I came from a small, urban city, a city that's one square mile to become the general manager for a Triple-A Baseball team. Looking back I wouldn't change a thing. Every situation, every instance that I have gone through on this journey has helped me get to here.

I had some sad moments, such as the time I went to the winter meetings in Boston to try and get a job and walked away saying *no* to a Triple-A team and wondering if I would ever get another chance. There are those moments such as the time I said *yes* to the usher job. A moment I will never forget because as far as I was concerned I had made it. Accepting the full time job with the Pawsox, what a moment, years of informational interviews, years of rejection letters after applying to so many positions, what a moment that was. Being recruited to work for Learfield sports and working at Brown, an Ivy League University. For a kid from Central Falls, I was shocked I was there amongst the large learning halls and historic playing fields. I've learned that life is going to knock you down, you will lose more often than you win, you will be rejected. It's how you respond to that that makes the difference in the life you will live. It was worth it. *It has been worth it.*

My final bit of advice, if you want to work in sports, then I suggest you go for it. It's a great industry and the opportunities are out there for you to chase your passion. Understand that we are a business, if you understand that you will excel, you will find happiness and achieve tremendous success.

GEAUX CAKES

Passion Creates Brand Advocates

David Lorenz
Vice President
Fort Wayne TinCaps
Midwest League, Class-A Baseball

About The Author

David A. Lorenz has worked in minor league baseball since 1995, a member of the Fort Wayne TinCaps since 1999. Lorenz's focus is dedicated toward leading the Corporate Sales Department at Parkview Field. Lorenz has also served his community for several years in local non-profits, serving the Boys & Girls Club of Fort Wayne for three years as a board member.

Whether I am selling group tickets or a corporate package, it is the passion that I bring to the table that helps me thrive by the end of the day. When you have a product that you believe in, when you love what you do, it shows in the product that you are selling. The client feels that energy from you too. They know when someone half-believes in their product, or doesn't really care about it at all. That's why every day, no matter how I might be personally feeling, I put those emotions aside to sell the product the best way that I know how. And that's with so much passionate energy that the client knows that I believe in this product as much as they should.

My first professional sports sales job in minor league baseball was all about my passion and energy. My first day working for the Chattanooga Lookouts is probably different than the person reading this. Mine started January 15, 1995 after driving all-night to Chattanooga, Tennessee, arriving at the ballpark around noon. My excitement carried me through the first day that I started. I was welcomed by the staff with open arms, and looked forward to starting my career in minor league baseball.

The training that I received consisted of showing me that my office was inside the Engel Stadium press box. It was complete with a phone book and telephone. And I was told to start selling group tickets. That was all my training consisted of. But my energy and passion for working in the industry that I love took hold. I didn't complain about where my office was, or what I was told to do. And I wouldn't have had it any other way. I realized that earning my stripes, learning to sell, and striving to be the best at selling the product that I loved would show through because of the passion that I exuded from the first day.

That entire summer had me working alongside two other interns who were also making group sales calls. We started feeding off of each other in a friendly, competitive manner. We pushed each other on goals, attempting to see who could make the most group ticket sales. To this day, I still have great friends who came from that Chattanooga experience. That first year in minor league baseball was the best year of my life. Because I was selling a product that I believed in, and loved. I still won't forget Opening Day 1995, during batting practice, where I was continuing to paint the outfield signs while constantly wondering if I would be clocked by a fly ball hitting the back of my head. I still wouldn't trade that memory for anything.

That summer was about learning who I truly was within the sports industry. I believe that 1995 defined me as a minor league baseball sales professional because I was open to the suggestions on how to grow in my job, and I haven't stopped learning since. I didn't have my sales "*wrap*" down pat yet, nor did I use a sales script. But I was willing to learn, especially from the two interns who sat beside me in the Engel Stadium press box that summer, and I developed my own style of selling. It's about fostering a belief in building a personal rapport with my clients, while listening to their wants and needs, that allows me now to supply them with a proposal that they will love. Mainly because I love the product enough to believe in selling it.

Love What You Sell

I enjoy making my sales presentations because it features a product that I absolutely love and believe in. My passion shows through. Every presentation may be different based on what each prospective client hears, and depends on budget, but the one thing that never changes is the passion that is hard-wired into my delivery. The quickest recipe for disaster is to lose excitement for the product that you are selling. A client wants to feel that passion from you, to see that you love it even more than they do, so that they can invest their budget into a product that you also believe in.

Sales serves as the lifeblood of any great sports organization and to be truly successful, you should be focusing a 100 percent of your effort on how you strategically manage your time equitably. This includes finalizing deals, creating activation points, managing inventory, working with other team members, cultivating prospects, being a visible respected individual in the community, building your personal family time, solidifying valued relationships with co-workers and clients, serving on non-profits, adhering to your religious beliefs, and becoming the face of the organization. That is a ton of spinning plates to keep from crashing down on your head. It takes a true professional to work in the sales and create an effective work-life balance that reflects your personal values as well as relationships.

Sales is not about learning gossip or spreading it. It is not about learning what is going on in your office or department. It is about generating an entire team effort toward a common goal of success. What happens in other departments within your organization can easily affect yours and may be more important. But those goals should be shaped together to serve a common purpose. And it is important for those success points to be shared by everyone when there is a "*win*" to be had.

An example of a team "*win*" can be ticket sales. Because if the ticket sales department does not "*win*," then other departments will suffer. Less fans through the turnstiles hurts everyone equally across the board. If ticket sales plummet, expect corporate sponsorship clients not to renew because the team no longer has the eyeballs of the community focused on it. Less ticket sales means less merchandise and concessions sold. Parking takes a hit because no one is paying to pack the lot when the stands are empty.

Celebrate Wins

Working in minor league baseball is a humbling experience. Mainly because you learn quickly that it is not about you as an individual member of the sales staff. The entire organization either wins together, or it does not. All departments should be working together toward that common goal of success, building up everyone together. That means an entire front office working to have each other's back, to avoid gossip or tearing each other down, and creating a culture where everyone feels they earned a piece of any "*win*" that the organization celebrates. A general manager should be a cheerleader for all of their departments to foster a winning culture further.

Some of the people who enter into minor league baseball don't tend to understand this. They get too competitive, especially with their co-workers, and they do not last long. Mainly because selling minor league baseball should be fun. That feeling of fun should be felt by your fans, and your corporate partners, each investing in the team to experience that emotion for themselves. The majority of companies will welcome any opportunity with open arms if the front office employees selling to them love the baseball product as much as the companies do.

Too often we forget that emotional check. We tend to focus on the routine, the mundane. And it costs us sales with our corporate clients as well as fans. If we treat minor league baseball as a normal business, the shine comes off for the public buying from us. When we call and set up appointments with our decision-makers and community leaders, they are taking our meeting because we are selling exciting product full of energy. We are not selling insurance. We are selling fun. An intangible that everyone wants to experience, and cannot get enough of.

I always attempt to speak to decision-makers when I am entering into the sales process. Luckily, it is easier with sports because it isn't insurance. It is something that everyone tends to like and want to talk about. When I'm in that sales process, I inch closer to the sale with a decision-maker because I am building that relationship with the top echelon of the company. It doesn't mean that I don't value non-decision-makers within the company either. Nor do I treat them differently in a personal relationship. But my focus on a relationship built with them cannot come at the expense of a CEO or President who will be making the ultimate decision on partnering with my team. It all comes down to focus.

It is important to remember that this game is about selling the idea of fun, the thrill of entertainment and above all, a great experience. It is not about whether you win or lose. The ballpark represents a cathedral of culture, where everyone is destined to have the time of their lives in a three-hour escape to forget about their daily troubles. It is imperative that your entertainment promotions team has a rock solid program each night because this may be the first experience for a fan at your facility. None of your front office can slack or take a game off when it comes to how they present the passion of the game toward the fans. If your fans show up, so should you.

Share Success Stories

Success stories are the best ways for your internal culture to thrive around the front office. That means celebrating the wins collectively, and talking about what went right with the sale. Everything should be positive, especially when a co-worker needs to hear it. This means getting down to the good, the bad and the ugly of what it took to make that sale happen. We learn from our mistakes more than we do our successes. It is important to share those stories in person with a co-worker, or even send them out in a company-wide e-mail. I encourage front office staff to talk about what occurred to make that win possible.

Understand that this is a long-game play for the front office and organization. I guarantee that someone within the office, upon hearing of how a win went down, will use that experience to make a new sale. Or it will end up assisting them in the sales process. This serves as the basis of creating a thriving culture of engagement within the organization. If the office culture isn't up to standards, then you need to be the change that you want to see. Challenge yourself as a team member within the organization to see how that organizational culture can be positioned toward everyone sharing a win together. It is an easy task if you focus your energy on making sure this is possible.

Celebrating your successes with others does not mean glorifying nonsense. It does not mean gloating or showboating obnoxious behavior. Share those stories to better the performance of the group around you. When you are with your client or co-worker, whether in an office setting or at lunch, sound encouraging. It is that easy. When your workplace culture showcases a bigger picture of the organization with employees who are working together toward a common goal, you start to build something special. Your clients are their clients. Introduce those clients to your staff. Let them know that each team member will have a contributing impact on the relationship during the success of your partnership.

Don't Be Territorial

A key facet to bringing in a team *"win"* is phrasing. This works for both the organization's staff as well as the client. It is *"our"* partner, not *"my"* partner when you speak about the client. This is a team win because the client is partnering with the organization. The partner is not solely *"yours"* alone. They never are.

You may have an extensive relationship with the client, but the logo and brand of the team are what they are affiliating with at the end of the day. When you segment out whose client it is, rather than provide a collective *"we"* to the equation, you are limiting the potential for a team "win" to flourish and effectively killing the organizational culture.

Let's set up a scenario where *xyz* company has signed a 5-year, $150,000 branding package. They want to buy season tickets and book a company picnic with your organization. You may not have the ability to go *"full menu"* or want to handle the ticket sales transaction personally.

Here is the way that you can phrase a conversation with a client to ensure that they will always receive the best service and experience, regardless of the point of contact within the organization: *"I'm going to have our specialized ticket sales representative contact you. He will take great care of you going forward with your ticket and hospitality needs. Remember, I'm always here if you need something or in case the contact that I'm giving you isn't available."*

This is how you setup the foundation of teamwork within your organization. Build up your co-workers as opposed to tearing them down or isolating them. Silos don't work for anything but agriculture. You should be open to sharing leads because everyone wins.

The client gets to work with two or more team representatives, allowing them to gain a feel of your vibrant office culture. No one has the ability to activate all of their client's needs solely anyway. By working in a silo, you tend to fail and drop the ball, harming the client relationship because you are forcing yourself to sell outside your expertise or comfort zone.

Focus

I'm a huge advocate of focusing on your expertise. This does not mean that you will not grow by honing some of the skills that you may be deficient at. However, you cannot abide by the notion that you are perfect in every skill set. You should want to share your clients with your co-workers from the start.

There are people who excel in specializing in hospitality or ticket sales. Let them gain momentum for your organization by developing a deeper relationship with your client. Not only are you setting up your co-workers for success, but you are strengthening your bond with them as well as your client. It is a priceless opportunity that you need to have flourish and can pay dividends back to you when your co-workers refer their clients to you as well.

This also re-enforces why your client does business with your organization. When its renewal time, you can be more certain of a slam dunk success and it is easier for a client to say "*yes*" when they have three great contacts within a team rather than saying "*no*" because they only have one.

If that team contact leaves, it means that the organization may not renew that client at all or have to rebuild the relationship entirely to keep the renewal possible. By practicing these methods of sharing success you are also setting yourself, as well as your organization and staff, up for dividends to be paid out later.

People always buy from people that they like. It is important to be likeable. To be a person that others want to meet and talk to. You need to avoid projecting negativity to anyone, especially a client, regardless of the day that you are having. You should go out of your way to be as likeable as possible.

Make the difference in how you project your attitude as the client is watching how you act through multiple sets of eyes. That administrative assistant, that low-level mailroom worker or that middle management employee are all watching how you react. This can get up to the decision-maker quick, especially if you are not likeable or project a negative attitude.

Be Involved

I would highly encourage anyone seeking to broaden their scope of sales in the community to be part of the community. This is about being different than the other sales people in the area, setting yourself apart because the client is buying from you, seeking out a fun, exciting entertainment product that will enhance their joy. It is important that you give back by being visible in your community as well. You should want to be an active part of the city that you live, work and play in. Serve on at least one non-profit board at all times.

Donate your time, knowledge and finances so that you can be proud of what organization you represent as well as the public good it provides back to the community that you serve. Giving back is the ultimate measure of a person.

Whenever I speak to a young professional about gaining momentum in the community that they are selling to, I focus on being known for doing the right things. That means doing business with the very best companies and contacts that you can find in your area. You want to be proud to share your client activity with your co-workers, because their reputation is renowned in your area.

Not only will the clients receive greater customer service, but your co-workers will "*win*" as they make more sales. This helps your organization employee retention, preventing them from looking for other job opportunities outside of your team. If everyone is happy and renewing, the office culture will be thriving.

Culture is not to be taken lightly. This means that you have to be a caretaker of building and maintaining it. Your co-workers may have game responsibilities and may not be able to provide a client with a facility tour. Or they cannot attend to a fan who requires assistance with ticket, concessions or parking needs. This is where you become a true caretaker of the "*win*" culture in your organization.

You should want to have your co-worker's back. If you see something in need of attention such as a client or fan assistance, be the immediate point of contact for it. Do not make an attempt to "*expose*" a co-worker for not caring for that issue. Do not undercut your co-worker with gossip, or complain to a supervisor. This is how toxicity kills culture.

If you see an issue, embrace this opportunity to make that client or fan's gameday experience better. Do not try to bring office politics to your client or fan. They should feel positive, not negative energy coming from you at all times. You are a point of contact for how a client or fan ultimately feels about your team long-term.

The experience that you provide them ends up shaping whether they ever buy from your organization again. Embrace the moment of meeting a future client or fan because they love the product as much as you do.

Embrace Opportunities

These are the opportunities that you should welcome every time they occur. This is a way to solidify your relationship with your co-worker as well as your office culture. Always make eye contact with your fans. Be looking for chances to meet new people. Be the organizational brand that makes your fans think of fun first. Every fan that you meet may be a potential sponsorship client. It is important that they see you as an asset, not a liability. When the client welcomes your presence, they are happier to renew with a simple phone call, a face-to-face meeting or a sit-down meal. If you end up taking them bowling or golfing, you may end up signing the next sponsorship deal at a luncheon for a Rotary that you both serve on.

Never leave your sales process to chance. The success rate for random not strategic sales is a poor one. If you don't work in a relentless fashion as continuing to build the relationship with a client, you may need to discover a new career path. It is imperative that you avoid becoming every other sales person that you have ever met who didn't care about the product that they were selling. Think about those people who sold something that they didn't have passion for.

You are selling a fun experience within an entertainment option. This is about treating every client like you would your mother. Trying to ensure their happiness and care, so that you can transform into a sales rock star. It also speaks to the office culture that you establish because you eliminate the fear of your co-workers not having your back. If you continue to focus and deliver on every detail, you will have a raving fan who serves as a client forever.

I recommend that every professional within an organization, regardless of title, act as if they are going to retire with that team. Even if there is no way that they are going to actually do so. You want to sell, but you want to build relationships within your work culture enough to build a mindset of success for everyone around you. Doesn't matter if they are an intern or the top executive at the team. Your thought process should center around becoming a lifetime member of the team, where you take ownership of each and every client that exists in partnership with that organization. This isn't "*your*" client, it's "*our*" client.

If you perform this broadening scope of projecting a dynamic office culture correctly, you will create lasting relationships with all of your organization's clients, whether they started with you or simply have worked with you at some point along the way. Clients are more comfortable with employee transitions when people do decide to leave the team, specifically because they know that they will be taken care of by those front office staff who have had encounters with them in the past, regardless if those conversations are in-depth sit-down meetings or random encounters at the ballpark on gameday.

A 24/7 Renewal Mentality

Quite frankly, I love renewal time, and so does everyone else within the organization. We host 125-150 corporate sponsors annually for a game, complete with high-end picnic fare, and allow them to network with our other partners. This is a great way to foster an environment where we ensure that they attend at least one game per summer without being asked to sign a check or agreement. When we host these events, we also invite 25-50 prospective clients, allowing them to network with our current clients, enjoying the game on the team. It creates a dynamic where our clients do the selling for us to prospects. They love our product enough to invest in it, typically sing our praises to the prospects, and create an easier buying decision on new business.

In June 2013, the TinCaps hosted our clients at the ballpark with door prizes, food, and spirits. One of our companies had a concourse sing at the park which elicited another client to inquire how they could replicate the same type of exposure the company was gaining. Having known this client over the previous 6-7 years, I replied "*multiply what you are currently doing by five times.*" I wouldn't have said that to a prospect, but I felt certain this was an appropriate reply. I wanted him to know that the investment level was also significant before we started talking actual price. Within 90 days, we had a signed agreement for a 6-year partnership at $32,500 annually. If we hadn't done that client appreciation night for our clients, we would have never had this type of inquiry or investment upgrade.

April 2012 was no different. We hosted a small event with only 65 prospects who came out to the ballpark. We had one outfield sign available, sitting there, unused. One of the prospective companies that had come out that day had told me previously that they didn't have the budget to work with us in 2012. I had been working at building the relationship with this prospective company for the past 2-3 years, and didn't give up, even when I was told there was zero budget available. That April 2012 event had the prospective company send out four representatives. I didn't concern myself with selling them directly, instead letting the ballpark do the selling for me. I allowed them to enjoy the game, foster networking opportunities with other prospective clients, taking in food and spirits. When I spoke to the four guys, I casually mentioned that I hoped we would work together next year, getting a proposal to that prospective company prior their budget being set. One of the guys from the prospective company mentioned the empty outfield sign, asking if it was available. I told him it was open. His reply "*We'll take it. I'm the finance guy and I sign the checks.*" Six years later, they've stayed with us and signed a new three-year deal that will last until 2019.

Renewals are a 364-day process that starts the moment the ink is dry on the last deal. The goal is to always be attentive, providing outstanding service along the journey. We should all love renewal time because it shows when you have put forth the effort, concentrating on all of the details of the agreement, building that relationship, and adding value to the partnership along the way. When you do those little things, a renewal is inevitable. You should be calling your client at different times, not solely for a renewal of their agreement. When you care about your client beyond the agreement, it separates you from every other sales person.

"We" Not "Me" Culture

This is a mentality that you have to adopt. It does not come easy. You must be open to working hard and over-delivering. You should be committed to excellence at your job, pushing a "*team culture*" over a "*me culture,*" creating sponsorship execution as well as activation. That requires you to undertake hand-written thank you notes, provide t-shirts and hats to your client's children when they come to the ballpark, help them gain access to batting practice or a pre-game dugout or field tour. If you perform your job well over the next 364 days, you will never have to sell another client on why they should renew with you. They will renew without question.

If you cannot do these little things, I would strongly suggest that you explore other career paths. This is a blunt assessment that is always an internal struggle. This industry is built on special people running a team who have the abilities to multi-task, focus on the team's big picture, and foster a working clientele base of over 100 companies. Not to mention all of the fans who come through the gates by the thousands for 71 home games, plus playoffs. Or the speaking engagements and other time commitments to show your community that you care. It is a challenging position to work in sports. It is not for everyone. If you are organized, driven by success and can pay extra attention to detail, you can shine in this industry long-term.

Every time those ballpark gates open is an opportunity. Whether the facility is sold out or not, this is the organization's chance to project a positive atmosphere to your community and fan base. It doesn't happen if you are frowning or negative. Do the little things for your clients when they are at the ballpark. You only have a finite period of 2-3 hours to engage with your community and fan base prior to lights being turned off, the opportunity to shine being over. Don't waste that moment with each fan by projecting an attitude that hurts your team long-term.

Be Excited To Work In Sports

It should feel like an absolute privilege and honor to work for a sports team. There are millions of people who would kill for an opportunity. You wouldn't even have to pay them to work it. And if it does not feel that way for you, that should be an indicator that there is a problem. There are going to be times when things do not go your way. When sales do not happen even when you thought you were about to close on a client who turned you down. Or worse, your best client moves out of state, and now you have to start the relationship process over again with a brand new set of people to earn back the revenue that you are losing.

This is a business that requires a tough skin. We want every client to buy our product. We think every client should absolutely buy our product. Mainly because we love our product so much, we cannot see any alternative other than consuming our product. But this isn't the case with every prospective client that we meet. You should embrace the opportunity when your clients choose to say "*yes*" to your proposal, and be able to handle those who tell you "*no*."

When someone doesn't buy your product, that means that you have to work harder at building the relationship so they will decide to purchase what you are selling over time. This is not an easy career. If it were easy, those fans in the stands who swear they would kill for the opportunity to sell your sport would be doing it. They aren't for good reason. Not everyone is equipped to handle the trials and tribulations of selling the sports product.

Your excitement needs to shine at the ballpark, especially when you give stadium tours. I love giving tours of our facility to prospective or current clients. You should as well. When you are touring a ballpark for a prospective client, it is a great opportunity to introduce all of your team members that you see on tour in a friendly manner. This creates the sense of a great office culture. It also transforms the experience for your prospective client into a friendly sales and buying atmosphere.

There should be no reason to hide your client from the other members on staff. If you are doing that, consider how it would feel not to be introduced to a client when someone else had them on tour. Isolation is never a way to warm up the office culture in a vibrant environment of fun and excitement.

Treat your tours as a way to help you bond with your client as well as your co-workers. This creates a family atmosphere with the team that your customers can feel, and pushes them to want to buy in. Your official presentation is secondary to the tour anyway. Sponsorship decks are formalities. The ballpark is the best deck you have to offer. The conversations between your prospective client and your co-workers serve as priceless opportunities to gain a "*yes*" toward the environment that they are buying into. There is no word that holds more magic than "*yes*" when it comes to sponsorship. Nothing even comes close.

A facility tour often creates the interaction that you need to foster a buying opportunity for the client to say "*yes*" to. It is the experience that they've had such as meeting your funny food and beverage manager who has a following in the community because everyone raves about their food. Your presentation is not one that comes from a sponsorship deck. Leave that nonsense for the sports management or corporate sales class in college. You've actually started your presentation by introducing the client to everyone else on the team. Because chances are, these are the points of contact that the client will require when working toward achieving activation. This also eases the client's apprehension toward being a partner with the organization. They earn the ability to feel comfortable with you, with your team, because you've even started the "*dating*" period of the sales process.

Know Your Client

There is an evolution consistently occurring with every client. Some clients react differently than others, and that renewal process alters the client's wants and needs. When you meet with a client, it is important that you be willing to adjust the partnership so it continues to meet their needs, even if those needs are a 180 degrees from where they were only three years ago. If a client doesn't absolutely love the sponsorship elements that the team has provided them over the terms of the original contract it should not be viewed as a death knell toward a renewal. This actually places the team in a position of strength. Now, they can drill down to fit the exact needs, as well as deliverables sought to achieve those needs, in a renewal contract.

When you dig down with your questioning of your client's sponsorship activation intentions during the renewal process, you discover what it is that they truly are seeking to implement over the next 3-to-5 years of the contract. All contracts change, and so do the needs of the clients that are agreeing to them. You have to be willing to change with your client in order to keep them on board. Getting upset, or walking away from a deal, or attempting to be dogmatic toward the original deal helps no one. Least of all the team cannot lose a sponsor who already loves them, the product and wants to work with you. You need to keep these clients on board because they are your best advocates for why other clients should invest in your team long-term.

During this process, I encourage all corporate sales professionals to re-examine the other options and elements that may have also changed in their portfolio from the time when the original deal was signed with the client. If the client already loves what you are doing, this is a great opportunity to not only increase the contract's value, but build a stronger, deeper relationship. You also end up selling more by doing more, meaning that your additional options and elements put in front of your renewing clients now allows you to sell more inventory to them. Every client feels taken care of, as they have been helped in building a larger brand within the ballpark, and with the team itself. By selling more, sure, your commission goes up, and you clear more inventory, but you're also increasing the renewal factor with the client. Because you are showing them that you aren't focused on merely providing them with the same product without re-examining their overall needs during the renewal cycle.

I've always found that the sales process compares a lot to the ritual of dating. No one sells marriage on a first date. No one closes a sponsorship deal on the first meeting. If it happens, it is an outlier, not a norm. And most of those quick type of deals often result in some type of divorce or separation, because the two partners came together too quickly to understand what they were getting themselves into. Corporate sales is always about the long-game play with a client. There is a process with minor league corporate sales that doesn't simply occur over the phone. It requires a face-to-face meeting, where the client becomes comfortable with you.

Sure, the meeting is setup by phone, e-mail or text message. But it takes a face-to-face meeting where the real sales process gets closed. I recommend trying to get that face-to-face meeting in the ballpark for the first encounter with a client. Tell your prospective client that they should plan on staying for an hour or so. Ask your ballpark chef to prepare a ballpark staple such as a *Philly Steak & Cheese* with house-made potato chips for both you and your client to eat at lunch while overlooking the baseball field. *The Philly Steak & Cheese* also happens to be our No. 1 concessions item at Parkview Field.[1] Every corporate sales person should always be playing to their strengths during this meeting. Make sure that everything you do results in the best version of what your organization offers to the general fan when you sit down a client in your ballpark.

Go The Extra Mile

Sweat equity often provides more tangible goods than anything else. Speak to your ballpark video production team prior to the client meeting. Get a welcome sign on your video scoreboard announcing the client's visit. Think about how this would impress you, to enter unexpectedly into a ballpark, and have your business as well as your name, welcomed on a 400-square-foot video scoreboard. With all of the video resources at your fingerprints, there is little excuse not to do this. Your sponsorship deck presentation is simply you, being able to sell yourself, as well as the organization, without screwing up on the little things. It's about creating that first impression for the client, making them understand why investing in your organization is one of the best decisions that they can make with the budget that they have.

It amazes me how few corporate sales people try to go the extra mile for their prospective clients. Selling sports is about selling the experience. Doesn't matter if it's the seventh inning for a general fan or the off-day lunch of a high-end sponsorship prospective client. When you tour the facility with your client, you should know what to say and what is supposed to happen within those confines during the period that your client is there. If the field crew is spraying chemicals on the grass or utilizing leaf blowers that possess deafening sounds, that isn't the time to schedule a facility tour with you client. Too many people do not know when to shut up either. Great sales people shut their trap, letting their client talk 95 percent of the time. It's the only way that the client will bluntly tell you exactly what they are looking for in a sponsorship package. If they love what they are seeing, they will renew with you. Most of the clients already have pre-determined whether they are going to buy or renew with you prior to stepping foot into the ballpark.

They can change their mind during that ballpark visit even if they are pre-determined to be against buying. Most if it depends on whether you can *"kick the tires"* by suggesting different sponsorship ideas as you tour the facility. If you sold them something that they didn't love or find helpful during the first contract though, you likely have a snowball's chance in heck of renewing that partnership. It's important that you listen instead of lecture while doing your tour.

You are the maestro of your own facility tour. The production must appear seamless, but help motivate the client toward a buying decision. While they are talking 95 percent of the time, you are conducting an orchestra of insight with your questioning. It leads them down the path toward opening their checkbook up to your opportunities.

I start off by asking them about their own experience in our facility: *What types of sponsorship options would you like to see in your package?*

I ask them about their community involvement, inquiring about the types of other sponsorships they have with other groups. Some clients want permanent signage, or 4-8 season tickets in seats facing their outfield sign. This is the point when I mention our annual summer picnic, ask in what location it has been held in the past, and who the point of contact is for that logistical component of the company employee retention program. All of these inquiries are brief in order to get the client thinking as well as talking.

This is where the team *"win"* comes in. You do not want to isolate your client at your facility from your other co-workers. This includes your rock star ticket sales representative, Jared or Jane, who you will introduce the client to during the tour. It is important that this engagement appear spontaneous enough to avoid sounding planned. You want the interaction between your client and the co-worker that you are introducing them to as seamless as possible, without sounding scripted. This is where the client lets their guard down, and ends up reserving a time for the ticket sales representative to be meeting up with them at a later date. You want to keep the touch points going, keep the conversation going into the weeks following, with new points of contact that ensure that the organization is viewed as having a wider relationship with the client than simply yourself.

Package Creatively

Having a written down agenda that you follow while taking your client on a ballpark tour makes the relationship feel forced. You are on a fact-finding mission with the client, but the conversation between you and the client, as well as the client and your co-workers, has to feel organic. It's learning about them, their interests and tastes when it comes to a sponsorship proposal, that makes the package work. This should be low-key enough that your client is eager to set another time to meet with you, after the facility tour is over.

You shouldn't be setting meetings in order to make your call sheets appear better.

If you are doing this, or your co-workers are adhering to this principle, please stop. It is beneath everyone in our industry to sell this way. You should be setting meetings to sell your product. Not dance around it. And if you don't absolutely love your product, you shouldn't be having ballpark tours or try to sit down with clients until you do love it. And if you cannot get in that frame of mind, consider another industry. Baseball is a passion play. If you are not passionate, then you aren't playing the game and should sit in the dugout with *"the Wally Pipps of the world."* Even with your passion on high alert, you should not be pushing the client into a *one-size-fits-all* package that they don't want. Way too many sales people try to carbon copy their packaging to individual clients. Pigeon holing your clients into something that they do not want is a recipe for disaster. Sure, the client may even buy this first contract renewal with whatever you are selling.

And you can offer the same sponsorship that you offer everyone else. But once they've experienced that package, and realized that it didn't fit them, it comes off like a mistake. It shows that you weren't listening to their needs, instead focusing what you needed out of them. And that's when you lose those clients forever or they decide to transition to budgeting those funds for other sponsorship opportunities with other organizations. Your packaging needs to be created and crafted in a unique way for every client. Partially, it is so other clients that you are cultivating constantly see something different that they could have had. It provides opportunities for discussion and engagement with the product in a different way. This perfect package honed specifically for a client means that once they sign on the dotted line of the contract, you will be on the clock for the next 364 days in a method of renewal with that client. Don't let up on the relationship or take it for granted. Instead, work at it, every day, in order to make sure that your client feels that you are earning their business as well as their trust.

In January 2015, I provided a ballpark tour for two marketing people with a bank. It was an initial meeting that fostered a great conversation. Breakfast meetings are unique in how they are perceived by the client, because you get that fog rolling off of the outfield lawn, that crispness of air as you sit overlooking the cathedral of whatever ballpark you are selling in. I had been prospecting that bank for several years prior, but had little success in getting a sponsorship out of them. The previous contact that I had, who did not buy from me, had left for other opportunities. That previous contact wouldn't provide me with the time of day, let alone a meeting, while at that bank. It is always music to my ears when opportunities start singing and this created a new opportunity for me to build a relationship with the bank overall.

It was a few days after the initial meeting when I actually received a hand-written note from one of the two marketing people who sat down for breakfast with me that day. They loved the tour and thanked me for it. My time was valuable to them, enough that they felt appreciated in thinking that I needed a note on how they felt during my time with them.

I still have the message etched into my brain: *"Your love of the TinCaps is evident and your enthusiasm is contagious. It's plain to see how much you love your job."*

By February 2015, the bank had signed a 3-year deal with our team. They signed up for another 3-year deal in January 2017. This is a great example of waiting out those contacts who won't provide you with the time of day. They may depart after a while, leaving you with an opportunity to re-engage down the line.

All of our meetings do not go this way. That would be a perfect world that does not exist. It is an example however of long-term thinking in a relationship model. You are required to have a vision that you can transform in front of any client during your meetings that allows them to see your passion. You aren't the only ones prospecting in the relationship either. The client is also prospecting you, to see if they want to do business with you. It's about the mutual trust going both ways in the relationship.

The beauty of scenarios such as the bank agreement was that they renewed a year prior to the original agreement being completed. This is a long-term thinking mechanism of creating a renewal cycle. It fosters a belief that there is no reason to wait until the original deal had fully expired. If you do that, the budget allocated today may be slashed before you reach the renewal date. Instead, the purpose is to never let the deal actually expire.

If you have a 3-year deal, you should be renewing at the end of two years, and keep it fresh with new activation points each time. When your client loves the partnership, they will want to keep it going and get the extension signed before you even ask. If they move on from the company themselves, by signing that extension early, they are helping ensure that you can establish that relationship with the new points of contact in that same company. It also allows you to focus on other renewals, as well as new business, because they renewed so early on.

Provide Options

You do have to ask the toughest questions when you are in a sit-down with the client. You cannot get away with not asking about a client's budget, what they have in mind, but you should be subtle about it. They know this question is coming, and they are waiting to respond to how you phrase it. This is where some younger sponsorship staff members get into trouble. They ask it so firmly that it ends up coming through as a caustic, blunt smack across the face. And it becomes a turn-off in the relationship overall. Having a modicum of patience, while strategically asking the budget question, is how you discover what the client intends to spend.

Shocking your client always happens when you do not ask the budget question. Because no matter what you say to them, it is always too high. Or you didn't ask for high enough, which causes the client to question whether your package is worth buying into. Some of this is a psychological gamesmanship. And it comes down to the subtle nature of creating a perfect package for your client by already knowing what amount of money they are comfortable spending with your team overall.

Too many sales representatives screw up the budget question from the outset. They either ask it too forcefully, or they do not ask it at all. When they refrain from asking, it tends to be an issue of fear. The idea that they are being rude or too nosy with their client. What in fact they are doing is protecting the client, as well as themselves, from a negative conversation scenario.

When you do not ask the budget question, you end up proposing a package that creates immediate sticker shock. It shuts down the conversation totally. Alternatively, if you know the budget number from the client, you end up getting the client to spend a higher amount by blowing them away with a package that they cannot say "*no*" to.

I encourage every sales sponsorship professional to share options with their clients. It tells them that you are willing to work with them. That you are actually listening to their needs to craft the perfect sponsorship package for them. This may sound awkward, but imagine how you embrace choice as a consumer. When you walk into a shoe store, there are more than two or three pairs to choose from in the place. There are dozens of choices, and the more attentive the shoe store representative is to your feet, the more willing you are to test out the shoes, give them a chance and bring them your business. It doesn't matter whether the consumer is buying shoes or sponsorship, it comes down to having their opinion matter in the environment that they are buying in.

The buyer is always in charge of the purchasing decision. You may feel that you have a superior product, but if you turn off the buyer, you won't convince them of anything except to walk away. As a sales representative, it is your duty to supply them with as many options as possible.

Retail is the perfect example on a small scale of what you, as the corporate sales representative, are attempting to offer: The ability to create a buying decision that resonates with the consumer making the choice of what they want by speaking to their needs and securing the transaction immediately by exceeding their expectations of those needs. It does not happen without the buyer saying *yes*.

There is a phobia that most sales representatives possess. And it kills the magic of the sales process. That's not being able to know when to *stop* selling. When the client agrees to what you want, saying the magic word of *"yes,"* it is important that sales representative stop selling the client. Too many sales representatives do not understand that their phobia of shutting up is exactly what harms the sales process. You should shut up more than speak.

You have two ears, one mouth for a reason. Use them accordingly especially after the client says *"yes"* by shaking the client's hand, replying *"thank you,"* welcome them to the team, and tell them that you will forward an agreement to them first thing in the morning. You want to give them the illusion that you are taking your time before sending them the agreement, so that they believe you are creating a special package for them personally based on what they told you during the ballpark tour.

Playing the long-game also means cracking open the door further on the team's front office to the client. Extending it to the people that they didn't meet during the ballpark tour. Have the team owner, president, or general manager mail them a hand-written note, welcoming them to the organization. Why? Because no other organization in the community will do that. The TinCaps implemented this idea several years ago. It has enhanced our relationship immediately with our client right after the hand-written note is received in the mail. This is a sales process of showcasing the type of avenues of representative power that are opened up to the client upon signing the agreement.

Another facet is how you treat the client's business from now on. Beyond the agreement. Put up the company logo on the video board during that second meeting at the ballpark, after the agreement is signed. Welcome that team to your social media channels. This is about earning that renewal that may be more than two or three years away. Everything should be geared toward that renewal happening with more than a year left on the original contract. Until then, that's when the hard work for the sponsorship sales representative begins.

There is a process to fulfilling activation as well. This includes involvement from the client. Something that they will welcome as it creates extra touch points and shows that you care. I would recommend giving your client marching orders, leaning on them for activation.

Once they get their artwork approved by signature, you can schedule the installation. It is important to also stay organized, making a list of everything that you need from your client, updating it daily. After they do their part, you should be sending them a digital picture of the sign being installed, as well as a picture of the finished product. A few days later, they should receive a professionally photographed picture printed and framed that is hand-delivered by you for them to put in their office breakroom. You are selling them, as well as the rest of the company, some of whom may be your future points of contact if your current point of contact departs for other endeavors.

Do not fail to act on any of your activation. The printed specifications for signage and other activation points e-mailed to them at least 15 days prior to the agreed upon deadline. That includes your client's season ticket requests. Locations should be finalized. This is no different than anything to do with activation. It isn't your client's responsibility to get you their artwork or meet their deadlines. It is yours. This is about being so relentless that it keeps them on task, and helps you gain that renewal long before that agreement has expired.

Increase your amount of touch points during this agreement process. Hand-deliver the season tickets to your client in person. Drop in, say hello, give them a few hats, shirts or a bag of peanuts. Remind them that you are fun, right around the corner, as the season is about to start. You are the person that everyone should want to see and meet. You are fun, passionate and exciting.

This is your chance to shine, get introduced to other potential points of contact within your client's company, and talk up the partnership agreement. Some of the highest-ranking members of the company may not even know what your partnership entails, and you want them engaged. You want company employees, especially the C.E.O., fighting over the tickets and excited about their investment in the team. It helps to showcase reasoning as to why the partnership exists in the first place.

The Signature Process

I am a big fan of agreement escalators. Those are put into place for the purposes of assisting teams in building a client's business. Clients will understand that the cost of doing business increases each and every year of the deal. Ticket prices go up, so does the cost of merchandise, and concessions prices certainly flatten out. Sponsorship sales are no different, hence, the escalator exists and permeates in most client agreements.

When a client partnership expires, you should be able to offer them last year's price for the next season as a considerable thank you for doing business with the team. However, you should include an escalator that, for the next period of 2-to-4 years, makes up for that price break that you are offering in the first year of the renewal. The escalator can be a percentage or monetary model that goes across the board, but it needs to be consistent with every other client, treating everyone fairly in the process. Also, clients talk, and if you *increase* an escalator for one client over another one, it will get around and you will lose more than you will gain.

Personally, the word *"contract"* sounds rough and abrasive to me. This is about opening up a new *relationship/partnership* in my mind. I love terminology that presents a warm, welcoming way to engage with a client. The term *"agreement"* is necessary as it lays out all of the sponsorship elements that have been mutually agreed upon, including payment terms and length of the agreement. But none of this is final until you actually receive the signed agreement. And you do need to realize that sometimes, these things take time to get signed. There's always a big black hole within the company when 4-5 different signatures are required, meaning internal discussion, budgeting as well as some signature authorities who are either on vacation, sick leave, or unavailable during the initial period when the contract is sent over.

You should be wary of thinking that an agreement is finalized without a signature. There are several times when a *"done deal"* ends up with a team fulfilling elements such as ballpark outfield signage, only to discover that the agreement is kicked back or never going to be signed by one signature authority. As frustrating as this is, you should be straight-forward if there are complaints from a client, where they haven't signed the agreement, yet still want their elements activated. Until you have a signed agreement, you cannot have the branding designed or installed.

During this signature process, you still need to work on ensuring that your client feels taken care of. Have the client forward on the company logo or design, so that your graphics team can begin the creative process. This actually helps accomplish two things; first, you get the artwork in the design pipeline for the client to approve once the agreement is signed. And second, this speeds up the signature process because the client starts creating internal advocacy on any signature authority with the anticipation of seeing their branding up at the ballpark.

Every follow up meeting with the client requires you to have a copy of the agreement in hand, ready for approval and the client's signature. During your final meeting, if there are some sticking points to be hammered out or an element required to be added, use your pen to write it in. A great sales person always has a pen for this, along with the ability to hand that pen over to the client, for them to sign right then. Some of this is a psychological play, as you are showing that you are giving them more value on the contract, and then impulse takes over for them to sign that deal while the ink is still drying in the agreement's margins.

All of this is great theater for what you are truly after: *A signed agreement.*

This final meeting allows you to mutually agree with all of the elements, walk out of the meeting with the client's signature, and start moving toward that renewal process. You should also provide your client with a copy of the agreement, both hardcopy and digital, along with a team-branded folder so that they can start the process of becoming a sponsor. Be the sales person who looks at the long-term play, ensuring that the renewal is right around the corner for you.

Engage In Your Industry

I mentioned previously about volunteerism in your community by working with non-profits and serving on their boards. It is important to be seen as a part of the community beyond simply a face at networking events. You should be actively involved for the good of your area. Volunteer your time to coach little league, serve on a local city parks board, or become a Big Brother or Big Sister. This goes beyond the idea of cultivating new sponsors. It goes to the reputation you have with your community. They should see you as a part of it, not simply as a sales trespasser. If you want people to be involved with your team, you need to be involved in their communities. *The Minor League Baseball Promotional Seminar* in late September is a great asset at learning ways to engage with your community. Both in the Minor League Baseball industry and in the general public groups as well.

The Promotional Seminar has been a great asset and staple for me to attend annually, and I recommend those serious about working in Minor League Baseball do the same. I've spoken at two seminars in front of my peers (*Birmingham, Alabama and*

Greenville, South Carolina). It has not only been an honor but a learning experience about how to grow my career, my co-workers, and speak about the sport that I love to sell.

These types of conferences hold the key to establishing great networking opportunities, foster new ideas and meet different people. It helps fine-tune your craft as you continue to learn creative ways to develop your sales approach and it's great at building industry relationships that can help you along the way. When you attend these events, you show value to your career and your team. Because we never stop learning or growing. Even if you cannot afford these conferences, I recommend seeking out any opportunities (*such as this book*) to study up on your craft. Selling baseball or sports in general is not simple. It is something that you have to work at every day, in order to be better at it, and continue to learn from it. There is never a stopping point in learning how to sell, or improve what you are doing.

I always suggest a personal growth tactic which has helped me learn from others. I open up a word processing file on my computer, and write down five minutes worth of thoughts each day. This can include inspirational messages, ideas about how to increase your sales or even new sponsorship activation points. If you stick with this mode of crowdsourcing your personal growth and do it daily, you will have a treasure trove of information within six months. You will also use these inspirational phrases, new ideas and different sales tactics as the backbone of any daily meetings and presentations that you have to run. It will show you as a lifelong learner of the sales process that is built to last.

Too many people are insular to their surroundings. Every day, there are people that you encounter that you can learn from. All you have to do is start to listen. It comes back to the two ears, one mouth concept that I mentioned earlier. Everything going on around you has teachable moments. It can provide context to what you are personally dealing with. Your customers, clients, fans, co-workers, interns and community leaders each have different viewpoints than you. Always a story to share, offering up a way to re-examine more about yourself and the person that you are with. Learning from them, both good and bad examples, improves your sales acumen in how you approach future clients. When you speak with employees, community leaders, clients or family members, use real life stories to make your point. People remember stories easier and it makes you more genuine and engaged.

Storytelling

The gift of gab is not bestowed on everyone. Some people cannot tell a story to save their life. Yet, storytelling is so essential in the sales process that people see the natural way in which a narrative is spun that they dismiss the hard work to create it. Storytelling helps assist a customer to remember the narrative, the points of entry as well as the highlights, as why your presentation mattered.

You can also insert specific lessons learned which illustrate why this client should be looking at a point of activation with your team, because of both good and bad examples of those who either signed an agreement or those who declined to sign an agreement. These examples help your client in the decision-making process use these key examples as a way to avoid specific pain points, instead enjoying the successes that a sponsorship with your team provides.

Your presentations should have stories that you can tell without having to look at notes. That feel real. That are shaped, honed and crafted to deliver within a minute or two of total talk time. They need to have a setup and punchline, highlighting a way to pound your chest on sharing the story of success about another client who worked with your team and won with their activation. All of these stories should showcase that no one offers a product like you do. It is about believing in your team's brand, being passionate about the product you sell and delivering that messaging in a fun way for your client.

It either comes natural or it does not. Much like writing. Either you have it, or you don't. Simple as that. And if you do not "*have it*" then you have to figure out how to "*get it*" or you should get out of sales. Storytelling is intrinsic to sales. You simply cannot get by on your charm alone. You have to be able to offer up stories that have a beginning, middle and an end. All which sum up into a set point that the client will remember. That does not sound like "*sales*" but as wisdom of past examples that you want your client to know about.

Storytelling is also a way to understand how spontaneity works. Until we grow older, we do not see enough situations to gauge how to react to them. Young professionals typically become unnerved when a sponsorship sales process derails or an element of the agreement goes wrong.

When you deal with enough inventory and sales, you see everything, literally, and witness every type of issue that crops up. It prepares you for the worst, because the odds suggest that at some point, the worst will in fact happen. Sales people should always be organized and open-minded to ever-changing situations in order to adapt. The worst client situations become magnified by unprepared or unorganized sales representatives being unable to adapt to the change in situation.

A typical scenario is when, in the middle of an agreement, a point of contact for your client company departs for another employment opportunity and you have no other point of contact within the company to keep the relationship going. It is important to know as many people as possible within that company's organizational chart prior to your point of contact disappearing, in order for you to build another key relationship who can become your advocate.

Another door opens when you start to call decision-makers, the C.E.O., or the people within the company who are least likely to expect to hear from you. Do this while your original point of contact is still with the company. Ask your point of contact who else you should meet or who would get a kick out of meeting a team representative. Chances are, they'll have about 10 referrals for you in a week. I would strongly suggest differentiating yourself from other sales people, who don't try to build more points of contact until after it's too late and they are starting from scratch again.

The unexpected does wonders for a company organizational chart. I deliver donuts, cookies, team-branded calendars, picture frames and have the team mascot appear at the client's office. Make it so that the entire organization is pleasantly surprised by your presence and sees the team as a friend of their company.

I would also invite your client's employees to games as they already have tickets but may not know to request them, give out gift bags for the children of employees, offer up an in-game facility tour to any employee of your sponsor who attends a game, and do anything possible to make them feel welcome. This type of kindness goes a long way with even the employees who will never be your point of contact, but may be a signature authority for a renewal down the road.

You Are The Brand

Touchpoints are the king of getting that renewal done. This is about not calling your clients when you need signed agreement or extensions, but welcoming them into a world that they never want to leave. You want to have opportunities to invite them to play golf, eat breakfast or simply build relationships with them. Think out the long-term goal here of making them ready for a renewal opportunity before the renewal is even up.

I always send out birthday cards, personalize holiday messages, write down family names, special dates and congratulate our sponsors when they have other major deals or achievements that have nothing to do with the team. This is about them finding out you are thinking about them as much as they are thinking about you. It is a discovery process. Too many sales professionals fall into the trap of contacting their clients only when it conveniences the sales professional. Usually that results in making a sales person's lack of preparation a matter of the client's emergency. I send out random thank you cards, invite them out to a game and connect with them on social media.

Even if the agreement falls apart, this is a great way to re-invest in that prospective client for the next period when the agreement may be solidified. If you see a lapsed-agreement client in a hospitality area or suite during a game, this is a chance to say "*hello*." They are investing in your product at a low-level and this is an opportunity to initiate a conversation. This extends out to your employees, who should be investing in their community as well. They should be viewed as a piece of the brand. They are generally a front-line ambassador for your team because the public tends to see the newest account representatives more than they will the C-suite executives.

When you hire these young professionals, they should exhibit a strong work ethic, believing in your product with as much passion as you do. Otherwise, they will turn people off from buying your product and be useless to you. I aim to hire for attitude, train for skill, and want people who try to take the position to the next level. If the new employee cannot add value as well as grasp the team brand, they will not be a contributor to your overall operation. Striving to build a championship culture daily is about seeing excellence in your organization. You achieve this by asking your staff to focus on ways to improve themselves as well as the team. Every member of the staff should know what the team revenues are, and how to create more revenue for the organization as a whole. No one wants to be associated with an unsuccessful organization. Including clients, fans and employees.

I've built a checklist on how I believe every employee should view themselves and their brand, when representing a team. Some of these are attitude, others are intrinsic to the overall success of the person themself: *P.E.A.R.L.*

P.E.A.R.L. Checklist

Personal branding is hard to teach when you have a resistant employee. If this happens, they are not going to change. Branding yourself into becoming one of the best corporate sales representatives means taking accountability for your organizational skills.

It also means being engaged in how the team operates and sees itself. I encourage any on-board staff member to learn as much as they can about ticket sales, marketing, food and beverage, picnics, budgets, ballpark improvements, parking, facilities and their fellow co-workers. This means that you are investing in an organization that invested in you. It also makes you a well-rounded, valuable employee who shows a team-oriented focus on putting the organization first each and every day that you come into work for the brand.

After 24 years of working in minor league baseball, with a career in five different cities, including 19 years currently in Fort Wayne, Indiana, I've developed a speech that I give about the sport of baseball. I've devoted my life to the sport, and after my playing days ended, I wanted to stay involved and make it a career in the industry that I love. This speech is shaped around **P.E.A.R.L.**, a concept of understanding baseball along with the experiences that I've had within the sport itself.

I have been blessed frankly to work with great people who have assisted me in growing on a personal and professional manner. I would not be in a position of strength in either category without the guidance that they have provided along the way. I would challenge anyone reading this to seek out great co-workers and mentors, as no one does this journey alone, nor should they. With the **P.E.A.R.L.** concept, I ask everyone to picture a baseball, to see the pristine object with a 108 hand-sewn stitches, and I start to talk about that "*pearl*" they are envisioning.

Developing Your Individual Brand

I am a very passionate individual. I absolutely love my career. I continue to learn daily, sharpening my craft. Passion means becoming a life-long learner in the field. You should always work in an environment where you can bring your passion, your expertise, and embrace the culture. That means striving to make your passion mesh with that of the passion brought by your co-workers, making the organization that you work for the best each and every day that you are employed there.

Lorenz's Employee Brand Checklist

✓ Attire

✓ Be kind

✓ Great listener

✓ Competitive

✓ Self-motivated

✓ Outgoing

✓ Helpful

✓ Charismatic

✓ Service-oriented

✓ Determined

✓ Energetic

✓ Enthusiastic

✓ Persistent

✓ Confident

✓ Organized

The "P" of P.E.A.R.L. Is "Passion"

- Loving My Career.

- Loving Coaching Youth Sports.

- Loving My Volunteer Groups I work with.

- Loving My Children's Interest and Hobbies.

I'm very fortunate…I have been blessed in my career in that I have worked for five MiLB teams and my office is at Parkview Field…The No. 1 Rated Minor League Baseball Facility in the Country[2]…If I can't get passionate here…I never will.

Jay Tuthill, President of Tuthill Corporation[3] spoke at a conference I attended and talked about passion and I want to share a few of his thoughts:

"When you settle you may lose your passion and drive."

Don't Settle…Always be your best…Every day.

"What are you passionate about and bring it to work every day."

The "E" of P.E.A.R.L. Is "Engagement"

- Get to know your clients and co-workers.

- Get comfortable with one another.

- You will learn something from each individual. Be ready for that moment.

- Take the time to send thank you notes to your clients as it's a great way to make an impression. Don't let these opportunities pass you by.

- **I want to quote Jay Tuthill, President of Tuthill Corporation[3] again who said earlier this Spring in LFW:** *"Be Authentic as a Leader."* (*People can tell when you're fake or trying too hard*)

Tom Henry, Mayor of Fort Wayne[4]: *"Take advantage of your time while you are in Fort Wayne and get involved in the city you live in"*

The "A" Of P.E.A.R.L. is "Attitude"

- A positive attitude is the way you dedicate yourself to the way you think and act.

- Go into each meeting with a client or co-worker with an open mind and the willingness to learn and listen to their wants and needs.

- I'm positive that you are all currently doing this right now. Carry yourself with pride and a positive attitude every day.

- My goal each and every day is to be **Likeable**.

- People want to do business with people they *LIKE*.

- Show up every day with a positive attitude.

- Work hard every day and give your best.

Complete each of these 3 steps and I believe good things will happen.

I couldn't do my job and be successful without the hard work done by others within our organization as well as our part-time employees.

One Phrase that I try and say several times a day is... *Thank You.*

Say *Thank you.*

Mean It when you say it.

AND...Use It often.

Thank you...evokes power.

Tom Henry, Mayor of Fort Wayne[4]: *"You want change...change the nature of who you are...Change your attitude."*

The "R" Of P.E.A.R.L. is "Relationship"

Relationship Building:

- Continue to make connections with influential community leaders.

- Be known for doing business with the best.

- Random acts of kindness wins.

Anthony Juliano, Vice President of Marketing and Social Media Strategy at Asher Agency asked us what do I do.

I'm in sales with the TinCaps:

- Corporate Suite Sales

- Sponsorship and Advertising Sales

- Signs/Radio and TV Spots

- Connecting two great brands together is what I do.

After thinking about what Anthony Juliano asked me to do I wrote this:

What do I do?

I'm David Lorenz: *While sales is my main focus, I'm passionate in strengthening the Fort Wayne TinCaps relationships with the fans at Parkview Field and our Corporate Partners and I pride myself in building long lasting relationships.*

The "L" Of P.E.A.R.L. is "Leadership"

- Leaders come with all types of backgrounds, education and life experiences.

- You don't have to be the President or CEO of your company to be a leader within your organization.

- I want to be a lifelong learner and sharpen my leadership skills every day. What drives you?

I believe Great Leaders Listen:

- Learn from customers, clients, fans, co-workers, community leaders, interns... everyone has a story to share and you will learn more about yourself and the people you're speaking with sharing moments with as many people as you can.

Leaders pay attention to their surroundings:

- You can learn from so many people if you just listen and observe to what is going on around you.

- Each team member of the TinCaps organization is asked to contribute to the overall operation of the team and is asked to join at least two non-profit organizations.

- We have 30 full-time staff members making a difference in the community we live, work and play in.

- We're all leaders and we all have the power, knowledge and opportunity to be difference makes.

- Leaders join non-profits, charities, donate their time, knowledge and finances and strive for excellence...Be the best at what you do.

Scott Glaze, Fort Wayne Metals: "*Leaders create a work place and a culture people want to be in.*"

The late Dick Enberg, Hall of Fame Broadcaster[5]**:** "*Giving back is the ultimate measure of a man or woman.*"

Never Give Up On The Dream

Derek Franks

President
Fresno Grizzlies
Pacific Coast League, Triple-A Baseball

About The Author

Derek Franks has served his entire career with the Fresno Grizzlies, from Ticket Office Intern in 2004 to being named team president in 2018. In 2015, Franks was chosen as the Pacific Coast League's Executive of the Year. Franks has overseen a continued bolstering of the Fresno Grizzlies and "Fresno Tacos" brand both in Central California and nationwide; with 2016 setting a new bar thanks to another all-time merchandise sales record for the franchise. In 2017, for the first time in franchise history, the Fresno Grizzlies were chosen as the Bob Freitas Award winner by national industry publication Baseball America. The honor recognizes the top overall operations in Minor League Baseball in each classification.

After I decided to work for the Triple-A Fresno Grizzlies in my hometown as an entry-level employee, it took me two tries to get hired by the team. Fifteen years later, I serve as the team's president. Looking back now, it was never my intention to stay in Fresno at all. I still lived in nearby Kingsburg with my family and was attending Reedley College, a JC close to home (*Go Tigers!*). I simply wanted to gain experience working in baseball. My goal was to transfer to whatever four-year university nowhere near Fresno, and have the ability to work for whatever local baseball team was nearby after I earned some resume experience with the Grizzlies. I figured, with baseball experience on my resume, I would have exciting opportunities in the future. And, I was willing to do anything to make it happen. I'd planned to tear tickets, sling hotdogs--hell, polish the mini-helmets for the Dippin' Dots, if it got me a job in baseball. At the 2003 Fresno Grizzlies job fair, I thought I'd exhibited my readiness. I imagined I'd conveyed my commitment. I felt I'd demonstrated my worth. I drove home with my buddy, Jordan, who also applied, feeling great about my future in baseball. I was a shoe-in. The folks that did the hiring back then didn't seem to have the same feeling. (*They did, however, offer Jordan a job. He declined--said he only wanted to do it if we could work together.*)

As I often did when plans didn't go according to...well, plan, I thought of Michael Jordan. I heard that he was cut from his high school team, and still, with triumphant grit, went on to be perhaps the greatest basketball player of all time. It served as a motivating factor to never give up. I'm not even certain if that story about him is actually true by the way. I may have read that Jordan actually got put on the JV squad instead of the varsity as a sophomore. But it doesn't matter. War stories aren't about the actual events. They're about providing examples that you can use to push yourself forward, because they offer a foundation for the results you can expect given a certain level of effort and not giving up.

Minor league baseball is full of transplants. People from all over the country end up working for multiple clubs so I have been fortunate to work in my hometown in a community that I have cared about my entire life. Now, if you hate a feel-good story you may want to stop reading. Mine could make you sick it's so cheesy. The local guy who goes from box office intern to general manager, starting with that same kid going to the team's job fair and not getting hired. I didn't even receive a phone call turning me down. I got nothing from the team whatsoever. And the job fair was for seasonal positions like ticket takers and ushers. But, I didn't give up on the goal of working in minor league baseball. And that 2003 job fair experience showed me that getting a job in baseball was pretty darn hard. It was worse to see that while not earning a position with my hometown team, I had a friend turning down the same opportunity, shrugging it off as no big deal. I returned to the job fair in 2004, stood in a line of over 800 applicants, a man possessed with the single goal of getting hired.

The year prior, I had handed my resume to one of the attendees and went home. In 2004, I looked all of them in the eye, shook their hand, and said, "*I'm Derek Franks, and I want to be on your team.*" Not earning a position the first time taught me a valuable lesson. When you want a job, get a job. And this time, I was hired. I'm glad MJ got cut, or whatever actually happened. Those motivational things work sometimes. And I learned a lot from the Grizzlies, especially my second day on the job as a ticket office intern. My boss told me to bring my golf clubs, said we were on pocket schedule duty, and that we could squeeze in 9 holes while we were at it. My dad called me that evening, asked how things were going. I told him "*I could do this job forever.*"

My Grizzlies Mug

My father is responsible for my first sale in this industry. I sold a 200-plus picnic outing to one of his friends during my internship year with the Grizzlies in 2004. I had no sales responsibilities at the time, but this showed initiative. Anything that brings in revenue for the team, regardless of a person's job duties, gets attention. When I became a salesman, however, I realized that it's one thing to make a sale when nobody's expecting it, and quite another to generate sales in order to eat, to demonstrate value and accountability, and to keep the dream of working in baseball alive.

I wasn't so green that I didn't know what a general manager did in minor league baseball. At this point, with all of the information out there, an entry-level person has no excuse to not know that general managers are in charge of running the business side of the game, and have zero say about the team on the field. There were/are some things that hit people even with general manager experience between the eyes, including myself. Especially realizing how much local politics comes into play for a general manager when you are running a team in a taxpayer-funded stadium.

In 2005, I returned to the Grizzlies as an inside sales representative. I had applied to Fresno State as a transfer student, originally applying as a back-up plan with all of those visions of leaving for some other big school in another big city. Instead, I elected to stay close to home because I loved my internship year with the Grizzlies. I was asked to stick around by my boss and started selling tickets. To be clear, I had zero desire to be a salesperson. I had never really sold anything aside from that big picnic to my dad's friend. But my mentor, Ash Anunsen, informed me that if I wanted to stick in sports, I had to sell.

I was a wreck at selling from the start. The art of the deal didn't come naturally to me. I had to work at it. There were eight other sales representatives hired along with me, but I was the only person that the front office employees knew personally because of my internship year. It placed added pressure on me, as I had colleagues from inside sales who were watching what I was doing. True to form, I was the last in my inside sales group of nine employees to make my first sale.

I'd bang calls in the bullpen, drinking coffee from my styrofoam cup, watching my peers, one by one, make their first sale. Upon doing so, they earned a Grizzlies coffee mug. The mugs multiplied around me, and the styrofoam scratched and squeaked in my hand when I'd take a drink--an omnipresent reminder to all in earshot, that I had not yet done my job. I wanted that Grizzlies mug. I needed a sale.

My first week on the phone I was so bad that some guy who owned a business in Shaver Lake, a city in which buying Grizzlies tickets is less likely due to the distance to the ballpark, laughed at me and asked me if I was reading from a script. I answered him with a nervous a flustered "*NO*" right before he hung up on me. This sucked. I sucked. My experience was a complete 180 degrees from my internship year in the ticket office. My boss was standing behind me when the Shaver Lake incident happened and coached me through it for all of the other eight inside sales representatives to hear. Did I mention this time in my life sucked? Not selling sucks! I thought about quitting every day, but I was too afraid to give up my baseball dream. I actually was more worried about disappointing my dad and some of the friends I had made at the Grizzlies.

At the time, Ash Anunsen was my boss. He had given me this chance and I was too afraid to quit. So finally, I get this guy on a call and when I tell him that I am Derek from the Fresno Grizzlies, he responds by telling me he was glad I called because he wanted to tell me how stupid the Grizzlies were. Great... this nightmare won't end, will it? He goes on to tell me that he wanted to buy club level tickets for the last three years but we only sold full and half season plans in the club level and he thought that was stupid. He only wanted a partial season. The reason he thought this was stupid was because he came to games and he never saw the club level sold out.

So, we are idiots because he was begging to give us his money for a partial season and he had been told *no* many times by our premium seat director. But I was lucky because we had just introduced 18 game plans and I basically told the guy I could solve his problem – and sold him the partial plan. I looked like a hero even though the partial plans had already been created going into the 2005 season.

The *no* sale monkey was off my back. I got my coffee mug. I walked up to the white board in the bullpen, rang the bell and put up the total revenue next to my name… *$666.67*. My bosses didn't quite get the pricing concept at that time, so it was this weird prorated looking rate instead of a sexy round number. So, in spite of throwing up *the mark of the beast* by my name after a miserable road to my first sale, it was the first of many. Looking back, there are three other people that have worked at the Grizzlies before I did that are still working with me now. Doug Greenwald, our radio announcer predates me by one season. Harvey Kawasaki and Ira Calvin are still on our operations team and they are originals. A lot of my colleagues still work in sports though. I can think of at least 7-8 people from that first year in 2005 that still work in sports, not all of them in baseball.

You have to be prepared to manage different personalities and communicate in a way that adapts to those different personalities. You have to be used to setbacks and challenges. Way too many people give up quickly when facing adversity, and they don't succeed because of it. Michael Jordan's story resonates because he obviously didn't give up, and despite being told "*no*" kept pushing forward until he was at the top of his game. Then, his challenge was to stay at the top as long as possible.

The thing about the folks who have stuck in sports is that a lot of us became the best sales guy of our group. Our bosses, in turn, wanted to keep us interested in staying with the organization, so they start letting us manage people and other stuff, often without a lot of management training. Best advice I can give is to read books. Find someone you can call a mentor and ask questions. Read more books. If you go into management knowing that you don't have all the answers and willing to learn every day of your career to get better, you'll have a better chance of being a leader. I've never seen the guy with all the answers be the best manager, let alone become a solid leader. There's a big difference between the two.

Other than my first month making cold calls and never making a sale, the urge to quit hasn't happened often. The times I thought about hanging it up were mostly from 2008-2011. After the housing market crashed, selling sports was a lot harder and we went through some interesting struggles trying to find ways to combat the steep drop off of revenue. I remember being around $490,000 down in season tickets in December. The other categories were ugly as well. Talk about a hopeless feeling. People were dropping their entertainment budgets, but also a lot of these companies were just flat out going out of business.

I Almost Quit

In December of 2010 after an insane management change, I actually lost my mind for a short time over my boss. I am a reasonable person, but I convinced myself to walk in and quit in a rage one morning after feeling blatantly disrespected by my boss. This was following months of frustration and a hopeless feeling after an off-season of no productivity and a lot of turmoil in the front office.

I woke up that morning, had some coffee with my close friend and decided I had had enough. I walked in wearing a pair of warm-up type pants – clearly out of dress code for good measure – and attempted to storm into the President/CEO's office to let him have it. As I type this, I can hardly believe it got that bad. I am not that guy… Luckily for me, his door was locked and he was out giving a massive group a tour of the ballpark. By the time he got done, he was late for a flight and when I tried to stop him, he zoomed past me, asked me to call him because he had to race to the airport. I went home for the weekend after that and talked myself back into reality and went back to work Monday and kept plugging along.

Communication is tough because in any organization, good or bad, it's probably one of the top things that people want to be better at. You can't communicate enough in a company and good communication makes employees happy. People like knowing what the hell is going on and do their job better when they do. A big one is to actually communicate. Passive aggressive behavior runs rampant in the workplace – especially with young people – so I learned early on to get comfortable having those interactions you dread and actually talk to people. As a manager, I learned to always check for understanding after you give direction to someone. I think this works even when you aren't the boss. Last step before you leave a conversation with someone that requires action is to simply recap and make sure everyone has the same understanding of the next steps.

When The Affiliation Ends

Communication is key. I don't like to have too much time between a big termination and a time in which you have either your entire team together or the department that the person was working in. From my experience, most of the time you have a separation, the rest of the team knows why and mostly agrees but there is sometimes that "*who's next?*" or "*now what?*" feeling that can be avoided by communicating with your team. It is no different when marketing affiliation with a parent MLB club or when talking to your community. They have to know where you stand at all times. For us, building a local brand was key to our change. Our market is full of Giants fans, so we let our fans know until the end that we were making our best efforts to renew with the Giants.

Once we changed, we made sure that our fans knew the exact reasons why Houston chose us and why were excited to sign with them. In fact, Reid Ryan told me he knew they were coming into Giants territory and he wanted to win over Fresno. Reid is my hero. He and the farm directors came to Fresno to do a press conference and other media appearances. This further helped educate the market and get people excited about our new partners. We hosted a dinner called "*Meet the Astros*" and they did Q&A with our fans. There is a lot of confusion when you change affiliates unless you're in a market that's gone through some changes and has already learned. Ours hadn't so we had to make sure people didn't think we were just gone. I took our team bowling during the holidays and we printed shirts for everyone. A lady that was coming off of the lanes before we started walked up and pointed to the Grizzlies logo on my shirt and said, "*It's too bad the Grizzlies are gone now.*" Just as matter a fact as could be. I explained that the Grizzlies were not gone and pointed to the dozens of others putting on the same shirt and explained this was the front office team and that we just had a new MLB affiliate. She nodded her head, appearing to understand. When she walked away from me, she approached Ray Ortiz, our entertainment manager and pointed at me and said "*That guy said the Grizzlies are still here. He doesn't understand they are gone.*"

We did a lot of PR that year to make sure people kept hearing about us. In 2015, we did some of the most outrageous stuff I had ever done in my career with the goal of just being on the news all the time because it seemed like, just like that old lady at the bowling alley, a lot of people needed to hear it more than once. At the end of the day, our goal is to build a local brand that is so strong, fun and gives back so much to the community that people aren't looking for reasons not to go.

There was a lot of low hanging fruit for us when we were with the Giants because the local fan base was so heavy Giants. It's tough to live up to the brand image of the Giants, but it was easy to piggyback off of their success. Three out of five World Series wins and a bunch of guys from Fresno that made it on those teams makes for some great opportunities. Your hardcore fans care about winning. Your general fans less so. I think those general fans are intelligent and know that the farm team just wears our uniform and the success from top to bottom really belongs to the big-league club. The home team winning is fun for our fans – it's in the song!! "… *if they don't win it's a shame!*" However, the needle doesn't move a ton on a season long basis based on winning, if at all.

When a team decides to change affiliations, you have to stick to the basics – family, fun, affordable entertainment. If you nail that stuff, it's hard to get too worked up about who the parent club is for anyone that's not in your hardcore base. I think ours here is around 20 percent of the fan base… the rest come once or twice a year and come no matter what as long as it's one of those three things, preferably all of them.

The Art of the PDC

In theory, you can change affiliates every two years if you're one of the unlucky clubs. The player development contract (PDC) terms are two or four years at a time. We didn't change from orange and black when we signed with Houston. When fans asked us why we still wore Giants colors, we looked them in the eye and said, "*These are OUR colors.*" I think people in Fresno appreciate a gritty approach like that one. We certainly evolved our look and incorporated some different branding elements to complement our primary logo and colors – including the Fresno Tacos alter ego. Some clubs don't have to worry about this, so it just all depends on your situation. In some cases, a rebrand to align with an affiliation change might make sense too, it just didn't for us during that time.

We marketed like crazy during the affiliate change to Houston to make sure that people knew the team was still in Fresno. The average person doesn't understand the PDC and how the deal works between the MLB and MiLB clubs, so after 17 years with the same affiliate, people didn't know what it meant and a lot of people thought that the team was gone. Our club was also for sale during this time and so the marketing we did to make sure that Fresno knew there was still a baseball team – we did outrageous stuff and held a lot of press conferences to get everyone's attention. We called the media to join us to reveal our new home uniform - we dropped "*Grizzlies*" from the front of the jersey and went with "*Fresno*" to make our City proud. I drove up to the podium for a Back to the Future promotion announcement in a Delorean. We renamed our team *the Tacos* for a day! This got us a two and a half minute segment on ESPN SportsCenter and a ton of other national media coverage.[1] The marketing helped get people's minds off the club being for sale. We put the emphasis back on Fresno and focused on making things more fun than they had ever been and that helped us change the narrative from the team selling – to the first mascot to become an ordained minister and officiate weddings at a baseball game, and so on.

Fresno is not a place where any team of any affiliation or sport is safely secure. There have been a lot of teams that have died. Hockey has had two teams in the marketplace. You have to commit to your market and not let your brand get too wrapped up in the affiliate. For a lot of years, we rode the wave of the success of our MLB affiliate (*three World Series wins in five years*)[2] and I think we lost the connection to the community. Changing affiliations from the Giants to the Astros was a great reminder of how lucky we were to have sustained success with the Giants, but there is recovery needed to unwind that when it suddenly changes. We won the Triple-A National Championship in our first year with the Astros[3] and celebrated them winning the 2017 World Series with a lot of guys that played in Fresno on that winning team.[4] We found a better balance between being a community team and celebrating the Astros success than we had previously.

Everyone Wears The Suit Once

Our mascot "*Parker*" goes everywhere in the Fresno community, continuing to establish our brand locally. We take requests for mascot appearances and keep a calendar of community events. The Grizzlies have a reading program that reaches over 100,000 students per year and in 2018 reached the 1 million cumulative student mark on the life of the program… so Parker has been to nearly every school in the Central Valley in the last 12 years. We keep our mascot visible by being at major community events, youth sports leagues, hospital visits and around town doing grassroots marketing.

There are a lot of mascots out there, so anything your mascot can do to set itself apart is huge. Parker is a great performer, but I really love to watch him interact with our fans. I think that part of his personality is so special and is one of the big reasons Parker is so beloved in Fresno. Parker knows that a mascot can get away with anything. Some of the stuff I've seen over the years is so funny, and so uncomfortable or awkward, I can hardly believe it.

Back in 2004 as an intern, our mascot was a grizzly bear named "*Wild Thing*." In those days we did mascot tryouts every year and that person performed during the season. This meant that all off-season and non-game day appearances were just done by whoever A.) needed the appearance or B.) whoever the sucker was that would jump in the suit for that person. I was "B" for a lot of people because I wanted to make a name for myself with the organization as a person that would step up and do anything to help the team.

I went to a lot of hospitals, schools and community events as Wild Thing – a dark brown grizzly bear with a large head. My go-to moves consisted of waving, lots of thumbs ups and of course the confused shrugging of the shoulders. I wasn't very good at it, but I was willing and available. One day at a big school rally, I had some kids – 8 or 9 years old – that were particularly interested in Wild Thing.

I think they realized that I sucked at this mascot thing and decided to make me pay. After a bunch of criticism and juvenile pranks aimed in my direction, one of the kids had an epiphany. He hadn't seen the school janitor, Mr. Carter, all day. So, after some discussion among the boys, they decided that Wild Thing, was in fact being played by Mr. Carter. My hand motions indicating that I was not in fact Mr. Carter were ignored. Soon a large group of students began chanting "*Mr. Carter, Mr. Carter!!!*" It took over the assembly and we left shortly thereafter. I don't know who this Mr. Carter guy was, but I got buried by a bunch of students because they thought I was him. To this day, the guy who wrangled me out to that event calls me "*Mr. Carter.*"

When you work in sports, you have to be willing to do anything and everything to help the team promote itself. There are no job descriptions or exceptions. When you decide to marginalize your duties, or eliminate what you are willing to do, you eliminate the value that you bring to the organization.

I could have always said "*no*" to being Wild Thing, or a million other tasks, but that would have eliminated the value that I brought to the organization, and made me less important toward getting hired full-time later on as an inside sales representative. Value is also what the team brings to the community. With our previous ownership group, it was always a struggle to show the value, because of the financial issues the team always had that got out into the community through the media.

Ownership Changes

In 2017, we finally had our team sell to a new ownership group. In our case it has helped generate more ticket sales. If there is one thing I know it is that your community doesn't want to see a team's financial struggles being printed in the newspaper four times a year and constantly have to think about other political nonsense surrounding the team.

It's depressing and gives people a reason to become disinterested. If the ownership can truly create a partnership with the city, that's when you really win. After years of that, people are ready for something new and if you roll out the ownership change in the right way, it can really impact your sales the first year.

The new ownership in Fresno announced $1.2 million in improvements to the ballpark and lowered the draft beer prices to $5 at every game. We were able to tell our fans that our plan is to treat them two steps better than fair. That's where you get the hearts and minds of the fans right off of the bat. In addition, we committed to donating the ballpark up to 100 times to nonprofits to use for their own events, free of charge. Because of that, there is an immediate excitement and people see that we aren't trying to monetize the community at every turn and that as citizens of Fresno - they truly own this ballpark. The sale of the team can certainly work against you as well, but with the proper roll out strategy and the right ownership, it can be a huge boon.

Everything about pushing your community brand message and development loyalty to that brand beyond all else. We changed our home jerseys to say "Fresno" on the front instead of the team name, which is more traditional. This was symbolic and part of the message that we are a Fresno team first. Fresno owners, Fresno employees, Fresno taxpayer stadium, Fresno charities. It's easy to debate about your favorite MLB teams. Our hope was that it wasn't that easy to debate on if you like your community.

Our community does not mean ignoring our Spanish-speaking population. Every season we produce a Spanish version of our pocket schedule. We run billboards throughout Fresno in English and Spanish. *The Fresno Tacos* brand was created to celebrate Fresno culture. Hispanics are part of Fresno culture and always have been. We have found that Hispanics prefer to be acknowledged as part of the community as a whole rather than pandered to.

Words like *"Outreach"* can be offensive because a reaching arm symbolizes distance between two groups of people. In Fresno we believe in Hispanic inclusion rather reach. Many members of our front office are Hispanic and are included in the marketing process from conceptual ideas to design to implementation.

We treat our team store like a flagship store for a fashion brand as opposed to a novelty gift shop. Knowing that if we stock apparel designed to be functional as *lifestyle/active* wear; our fans will wear the product more often. Fans can easily tell if a design is a stock or generic template made by a national distributor. The majority of our apparel product mix is designed in house by designers with an active pulse read on the Fresno market.

The Tacos of Fresno

Creating designs that become symbols of regional pride while staying on trend has become our strong point. Stocking limited amounts of particular designs also helps create energy and demand for the product. Limited runs also help create a sense of urgency to make purchases. Limited release strategies have made our brand a favorite amongst local trend setters and influencers.

Promo graphics are posted on social media platforms such as our Team Store's Instagram account (wearthebear_IG) followers help spread awareness by keeping the buzz going about it. The more a design resonates with the market or the more on-trend the design is: the louder the buzz. Creating merchandise to coincide with themed uniforms and in-park promotions is another strong point for us that helps drive traffic to the team store. *Taco Truck Throwdown* merchandise eventually became "*Fresno Tacos*" merchandise.

The "*Fresno Tacos*" brand has become a staple in our team store with a wide array of design choices for men, women, and children. We have shipped *Fresno Tacos* merchandise to every continent minus Antarctica. Every year during Taco Truck Throwdown, we unveil a new *Fresno Tacos Uniform Kit*. The *Fresno Tacos* then wear that uniform the following season for Tuesday home games. Our team store stocks new merchandise in the kit colorways every season. In 2017, The Fourth Of July fell on a Tuesday so naturally we played as *The American Tacos*. Red, White, and Blue Tacos merchandise was also produced for the team store.

With the change from the Giants to Astros, we get fewer rehab appearances because of location. Houston can much more easily send players to Corpus Christi, so while we have had some big-time rehabs in recent years – including a return from Carlos Correa (*he did a stint with us on his way up*) – it's not as big of a thing for us now as it was when the Giants were the affiliate. With the local parent club, less prominent players move the needle because the fan base has an affinity for certain guys. With a non-local affiliate, it takes a bigger star to get your market to come out. I always love to get pitchers more than position players because you know when they will start and you can market it without as many contingencies. However, if you get a big star like Nomar Garciaparra – it's nice to have the 3-4 nights worth of draw.

Taco Truck Throwdown

One of the challenges that has actually come from having a huge annual event like *Taco Truck Throwdown* (TTT) is that it can actually cannibalize some of the other promotions on the schedule around it. For that reason, we have to be strategic about how to keep the life in our other games/promotions the week before and after. For us, the evolution of the event including the *Fresno Tacos* rebrand was the answer on how to increase sales beyond the event date. The '*alter-ego*' of the Grizzlies has played well and the *Tacos* brand has been around 40 percent of the overall merchandise sales of the team since 2015.

The popularity of the brand (*and local taco trucks*) extended to a *Taco Tuesday* promotion so that we can extend the brand and increase sales on other nights – in this case slower Tuesday games. In the early years of the event, we did the old school voting format of dropping a piece of paper in a box. Two years ago, we moved to a text-to-vote platform, which gives us a database of over nearly 10,000 to market our other events too – and specifically target *Tacos* merchandise, nights, etc. From there a new mascot was created for the *Fresno Tacos*; fans were asked to vote online and they chose the name "*Cilantro Gomez*." Cilantro Gomez merchandise is sold along with *Fresno Tacos* merch.

In 2017 we introduced a new taco themed character called "*Tacosaurus*". We collaborated with the Lehigh Valley Iron Pigs and did a national *Bacon vs Tacos* campaign. We entered the Nabisco "*My Oreo Creation*" Contest and submitted an Oreo Taco. We then created an *Oreo Themed Fresno Tacos* uniform and sold the world's first and only Oreo tacos at the game. This year we are going to ask fans to vote for their favorite type of Taco (*asada, carnitas, pollo, etc*) we will then design a *Fresno Tacos* jersey themed around the winning meat choice. There are always ways to evolve your brand. We believe that if you aren't growing you're dying. Growing too big too fast can over saturate and burn out a trend. We have found more success by gradually evolving our tacos brand organically.

TTT has its own budget and marketing plan. We have a committee that works on this event year around that includes an outside collaborator - a local taste maker – who is the co-creator of the event. The marketing for this event really goes on all year long as we engage with fans on Twitter about topical taco news or just simply create dialogue with fans that are trying to figure out where to find the best tacos in Fresno.

After the wild success, we've had with TTT, you can imagine the amount of people that have told us to do it 3-4 times a year. *"Why don't you do one every month and sell out the ballpark 5 more times!?"* We've had the discipline to not do that because you over expose it and ruin a good thing. Having the Super Bowl of Taco Truck contest/events is called the Super Bowl for a reason – it can only happen once a year to stay a big deal. We have also had to challenge ourselves by asking what's new this year to keep people interested? That's really how the *Fresno Tacos* brand was born… looking for ways to add to this event and keep it fresh each year. The key to not over saturate is to not only grow but to evolve. Every year we add new elements to *Taco Truck Throwdown*. In 2015, we became *"The Fresno Tacos"* in 2017 we added the *World Taco Eating Championship*, this year we will add something new as well.

Selling The Experience

Being at an older ballpark means trying to freshen it up continually. You have to keep up on the little things consistently. Budget for paint. It's amazing how much a fresh coat of paint can make a difference in an aging ballpark. When we couldn't afford anymore paint in the lean years, we traded sign companies and wrapped doors and added branding wherever we could to freshen up the place. In recent years, we have added more premium seat areas and hospitality. I think that's the biggest difference between the ballparks built in the early 2000's and those built in Reno, El Paso, and Nashville in recent years.

Our stadium is 12,500 seats, with 33 suites (*good*) and 3 party areas (*not enough*). We added the Dugout Club 4 years ago behind home plate by taking out some meaningless looking seats and adding high tops, in-seat service and parking passes. The results were good but when we dropped a bit, we adjusted pricing and made the area all-inclusive – beer and wine, and a comp meal each night. We're now sold to capacity.

In 2018, we took out some seats at the top of a section in the upper level behind home plate and bought about $8,000 worth of new seats, a drink rail and high tops. The package comes with a meal and attendant. We have the naming rights for The Landing sold and it's been booked every night but one so far, this season. We are looking for more areas to create destinations in the ballpark. I think another important thing that's helped the experience feel new is the addition of portable carts with branded themes over the years. If your fans arrive and see new concepts every year, it goes a long way and the more portables you add, you get the smells and sight of food that makes the experience even better.

During the most difficult times of the economy in Fresno, we had to completely refocus on value. One of the most successful ticket deals we did from 2009-2011 was *Monday Madness* – we have done this promotion in different variations for the entire history of the team at the downtown ballpark. However, during this time we were able to partner with the local water park to add their passes into our deal.

Two tickets, two hot dogs, two sodas and two water park passes for $28 was such a great value, we went nuts on Monday nights. I make the case that during tough economic times, the companies that continue to treat their clients to Grizzlies games or take their employees on a company picnic, are the ones that stand out and separate themselves among the competition. This stuff gets cut so quickly when times are tough and every edge you can create as a business owner to attract new business, keep your current customers happy and keep your employees from leaving you, are so important.

Selling In A Depressed Market

The economy has improved but Fresno is still a depressed market. We can't let our clients forget that that's the purpose for buying tickets and it's not a donation. We have to market to both ends of the spectrum and make the games very affordable for the larger portion of the market that has a lower household income. There are also more millionaires, per capita in Fresno County than any other county in the US. This is mostly due to the agriculture industry here. It's still a price conscious community and without the packed value, we can lose quickly in this market.

Fresno is interesting because there is a lot of wealth in a small part of the population. We have actually continued to see growth in recent years with the premium and all-inclusive packages. You have to target the right groups and premium sells. I am amazed in this economy how much disposable income there is at all economic levels for experiences though. There are 4-5 premium boutique ice cream places within a 4-mile radius of my house. It costs me over $40 to take my wife and kids out for some ice cream that looks like some scientists made it from scratch! It's something else.

With the high summer temperatures, our club and suites stay full, especially late in the summer. We still offer midweek suites to season ticket holders as an early-bird renewal perk. This helps us fill the roughly 40-50 percent that are not sold in lease deals each year. It's been a big hit with our loyal fans and we can sell food packages to these groups. We have done things like variable pricing on midweeks to keep the other nights full. Having the right mix of rentals, large party suites and a good suite lease program is the key – once we sprinkle in the STH perks, we have very little inventory left and there is a real urgency to get your deposit down on a rental, because they sell quickly.

Never Give Up

Our staff goes through separate training sessions for ticket packages and group sales. They go full menu, but do have some specific territories that they are responsible for. Once they know how to do both types of sales, we really dial in to assessing and tailoring the needs of the customer so they know which direction to go. Full menu sales reps have to be good for this to work. It's worked better for us to set goals in each category or we've run into the issue that everyone tries to sell premium. For a sales person, this is the most bang for your buck and the fastest way to hitting your goal. If you don't manage it properly, all you have is a bunch of premium sales reps. Not good.

One year in early April, my sales director told me that he had five full season suites still pending in his department. I couldn't remember a year in which we sold five new full season suites – and that year we already sold one or two. Guess what? One of them closed and it was our sales director that closed it. He had experience closing high dollar accounts and was a veteran. The rest of the crew that had these high valued prospects in their pipeline all didn't close them on full season suites – but they babied them along for months and kept talking about it.

I am sure all these guys also spent the hottest sales months (*Feb-April*) thinking they had another $25,000 coming in soon. That mentally can make a sales rep let up on cold calls and filling their pipeline and spend a lot of time chasing something that really doesn't exist. We had to make some adjustments after that year. Today, we have group-specific sales representatives and someone that specializes in premium to create a better balance and set the goals in a more balanced way. However, we still train all of the reps to sell full menu.

When I think back to 2003, I remember who I thought I was. My friend got the job offer that I wanted from the Grizzlies. I didn't give up when I was told "*no*" or told nothing at all. Instead, I got to work. And it took a year of being aggressive in my job search to finally earn the internship that I wanted. But I didn't remain satisfied with simply getting the job, but really showing that I was worth it. That's where the Michael Jordan story still hits home for me. Even if it's untrue, it's something that I remember fondly. Because even after Jordan made his high school team, it was simply another step toward his overall goal. And it never stops until you decide that you're ready to quit entirely.

From Bottom
To Top

C. Ryan Shelton
President / General Manager
Salem Red Sox
Carolina League, Class-A Baseball

About The Author

C. Ryan Shelton has worked in sports since 2008, when he began as an Inside Sales representative for the Florida Marlins. Since that time, he has worked in minor league hockey and baseball, with the Augusta Lynx (2008), South Carolina Stingrays (2008-10), Manchester Monarchs (2010-2013), and now as President/General Manager of the Salem Red Sox since 2013. Shelton was awarded the Carolina League Executive of the Year in 2015.

It has been ten years since I broke into the sports industry. Currently, I am the President and General Manager of the Salem Red Sox, the Advanced-A affiliate of the Boston Red Sox located in Salem, Virginia (*not Massachusetts, New Hampshire or Maine as many assume*). We are an interesting case. We were purchased in 2008 for player development after Theo Epstein pressed the Red Sox ownership to secure our future in the Carolina League. Typically in these situations the team is operated solely from the perspective of player development with business development not really being a factor. If the team breaks even, that's a win.

In our case, we are largely owned and wholly managed by Fenway Sports Management, which like any business, prioritizes bottom line results, achieved by creating a memorable fan experience and outstanding sales and service. My role is to ensure we are creating the best environment for our player development staff while being a budget conscious revenue generator. This situation has been an amazing learning experience, having to manage so many different paradigms in order to achieve all of our stakeholder goals.

My career success during the years prior to joining Salem and particularly over the past five seasons since has been built on recruiting, hiring and developing a talented staff. It is cliché to say that an organization's most valuable asset is its people, but I firmly believe that is true. However, with the limited resources available to a minor league organization managing this asset requires patience, inspiration, foresight and the wisdom of the stoics to keep everything moving forward.

In this chapter I will share my personal experience, techniques and anecdotes from a decade of recruiting, managing and leading. I will preface this by saying that I am constantly learning, growing and evolving (*as is our industry*). If I were asked to write this chapter again ten years from now for a new edition it would likely look very different.

My career in sports began in 2008 when I was hired as an Inside Sales Rep for the then Florida Marlins. I was one of fourteen reps hired to sell season tickets and to a lesser degree, groups. We were given a week of "*boot camp*" training and then thrown on the phones.

We were, for the most part hired by the Director of Ticket Sales, though there was an Inside Sales Manager and an Assistant Inside Sales Manager. The week of training was almost entirely led by the director with the two managers observing and handling small groups. After that week, the training ended, we were off to sink or swim. Daily reports would be sent and if your calls dropped too low an encouraging or scolding email would follow. If you needed advice or a shoulder to cry on the managers or other senior reps were always available.

The program was 24 weeks and along the way a few had dropped off, choosing to go home, back to school or *Enterprise Rent-a-Car*. As we approached the end, the bottom half of the leader board, knowing they would not be offered a position, began leaving one by one for other teams in similar roles or internships. The top three or four on the leaderboard fought until the last.

I distinctly remember coming to work on the last day of the program not knowing if I would be offered the coveted Account Executive position or if I was leaving with my belongings in a box. There was great speculation among the leaders as to which of us would be going out for celebratory beers and who would be calling home to break the bad news.

Around lunchtime our curiosity abated as word began to spread who was staying and who was going. I did not receive a golden ticket that day. I finished second in ticket revenue despite having the most accounts sold. While we had been told for 24 weeks, clearly to keep us motivated, that the total ticket revenue would not be the determining factor, it clearly was.

The "*winner*" was not in the top five in accounts sold, but happened to receive a lucrative in-bound call the day after the Miami-Dade Commission approved the new ballpark at the Orange Bowl site. The caller was an original premium season ticket holder who had become disenchanted with the organization over the years. Seeing the future of a beautiful new ballpark in Miami, she wanted back in. She asked what it would take to get the best seats in the new ballpark. The answer, at that time, was to buy and maintain the best seats at then Dolphin Stadium. Boom, a $25,000 sale.

The next week the same rep received an in-bound call for a group sale upwards of $10,000. After those two sales his spot in first place was fairly solid, though a couple of us made a strong run and got very close. At the end of the day he finished a few thousand dollars ahead of a close race for second. We realized later that had management told us this job would go to the person with the highest revenue, production would have cratered the day after those in-bound calls.

The Shelton Equation

Now that I am an operator, I understand that we were the front end of an equation:

✓ X sales reps (Y attrition rate) x Dollars per rep = Ticket Revenue

✓ Ticket Revenue > 24 week Budget is a success

✓ Ticket Revenue < 24 week Budget is a failure

The 24 Week Budget Issue

There was no thought put into the next 24 weeks or year or five years. Only hitting the 24-week budget. By that evaluation, the rep with the highest sales equals *"best."* I tell that story, not out of bitterness or because I didn't *"win"* the job. I am incredibly grateful for my time in South Florida. That experience taught me many lessons, good and bad.

In the spring of 2009, I was given my chance to take what I learned from my Inside Sales experience and apply it to my own program. I'm not talking about sales techniques; I'm referring to the program itself. I had just been promoted to Season Ticket Sales Manager for the South Carolina Stingrays in the ECHL after about nine months as an Account Executive. The purpose of the program was two-fold. First it was a low cost way to boost our season ticket revenue for the coming season. These reps would be on a 24-week program making $8 an hour attempting to earn a full-time staff position as an Account Executive.

That leads to the second reason for the program. Over the years our team President, one of my early mentors, said he had *"kissed a lot of frogs."* For every good hire, there were three to five bad hires. Unfortunately, once you've hired someone in a full-time position it's harder to get rid of him or her if things aren't working out. Inside Sales re-positioned the hiring process. After six months we were determining whether to hire you or not, rather than fire you or not. It was during this program that I began developing the three key tenants of my B2C (*Business to Consumer*) sales program. While the program has improved and evolved over the years, these three pieces have remained at its core.

In every league I've worked in I'm proud to say my teams are always the first to be on-sale with season tickets for the following season. During my years in hockey the campaign would begin at our New Year's Eve game (*a tradition with both hockey teams with whom I worked*). You cannot make more time. By going on sale early you will absolutely sell more season tickets. Trying to *"time the market,"* going on sale when the team is hot or waiting until after a playoff run will cost you package sales.

Trying to craft the perfect pricing model leading to endless debate on ticket structure will cost you package sales. The year prior to my arrival in Salem there was an internal debate on pricing that lasted months. Season tickets did not go on-sale until Thanksgiving for a baseball season beginning in April. The *"early bird"* campaign ran until January. I'm not sure I would consider that *"early."* The following year, my first in Salem when I was still Vice President of Ticket Sales and Service, I put together a thoughtful narrative and case for pricing for the 2014 season. It was circulated and debated, which I welcomed.

A call was scheduled to discuss with many stakeholders including investors, members of the finance team, analysts and our leadership on the ground. We discussed and debated. At the end of the call, having not reached consensus it was agreed that we would table the conversation for two weeks. On the next call we still failed to reach consensus. There was general support, but it didn't seem quite perfect, so we tabled the conversation for another two weeks.

Seeing that history was going to repeat itself on the third call I said to the group, respectfully, *"I understand the desire to make a well-thought out decision on pricing. It's not my money on the line, so we can continue to discuss this if the group would like. But, I was hired to advise in this area and I have had great success growing season ticket bases. I am telling you there is no doubt in my mind that every day we are not on sale after July 15 you are losing money. There are sales we will miss and opportunities we cannot get back. It is better to go on sale early with a less than perfect pricing model and leave some nickels on the table than to delay and miss out on dollars."*

We approved pricing on that call and we sold season tickets during every game the rest of the season. As a side note, there is no such thing as a perfect pricing model.

Why is going on sale early so important? *That leads to the second pillar, getting face-to-face.*

Bench Tour

My training with the Florida Marlins was completely based on telemarketing. We were essentially in a call center. Our success or failure for the most part was determined by how many calls you could make in a day. We had an endless supply of leads and a lot of bodies to throw at them. While some of us had better technique than others, the real differentiator was your focus and willingness to *"smile and dial."* The top reps in terms of transactions were the top reps in call volume. It was that simple, a math equation.

I continued to use that approach, with success, with the Stingrays. I showed up early, worked late, and more than anything, made more calls than anyone else in the office. It was after my first couple of months with the team that I thought back to how the Marlins would *"allow"* us to bring a prospect out to a game as a carrot to close the sale.

We were also *"allowed"* in special situations to bring a prospect down to the field to watch batting practice. There was a roped off area along the warning track behind the cage. After hitting, many players would walk over, say hello and sign a few autographs. If you had a prospect on the field for this, it was nearly an automatic sale. You'll notice I said we were *"allowed"* to bring prospects to the ballpark. I say that because it was not part of our process. It was not an expectation. It was something we could do if we felt it would help akin to giving a prospect's kid a signed baseball. The phone was still where we did business.

As I thought back on this it occurred to me that my biggest sales were all fans that I met face-to-face. The first time I sold two full season seats for $5,000 it was to a fan that I brought to, what at the time was called Dolphin Stadium and gave a makeshift tour. I actually closed the sale sitting in the Marlins dugout while the field was being re-sod two weeks after the Orange Bowl. I realized I had literally closed 100 percent of the guests I brought down to batting practice. The phone was for selling ten ticket flex books, quick transactional business. The real money was in getting face-to-face. Being a relatively new hockey fan (*I attended my first game only three years prior*) I asked my boss what hockey had that was comparable to the batting practice experience. It was at this point that the *"bench tour"* was born.

Over the next week my team and I invited guests out to Friday night's game as our guest. The guests were asked to please arrive early because we were actually going to sit on the bench during warm ups. We were all very nervous about how this would go. Letting a fan that close to players in a game setting was a new concept for us. Fortunately, our Team President regarded season ticket sales as the highest priority item in our organization.

When Friday arrived and the first fans sat on the bench of the North Charleston Coliseum there was excitement from the guests and tightness in my chest. Either the players were going to be distant or worse, offended that *"their space"* was being invaded, or they would join in our reindeer games. As the first players approached the ice they saw our group on the bench. One of our families had a son around eight-years-old. He began holding his hand out to high five the players as they passed.

To my great relief one by one the guys started tapping this kid on the hand as they headed out to the ice. The energy, the music, the excitement of the family, everything was perfect. It was at this moment that one of the players decided to have a little fun with us. Coming from the far side of the ice one of our popular defensemen skated as hard as he could toward us, stopping a few feet away with his skate running parallel to the bench. The effect was a snow shower of shaved ice all over the young boy. He was drenched, but he was laughing uncontrollably, screaming, *"Again, again!"* This was magical. After warm-ups I walked the family to our guest services table, filled out the contract and took their deposit for three full season seats for the following season.

Get The Face-To-Face

That spring we sold more new season ticket seats than at any other point since the team began play more than twenty years prior. Since that time, my reps are required to have a minimum number of guests out to each game. In-game sales became the most effective piece of our campaign each year. Despite having so much success meeting face-to-face, we still spent 90 percent of our effort on selling over the phone. The in-game, face-to-face opportunity felt like a gift, like something that was only available to us for a limited time.

I met Charlie Chislaghi during the winter of 2012 at a sales leadership event in Charlotte put on by the AHL. Charlie had spent thirty plus years crafting a face-to-face sales program beginning with a specific, relationship building phone call that led to an invitation to meet in person. From Charlie we learned how to get more guests to the arena for game invites. By delivering this new phone call we had more guests accept our invitation, and when they did, they were more prepared to make a purchase.

Our in-game closing rates were good before, closing more than half of our guests. After bringing him in to work with our staff those rates shot up to nearly 80 percent. The biggest benefit was not in our closing rates it was that he changed our way of thinking about our building and our opportunities. The summer after meeting Charlie we began inviting guests out to the arena for a *private, exclusive, behind the scenes tour of the arena.* On the tour we would take them through the locker room, weight room, coaches' offices and even sit on the bench. We would take them up to the President's Suite and from that view of the arena, have the guest tell us where they would sit if they had their pick. We would move to that location, paint a picture of what it is like to watch from that vantage point and move into our pitch. That summer our season ticket sales increased tenfold.

Getting face-to-face early with an offer they can't refuse has resulted in our team having more new business closed before the end of the season than many teams do in a year.

The Exploding Ticket

The third leg of our trip-pod is often the hardest to swallow and most easily misunderstood. From the time we go on sale the sales staff has the ability to offer the rest of the current season for *FREE* in exchange for signing up for next season. You'll notice, I say they have the *"ability to offer"* not *"everyone who signs up gets the rest of the season."* This is not advertised. It is not meant to be a marketing piece used to drive in-bound calls. This is a tool that a sales rep can use while sitting with their prospect in the seats during a game. We know that we must get a commitment in the seats or we may lose the prospect for good.

It often takes four, five, six or more phone calls to speak to a prospect for the first time. Once you speak with them you need them to accept your invitation to be your guest at a game. Now that you've left tickets for them, you need them to show up. If all of that happens and you don't close them in the ballpark, the chance of making the sale drops significantly. From our tracking we've found that if the prospect leaves the stadium without purchasing the chance of closing drops to less than 10 percent. Using these tools, we've seen closing rates as high as 80 percent.

The free ticket offer lines up with the product they are being presented. If they are looking at half season seats for next season the rep would offer half of the remaining games. If they are considering a quarter season plan and there are twenty games left this year the rep will offer five games.

The exploding ticket was born when I was selling in South Carolina with the Stingrays. I had a particularly challenging prospect in the seats for a second go-round. He and I had spoken on the phone multiple times over two seasons. This is an admittedly long sales cycle for season tickets. The gentleman was a relatively new business owner and while he was a huge hockey fan, he wasn't able to attend as much as in the past due to his new responsibilities. He wanted the tickets for his business.

His employees could use the seats for their own prospects, they could be used as an incentive or reward for his office staff and on occasion, he could attend himself. For some reason, he was having an incredibly difficult time with this decision. I met with him during the first period and he gave every indication he was ready to buy. We found the perfect seats. We discussed putting them in the business name. He did everything but hand over the card.

He said he "*needed to think about it*" a little more. I told him I'd be back around shortly. I left the seats, went back to the office and printed four seats for the rest of the season. I walked back down to his seats right before the second period began, handed him the bundled stack of tickets and said I'd be back in the third period for the card. If he decided not to buy the seats, I'd just *deactivate* the barcodes. Before I could even make it back he texted me his credit card number.

Motivating The Buyer

The thought of potentially giving away so many tickets can be unnerving to some. I should say that I am one of the biggest price integrity hawks around. My teams do not take comps lightly. Baseball has an epidemic issue with comping tickets. A few years back there was a session at one of our gatherings titled "*Empty Seats Don't Eat.*" It was predictably 60 minutes of teams sharing ideas for the best ways to give away or steeply discount tickets in order to get the all mighty food and beverage dollar.

Ironically, teams who also comp heavily have challenged the exploding ticket. It's not the comp itself so much as comping tickets to people who are clearly predisposed to buying tickets. I have encouraged to increase ticket prices and comp more to boost the turnstile in the same season. The belief being that the people who are paying can and will pay more, but since there are not enough of those people we need to give away tickets to everyone else in order to maintain the turnstile. I do distinguish between "*papering*" and strategic sampling or using comps to gain data, additional sales, or in the case of the exploding ticket, to motivate a buyer.

Minor league sports sales (*particularly in a small market, even by minor league standards*) is hand-to-hand combat. If you are following the steps that lead to having a guest in the ballpark considering a purchase, you also need to know that this is not a person who "*would be buying anyway.*" These are people plucked from a jumbled pile of *Enter to Win* leads or a list of on-line buyers from two seasons ago. These are fans (*used very loosely*) that may have only attended a game or two last season.

Maybe their son was in the choir that performed the national anthem or their daughter was there for the *Girl Scout* sleep over. These individuals are being asked to join us for a few more games this season as a family or with friends. In minor league markets tickets sales don't just happen. For that reason sales reps need every available tool at their disposal. The exchange is often viewed in terms of free tickets for this season for however many tickets they buy next season. It is also viewed as a potential hindrance to hitting budgets the rest of the current season. This is very short sighted. In our experience we've been able to renew season tickets at roughly 80 percent meaning this new season ticket holder will likely be around for a few years at least.

In 2015, the year after introducing the quarter season plan in Salem, we actually had a renewal rate of more than 100 percent on quarters due to the number of accounts that upgraded to half and full season plans. If you are in a situation that your current year budget is taking a noticeable hit due to all of these exploding tickets, guess what, you are in store for a great year next season and beyond.

Having these three elements as the core of our season ticket sales process and Inside Sales program has led to unprecedented season ticket growth. I have been in sales leadership or an operator of a team for more than a decade in three markets and to date my team has never failed to grow our season ticket base. I know we will hit a ceiling in the coming years in Salem, but we're not there yet.

The 2018 season will mark the fifth straight year of season ticket growth with our base growing nearly *six-times* since 2013. Getting face-to-face early with an offer they can't refuse has resulted in our team having more new business closed before the end of the season than many teams do in a year. It takes a specific type of person to be able to execute this plan at a high level.

Workplace Motivators

In 2009, not long after becoming the Season Ticket Sales Manager with the Stingrays, I was introduced to a gentleman named Bill Gelderman with the Steering Group. It was Bill who first introduced me to the *DISC*[1] and *Workplace Motivators Assessments*.[2] One reason we may have kissed so many frogs in the past was that the individuals we were hiring were not ideally suited for the role they were being put in. Sales is viewed as a way to "*break into*" the industry. It is so transparent that many candidates will tell me during an interview (for a sales job) that they are "*willing*" to do sales as a way to get in and work "*up*" to the job they really want. Those people are easy to weed out and trust me, if you are "*willing*" to accept a sales role, I won't be offering one.

Our challenge comes from the people who have the wherewithal to not share their disdain for sales in an interview. We also have a challenge when evaluating the out-going individual who wants the sales job because of the social aspects. How do we evaluate the ability to ask for the sale? How do we determine in an interview if the candidate will thrive when challenged in a sales competition or will shrink back when another sales rep finds success? The answer we found was the *DISC* and *Workplace Motivators Assessments*. I should say that there is a great deal of study and training required to truly understand all the nuances of these assessments. What I will do now is give a layman's overview of how to use the assessment for quick decision-making in the hiring process.

The letters in *DISC* stand for **D**ominance, **I**nfluence, **S**teadiness and **C**ompliance. We are looking for a high "*D*" and a high "*I*." Those determine if you are hirable or not. The "*S*" and "*C*" relate to how you need to be managed. Dominance essentially tells us if you are willing to ask for the sale. Until you are in that situation, shaking, with your heart pumping you don't know how you will respond.

Many new sales reps simply create a scenario by which the prospect eventually asks how to buy. This can help you stay afloat, but it will not lead to high-level sales results. We are looking for efficiency. Remember, my experience is primarily in the minor leagues, in small markets even by minor league standards. We don't have enough leads or reps to waste only on prospects who ask us to buy. We need a high percentage of our face-to-face encounters to lead to sales. Our reps need to "*ask for the sale*" every time. A rep with a high "*D*" will do that.

Individualistic & Utilitarian

Influence is a reflection of how social the candidate is, how comfortable they are engaging the prospect. The high "*I*" individual is exactly why I love this assessment so much. You see, a high "*I*" will always interview well. They will be able to talk the talk and say what you want to hear. I don't mean to say they will mislead intentionally, they just have a charm and charisma that makes you like them. That's the gift of the high "I." A high "*I*" rating without a moderate to high "*D*" means they will never ask for the sale.

Though it may be subconscious, they will be afraid to ask for the sale out of fear of losing their new friend. They won't want to come off as pushy or "*sales-y.*" The high "*I*" energy will put them in plenty of situations to have the buyer ask them how to buy or even have the buyer want to "*help out*" the rep because they like him/her. This individual will become a moderate success as a sales rep and will generally be well liked in the office, but moderate success is not what we're going for. The assessment is split into two parts, *DISC* and *Workplace Motivators*. We are looking for four characteristics in a candidate. The first two were mentioned above. The next two are part of the *Workplace Motivators Assessment*.

This assessment is broken down into six parts: Individualistic, Utilitarian, Theoretical, Aesthetic, Social, and Traditional.

I will only focus on the first two listed. There are countless blogs and videos online as well as courses to become certified in evaluating personality profiles. For our purposes we are looking at Individualistic and Utilitarian. The others are important, but again, they are factors for how you need to manage this individual, not whether you will hire the candidate. Individualistic is what I like to refer to as "*leader board motivation.*" A high Individualistic wants to be seen as a leader more than anything else. Not being on the top of the sales board can almost become painful. Trust me, I lost sleep with the Marlins when I lost the top spot. This person will push themselves into sales success.

The next motivator is Utilitarian. This is money motivation, not just money, but control over their earning potential. Someone with a high Utilitarian ethic will always be motivated by the "*upside.*" They will do calculations in their head like number of seats in the building x cost per seat x commission rate just for fun to see how much they could earn by selling the place out. They are motivated by the possibility of what they can earn as much as what they do earn.

A Good Problem To Have

In order to be offered a spot in our Inside Sales program a candidate must hit three of the four lines I mentioned on the assessment. In my time reviewing assessments I have had four candidates hit all four lines. All four of these were rock stars and are now in management with major sports organizations. By having three of the four key areas you are deemed well suited for the face-to-face sales program we run. This is not to say someone cannot find sales success without all of these, however, they will be fighting their nature every day, every call, every meeting. Factors such as environment, time or simply being exceptionally strong in one area of the assessment can lead to a rep having "good" sales numbers.

With that said, efficiency is the key. We have a finite amount of leads. A candidate with three of four assessment factors will give you the best chance of high-level success. Using what I've shared it is possible to review an assessment for two minutes and make a comfortable decision, yay or nay. Now that you have the right people in the program, it's time that you follow through on your commitment to promote the right person at the end.

Let's talk about Charlie. At the end of the 2016 season I was faced with the same difficult choice as the Marlins eight years prior. The summer Inside Sales Class with the Salem Red Sox was one of the strongest I've had. All three reps were outstanding. They worked well together while also being very competitive. Their dynamic of constantly pushing each other drove the highest new season ticket sales during my five-year tenure with the team.

Despite all three being very close in revenue, one rep led wire-to-wire. The other two fought for second place and tried to stay as close to first as possible. On paper there really didn't seem to be a decision to make, first place gets the job. This would have been easy to do. It would have been a safe choice we could have made without much thought. It wasn't going be that easy though.

Charlie Changes The Hiring Model

Halfway through the program my Vice President and Director of Ticket Sales and I began discussing who we thought would make the best addition to our full time staff. We really liked all three and were it not for headcount restrictions they would have all received job offers. As we debated the merits of each rep we kept coming back to one, Charlie. Charlie had strong sales numbers; in any other year he would have been the leader. He was a team player, really good culture guy in the office. He volunteered for events on the weekends. He never missed a tarp pull. And more than anything else, he cared deeply about the job he was doing.

Not being in first place really bothered him. I think he felt like he was letting us down in some way. He came in earlier, worked later and took shorter lunches than anyone else, doing whatever it took to work his way to the top. This did not go unnoticed.

In minor league sports you need people who truly want to be here. Not just earn an account executive position because it pays slightly more and provides healthcare, but really, truly wants to be a part of the team.

Our payroll is low, so the bump from Inside Sales to Account Executive is minimal. The staff is small, so we all have to work harder, longer and wear many hats. The games aren't televised and the players aren't household names... yet. There is not as much prestige as a major league job and often you have to explain to friends and family that, yes, we are still professional, this is not amateur, this is not a club team. For all of those reasons we need believers. Charlie was that.

Periodically we would get together and discuss the candidates. While we tried to talk ourselves into the easy decision, we kept returning to Charlie. As the end of their program approached we began preparing the other two reps and helping facilitate offers with other teams. Finally, with about a month remaining we brought Charlie in and made our offer. To say he was stunned would be an understatement. We had honored our commitment from the beginning to hire the most well suited individual for the future role we had in store rather than simply the top seller.

In his first year Charlie became the top selling group rep during our ownership's history. After two seasons he left Salem to pursue his desire to work in collegiate sports taking a position in California with The Aspire Group.

Charlie Changes The Hiring Model

One and done is not just for college basketball. Employing the system we use for hiring and the program we use for selling it is incredibly difficult to keep a good sales rep for more than a season or two. What may actually be a bigger problem is that minor league teams don't necessarily see this as a problem. Sales people are dispensable and easily replaced. That may be true if you are looking for people who are "*willing*" to sell on their way to the job they want, but that won't lead to high-level sales success.

In September of 2017 at the *MiLB Promo Seminar* Eric Platte of the Atlanta Hawks gave a presentation on sales staff retention. He shared NBA TMBO data showing a dramatic increase in sales production between years two and three for reps around the league. He talked about the retention process beginning on day one of employment and the different steps they take to keep their sales staff intact.

In my experience the only individuals whom I hired in Inside Sales to still be with me in year three had all moved into management positions. While they were still selling (*and doing so extremely effectively*) they were also charged with leading a staff. Having someone exclusively dedicated to selling for three seasons is something I have not seen. It's hard to not see this as an opportunity for our industry. If we simply see our sales staff as disposable cogs in the wheel or act as though "*sales happen*" and it doesn't matter who takes the order we will never see year three success.

While "*Year 3*" is not something I've experienced yet, Eric's presentation caused me to re-evaluate our on-boarding practices and take a close look at why our sales staff life cycle is so short. In Salem we hired three new sales reps in the fall of 2017 and two Inside Sales reps in early 2018. All are being managed with a "*Year 3*" perspective.

Check back with me in early 2021 and I'll let you know how things worked out.

Feeding Fan Ballpark Experiences

Joe Hudson
General Manager
Inland Empire 66ers
California League, Advanced Class-A Baseball

About The Author

Joe Hudson has worked in professional baseball for 17 years, primarily with his hometown baseball franchise in San Bernardino. Hudson assumed day-to-day operations of the Inland Empire 66ers in 2012 when he was named the General Manager. Hudson has had stints in Helena, Montana and Salt Lake City, Utah while working in the food and beverage operation. While currently the General Manager for the 66ers, Hudson still maintains the role of President of Diamond Creations with the Elmore Sports Group where he oversees all food and beverage operations for the group.

No kid ever says that he wants to make a minor league baseball career out of working in food & beverage. Making a career out of working in food and beverage had never been a goal of mine. Matter of fact, working in food and beverage was never the goal even after accepting my first job at the minor league ballpark in town.

It is the forgotten side of the house, but one of the major ancillaries where minor league franchises make their money. Talk tickets all day long, but the second the tickets are bought, it comes down to what else you can sell them, to capitalize on their stay at the ballpark.

My drive to work in minor league baseball was pretty simple: I was sixteen, looking for a way to pay for my first cell phone and have some pocket cash. And a friend's dad worked for the local minor league team in San Bernardino, CA.

My friend mentioned to me that he was going to get a job working with the team that summer and I asked if I could get one too. Pretty simple. No major fixation with working in sports. No handwringing over which team to choose. My basic intentions, looking back on it now decades later, was to have the ability to work a summer job. And somehow, I've stuck with it enough to have a career.

Arriving at the ballpark a few weeks later to apply for the job, I found that the only available position being hired for was concessions. It wasn't what I imagined me or my friend doing when I was asking about working for the summer. But I had little idea of what working in sports actually meant. I envisioned myself working as a batboy or something, I don't know, but I guess I figured everything they offered was minimum wage anyway and I was just excited for my first job. Over the next seven years, amid several internal company opportunities to move up in duties, I was offered the Food & Beverage Director position with the Inland Empire 66ers.

My Summer Job Became A Career

I don't have a culinary background. All of my time has been spent with the Elmore Sports Group. In 16 years, I've experienced every type of management philosophy, including a little in Utah serving food and beverage to hockey fans at the Utah Grizzlies games and an outdoor amphitheater. Now, as President of Diamond Concessions, overseeing the entire Elmore Sports Group food and beverage operations for several teams, I can safely say that trying to get that first cell phone and extra pocket cash as a teenager gave me a career. It wasn't the career that I thought I was going to have when I started, but who envisions staying in food and beverage or minor league baseball as an employee when they are sixteen? Certainly, I wasn't at the time, but at this point in my career, I can't see doing anything else.

Back when I was 16, the San Bernandino owner, Dave Elmore, sat me down to discuss the position with food and beverage. He mentioned that they had continued to struggle to hit expected profitability numbers in over a decade at that point, and he didn't think they had ever made the money that Elmore thought that the San Bernandino team should have made in food and beverage. At the time, Elmore owned a number of other minor league teams, each self-operating their own food and beverage. Meaning that he had a great knack for knowing what yield to expect from profit margins. San Bernardino had never quite hit that threshold.

Elmore's definitive question to me was pretty clear. *"Do you think you can make the concessions operation make money in San Bernardino?"* It was a challenge to me that I accepted from the start. I said I did. I was nervous in taking over an operation that had never truly been profitable according to the owner. After a season of struggles, learning and successes, food & beverage started to move the needle toward profitability.

San Bernardino is home to the original McDonald's Brothers restaurant that was founded in 1948.[1] They created a fast food system, complete with profit margins and the elimination of waste, to ensure customer service in a clean, efficient environment. It is strange that fast food, which is as American as baseball, would have such a differing effect when considering that the San Bernardino ballpark was losing money at the one industry where internationally, it was recognized as one of the pioneers. That's how tricky food and beverage is. You can master it in one place such as McDonald's, and down the road, you can almost be totally oblivious on how to operate it in the ballpark.

Through every stage of my 16 years in food and beverage, there have been a lot challenges from starting entirely new operations from the ground up, to taking over existing operations that have struggled and it is my job to find ways to get it back on track. Each new challenge brings new opportunities to learn and grow in this industry. One thing is for certain, the food and beverage industry is always evolving. There is always something different and new about each season and maybe even each event. It's the aspect that each day brings new challenges that I truly enjoy, and maybe why I keep doing it.

Know Your Numbers

When I think about my first season in San Bernardino running the concessions I remember how focused I was on profitability. Every decision I made was purely about dollars and cents; which I can now admittedly say isn't always the smartest way to run any business, especially concessions. But this season was an exception and I felt like I had to do everything I could to increase profit quickly, I mean this is what I committed to when I took the job. The goal was simple, at least on paper, bring food cost down from 32 percent the previous year to within 25-26 percent, and bring overall profitability up to 47-48 percent from roughly 36 percent.

Walking into an operation that had struggled financially and operationally previously there were a lot of areas that I knew needed attention, but my goal in the first season was to focus on cost of goods. The team we operated, like many minor league teams, did a number of food and beverage based promotions to help turn the gate, one being $0.50 cent hot dogs every Friday. We were selling four thousand hot dogs every night for $0.50 and they were costing us somewhere around $0.45 cents just to make. So right away I was starting from behind. But I knew we weren't the only team in the ownership group with these promotional nights, and so if they were making it work, we could as well.

With the challenges of the food and beverage promotions, and in order to hit that 25-26 percent COGS (*cost of goods sold*), I felt the best way to hit our cost numbers was going to be a balance of first minimizing waste as much as possible, and second raising prices. It was tough not really knowing how much waste had an impact on the previous years' numbers. I started with evaluating the menu and heavily simplifying it that year. The more items you have, the more products you need to have on hand, the more waste you will inevitably have.

Of course this doesn't mean we only sold hot dogs and hamburgers, we still had a few specialty items, but what we did was focus on creating menus that maintained all the basic concessions fare (*nachos, hot dogs, popcorn etc.*) while strategically adding one or two specialty items per location, and focused on trying to use products we already had on site to create these specialty items to minimize waste.

For example, instead of doing a super nacho with steak or chicken, we would do a pulled pork nacho because we were already using pulled pork in that location for a pulled pork sandwich. I felt like this was a good way to add variety at the same time not adding additional items that we would need to prep, cook and have on hand. This process worked for the most part. We were able to keep a menu that provided a good size offering, and still lower the amount of items needed to have on hand.

Managing Food Waste

Our next step in helping to minimize waste was focusing on how much our game day staff was prepping and cooking, when they were producing the food, and how much was wasted at the end of each night. We created *"event notes"* that would give cooks and managers a guide of what projected sales would be for each cooked item sold in their stand, as well as how much they should start with.

By implementing the event notes it took the control out of cooks' hands and into mine. I didn't want our cooks and prep staff cooking based off of what happened last night, or how last Friday was, but rather what this event was projected to be. Sometimes I would find that staff, after a busy night before, would really ramp up for a game because they wanted to get ahead and make sure they were prepared. Unfortunately this isn't always great when you know tonight isn't going to be as busy as last night. So the event notes really helped with that communication and with giving the stand managers and cooks a guide as to where to start in terms of food preparation.

We implemented strict inventory guidelines and made sure that we did a cash to inventory reconciliation at each location after each event. This helped us with not only the goal of minimizing theft, but also in having a constant conversation with our managers each night during our reconciliation or *"cash out"* about food spoilage, leftovers and what we could do to minimize it.

Another important aspect I tried to convey to my staff was the better I knew what inventory was in the stand at the end of the night, the better I could make sure that they were stocked and properly prepared for the next night, and when you are in the middle of a busy game with long lines and fans anxious to get back to their seat, the worst feeling is running out of something and having to run to the warehouse and get it; or worse tell a customer that you are out.

We would ensure to the best of our ability that all food was accounted for through some form of tracking. Either through sales, spoilage, comp or waste. Of course this wasn't the easiest at the time without a great POS system that could help track sales through registers and sales. So we were using excel spreadsheets and lot and lots of counting. Sometimes the stands matched their inventory to cash great. Many times they didn't balance, especially in the beginning when it was new. We just kept trying and working at it until eventually it got better and better. By no means were these new implementations easily received by staff.

There were plenty of times that I would go into a concession stand and the cook would not have followed the notes, or that my stand managers would forget to write down waste items that occurred during the event and so their cash to inventory wouldn't balance. The first season of training a staff that had never had these checks and balances, to now use these new spreadsheets and follow these new policies was tough. Yet as the season went on, and you weed out the good staff from the bad, our waste went down significantly, and things seemed to really operate much more smoothly. Stand managers began to realize that if they filled out their inventory sheets correctly at the end of the night they would get out faster and they would be more prepared for the next game.

Cooks began to realize the event notes were there to help and keep them from cooking too much, or worse cooking too little and getting caught off guard. Fast forward four or five years and even when I would make a mistake and assume an event was too small and they could "*just start low*" as I would say to the cooks, some of my better managers would correct me and tell me to hurry up and make them event notes, because they wanted this information no matter how slow it was. They needed it. To me the first time this happened, it was a realization that the staff not only needs these helpful guides, but they truly want this communication because they realize that it makes them better at their jobs!

At the end of the day everyone whether they are the general manager of a team, the parking attendant or the cashier at a concession stand wants to be good at their job. Giving employees the tools to succeed, which in this case is information and training, is the best thing a manager can do for any of their employees.

Pricing

One of the common misconceptions I would run into throughout my career about the food and beverage industry is that when a company is running high costs the first thing a lot of people think is that their suppliers might be charging them too much.

This may be the issue with small restaurants, but in mid to high volume venues what I have encountered more often is the first thing that should be evaluated is the pricing:

✓   Are we accounting for reasonable waste levels?

✓   Have we properly measured the portion sizes and then trained our staff to make sure that we are actually following these portion sizes?

✓   When setting the price, are you accounting for reasonable fluctuations in purchase costs of items like produce and meats?

These are things that typically more often than not are the root of high food costs, not necessarily the cost at which we are purchasing goods. Most venues are likely set up on a national purchasing group, which means that you are already getting extremely competitive pricing from your suppliers. Now of course we do not want to lose sight on the purchasing side. I can tell numerous stories where I have found a supplier who I feel is charging too much for a particular product that I can find for much less, or worse charging higher than their contracted margin schedule.

One of the better tools to handling this simple issue is to update your inventory price sheets once a month with your new invoice price. If you notice items continually going up, or an item increasing when you felt like it shouldn't have it may be time to do a pricing quote with other suppliers to see if there is an issue. With those issues being said, it is far less likely the cause of high cost. Once or twice a year it is always good to get updated pricing from your suppliers and compare them to each other to see if there are opportunities to save money by purchasing select items from one supplier and some from another. Yet at the end of the day, from my experience, the first place to look when addressing costs above your goal is always at the start, pricing.

As a *"food guy"* every time I go to a ballpark, or a concert, or even the movies, I always find myself walking around checking out their prices. This is something that my wife would always catch me doing and laugh at me for. I guess I just liked that I had some insight into what their costs were, so I could figure out how much I was going to be paying above the real "*hard costs*". Setting menu pricing is always tough. The operator wants to make sure that they are setting it at a price that will keep their costs in line, and the client or team wants to make sure that pricing isn't too high where we are going to scare patrons away.

There is a fine balance when it comes to this issue. We always want to show a value, and the truth is in the entertainment based food and beverage arena the best way we can do this is through quality, not necessarily price. I feel like many times people who do not have a lot of experience in food and beverage are very hesitant to set pricing to the level it should be. I could be wrong about this, but I think the most common mistake is that people create pricing based off of what they "*feel*" or think it should be rather than what the math dictates it to be.

High Quality Over Low Priced

The math will dictate what the price should be based off of the costs and then just calculating the desired margin. We shouldn't get caught up in the idea that "*$7 for a cheeseburger just seems like a lot*", or people don't want to pay $5 for a soda they can buy for $1 at the convenience store. Again, we can only control so much of what the purchasing cost is, so don't feel bad if you do have to charge $7 for a cheeseburger.

My friends that criticize me for the pricing always like to compare the soda we sell for $5 to the $1 soda at *Costco* or *7-Eleven*. I always like to ask them if a baseball game happens to break out right in the middle of *Costco* when they are buying their soda; I sure hope not. The point is, in most entertainment venues we only have so many days we can drive revenue compared to these places we are commonly compared to. In baseball there are 70-72 openings a year, and for only four hours of that day, to really make money. Last time I checked *Costco* and *7-Eleven* are open quite a bit more than the 280 or so hours that we operate in. So of course we are going to have to make more per sell than these other companies.

We have the ability to manipulate the size of the product and the quality, not necessarily the price at which we buy it: *If you take a cheeseburger as an example.*

Let's say you are currently charging $7 for a standard cheeseburger using a 5-ounce patty, cheddar cheese, leaf lettuce, tomato and a quality flour dusted bun. Now in this scenario if you wanted to be able to charge less than $7 because you just feel that is too much to charge for a burger at a minor league ballpark, you could of course make adjustments to the ingredients to bring the cost down. You can go from a 5-ounce hamburger patty to a 4-ounce, instead of cheddar cheese use American cheese, and you can eliminate the lettuce and tomato entirely. This of course would bring your cost of the product down, and in return you can lower the burger price down to maybe $5.00 or $5.50. Now this is not a model that I believe in or would recommend, but I have seen it done. My feelings toward this model of menu development and why I necessarily do not like it is that it is the vocal minority that complain about menu pricing, and it is this vocal minority that would probably still complain about a $5 price as much as they would a $7 price.

So rather than appease the vocal minority and provide a less than desirable product at $5 that would still be deemed high priced, and now also poor quality, I would much rather provide a quality product that while it may be considered high priced it is still considered high quality. Most patrons that attend an entertainment venue, whether it be a sporting event or a concert, expect to pay a little more and can accept that. What patrons don't want to do is pay a little more and still receive a subpar product. At the end of the day food and beverage is not just an amenity within the facility like restrooms or customer service. The food and beverage operation is a part of the overall entertainment and experience when attending these events. If we treat it as part of the entertainment then we will constantly be trying to improve the quality, the service, and the experience similar to how we do in other aspects of our industry.

Staffing & NPOs

Menu development and pricing are only a small piece of the overall equation to a well-run food and beverage operation. One of the biggest challenges in any business, but maybe more so in food and beverage, is staffing. Of course without proper staff, and well-trained staff, you can have the most unique menu as well as the highest quality food and it will all be for nothing without the right staff to execute it. When most teams do job fairs, or have applications come in, concessions and catering is usually the last box check for staff.

It's just not a glamorous position; and in many cases one of the more stressful jobs in the ballpark: *Let's be honest here, if you are starting at minimum wage, which is what most organizations pay their first year part time staff, would you rather be behind a hot grill in the middle of summer or would you rather be an usher out helping fans and watching the event?*

Finding quality staff is difficult, even more so when the economy is doing well because you don't necessarily have career oriented men and women looking for second jobs for supplemental income: *So how do we handle this challenge?*

There are a lot of things that can be done to help with staffing challenges, but not a single one that will solve all your problems: *Some organizations go with non-profit organizations (NPO's) to run all their stands.*

Some organizations do constant hiring and training all year long. Some teams work with staffing agencies to hire and control all their staffing needs. In reality, I think it is a combination of all of these that makes it work. In most the venues I am involved with our typical approach is to try and balance our staff between 60-75 percent self-operated stands and the rest NPO's. Of course this isn't going to work everywhere.

In Utah, one of the operations I was involved in a number of years back, we ran a 20,000 capacity outdoor amphitheater. Over the course of five months we would run roughly 10-12 shows when I was there, today it is closer to 30-35 shows a summer. The constant struggle at this location was that with so few dates to work over the course of five months, and with the demand to operate 40-45 locations, there was no way to maintain a staff of 150-200 people willing to work such limited dates.

So of course in this scenario we relied on roughly 90 percent NPO labor, and these groups are not always easy to find. Not only do you need a group that is committed to showing up each date with the proper level of volunteers that are needed, but you also need to find groups that will truly take the job seriously and provide the quality in service you would expect from your own staff.

Over the years what I have found is that the key to keeping and maintaining quality non profit groups is to pay them well, be fair with them, and make sure that they are making money in the process, because at the end of the day they are volunteering their time to raise money not for themselves but for their cause. In fact I recently visited that same amphitheater operation and 12 years after I had left there are still a number of great NPOs still working there today.

Building Staff Rewards

Maintaining good part time staff with the limited hours as well as the uncertain schedules that are provided in the entertainment world can also be a real struggle. In a lot of other part time jobs there is a relative stable number of hours that an employee will receive as well as a somewhat consistent work schedule. Many minor league baseball and entertainment venues in general just don't have this same consistency when it comes to schedules.

One week an employee may have the opportunity to pick up a shift each day that week, the next there may be no shifts available because there are no events to work. This creates a constant struggle to find good staff that you can maintain not only for a season, but year after year which is the ultimate goal. In many of the locations I have been a part of most of the staff is comprised of either high school kids working their first jobs or middle aged men and women who are picking up a second job for supplemental income.

Typically both of these roles have relatively high turnover because a high school kid is always looking to make more and find a better job and a middle aged employee is usually only working as long as they need to for that supplemental income and then they are done. Added the limited number of hours and it can make it even that much more difficult to keep staff long term. Some of the best ways to combat these issues is by creating a fun and flexible work environment. I have always tried to tell employees that I will work around their other commitments. When I can only provide a limited number of hours in month, it's hard for me to be demanding of the employee on the days that I need them, but then not provide hours on all the days he is available but we do not have an event.

Obviously this leaves me open to having people not be able to work on key dates because they are not available, but we try and hire above the hard number of staff needed by a significant amount and consistently hire throughout the season, but there will always be turnover and need to hire. The key that I have found is to make sure that we can find a way to keep good stand leads and good cooks. We pay them a little better than what they would potentially receive elsewhere with the hopes that it will keep them around a little longer, and for the most part it does.

And even more recently I have started implementing employee reward and acknowledgment programs for even our part time staff members. It amazes me that some of the best feedback I have received from employees on how we can help them enjoy their jobs more has to do with more communication and acknowledgment. Of course what I am saying is nothing new here. Men and women far smarter than I have been talking about the benefits of communication and acknowledgment for a long time and how that can improve the culture of a work place.

After recently implementing our employee acknowledgment and engagement program I was impressed with how many of my employees took time to personally go out of their way and comment on the program to me. I think it shows that whether or not our part time staff views this job as important to them financially, they still want to be appreciated for their efforts.

Staffing Agencies

Outside of your own staff and NPOs, staffing agencies are sometimes the last option, and when caught in a bind very much so needed. Using a staffing agency is typically a last resort when we just don't have the bodies necessary to operate, but of course it is never a great solution as these staff members do not have the operational knowledge and training of your own staff. In that same operation in Utah back 12 years ago, we consistently ran into staffing issues. It was around 2005 and the economy was at its peak which means unemployment was extremely low and staff willing to work part time hours difficult to find.

There were a number of times we used staffing agencies to fill holes in the schedule because sometimes a body with limited knowledge and experience is better than nothing at all. At the end of the day, what we realized was in order to compete and get people hired, we just needed to pay more than the competition which meant paying higher than minimum wage. That year we decided to raise our wages $0.50 - $1.00 more than the minimum wage based off of the job requirements and with this the wages of our existing employees to ensure they stayed with us.

What we saw pretty quickly was that we were having less turnover and were getting more referrals from existing staff for their friends or family that were looking for work. We slowly were able to hire more and rely less on the temp agencies, which in turn provided better customer service and faster wait times and quality. Every location and every economy brings its own set of challenges when it comes to staffing. Ultimately it is being flexible and adapting to the situation that is going to be the right path.

Menu Simplification

One of the things that really drives a fan crazy is going to an event, expecting to enjoy the entertainment, and finding themselves stuck in long lines at the concession stands. Speed of service can be a common challenge in food and beverage. In entertainment many facilities were built inadequate for what the demand is. When they build these venues they are working with limited budgets and they need to provide some of the absolutely necessary amenities like restrooms, seating, locker rooms etc., sometimes food and beverage is on the short stack when it comes to level of funding available.

I can list facility after facility that just don't have the infrastructure required to provide a quality and unique culinary experience. As a food and beverage operator our goal is to always provide the most variety and the best quality as we can with the facilities we are provided. Sometimes this is easy, but a lot of times this is tough. So we try and make do with what we have. We create diverse menus that stretch the boundaries of what the facilities can handle operationally, and sometimes this comes back to haunt us later. Sometimes the simple menu with the high quality is the better route over say the more complex menu that offers customers a more diverse offering.

I like to use In-N-Out burgers as an example. They are one of the more successful food chains in Southern California, and now maybe the west coast in general when it comes to rankings of quality and speed of service. When you look at In-N-Out's menu what stands out the most compared to other hamburger fast food competitors is the simplicity of the menu.

There are three offerings: *cheeseburgers, fries and milkshakes.*

They have this simple menu that they push out mass amounts of volume with because they are quick, accurate and provide a quality product each time. When compared to other fast food chains In-N-Out tops the list with quality and service and I think the simplicity of the menu has a lot to do with it. Of course this is a struggle for concessions. We can't simply provide one style of food and beverage like In-N-Out does because people go to In-N-Out specifically for the purpose to eat there so they know what they are getting whereas fans who go to a ballpark or an arena are going for the game and the food is just one piece of the overall experience.

With that said, I think there is a lesson learned with the In-N-Out model of simplistic menu. Taking that same overall concept and applying to concessions means that we shouldn't put so much onto the menu that we can't provide the quick, accurate and quality service. Once we start failing at the service level it no longer matters that we have a great variety in offerings if we can't provide a quality experience once the product is ordered.

Working With The Facility You Have

As I have said, one of the areas I enjoy about this job is the fact that there are no two days exactly the same. The struggle with slow concessions lines can be brought on from the beginning with a menu that may just be too extensive for a certain area, or it could be something extremely simple and small like an issue I dealt with in Eugene once. I recall a situation we were having with the concessions just constantly being backed up and providing slow service. At this time I was acting in a role of overseeing the operation for the Eugene Emeralds from more of a regional manager position.

To give a little background on Eugene, we were operating out of a ballpark that had a capacity of 3,500 or so and only one small concession stand with about five registers and no onsite cooking facilities anywhere in the ballpark. To put this in perspective, our general goal is to have one register in a permanent concessions stand for every 100-125 seats, so this facility was definitely lacking some infrastructure. Now of course this was not ideal, and so we were constantly building portable point of sale locations using tents, grill kiosks and even a food truck to provide the much needed additional points of sale.

Eventually we had created enough portable locations where we were able to provide enough points of sale that we should have been able to get fans through the lines in the desired time. One season, despite the efforts of the added points of sale locations throughout the ballpark, we were still struggling getting fans through the lines at the sole permanent concession stand that we operated out of. Allan, the General Manager of the facility, was concerned about a big game on the schedule and asked if I could fly out and help figure out why the stand just wasn't able to keep up with the demand.

We both felt they should be able to handle the demand with the added points of sale and the basic menu we were operating at the location. After making the trip out there the first thing I wanted to do was speak with the food and beverage director and stand manager directly prior to the next game to get their opinion on what was potentially slowing them down. I had already checked the menu and didn't think there was anything on there that was too complex or time consuming, and so there had to be something operationally that was catching them up. What the stand manager and I both came to as the conclusion together was that the process of building and making the nachos and super nachos had to be the reason lines were slow. I went through the process of asking her how she set up the stand and the prep area, what part of the ordering process was taking the longest, where we could be faster etc.

What we found was that with a few tweaks in the setup of the stand, moving some equipment around for a better flow, as well as prepping the number of expected sales for nachos in advance we were able to push out more nachos and faster which ultimately helped the lines dramatically moved quicker. It's funny how something as small as moving a few pieces of equipment and traying up nachos in advance made the difference for this location. I've realized over the 16 years that I have worked in this industry that it isn't always massive changes and grand ideas that fix issues within most food and beverage operations; it's a lot of small things that add up.

I truly enjoy every aspect of this industry. I enjoy the planning of a big event and doing your best to strategize as best you can on what to expect and how to be prepared for it. I enjoy the feeling right at gates when you feel like you've "*crossed all your T's and dotted all your I's*" as best you can and you are just waiting for the controlled chaos to happen. I love the feeling post event while you are sitting back checking out vendors and stand managers after a long day and that is the first moment you have been able to relax all day and have a well-deserved beer.

My favorite part of any game day is right at gates when you just get to watch the hard work you have done take shape as people stream in. Maybe the aspect I love the most in this job is the interaction with all your staff and the relationships you build in those busy and sometimes hectic times. Concessions can be a hard industry. There are times you can't anticipate all the things that can go wrong, and when they do it throws a wrench into all the planning and preparations you've made. It's like that theory, if something can go wrong it will.

Learning Never Stops

Sometimes this happens and in that moment it sucks and all you can do is grind through it. But in those moments after a day where things go wrong at no fault of your own, and with those men and women that were right there grinding it out with you, it's those moments that you really appreciate great people and their commitment to their jobs and to you as a manager. I have learned a lot from the people that I have worked under and maybe even more from the people that I have managed.

Yet I can tell you there will still be crazy days, there will be new unforeseeable wrenches thrown in my seemingly well thought out plans, and hopefully plenty of relaxing moments at the end of a long day and a successful night with a cold drink in my hand. I am still bewildered at the adventures that I have had over the past 16 years. I was a kid back then, looking for a way to pay for a cell phone. Now, I have a knowledge of a part of the industry that few people think about, but every one should be well-versed in.

It's a wild contradiction of sorts, but one that matters to address. Since that time when Dave Elmore first challenged me with making San Bernardino's food and beverage operation profitable, my knowledge base on how to make it a viable revenue stream has changed. But that doesn't mean I answered incorrectly when I told him that I could do it. That I could change around a decade of bad numbers in food and beverage. As with anything, it takes trying to learn in-depth everything about the job you are in, down to the nuts and bolts of profit and cost. If you can master food and beverage, you are really suited for any position in minor league baseball that's available.

Market Your Assets Off

Greg Coleman
President
Erie Seawolves
Eastern League, Double-A Baseball

About The Author

Since 2011, Greg Coleman has served as President of the Erie SeaWolves, the Double-A Eastern League's top promotional team in 2017. As Vice President and General Manager of the Modesto A's, Greg led the team to record attendance and received the 2003 Bob Freitas Award for franchise excellence. He helped open a new ballpark as Assistant General Manager of the Bowling Green Hot Rods, and the franchise was awarded 2009 MiLB.com Promotion of the Year during his tenure. Coleman's career spans more than two decades including stops with the Daytona Cubs, Orlando Rays, Golden Baseball League and Trenton Thunder.

It was a Friday afternoon, in the Central Valley town of Modesto, California and a few people in the front office of the 2002's Modesto Athletics were sweating. The perspiration had nothing to do with the hot summer temperatures. On the following night, the Class A-Advanced affiliate of the Oakland Athletics was scheduled to give out seat cushions to the first 1,000 fans. Seat cushions may not go down in baseball history for promotional originality, but any fan who has tried to sit in a seat at John Thurman Field or another sun-soaked ballpark can appreciate the value of not burning his or her bottom.

The end of the business day had arrived, but the seat cushions hadn't. The shipment was tracked to a distribution center about ten minutes from the stadium, but the cushions weren't scheduled to be delivered until the next business day: Monday. At the time, as General Manager of The Modesto Athletics, both I and my staff needed to pull a rabbit out of a hat or prepare apologies for both the fans and the sponsor. Presented by a local health services agency to promote smoking cessation, the missing cushions were to read *The Butt Stops Here*.

After unsuccessfully trying to reach the distribution center by phone, we planned to go there on Saturday morning to see if we could conjure up a miracle. After getting into the building through a door that was ajar, we were able to locate a well-meaning employee who informed us that our ten boxes were on a locked trailer that was waiting to be sorted. He wouldn't be able to sort the trailer, but he was willing to open the back of the 18-wheeler and allow our staff to search for the boxes ourselves. We called in our 10-person staff, along with friends and family, and started unloading items – boxes, tires, lamps and more. The trailer was packed from floor to ceiling. It was a sweltering day, and it was even worse crawling around inside the truck. About halfway through fully excavating the trailer, we located our first box of cushions. It was like we'd won the World Series – high fives and hugs all around. Unfortunately, the boxes weren't together, but we soon found four more boxes of cushions.

While we continued to search for the remaining boxes, one of our two Assistant General Managers decided to take a quick break and a sip of Gatorade. During this break in the action, he decided that he wanted to see the cushions we'd been working so hard to extract. He opened one of the boxes and pulled out a seat cushion. Much to our surprise, the giveaway we'd worked so hard to execute wasn't going to happen. The vendor and our merchandise director both missed a typo in the design, which incorrectly read *The Butt Shops Here*. One letter can make a big difference.

We reloaded all of the packages back onto the truck (*far more quickly and far less carefully*) and headed to the stadium. We made amends to the sponsor and offered rain checks to the fans as they entered that night. We marched forward with the rest of our promotional plans for the game and then launched fireworks to cap the evening. Plenty of things went wrong that day, but most of our miscues would go unnoticed by the fans -- until they tried to drive home. Our promotional efforts, which were supposed to draw fans to the game and encourage those in attendance to stop smoking, ultimately ended with our fireworks setting a nearby riverbank on fire. It wasn't our finest promotion, but it was memorable.

Make Marketing FUNN Again

Running a Minor League Baseball team requires resilience. Some key factors in achieving your business goals are out of your control. You can do your best to manage inclement weather conditions, but *Mother Nature* will have her say. In the affiliated minor leagues, a General Manager has little impact on team performance. Major League teams determine which players are assigned to each level and which coaches and instructors help them develop. Every Minor League executive would love to have a championship season and a lineup packed with future Major League All-Stars, but you can't build a business plan on that premise. Fortunately, there are plenty of variables that can be controlled. You can hire talented, creative and hard-working people to sell and market family entertainment. You can make the ballpark a welcoming, comfortable place to spend a few leisurely hours. You can treat attendees as guests in your home and make their experience so much fun that they want to return as soon as they can.

Perhaps no word is more inextricably linked to Minor League Baseball than fun. Bowling Green Hot Rods Baseball was *Fueled By Fun* and later, to the chagrin of some English teachers, *FUNNER*. The El Paso Chihuahuas want their fans to *Fetch the Fun*. The Richmond Flying Squirrels don't just play at the Diamond, they play in *FUNNVILLE*. They have so much FUNN in Richmond, they require an extra N to contain it. Each of these teams is trying to increase awareness, create interest, generate sales and create brand loyalty. This is the very definition of promotion.

Major League teams enjoy many advantages. They play in the largest markets and have the most resources, and they can spend those resources on star power. A Minor League team's biggest star is typically its mascot. Despite the lack of star power and resources, good promotions and creative marketing can help a Minor League team cut through the clutter to draw an audience. Teams can use promotions to create the perception of value for the fans and create value for the team in the process.

Affiliated Minor League Baseball teams play 70 home games per season. While some games may be more attractive to fans because they fall on the weekend or feature an opponent of regional interest, most are unremarkable events until a team puts its own promotional stamp on it. A well-designed promotion can give a fan an additional reason to attend an event. Some promotions even can be *THE* reason a fan attends an event. Not every promotion will resonate with every fan, but teams can layer multiple promotions to give more fans a motivating reason to attend.

The Promotions Calendar

In 2011, I started as President of the Erie SeaWolves, the Double-A affiliate of the Detroit Tigers. In the years since, the SeaWolves have been committed to developing high-quality promotions that deliver added fan value while driving revenue growth for the team. We know we can't shape team performance, but we know our promotions can connect with fans, offer an enjoyable distraction from some of life's challenges, and encourage them to catch a game.

The way a team chooses and implements its promotions can have a far greater impact on a team's financial success than wins and losses. Promotions can become an anticipated part of the ballpark experience, and they can become more closely linked to the team than the players themselves, who may be promoted, demoted, released or traded at any time. Promotions, however, can become an inseparable part of the team's brand.

Promotions can create new opportunities for fans to buy or give them reasons to buy more often. Despite 70 home dates, promotions can also give fans the perception of scarcity. Fans may have dozens of games they can attend, but only one may feature a specific giveaway or featured entertainer. Teams also can use social media to generate online content and show fans who missed the game why they shouldn't miss the next one.

Every Game A Different Experience

Each year, Minor League Baseball hosts its *Promotional Seminar* as a way to share some of the best current promotional ideas in the industry. It's hard to imagine this type of exchange occurring in other industries. McDonald's and Wendy's aren't willingly sharing their best ideas with one another, yet that's exactly what occurs at the seminar.

As part of the festivities, Minor League Baseball allows seminar attendees to vote on the *Golden Bobblehead Awards*.[1] These honors are presented to the top promotion in each major category including *Best Theme Night, Best In-Game Promotion, Best Non-Gameday Event, and Best Community Promotion or Event*. Many promotions fall into these four categories, but it's not all encompassing.

Price Promotions: Everyone loves a great deal, and the right deal can drive sales. When considering a price promotion, it's important to consider the overall impact on the team. Will a discount that attracts some customers devalue the product for others? While price promotions on concessions can benefit the entire fan base, price promotions on tickets can discourage fans from purchasing season tickets or similar offerings.

The Erie SeaWolves' most notable price promotion is called *Buck Night*. It was created to address weak numbers on Mondays after Erie earned the opportunity to host Double-A Baseball. The move from the Short-Season New York-Penn League (NYPL) to the full-season Eastern League nearly doubled the number of games and seating inventory the team needed to sell. After being one of the top draws in the NYPL, Erie now found itself as one of the smallest Double-A markets in the country.

Most Minor League Baseball followers are familiar with beer and soft drink specials on *Thirsty Thursday*, a concept pioneered and trademarked by the Asheville Tourists. The SeaWolves went further, offering $1 specials on beer, soft drinks, hot dogs, popcorn and bleacher seats. The promotion was wildly successful in attracting thousands of value-minded consumers to each *Buck Night*. Monday ticket prices were increased over time to full price and craft beers increased too, but the offer was so impactful that it remains one of the most recognized features of the team's brand.

After the early success of *Buck Night*, the team received feedback from fans which led the team to create a family-friendly version of the promotion on Tuesdays called *Family Buck Night*. All of the features were the same as *Buck Night* except the team sold beer at full price and replaced it with $1 cotton candy. Attendance increased on Tuesdays as well, but profits did not. Whereas *Buck Night* sold thousands of tickets per game, *Family Buck Night* sold hundreds per game and encouraged full-priced group outings to migrate from other days of the week to the discounted night. *Family Buck Night* may have increased attendance on Tuesdays, but it eroded margins and profitability. It was soon replaced with a *Kids Eat Free* promotion on Tuesday. The new promotion yielded better overall results by giving away free hot dogs, drinks and chips to children (*ages 12 & under*) while charging regular prices to all other fans.

In most cases, our organization steers clear of ticket discounts. On occasion, we'll make an exception to drive results for a sponsor, such as a $2 discount to fans presenting a credit union's debit card or *AAA membership card*. These limited exceptions are always underwritten by the sponsor and will never be a better deal than what loyal season ticket holders already receive. Compared to other forms of entertainment, Minor League Baseball is relatively inexpensive and, in my opinion, worth every penny of the ticket price. We would rather deliver an excellent product at a fair value than an average product at a cheap price.

Value-Added Promotions: Baseball teams have an infinite number of ways to add value for their fans before, during and after a game. Fans can receive a free hat, T-shirt, jersey or bobblehead upon arrival at the game. They can listen to live music or watch on-field ceremonies until the game begins. During the game, fans are entertained by sound effects, between innings contests, touring entertainers like the Zooperstars, and celebrity autograph sessions. Post-game festivities might include fireworks, player autographs, or the opportunity to run around the bases.

Each of the elements above add value to the experience without relying on discounted prices. It's important to consider that some of the promotions carry costs, and some of those costs are notable. The costs of bringing in a notable celebrity or entertainer can be three times as expensive as a fireworks show. Unless a team has enough seating inventory to sell, it may not be worth investing in certain promotions or combining promotions in a way that limits the team's ability to get a suitable return on its investment. Even if a team receives sponsorship revenue for a specific promotion, it's important to consider whether a different date, day of the week, or promotion might be more impactful.

In 2016, the SeaWolves booked *Team Ghost Riders* for the first time.[2] In Minor League Baseball circles, they are better known as the *Cowboy Monkey Rodeo* –

capuchin monkeys that ride dogs and herd sheep. While some may argue against the use of animals in entertainment, we've seen first-hand the manner in which the operator cares for the animals as well as the gross misinformation spread by opposition groups. This promotion isn't for every market, but we support *Team Ghost Riders* and the SeaWolves fans have turned out by the thousands to see them in person.

We view entertainment acts like the baseball sabermetric community views *Wins Above Replacement*. When we place a promotion on the schedule, we ask ourselves how we project it will compare to the average for that day and time of year. We can forecast impact by consulting with other teams that have booked the act and by reviewing data on our past events, which we record following every game to ensure we have an accurate basis for future decisions. Some important data points include the number of tickets sold itemized by subset (*packages, groups, single-game tickets purchased in advance, and game day walk-up*), weather conditions, ticket use rates, and key promotional elements.

Erie has one of the smaller stadiums in the Eastern League, and we've found that we can better accommodate the larger increases that accompany an act like *Team Ghost Riders* on a Tuesday, Wednesday or Thursday and realize a better return than if we place it on a date that is more likely to be filled with larger group outings. While our model makes sense for Erie, each team's data will determine which days or dates are likely to yield the best return.

Tapping into Tribes: Promotions like fireworks and team-branded giveaways may not deliver added value for everyone, but those enhancements are often scheduled with the objective of reaching the broadest possible audience. However, another approach is to develop promotions that cater to the shared interests of a group or tribe. While the interests of a tribe may not appeal to the masses, a subset of individuals may share a deep passion for a specific interest area.

One of the most common examples of a tribal promotion is a *Dog Day* or *Bark at the Park Night*. Dog owners are passionate about their pets and consider them as family. The opportunity to share an experience with their pet, and others who share the same interests, carries appeal.

Bark at the Park is only one example of a tribal promotion. Fans will act on their passions to support shared causes and attend games to support cancer survivors, recognize veterans and active military, or connect with other alumni from a school or university.

Over the past few seasons, there has been rapid growth in the number of promotions based on licensed characters, products and films like *Star Wars, Harry Potter*, and *Teenage Mutant Ninja Turtles*. These interest groups are easy to identify and target via social media and they will share details about relevant promotions to others in their tribe. My family is likely to show added interest in *LEGO, Harry Potter, Star Wars*, and *Marvel*-themed events as we consider ourselves fans of those properties. Conversely, *Bark at the Park* or a *Star Trek* promotion would have little positive influence on our decision to attend an event.

Pop Culture Moments: Licensed characters and products are certainly a part of popular culture, so a single promotion can cross-over into other categories. With that said, some of the most powerful promotions are those developed in real-time and capture the moral or cultural climate of the time.

In 2015, the Myrtle Beach Pelicans announced a *Deflate Cancer Night* in response to the Deflategate controversy which resulted in the NFL suspending and fining Tom Brady for footballs which were presumably underinflated to the advantage of the New England Patriots. Fans were offered inflatable baseballs, most of which were properly inflated. A local tire store handed out pressure gauges and fans were offered the opportunity to ride in a deflated hot air balloon. At its core, the team used the opportunity to promote awareness for testicular cancer. *Deflate Cancer Night* is a great example of inserting your team into a national conversation. Publicly taking a position on some issues can carry some risks. In this instance, the Pelicans may have alienated some New England Patriots fans in the Myrtle Beach area. Conversely though, the team may have acquired legions of new fans while press coverage of the promotion drove people to the *Deflate Cancer* game and to their website, where prospective customers could buy both tickets and merchandise.

One of the most exciting days of the season is the day that next year's draft schedule arrives from the league office. In the Eastern League, this day typically arrives in May. Each team has two weeks to review the document and offer feedback. After the league makes a few changes, teams then have another two weeks to determine the times of their games. By the end of June, each team typically knows its schedule for the following year. Each team is then permitted to release its home schedule at its own discretion by early August. Upon receipt of the schedule, our first step is to identify dates for core annual promotions.

For the Erie SeaWolves, we determine which dates will be *Buck Nights (featuring $1 hot dogs, soft drinks, popcorn and domestic draft beers)*. *Buck Nights* typically coincide with every Monday home game, but some exceptions, like when a holiday falls on a Monday, may apply. In an average year, *Buck Nights* represent one-third of the team's single-game ticket sales, so we carefully consider any exceptions.

We also identify three home dates that can be played at 11:05 AM to accommodate school field trips. The SeaWolves provide area teachers with lessons that can be used in the classroom before and after the event. At the game, the team provides pre-game presentations on a variety of subjects and concourse displays from local agencies and universities. These *Education Day* games typically fall on the final weekday game of a May series, easing travel for one or both teams.

What Moves The Needle?

For the SeaWolves, the process of identifying core promotions isn't complete until we've identified our fireworks strategy. After years of conditioning, Erie fans have come to expect fireworks shows on summer Saturday nights. However, we always review the schedule for the opportunity to test the impact of other potential dates. Among all possible promotions, the SeaWolves have found fireworks consistently yield the best return on investment.

In addition to core promotions, our senior management team identifies potential trouble spots. Each team has competition in its market, and that competition comes from a variety of sources. Community festivals, holidays, graduations, and high school football are just a few examples that warrant consideration depending on the community you serve. In Erie, we have several annual summer events which bring thousands of tourists to the community. In some cases, we try to complement a community event to attract tourists. In other cases, we'll market to the local audience least likely to attend a competing event. Lastly, we identify dates most likely to host major group ticket initiatives. A team may have group outings which fill the majority of a game's seating inventory, and these outings may occur annually in the same approximate time frame. Depending on the size of the group, it may be best to avoid investing major promotional resources in a specific date as the team won't have enough available seats to realize a return on its promotional investment.

As the season progresses, the staff is encouraged to log ideas for new promotions and ways to enhance existing promotions. Near the end of the season, we ask all full-time staff members to complete a questionnaire about theme nights, price promotions, and game day entertainment. Each staff member replies, and these replies are compiled into a master document to be discussed immediately following the season.

Some example questions:

- *What theme night should be added for next season?*

- *What are four giveaways you'd like to see the SeaWolves issue next season?*

- *What annual or recurring promotion should not return next season?*

Once the replies are compiled, it's easy to identify some staff preferences. If a team has implemented a fan survey (*even an informal Twitter or Facebook query*), it makes sense to add any survey trends to the master list as well. Once this information is compiled, the team can meet to narrow down the pool of ideas to the best of the best.

Once postseason planning meetings are complete, it's time to figure out which ideas are truly financially viable. Since we have already placed our core game day promotions on the dates we believe they'll be most effective, we look at other key dates to see how we can positively impact them.

In Erie, our Director of Entertainment will contact vendors and entertainers to determine the costs associated with each potential promotion. While we go through the process of identifying these projected expenses, we look at historical numbers and determine the likely impact of each promotion.

We'll take into account potential sponsorship revenue for the promotion, the number of extra tickets we anticipate we'll sell, and the impact on ancillary revenue streams like merchandise and concessions. If the quotes we receive are in line with our expectations, we'll move forward with the promotion. If the return on investment is less than desirable, we'll consider replacing the promotion with one more likely to yield a better return.

By October, we know the majority of our promotional schedule. If we have priorities in other areas of the budget, we may decide to pull the plug on one or two promotions that we believe will yield the lowest return on investment. We also leave some budget flexibility to react to current events.

The Off-Season

One question that is asked repeatedly of Minor League Baseball executives: *"What do you do during the offseason?"*

While I would love to explain that I spend months on a tropical island, my standard response is much less exotic and far more honest: *I'm like a wedding planner.*

When an engaged couple plans their big day, they choose a date, time and location for their wedding and reception, invite their guests, book the entertainment, order wedding favors, decide on attire, select a caterer and menu, and so forth. For every Minor League game, someone in the front office schedules the game, prepares the venue, sells ticket, plans the entertainment (*before, during and after the game*), orders custom giveaways or prizes, determines which uniforms are to be worn, sets the concessions menu, and so forth. A full-season Minor League team has to prepare for at least 70 *"big days"* and possibly more if the team qualifies for the postseason. With 261 workdays in an average year (*for non-sports professionals, of course*), each game has to be planned, sold and executed in under four days. In reality, it's far less than four days as most teams schedule extra events at their facilities too.

In Erie, we begin the process of planning our promotional efforts shortly after we conclude our organizational planning meetings. For about an hour a week, we'll have representatives from each department meet together to further develop our initial promotional ideas. We'll discuss a couple of key dates during each session and determine how we're going to market the promotion and ways to enhance revenue opportunities. For theme nights, we might add a specialty concessions item or limited edition T-shirt. We'll identify local ticket sales targets who can help promote and purchase tickets to the game. Through this process, we're able to identify ancillary opportunities and give ourselves adequate lead time to sell sponsorships and tickets against our promotional schedule. We're also able to announce our promotional schedule at least a month before single-game tickets go on sale.

By the time Opening Day arrives, planning is complete and execution is well underway. If you ask a team's fans which promotions were their favorite or which one(s) specifically motivated them to attend a game, you're likely to get a diverse set of answers. For some, fireworks or cheap beer may drive purchase intent. For others, the opportunity to share an experience together is a powerful motivator.

You can't please all of the people all of the time, but you can seek to understand what will motivate large segments of your audience. You can compile this data through fan surveys, informal conversations, and by keeping excellent records to identify the impact of past promotions on sales.

Guiding Questions for Promotions:

Does the promotion encourage fans to purchase more or sooner? Single-game ticket buyers have value, but their intent to purchase can be negatively altered by weather, team performance, or just the ever-changing nature of life itself. We want to encourage fans to purchase their tickets before overcast skies or the team's losing record can influence their decision. Promotions that encourage advance purchase eliminate some of the risks of operation.

Does the promotion have broad appeal? Thanks to creativity and current events, there's an endless source of material for new promotions. Not all ideas are created equal though. A theme night or a celebrity appearance can be successful if it appeals across a variety of ages and demographics. There's a reason so many Minor League Baseball teams host one or more *"Bring Your Dog"* nights – approximately 68 percent of U.S. households own a pet.

Does the promotion have deep appeal? Not every promotion can appeal to a broad audience. If the target audience is smaller, it needs to connect on a deeper or more personal level. Promotions centered on personal causes or affinity groups make this type of connection. Each season, the SeaWolves host a sensory-friendly game specifically to accommodate guests with autism. The team reduces the stadium audio levels and the number of in-game crowd prompts, and a comfortable space is provided to serve as a break area should anyone become over-stimulated by the environment. While the majority of families are not affected by autism, the majority of autism support groups in the Erie community attend this specific game.

Does the promotion provide more value than the price of admission? Minor League teams give away all sorts of things – bobbleheads, caps, jerseys, foam fingers and other items featuring the logos of the team and presenting sponsor. A giveaway item that is equal to or greater than the price of a ticket can increase a fan's purchase intent. A lesser value item such as a magnet or water bottle can still provide value to a sponsor, but it is far less likely to impact the team's ticket sales results. If a promotion doesn't increase purchase intent, there's a chance the team could be missing the opportunity to apply resources to another opportunity that does.

Does the promotion provide a shareable experience? Social media has changed the way we live, consume and share our experiences. Each social platform provides a means for teams to stay relevant on a season-long basis, and that means more opportunities to drive sales. Every experience leads to an emotional response, and that response may drive others to purchase tickets. A shareable promotion can be both simple and inexpensive, such as giving fans the opportunity to play catch on the field before the game or giving them a reason to dress up as their favorite super hero. In the end, a shareable experience will further cement the bond between the team and the fan and, thanks to social media, reach new prospective fans.

What's the risk of (not) doing the promotion? While social media has made it easier to target certain audiences, it also means that individuals are constantly being bombarded with messages. It's not enough to create a fun promotion that has value and resonates with a specific audience. Your promotion has to cut through the clutter and be processed by the target audience. Every promotion carries some risk. If you push the boundaries of good taste, you could alienate otherwise loyal fans. At the same time, a promotion can be equally or more ineffective if it's not noteworthy.

In 2017, the SeaWolves took a risk with a political promotion called *Alternative Facts Night*. The theme night threw a few jabs at politicians on both sides of the aisle, and it rankled a few people online who preached that baseball and politics shouldn't mix. However, USA Today, the Washington Post, and other major media outlets actively reported on the promotion because it captured the essence of the political landscape at the time and did it in a light-hearted way. We took a calculated risk and, thanks in part to *Alternative Facts Night*, the SeaWolves were honored as the Eastern League's top promotional club in 2017.

Every year, Minor League baseball teams churn out thousands of game day promotions. The best of those promotions capture the imagination or heart of the fans. However, there are amazing promotions that happen every year that never get their due. They may enjoy a degree of local success, such as an uptick in game day ticket sales or a mention on a local newscast, yet they never find a national audience. Not every idea will resonate on a national level, yet some ideas should garner more attention than they do. In 2017, the Gwinnett Braves (*now the Gwinnett Stripers*) presented a simple concept for a ballpark event to attendees at the *Minor League Baseball Promotional Seminar*. The event, *Goat Yoga*, gave attendees the chance to practice yoga with several goats meandering around and on them.

For many of the Minor League executives in attendance at the seminar, it was the first time they'd heard of *Goat Yoga*. It really captured the fun spirit of Minor League, which meant it was soon to be replicated by other teams. Not surprisingly, the Hartford Yard Goats were one of the first to follow suit. The promotions were fairly similar, yet Hartford's promotion was picked up by the Associated Press and other local and national outlets. Gwinnett may have been first to market, but Hartford used its media relationships to position the idea and their team in a more impactful way. Just as there are more options than ever for creating a promotional schedule, there are more options than ever for building excitement for promotions. In the past, a team may have simply printed it on a pocket-sized schedule. Thanks to changes in tools and technology, teams have more options than ever to introduce and highlight their promotions.

Press Release: Introducing your promotional schedule via press release is still a very common practice. A release can be posted on the team's website and circulated with key media outlets. The process can be more effective by pairing the release with supporting images to draw attention to highlight key promotions. Some teams take this process a step further and introduce their promotions through a series of releases. For instance, a team may release its giveaways on a Monday, entertainment acts on Tuesday, celebrity appearances on Wednesday, price promotions on Thursday, and fireworks schedule on Friday. The effectiveness of this strategy will vary from market to market and may prove to be a better strategy for social media than for media communications. It's worth noting that the timing of a team's release is very important as the release may receive less attention if it is competing with other major stories such as the Super Bowl.

Press Conference: Hosting a press conference can be an effective strategy if the team has visuals that may be communicated with greater emphasis in person. For instance, the Harrisburg Senators boast *The One & Only World Famous, Life Size Bobblehead Hall of Fame* at its stadium. The Senators induct past players into its Hall of Fame, and induction is typically accompanied by commemorative bobblehead giveaway to the fans and a player appearance when possible. The Senators introduced this idea by press release, but they also could have used a life-size example, such as a rendering printed on corrugated plastic to illustrate the sheer size of the Hall of Fame exhibits.

Social Media: Press releases and press conferences bring value, but neither is a complete solution. With the tools available through Facebook, Twitter, Instagram, Snapchat and other platforms, teams can quickly spread excitement for its ideas with assistance from engaged fans. Facebook continues to place increasing importance on live video, and events such as the release of a promotional schedule provide ideal native content for the platform. Teams can tease the announcement in advance to help build an audience. A picture is worth a thousand words, so prepare good quality images and/or infographics in advance to make it easy for others to share, and always include the team's brand prominently in those images.

Over the past few seasons, the SeaWolves have made it standard practice to order additional promotional giveaways to provide to media influencers such as television anchors and radio morning show hosts. We are fortunate to have very supportive media partners willing to show or wear our giveaways on-air for free. While this level of free publicity won't be attainable in many other markets, every market has influencers who could post or tweet about the promotion from their own social media accounts. In addition to giving our influencers items they can keep, we also provide them with copy points to ensure they understand the supporting details (*e.g., date, quantity, age restrictions, and sponsor*) of each promotion. These influencers' posts, tweets and snaps can be documented and used to demonstrate value to any sponsors associated with the promotion.

Website: For affiliated Minor League Baseball teams, Major League Baseball Advanced Media (MLBAM) provides the framework for team sites. However, teams are individually responsible for populating online promotional schedule content. A promotion is not effective unless the details that could persuade someone to buy reach the prospective buyer in time to act on it. I recently researched a sports team which hosted game day offers ranging from giveaways to specially priced tickets. I was aware that the team had promotions because its official social media accounts shared the information, yet the team's official website had no list of promotions. This one oversight reduced the effectiveness of the team's promotional efforts and shortchanged the team's promotional sponsors in the process. Quality images and descriptions can be the determining factor in whether or not a customer decides to purchase a ticket. Graphics need to be equally eye-catching on mobile devices as they are on a desktop, and teams should ensure that their sponsors are effectively and appropriately represented regardless of the viewer's device.

Advertising: No two teams share the same media mix. Teams will have certain priorities based on the relationships they value in their respective markets. Over the past few years, the SeaWolves have increased online spending while maintaining most of our traditional media mix.

While teams may vary in what they consider to be the ideal media mix, a lousy message will be largely ineffective regardless of medium. If you try to communicate too many ideas, you may fail to communicate a single one. If you communicate too little, your ad will be equally ineffective.

In September 2017, MLBAM surveyed users of MiLB.com and individual team websites about their interest in Minor League Baseball. Over 70 percent of respondents were interested in Minor League Baseball because of its value proposition, entertainment, family environment and local relevance. Fewer than 30 percent of respondents indicated player performance or prospect-watching influenced their interest level.

The results of the MLBAM survey are relevant because teams often omit promotional information from their advertising yet include details such as the opposing team or the opponent's affiliation. I am not suggesting that supporting game information is entirely without value. In northwest Pennsylvania, we always highlight when the Erie SeaWolves will be playing the Eastern League affiliate of regional favorites like the Pittsburgh Pirates (*Altoona Curve*) and the Cleveland Indians (*Akron RubberDucks*) because we know this information may influence a purchase decision. At the same time, we always make sure to highlight a key promotion, such as fireworks or a giveaway, which will resonate with the other 70 percent.

A full-season Minor League Baseball team has to plan to attract an audience to at least 70 stadium events. Compared to other sports, baseball requires an abundance of ideas to make the most of each opportunity. Fortunately, inspiration is everywhere.

Dates & Holidays. Baseball is a beautifully cyclical game. The season starts each spring and ends each fall. A team's schedule may be a little less reliable. A team may be home on Father's Day one season and may not be able to celebrate Dad on his day again for several seasons. With that noted, Minor League Baseball promoters love elasticity and may just celebrate Dad's day a week earlier.

Every baseball season offers hundreds of reasons to celebrate. It makes sense to seize any commonly celebrated holiday that falls on a game day – Mother's Day, Memorial Day, Father's Day, Independence Day, and Labor Day always fall within the Minor League season. For holidays that fall outside the season, it's easy to find a reason to celebrate. Teams regularly scare up some fun with Halfway to Halloween (*late April/early May*) and spread holiday cheer with Christmas in July.

One of the side effects of social media is that seemingly everything has its own holiday now. You can celebrate Grilled Cheese Day (*April 12*), Star Wars Day (*May 4*), National Doughnut Day (*first Friday in June*), National Cousins Day (*July 24*), or Left-Handers Day (*August 13*). There are numerous websites like *timeanddate. com* or *holidayinsights.com* that offer information about these unusual holidays. Be careful to cross-check the information though as some sites may be outdated or details may have changed based on a decision made by a trade organization or governing body. If you can't find the holiday you want, you can always make up your own reason to celebrate.

Movies & Television: If you're thinking of planning a *Super Hero Day*, it makes sense to find out when the next *Avengers* movie hits theatres and build off that excitement. Fortunately, Hollywood is always churning out a steady stream of sequels and prequels for its most beloved (*and profitable*) franchises and that information is easily found with a quick Google search.

Television is a little more difficult to project as a hyped-up show may not last very long on the fall TV schedule. Proven shows are easier to project, but they still carry some risk should public sentiment change about the show or one of its actors or actresses. In recent years, teams have created theme nights to tap into the loyal followings of shows like *The Walking Dead*, *Game of Thrones*, and *Stanger Things*.

Pop Culture Anniversaries: There's an old adage that says *"everything is new again."* Some posit there's a 30-year nostalgia cycle as people in the primes of their careers are in a position to introduce and consume pop culture inspired by their childhood or teenage years.

Every year provides another set of anniversaries to celebrate. In 2018, teams could celebrate the 50th anniversary of the Detroit Tigers' World Series championship, the 40th anniversary of *Grease* or *Animal House*, 30 years of *Die Hard*, the 20th anniversary of the *Seinfeld* finale, and yada, yada, yada. Dig into music and the most influential events of the day, and you'll have plenty to promote.

In 2018, multiple Minor League teams are working to celebrate the 25th anniversary of *The Sandlot*. The Richmond Flying Squirrels have really embraced the anniversary with five different promotions including a "*Bambino*" baseball giveaway, a "*Beast*" bobbledog giveaway on *Bark in the Park Night*, and an appearance by the actor who played "*Squints*" in the movie.

Local Celebrities and Anniversaries: Every community has its own history, heroes, and happenings. Teams can celebrate the accomplishments of current and past residents or celebrate the community itself. Each season, the Greenville Drive, Class A affiliate of the Boston Red Sox, hosts an event called *Green Day*. The annual celebration commemorates the South Carolina city's birthday and salutes an individual who made positive contributions to the community. The occasion is typically marked with a green giveaway item, such as a T-shirt or superhero cape.

Teams can and should also celebrate their milestones such as anniversaries and attendance achievements. A team can develop a custom logo, which can be used for promotional and merchandising purposes, to celebrate a longstanding relationship with its Major League affiliate or the number of years its ballpark or franchise has served the community. Using social media, a team can engage its fans by asking them to vote for the team's 25th anniversary team or award prizes to an attendee identified as the franchise's five millionth fan. A team's own personnel are celebrities too. It's common for teams to issue giveaways featuring past players who have gone on to achieve success. A team can also celebrate its mascot's birthday or recognize the retirement of a longtime employee.

The Tulsa Drillers, the Double-A affiliate of the Los Angeles Dodgers, game day experience features an in-game promotion called the *Usher Base Race*. During a designated inning break, two ballpark ushers race around the bases in head-to-head competition with a champion crowned at the end of the season. The titleholder receives the *Golden Walker Award*, a gag based on the not-so-spry condition of the average stadium usher. By the end of the season, fans were bringing signs to the ballpark to cheer on their favorite ushers.

Causes: Every community has organizations and agencies taking strides to improve the quality of life for its residents. By partnering with these entities, teams can create promotions which drive people to the ballpark and move their partners closer towards their objectives.

The Erie SeaWolves play at UPMC Park. UPMC, short for University of Pittsburgh Medical Center, partners with the SeaWolves on healthy living promotions that span the age spectrum. The SeaWolves and UPMC conduct school-based programming to encourage kids to make healthy dietary choices and participate in physical activity and reward them with a ticket to a ballgame. At the opposite end of the age spectrum, the partners host a *Senior Expo* at the ballpark in conjunction with a noon game to connect senior citizens with the health services they need. Area senior living communities attend the expo year after year as it provides both recreation and education.

Advances in jersey and cap manufacturing have offered teams the opportunity to create unique on-field wear which aesthetically promotes the cause and can be auctioned off to raise money for it. These promotions can connect with fans on a very personal level if they are emotionally tied to the cause, or they can simply give fans the opportunity to experience the game in a new way – such as taking home a jersey that was worn by a player during the game.

Current Events & Trends: Teams expend time and energy to plan the best promotional schedule they can. Some of the best promotions though are those that capture the attention of the masses because they are ripped from the headlines and capture the essence of a moment in time.

In 2017, several teams seized the opportunity to host games in conjunction with a total solar eclipse.[3] Teams located in the "*path of totality*" created detailed promotions including custom-designed jerseys, special viewing glasses, and in-game entertainment content courtesy of NASA. The next total solar eclipse is April 8, 2024, so teams will have time to prepare for the next occurrence.[4]

Unlike an eclipse, most current events aren't so rigidly scheduled. Events happen every day that affect our culture and our lives, and it's up to teams to seek out the right balance of contemporary relevance or humor for its audience. When an opportunity presents itself, it's critical to act quickly and own the moment. When building a promotion around current events, the team that is "*first to market*" with their idea is typically the one that enjoys the most media coverage. The team's brand is also often labeled by the public as creative in an industry known for its creativity, and this alone can attract new legions of fans.

Acting upon trends requires teams be equally nimble. In 2017, teams rushed to add team-branded fidget spinners to their promotional schedules.[5] At the start of the year, *fidget spinners* weren't on the average Minor League promoter's radar. By the end of the season, the fad had nearly expired. Those who jumped in early used the opportunity to sell more tickets before supply exceeded demand.

Building a promotional schedule is fun, but it requires plenty of inspiration, flexibility, and patience. If you include multiple people in the creative process, you're likely to yield a wide array of ideas stemming from the interests of your staff and fans. However, someone has to be responsible for making the final decision for which promotions make the cut and which ones get cut. For that person, I offer the following guidelines.

You Need to Take Risks to Get Rewards: Fans have entertainment options with them at all times – in their homes and via the mobile phones in their hands. Sports properties who only maintain the status quo will have an increasingly difficult time cutting through the clutter to capture the attention and imagination of prospective fans. Competency alone is not rewarded; it's an expectation. Unfortunately for

Minor League teams, it's the major entertainment entities, with far greater resources, who are setting that bar. Minor League teams can compete though by staying locally relevant and tapping into ideas that capture the imagination. Not every great idea will be rewarded with the attention it deserves, and sometimes a bigger story will rule the media cycle. If you take more chances though, you'll have a greater chance for success.

By advising teams to take chances, I am not recommending that teams risk lawsuits or compromise their standing in the community. I am suggesting though that teams should consider promotions that demonstrate wit or push the boundaries of the fans' expectations. In the end, a team can always decide a certain promotion isn't a good fit for them. Recently, a school district in Erie County announced that its superintendent had provided mini-bats to district teachers as a symbolic gesture to encourage their teachers to take action and make noise should an active shooter situation ever occur. With schools and our country seeking to end mass shootings, the late night talk shows couldn't resist the absurd visual of bringing a mini-bat to a gun fight.

As a Minor League team in Erie, it would've been easy to insert ourselves into the national conversation by staging a *School Safety Night* complete with a mini-bat giveaway. We would've gotten our fair share of Likes, Tweets, and media coverage, and we might have enjoyed a few extra ticket sales for the game. At the same time, we likely would've burned important bridges with the school district, which brings its students to games, supports our student learning initiatives, and rents the stadium for a few high school baseball games each season. The relationship we'd built wasn't worth sacrificing for a few laughs over a few days, even though we gave thorough consideration on how to best handle the opportunity.

Some Promotions Don't Yield Results: A promotion is intended to yield a result, and typically that result is to drive revenue for the team. In my office, I have a sign which reads *What Did I Do Today to Bring People to the Ballpark?* To me it's an essential guiding principle. No day should pass, even days away from the office, without making an effort to introduce someone to our brand and sell a ticket.

Younger Minor League executives often fall in love with the idea of staging a promotion around a fun theme or an idea that resonates with them personally. These ideas can have value, give the employee a sense of fulfillment, and even build camaraderie among the staff (*who may all be dressed as Elvis or their favorite super hero to complement the event's theme*). At the same time, the core purpose of a promotion is to sell tickets. It's important that any promotion added to the schedule have a target audience and a plan to bring that audience to the ballpark. If a promotion doesn't bring someone to the ballpark, it lessens the resources you can apply to one that may.

Focus Your Resources Where It Counts: A younger version of me once created a promotional schedule with a giveaway, fireworks show, entertainment act, or theme night on every day of the season. While my team was able to provide an extra reason for fans to attend every day of the season, we couldn't effectively devote the resources needed to marketing and producing 70 great events. Inevitably, some promotions didn't get the attention they needed to make an impact and we wasted an idea that might have delivered quality results in the future with the right support.

With the SeaWolves, we identify the 25-30 dates annually that give us the best chance of selling out the ballpark and devote the bulk of our advertising and promotional resources on those dates. From time to time, we'll test a promotion on an off-peak night, but we try to avoid scheduling promotions that we know we won't have the time or money to support. As a rule, we address the remaining dates through group sales, community programming and weekly promotions (*i.e. Thirsty Thursday*) that we can create once and use repeatedly.

Say It Again, Sam: Just when you're getting tired of hearing about a promotion, many fans are just starting to hear your message. Teams need to make sure they are delivering their key messages across multiple platforms and that fans will get the message early enough to act. The SeaWolves have found Facebook events to be particularly effective in reminding potential attendees of our games. We can plant a seed months in advance and add promotional resources, such as paying to boost a Facebook event, as the featured game nears.

Promotions Are For the Fans: This seems like a pretty simple concept. After all, the goal of a promotion is to attract fans to the game. With that said, there are plenty of teams that have allowed their sponsors to drive their promotional mix. Earlier in my career, I worked for a team that hosted five plastic water bottle giveaways in one season. No fan needs five water bottles, and a plastic bottle's perceived value is low enough that it's unlikely to change a prospective ticket buyer's behavior. Sponsors were attracted to the item though because the cost of execution was inexpensive. It certainly makes sense for a team to help its sponsors achieve their objectives, but a sponsor's objectives can often be accomplished while also drawing fans to the game.

Something Borrowed: Each year, our front office dedicates substantial time to planning our promotional schedule. We talk through our best concepts and set out to find sponsors who might benefit from sponsoring those promotions. When February hits, teams from across Minor League Baseball begin to officially release their promotional schedules. At this point, I experience a wide range of emotions. I am impressed by the creativity across Minor League Baseball and proud to be in an industry with so many great minds. At the same time, I also start to *hate* our own promotional schedule. I want our team's schedule to feature the best promotional ideas every year, and yet *so* many teams have *so* many great concepts.

It's impractical to think that every great idea will come from one team, but teams can learn from the successes and failures of other teams. In fact, it's flattering to have one of your team's promotions *borrowed* by another team.

The Infamous Cave Shrimp of MiLB

In 2009, I led marketing and promotions for the Bowling Green Hot Rods, Tampa Bay's Class A affiliate that was relocating and opening a new ballpark in South Central Kentucky. The team conducted a *Name the Team* contest and eventually became the Hot Rods, a nod to the fact that General Motors assembles Corvettes in the community.[6]

The second place name in the contest, *Cave Shrimp*, proved to be a very polarizing choice. Kentucky has an extensive network of underground caves, and cave shrimp are sightless, translucent crustaceans that live in subterranean springs and grow to be no more than about an inch. The community felt strongly about the potential name; they loved it or hated it. There really was no middle ground.

One person who hated the *Cave Shrimp* name was a local government official who had been key to bringing the team to Kentucky. As a gag, we asked the designer of the team's actual logo to sketch out a fake logo so we could trick the official into thinking that fans eventually would be heading to the ballpark to cheer on the *Cave Shrimp*. The gag worked (*to our enjoyment*), and the sketch, created by *Brandiose*, was really good. In fact, it was too good to just use for a private joke.

While building the promotional schedule for our inaugural season, I couldn't let go of the idea of doing something with the *Cave Shrimp* logo. If fans liked the fake logo as much as we did and remained as passionate about the name as they were during the contest, we might have a real winner on our hands.

During an after-hours brainstorming session with Hot Rods merchandise director Kyle Hanrahan and GM Brad Taylor, we eventually figured out how to pull it all together. We created a promotion built on the premise of the *Butterfly Effect*, a phenomenon whereby even a small, localized change can have large repercussions elsewhere. In essence, we asked *What else in the world might have been different if the Hot Rods had been named the Cave Shrimp?*

We sold hats and T-shirts featuring the *Cave Shrimp* logo, changed rosters and graphics in the new stadium to encourage fans to cheer on the *Cave Shrimp*, and used the video board to show video vignettes of recent events that had been altered by the team's decision to be the *Cave Shrimp*. It was funny, heady stuff -- so smart that some fans and sponsors wondered why we'd changed our name so soon! The promotion, dubbed *What Could've Been Night*, went on to be named MiLB.com's Promotion of the Year.[7] Around the same time, changes in uniform manufacturing technology made it easier and more cost-effective for teams to suit up as an alter-ego for one night. The promotion has been replicated many times since, and while some of the original concept has eroded, we created a new idea that every team in minor league sports could borrow and localize for its own fan base.

Every promoter in Minor League Baseball would love to create a promotion that's borrowed by the best teams in the industry. It's a validation of a promoter's work, but it's not nearly as important as filling the ballpark seats. Regardless of who spawned the original idea, success will come to promoters who deliver valuable, sharable experiences that resonate with their audience.

The Supervisor Grind Is Adapt Or Die

Michael Abramson
General Manager
Hartford Yard Goats
Eastern League, Double-A Baseball

About The Author

Mike Abramson has spent 15 years in baseball, and more than 20 working in the field of marketing & communications. As General Manager of the Hartford Yard Goats, Mike oversees all day-to-day operations for the team, including sponsorship & ticket sales, marketing, promotions, and operations. Prior to joining the Yard Goats, Mike spent six seasons with the Pawtucket Red Sox; Triple-A Affiliate of the Boston Red Sox. Mike began his career in sales with Sports Radio WEEI; then the highest-rated sports radio station in the country. Mike lives in Chester, CT with his wife and three daughters.

Perspective changes how you view the position you want, especially once you've obtained it and have seen the strings to the job that no one else does. So does the idea that you will somehow know when you have "*arrived*" after a successful journey. Because if you stop learning, if you stop moving for even a moment, someone else will be there, ready to step into your position. This is the life of a minor league general manager. The greatest difference between when I started as an account executive and now, as a general manager, is that I now realize there is always more work to be done. When I was young, I felt there was a finality to what I had to do. Now, I realize, it never stops.

My position as a minor league general manager is a daily challenge and rewarding, and I make every attempt to provide those employees that I supervise with the ability to be heard regardless of organization status. As a young account executive, I assumed every idea that I generated was perfect and that my input was immensely valuable to the success of the organization. But as I grew in my career toward the general manager role, I realized that listening more than talking, helped my acumen. Looking back, I understand that many of the managers who supervised me in the past were making the same effort that I make in the same role now, simply assuring that I was heard, and felt appreciated.

I started in baseball under three men who defined my career. Looking back on the past 11 years, I earned mentors, role models and friends from those who supervised me. Simply by listening more to what they had to say. Lou Schwechheimer, then-Pawtucket Red Sox owner, president and general manager, was an idea man, both charismatic and unshakable in his entertainment vision. Mike Tamburro was patriarchal in his delivery and shaped my career at the end of the line. And Ben Mondor, was tough, but fair, and unfailingly generous. Each of these men gave me life lessons and teachable moments. Mondor passed years ago, but his mentorship guides my decisions to this day.

I still recall the many pieces of advice the three men bestowed on me. Schwechheimer gave me one of the greatest pieces of advice that has shaped my career; in business, it is important to remain even-keeled. At your most excited, stay at a high of 60. At your lowest, put it at a low of 40. Throughout my career since that conversation, I've enjoyed great successes, and endured some large disappointments. But I've tried to remain at a high of 60, or a low of 40, whether it's achieved through promoting employees into peers, or dealing with the displeasure of letting other employees go.

Thinking back, I'm pretty fortunate not to have dealt with an egregious error or human resources issue, or with a lack of employee performance when letting someone go. Sometimes, employees simply do not work out at the position. They know it as much as you do. Understanding minor league baseball operations is more a product of showcasing that some people will not be able to perform at the high level that the organization needs. And in their heart, these employees tend to know it as well. They didn't have what it took to achieve that high level of success, and tended to opt-out on their own. And sometimes, as a manager for a minor league baseball front office, you are expected to help the employees who are not achieving the high level of success by making the decision to leave for them.

No One Wants To Supervise

Everyone wants to be a general manager. No one wants to be a supervisor. Because the first comes with a nice title that everyone feels is important. The second is a tough job that everyone knows comes with accountability. To be a general manager, you have to know how to truly supervise people, earn their trust and value their opinion. Barking orders gets no one to follow you. And if they do not follow you, there is no point in you being in a leadership role. Everything depends on you understanding that it begins with the people that you are managing.

You have to know who they are, what they want, and who they want to be. That means investing in them, engaging with their personalities, and pushing them to a higher level of success. It does not mean sitting in a nice big office, ordering people around, with zero accountability to yourself. The majority of the staff will show you how they want to be managed. And as a minor league baseball general manager, you have to show that you can identify sales talent, cultivate it further, and figure out how to teach them effectively. And it means accepting that your staff will make mistakes, especially teachable moments that will broaden their sales skills later on. The minor league baseball front office is as much a working lab for the future general managers of tomorrow as it is an organizational sales floor.

The front office staff should be treated as if they are your peers. Including the interns. Leaving people behind, or creating levels of respect does not help situations. It breaks down camaraderie. It is divisive. Opinions must be valued, even from the newest employee, regardless of their paycheck. And minor league baseball general managers should be seeking to incorporate ideas that are presented. The craziest idea that half of the old guard in the room feel is absolutely stupid may generate the most interest from the public. This is where a minor league general manager either excels or fails at their job. When a person is put into a position that can be considered higher-level, it is easy for them to setup a dynamic where everyone thinks that the boss has great ideas. But that type of environment serves no one. It is systematic fraud. It is better to treat yourself as an equal to everyone else in the room, and foster the belief that everyone has an equal stake in a successful outcome. Being genuine as a general manager or supervisor is how you earn respect, and how you generate the best ideas as a group.

Management is about instituting guidelines that work for you, as well as the employees that you supervise. That means monitoring their successes, while allowing them some independence toward learning from situations that they encounter. Too much freedom can actually lead to distraction, but it is also necessary when creating building blocks of experience for a future leader's foundational structure. There exists a line of demarcation with every staff member that, as a manager, you will have to engage with. Are they employed because "*they love the game*" or are they employed simply to collect a paycheck. There might be other answers, but those two reasons are specific to why someone chooses to work in the sports industry.

Unfortunately, there are situations where the staff member is working in a minor league front office for a goal that cannot be achieved. This is where you are expected to become the cheerleader to the cheerful, and occasionally, the cheerless. Expect your staff's culture to consume the majority of your day in different scenarios. There are never enough hours for what is truly required of a general manager when it comes to staff culture, nor is there ever enough supervisorial support when issues crop up. The key is to settle for "*good*" over "*great*" as long as it exists in a sustainable manner.

Job candidates are never simply being interviewed by our organization. They are interviewing us as well. This is important to share with those who apply and gain an interview with your organization. Specifically because it means finding a great fit on both sides. A job placement should never be advantageous for the employer and not the employee. When that happens, employees leave quickly and the organizational culture suffers long term. Every manager should speak about culture in their initial interviews with prospective employees. They should talk about it a lot. I do. There is a special breed of person that can endure the machinations of working a baseball season. That's 16-hour days with 30 people in the office. A lot of varying personalities and potential conflicts with how different people engage with each other. This is important to address, so that prospective employees who are working in baseball understand it is a unique place, in a unique industry. This extends to how you speak to those who get hired. One of my employees is a mother with teenagers at home. I sold her on the benefits of having her children attend games at the ballpark, and gaining a sense of ownership that their friends would not have. It all comes down to the culture and attitude that you project and maintain.

The Thankless Part

Being a manager is about understanding that, beyond the basics of running an organization, you have 30 pairs of eyes watching you. It is important to focus on revenue, expenses, operations, schedules and other daily fires that spring out of nowhere for you to put out. However, you also need to look beyond the basics. That means gaining a full sense that the organization, and its culture, is continually healthy. That the team in the front office is focused, happy and productive in order to position the organization for continual success. In the end, your process and product may be fantastic, but if your culture has diminished, it corrupts every positive that you do. Focus on your people beyond all else.

Diversity is sometimes misused when it comes to how to hire. Ethnic diversity is only one component of creating a diverse culture. I personally place a lot of emphasis on ensuring that we have a unique, diverse staff that shares the values of the area that we are selling to. We want our staff to reflect our city's values. Diversity of opinion, experience and culture allows us to share a bond of enthusiasm, friendliness, and engagement with our customers. This is about looking beyond the paycheck compensation, to how your staff views the bigger picture.

There are always more dollars to be had for an employee who is good, but as a manager, you want them to look beyond that point. Are they going to miss the environment that they have with your organization enough that the difference in pay or title with a new organization diminishes by comparison? All managers should want employees to seek to contribute in ways that take ownership over their sales territory or vertical, to be a part of something larger than themselves. This does not happen if your office culture, as well as your diversity, fails to value how an employee is going to feel about their place of employment.

This is a learned approach over time as a manager. It is not something that you can simply adopt from the beginning. Time creates the best experience for a manager, because you end up seeing everything. Being even-keeled in how you approach situations is important as a leader as well. I've always believed that no one should ever witness the strings of my job. Once they do, I am revealing too much. Complaining about the tough times, the uncertainty and the indecision, especially the wrong decisions, is not what someone wants to discover when dealing with a general manager. This is baseball. It is sports. Millions of people would kill to be in my position, and do it for less money. The least that I can do is respect that perspective, and not show the difficulties which are far less difficult than any of the public deal with on a daily basis who do not work in sports.

This also comes to the issue of emotional baggage. Not only for you, but your employees, who will bring baggage of their own to your doorstep. This can corrupt an organizational culture quickly. And it serves no benefit if your respective insecurities find a way to bump up against another employee's insecurities. As a general manager and supervisor, you need to earn your self-awareness. I have never felt that personally, I have been easy to manage as an employee. Partially, because I believe that my ideas or opinions are more than often correct, despite evidence to the contrary. This self-awareness has been a learned mechanism that I have honed overtime. We all have flaws, but it is how we ensure the overcoming of those flaws that help us become better employees, supervisors and people.

Realize You're Wrong Sometimes

Despite those flaws, I do know being self-aware has helped increase some of my attributes. I am a great listener. A good negotiator. And at the end of the day, I probably believe that I have the right answers to the majority of solutions, as well as the best ideas. Well, that last part is a flaw of mine as well, being over-confident. But I'm trying to become better at learning that what I am not good at, can be an attribute too if I understand it correctly. It is all about being a work in progress as a person, and growing. As a general manager or supervisor, the moment that you cease personal growth, you are no good to the organization, or your employees and you need to recalibrate yourself. Everyone grows until they stop existing.

When The New Britain Rock Cats decided to rebrand into the Hartford Yard Goats, I was one of the people in the organization that felt certain it was a bad choice. There is a specific integrity toward earning a team name with credibility in the marketplace; a moniker such as *The Senators* or *The Capitals* I felt, was the right choice for the team rebrand. And I fully admit how wrong I was when opposing The Yard Goats name for our organization. Hundreds of thousands of fans buying tickets, as well as a million pieces of merchandise sold later, boy, I was definitely wrong in what I thought was a sellable team name.

When someone comes to me with an idea that I am absolutely certain is wrong, I now stop and think about it. I listen and evaluate. This is part of the learning process. I run that idea by other people before automatically killing it. And sometimes end up fighting against my natural instinct of believing that I have to be right. The conflict that I experience stays inside my brain, where it runs head over heart, rather than the other way around. It is during this process that I begin to evaluate what becomes the best thing that I can do for the organization, the people that I work with, which helps me elevate my job. No one needs to see the strings at all, they simply need to see the results. And that includes having their ideas valued and used when appropriate.

It all comes down to leading by example that makes you a better manager or supervisor of people. When you ask someone to perform a task, they should know that you are also willing to do the same task. I believe in being present, being accessible, in order to show why a person was placed in a supervisor's role to begin with. That includes an open-door policy to my office, unless I'm on a conference call. It provides the ability for presence, with the staff knowing from the top manager to the newest intern, that they can come into my office at any time to see me on an issue.

Perspective Comes With Time

The worst type of manager hides in their office. Because they choose not to be present. That is why I spend an enormous amount of time in the common areas of the front office. Because if your staff cannot see you working hard, setting a tone, it can cause issues in the workplace. I never want to be perceived as a distant supervisor. One of my favorite memories is the two years that our entire organization spent crammed into a tiny office, waiting to open our new ballpark in Hartford. It provided me with the feeling that we were a start-up company then, and to some degree, I preach that we should never lose that energy and passion. But it comes back to being seen by your staff, who then feel that you are working as hard as they are for the same goal.

The hardest component of the general manager position is being removed from my staff. That happens when you choose not to engage or provide presence. At the end of each day, there are undercurrents of conversations, ebbs and flows of personal decisions that I'm not a part of. A portion of my position is about understanding whether people are truly happy, content or fulfilled while being employed in our organizational culture. When I was younger, I never gave any thought to how my supervisor felt, or the amount of energy they had to put into ensuring that I was responding correctly to the organizational culture that they had in the front office.

When I started in 2006, I would have probably misunderstood what it took to be a great general manager of a minor league baseball club. Eleven years since that time has brought perspective. I would have said something to the effect that being a great general manager was about power, presence and ability to answer a question definitively. But experience occurs with age, and enhances the perspective of what it truly takes to be a leader in a minor league baseball front office. There is no real power to speak of, only the ability to influence. There are not definitive answers, only educated guesses. Presence only occurs when you have the belief and confidence of your peers. These are the components that make a great general manager. And experience is the best teacher of how it is a continual education process in order to stay effective at your leadership position.

Throughout my journey as the Hartford Yard Goats general manager, I have had the pleasure of speaking at several events. This includes lunches, breakfasts, dinners, Rotary Clubs, Chambers of Commerce, universities and high schools. Quoting the late former mayor of Rhode Island and convicted felon, Vincent "*Buddy*" Cianci: '*If there is a letter opening, then I'm there.*'[1] Without fail, during the question and answer session of my speech, someone always asks me an actual baseball question about the game on the field, not the business. I hate to admit it, but I never know what they are referring to, because I don't actually follow the sport of baseball. I merely sell it.

Back in the late 1990s, while living in Boston, I went to more than 30 Boston Red Sox games and followed every other game each season on the radio or television. I listened to sports talk radio throughout the day on a small transistor radio that I carried around, watched ESPN every morning, and NESN in the afternoon. I also chewed large wads of gum, kept it packed in my cheek like Major League Baseball players do with sunflower seeds. I obsessively adjusted my watch band in a ritualistic fashion when I stepped up to my desk at work, participated in four fantasy baseball leagues by 2006, and even wore a baseball cap for a while.

But then I worked in baseball, had children, and lost my ability to carve out three hour chunks of time each night to devote to watching the sport for enjoyment.

I moved on from the game stories in the newspaper, to eventually not following the sport at all. Once you become immersed in a work environment such as minor league baseball, you tend to find other things to do. For me, I play guitar, occasionally bass. I practically live at the ballpark. My entire job is wrapped in selling the game of baseball. And if you are intent on working in the sports industry, be aware that you will desensitize yourself from watching the game intently for pure enjoyment. You'll do other things, because your baseball fix will be on overload within a year of working at a minor league baseball front office. That isn't a bad thing either.

You Are A Sales Supervisor

It's also not a bad thing to love the sport that you are trying to work in. Most of the people who work in minor league baseball love the sport itself. But I can honestly tell you that, when confronted with a job candidate who voices that they want to work in baseball because they've loved the game their entire life, I tend to groan. Mainly because I know that it isn't going to result in the way that the candidate wants it to look once they see what the sports industry is all about. They think about hanging out with players, talking about statistics and watching games. In truth, we are in a sales industry that could easily look like an insurance office with a nice backyard that a team plays on 71 times per year. And we have luxury suites to sell.

A Minor League Baseball general manager has few, if any, of the same duties of that of their counterpart in the Major Leagues. The top level focuses on player operations; they scout players, crunch statistics, make roster additions, sever contractual agreements and attempt to put together a team that can win a World Series. They focus on the field of play. And when it comes to the public hearing the term *"General Manager,"* this is what they think about.

Minor League general managers do not focus on the field of play unless it has to do with promotions and ensuring the grass is green. A general manager in the minor leagues oversees a sales staff in a front office that sells tickets and sponsorships. Helps engage a team to plan out promotions, operate the facility, and is the face of the organization for fans, the community and general public. A general manager in the minor leagues is a Chief Operating Officer rather than a *Chief Roster Builder*. It is an important connotation when starting out in a sports career, and something that separates those who are already prepared to begin that journey from those that are not during their initial interviews with the team they hope to be employed by.

The off-season for a minor league general manager is challenging. This comes down to idea creation, factoring in a lot of moving parts, and not enough time to catch your breath as the calendar peels away toward Opening Day. Everything is about maintaining a large amount of momentum to get the job done, when there are zero games of summer baseball played for the past three months and it is snowing outside. The in-season experience is no easier. It is a war of attrition, trying to maintain focus while executing all of the off-season planning, initiating those ideas, while the daily landscape changes and every idea put into motion now has to change with the variables of consumer taste and random occurrence. To me, it is much more fun being a minor league general manager than a major league one, because no one calls for your job when the team stinks on the field. The opposing viewpoint is that everyone in minor league baseball will call for your job if the tickets are over-priced, the beer is warm and the hot dogs are cold.

As mentioned previously, a minor league general manager is focused as a sales supervisor. The Hartford Yard Goats do a couple of weeks of sales and customer service training with new hires. We follow that up by doing weekly *training/meeting* sessions for the entire sales staff. This is a continual learning experience, where no one escapes redeveloping their skills to grow at their position. Part of controlling your sales training also means bringing in outside perspectives to garner new ideas and prevent stale ones from permeating.

My focus has been on bringing in high-level executives from our sponsor client pool, who engage with our sales staff. They share their wisdom on how they prospect, sell and maintain their client relationships. While they may not be selling the same exact product or be in the same industry as the Hartford Yard Goats, it is the perspective they bring and the information that they provide that helps a young sales staff broaden their acumen altogether. All of your sales training with business community folks needs to be of a mutual benefit. I always make the time to listen to their pitch before putting it in front of my sales staff as a presentation. If I don't feel it is a fit or benefit to engage upon, I'm honest with the presenter. This can be tricky when the meeting is political, or set-up through a sponsor with a current team relationship.

Grow Your Staff

I should preface the amount of meetings that a minor league general manager will have in a day. I average about six per day. Many young professionals aiming for the general manager's seat at a minor league baseball franchise don't seem to understand this. You will be in more meetings, ranging from internal managers meetings, to staff meetings, to sponsor meetings to other random meetings. There is no training module available for a person to handle that many meetings daily throughout the year. It is imperative to build up your preparation skills, so that when you come into a meeting, you aren't lost the second that the discussion starts.

This does not suggest that minor league general managers cannot learn from game managers, such as those you see in the dugout. A person who has had a profound impact on helping my skills as a supervisor has been Hartford Yard Goats manager Jerry Weinstein. He is a been-there, done-that type of guy who has seen virtually every type of situation.

He is a professional with post-graduate degrees, experience that ranges from Little League to the Major Leagues, an Olympic medalist, published author, and has the moniker of *"Hero Coach of The World Baseball Classic."* Impressive resume statistics that don't even mention that he is a member of the *Sacramento City College Athletic Hall of Fame.*[2] He has accomplished many things in his career, yet keeps learning, because he keeps trying more things.

If you asked Jerry to describe himself, he would use the term *"mentor"* long before describing himself as *"coach."* Standing on the top dugout steps in a baseball uniform with stirrups proudly displayed above his cleats along with two or three toothpicks jammed in his mouth at all times may be a nice visual. But his presence goes beyond what you see. It is what you learn from him. Much like bringing in business community members to show sports sales professionals how they prospect and close on deals, Weinstein's knowledge translates when it comes to understanding people, managing emotions, expectations and personalities effectively. The worst type of minor league general manager is one that does not take input from those outside of their niche of the industry, because it limits the amount of perspectives they can receive from others.

When you grow your staff in an effective culture, you will have those who are earning their promotions and touching what might become a ceiling within your organization. That is not an issue to be afraid of. The Hartford Yard Goats have two assistant general managers right now. One is destined to be a general manager for a minor league team someday if he chooses to stay in the business. And I want that for him if that's his choice, even if it means leaving our organization to achieve that goal. I spend valuable time with him, putting him into a position to either take my own job someday, or move on elsewhere to an organization that hires him for a general manager position.

Avoid "Yes, But" Attitudes

In my role, I cannot be afraid of others challenging for promotional opportunities as they grow, even if that means taking my position. Competition keeps me effective at my current position, and growing as well within the organization. Once you stop growing, you become less effective for the organization as a whole. When you build up your staff, especially young professionals who are growing, it shows to the rest of your organization. This means sharing information. Putting each person in a role that allows them to succeed and flourish. Our staff senior account representative runs a group of six ticket sales folks as a supervisor, in order to ensure that it is a culture where those who show sales results have earned the chance to lead their peers. I want those staff leaders to feel that they are allowed to make decisions, empowered by the opportunity with the culture we have created, and foster them into a dynamic of becoming that future general manager who leads their peers.

Team building is something that every minor league general manager and supervisor should put a huge emphasis on. And it starts with the culture that the general manager elicits when speaking to their staff. We have monthly full staff events; we take the entire staff out to dinner and a movie. There are staff parties in the breakout rooms during the season. It is very important for each staff member, down to the newest intern, to feel that they are part of a fun environment with an organization that is aiming for something bigger. This is how we also create staff energy for promotions, where everyone is involved and fostering new ideas to be implemented throughout the upcoming baseball season.

We get together with a white board a couple of times per month in the staff room. Everyone is involved. No one is allowed to say *"that's a bad idea"* or *"that won't work."* This creates that culture of creativity. That doesn't mean to suggest that there aren't a lot of bad ideas out there. I've heard a lot of them, and likely suggested a lot of them. There are also a lot of ideas that will not work. However, it is a therapeutic form of fostering creativity when people are allowed to put their thoughts out publicly in a safe manner. When everyone has a voice, everyone wins, even if their idea doesn't actually happen. And chances are, many of the promotional ideas we come up with actually do work, because when they aren't shot down immediately in a negative fashion, we find a way to make them work, incorporating those ideas into our promotional calendar.

Before I worked in minor league baseball, I was part of a different industry. I disagreed with a management decision that was made regarding the distribution of client accounts. It took away some accounts from co-workers, and gave those accounts to others, which I felt harmed the client relationship overall. I was called into a meeting, was told that I didn't understand the reasoning behind the decision. They said that I was too close to my peers to diagnose the issue, and that it wasn't my place to oppose it. In the end, looking back on it, management was actually correct in the decision, as well as my bias that clouded why that decision was a good one to make. I've always remembered that issue as well as how management handled it with me, privately in a meeting, rather than simply being told to not talk about it, or receiving a consequence. That scenario is something that I've thought about and appreciated when it comes to how I have conversations with my own staff, and the lengths necessary to over-explain why a management decision was made in order to ensure that staff members understand its reasoning.

Be A Great Co-Worker

Understanding how career promotion works in minor league baseball is simple. The better you can sell, the more you can ascend. This means being comfortable in a room full of strangers and selling them on yourself. Being a great general manager means being able to see the entire organization as well as being patient with the process. It is about anticipating without being reactionary. The general manager position requires you to learn the answers from your experience in climbing the organizational ladder. Because everyone you supervise, and some people who supervise you, will be seeking your guidance on answers to the questions that they have. You have to demonstrate an ability to remain calm, collected and sure of yourself when put under the enormous pressure of the position. This requires mental organization of your thoughts, as well as being organized in your presentation. These two skills are qualities that, above all else, can take anyone as high as they want to go on the organizational ladder.

It is easy for someone to sidetrack themselves and distract from their career path toward organizational promotion. All they have to do is be inconsistent. That means not taking their job as seriously in the second year with the organization as they did when they began a year earlier. A key problem that young professionals face which is harmful to their career aspirations is being too overly concerned with the social aspects of the job. Working in sports, especially minor league baseball, requires each individual to be moving forward in their career through a consistent effort of demonstrating growth and capitalizing on opportunity.

Another component that can sidetrack an employee's ascension within an organization is how they treat their co-workers. Are they someone who can be trusted, who while competitive is not toxic to be around? My advice here is for employees to stay in their own lane. That means not trying to snake business away from their co-workers for their own gain. Being too obnoxious about their success in a public manner turns everyone off and is unbecoming of a future supervisor. People have to want to be led by you in order to see you as a supervisor. Those employees within the front office who try to be the best versions of themselves are the ones who win. They are compassionate to their co-workers and they strive to make the organization better by their presence, not worse.

There is always going to be a factor of professional jealousy surrounding the success of co-workers. This comes with competition. When someone outperforms another person, it comes down to whether those who are professionally jealous are willing to step up their game, or complain. And if they are willing to complain about the successes of others, it is a sign that they are serving an excuse-making psyche. That is an issue for those who succeed. But can be a trap for those promoted within the organization if they feed that narrative by lending credence that their ascension was not fully earned. If you foster a situation where you are promoted, but do not provide humility in an organization to your success, you will provide reason for your co-workers to dislike you. And it harms your future success overall as the organization and your supervisors monitor how you handle your current achievements when considering you for future roles.

In 2017, the Hartford Yard Goats moved away from a commissioned-sales model that is fashionable throughout sports. By transforming the sales floor to a situation where the best person to answer a call that comes in actually takes the call, it has fostered a camaraderie within the organization. This decision on non-commissioned sales removed any and all infighting issues. It eliminated resentment. And I would strongly advise other minor league organizations to do the same. The difference in how your staff reacts under a commissioned-sales model to a non-commissioned sales model is amazing, and well worth examining.

A major league general manager won't be worried about the sales floor or removing the commissioned-sales model approach. They will be worried about the science of statistics for player development and data management concerning how to dissect those processed numbers for a great performance on the field of play. Minor league baseball general managers do the same thing, but their field of play is much different. I have a to-do list of almost 400 items that I begin to run through from January 1 to the start of the season. That is my full-time job, but does not include the other 400 items that may pop up, unannounced, in that time that I also have to do. And I'm always revising, reviewing and adding to that 400-item list of things that I know I have to do, in order get it done on time.

What Are You In This For?

Everyone has seen the 2011 film *"Moneyball"* and confuses the general manager position in Major League Baseball with its minor league baseball counterpart. But in that role, you need to know about kurtosis, variance, and scatterplot. All statistics that proved that laptops were the new notebooks and on-base percentage was the new batting average to achieve. Don't forget the mathematical theorems of regression analysis, logistical regression, and hierarchical regression.If you are looking to engage as a Major League general manager, and you did not play for 12 years as a shortstop, your best bet to achieving that goal is a solid understanding of statistical formulas, with a correlation toward sports. However, there are only 30 total jobs as a Major League Baseball general manager. There are 247 jobs in affiliated minor league baseball general manager and many more in unaffiliated minor league baseball that can be turned over at any one time. So the statistics show more opportunity in minor league baseball, but you have to know how to sell in order to get those jobs. Even if you did play shortstop for 12 years prior.

When I began in minor league baseball, I did not understand nor quantify the time commitment required to serve as a general manager. I do not think that I would have been as receptive toward processing what it took, and what it took away from, in order to fully perform the general manager role. No one can truly tell you what it takes to do something, until you are actually there, fully committed, doing it. This is why job shadowing is imperative, as it provides an experience to something that may otherwise have been willful ignorance to the challenges of the tasks at hand.

I do not think that the role was explained to me properly nor could it have been. When I first became a minor league general manager, there was a learning curve. To say that it was a shock in the amount of time and commitment it took to be a general manager would be an understatement. This is where not letting people see the strings comes into effect. You have to want to work long hours. You have to be willing to sacrifice for those long hours in order to achieve your goals. Because when the game happens, there are thousands of patrons who will see what you chose to neglect or did not accomplish. To me, that is the greatest opportunity to showcase accountability for what you did in your job as a general manager, and the greatest reason to put in the effort long before the game happens so no one sees your strings.

I am personally used to the long hours. I've always taught classes at night when I had a day job. Thus, I was not a stranger to the commitment of long hours at the office when it became required for my general manager role. A lot of work tends to appeal to me for some reason. When my children were very young, I enjoyed the option of being out of the house. Now that they have grown a little older, I have more things that I do not want to miss in their lives, thus the role of general manager becomes tougher.

Work-Life Balance

People are getting wise to understanding the overall sacrifice that you have to make in order to work at a minor league franchise. Keeping those good people working for you is another matter entirely. And that comes back to the culture that you foster within your organization. There are more people who want jobs in sports than actual positions available. That means that employees will work those long, arduous hours because they feel that they understand that going in. Then, the bloom comes off of the rose by year two. And that's when it becomes tougher for staff members to justify why they do what they do, along with whether or not to continue to do it. The culture is what can help them justify their reasoning to stay in the organization or leave it as soon as possible for more lucrative endeavors that may require less hours of their time.

I believe in work-life balance. So does the Hartford Yard Goats organization. We've been committed to giving employees more time off than any other team within affiliated minor league baseball. That includes giving non-gamedays off during seasonal home stands, allowing staff to achieve multiple 3-day weekends, being comfortable with late arrival days every week and shorter off-season hour commitments. We also allow staff to select certain game days off to handle personal commitments such as family events, milestone moments, etc.

Everyone knows what they are getting into working in minor league baseball, but it comes back to the cultural aspect. And when staff grow older, they tend to discuss those issues with their supervisors and management in order to achieve the best decision for them as well as the organization. No one wants to lose great employees, but as people get older, their priorities tend to change. They want to start families or do something else. It is whether they feel that they have enough flexibility in their lives to achieve their new priorities within your organization that will ultimately factor into whether they will stay or not long-term.

In minor league baseball, everybody does everything. From the time that a new employee enters into the organization as a young professional to the point where they are in a general manager role as a grizzled veteran of the industry, they are responsible for everything and involved in nothing at the same time. Everything funnels through your presence when you become a general manager. Everyone is involved to some degree in decisions, but the general manager is responsible for every decision. And a general manager's input is often required in order to move forward. And yet, a minor league general manager does not do a lot of things.

The Grind Never Stops

You don't maintain the field. You are not selling tickets. And you never cook the hot dogs. Yet, when people think of these things, it is suggested that I do them. When the general public asks what I do as a minor league baseball general manager, I tell them that I e-mail, talk on the phone, meet with people, and eat lunch. Because that's all true, to a degree. I could suggest that I do maintain the field, sell tickets and cook the hot dogs and that wouldn't necessarily be untrue. That's because minor league baseball general managers are responsible for everything, which is why the job is unique. Though some of us like to believe that we specialize, we end up being the go-to person for everything that happens, whether we personally do it or not.

I do spend the majority of my daily routine answering e-mails, talking on the phone, as well as having face-to-face meetings both externally and internally. As mentioned earlier, a typical daily scenario for me is participating in six meetings, some planned and some not. But I also respond to as well as receive more than 300 e-mails in that period of time, as well as make roughly ten phone calls. Each action that I take has relevance to the overall mission of running a minor league baseball team.

In-season, when the team is at home, I'll work the games, meaning more hours away from my family. This means pitching in where I can, talking to fans about their expectations and experience, as well as meeting with sponsors to ensure that they are enjoying the game because they are investors in our organization. This may seem as if it is an entirely different job, but it is merely a component of the same job; the day versus night responsibilities. That is one of the underlying issues with minor league baseball, regardless of what you do during the daylight hours during a gameday, there is still the night where the game is played, and you are expected to work that event as well.

I mentioned before the difference between in-season and off-season duties for a general manager. The off-season indicates the perplexing nature of the general manager's job description. Off-season is for planning while in-season is about the execution of that planning. It takes seven months of intense planning to create a five month season of promotions. This means selling sponsorships, tickets and hiring staff. Your best marketing promotions take time to build, as does the training of your gameday staff.

There is always a 30-minute commute, 60-minute roundtrip from the office. That doesn't include the 45 minutes to get ready to go to work every morning, the walk of 10 minutes from your house to your car to your office and repeat back each night. Nor does that count the 90 minutes of eating lunch, drinking coffee, or snacking while chatting. There is never a *"punch in, punch out"* mentality. E-mail is checked at home first-thing in the morning, along with responding to texts throughout dinner, before bed, and when you wake up again. Every sponsorship proposal occurs while you are sitting on the couch in front of the television each evening, with e-mailing documents at the breakfast table, while taking all of your important sales calls out on the back deck. There is never a *"clock"* because you are always on, all of the time.

Off-season hours are harder than in-season, because it requires thought, creativity and drive. In-season, you get to simply execute, learn from those mistakes that occur, and troubleshoot for next time you have that same promotion. While in-season requires nearly 100 hours of a week of full commitment toward execution, the off-season is a general 40-hour work week of recharging the batteries and creating better promotions for the upcoming season.

Do You Love It Enough?

There is no specific educational track to help you develop the skills of becoming a minor league general manager except experience, which teaches perspective. There is a slow burn process involved, and a lot of intangibles required in order to earn your stripes. While sports management majors are exploding for the American university system, you cannot rely on the classroom to gain the majority of your experience. This is a war of attrition that will showcase whether you love working in minor league baseball, as well as the culture that you gained your experience under.

It is a shared success of seeing the outcome of the planning that you and your employees initiated. While there is no shortage of young professionals willing to take the job, it is keeping them with an organization that becomes tougher. This is all part of the perspective that you earn, working in sports, that cannot be generated out of any text, including this one that you are reading.

If you truly desire to be a minor league general manager, you have to want to supervise people. This means helping guide people who are in their twenties, recently out of high school or college, and working in an entry-level pay situation for your front office. By the year 2030, over 75 percent of the workforce will be millennials, who will complain about the generations that come after them. The millennials will make the same claims and slights against those incoming generations that were made about them. Baby Boomers said the same about Generation Xers, who said the same thing about millennials. Because the young always have it easier than the generation that came before it, or at least, that's the perception offered up by whatever older generation is in power at the moment.

Everything dissects the same down to the issues that separate people and harm organizational culture. No generation is above the dreaded facet of gossip, which is so toxic to the front office environment. Fortunately, the Hartford Yard Goats has a human resources director who understands how to quell these issues before they permeate further. She is trained to get involved with the culprits of gossip, those poison-spreaders, in a way that ends underlying issues without the conversation between her and the employee feeling disciplinary. Firing only happens if a situation calls for it. But the worst mistake that you can make in protecting your office culture is to hang onto someone too long because you're afraid to make that personnel change. Letting their actions fester corrodes the fabric of your organization worse than any positive value that they bring to the club.

"Talent" Can Equal "Underachiever"

Friction is unavoidable. The single most demoralizing characteristic in workplace culture is the spread of negativity. It lies in wait like black mold, spreading like cancer, and murders more effectively than the plague. Negativity eats away at the harmony of your organizational culture until the weight of it collapses the entire structure of your staff confidence in the team brand. It is a slow, effective and silent killer that creeps along until it is dealt with. Great employees transform into bad employees when they are overtaken by negativity, gossip and defeatism. And those who don't feed into that bad environment tend to leave it as quickly as possible.

Ego is another career-killer for young professionals. Removing it from the situation, especially when it comes to idea creation for promotions. This is where a *"yes, but"* person exists to stop all creative ideas that harms the culture of the office environment. My least favorite phrases to hear is *"we tried that before and it didn't work"* which translates to, they personally tried it, and since it didn't work for them, they cannot possibly believe it can work with a different viewpoint on an idea's implementation. This is ego. It strangles a lot of young professionals, and creates factions within your front office.

I highly encourage those young professionals who turn into the *"yes, but"* person to remove ego from their vocabulary and mindset. They need to empathize with their co-worker's approach to the same idea, which may result in a success that the *"yes, but"* person did not have when they attempted to initiate the idea. I truly believe that people often say *"no"* because they do not want to put in the work of exploring something that they are not confident will work in someone else's hands.

Innovation is messy. Innovation doesn't always translate into a successful product during the first try, or the hundredth try. Everything can be re-written. And true innovators know this. Innovators have to be willing to go down the path and experience failure first-hand, in order to understand how to make something more successful during future attempts. Failure is one of the better teachers toward innovation and execution, and you often learn more from failure than you would have if everything had gone perfectly from the start.

When you are innovating, there is no ability for people to simply offer an objection. The *"yes, but"* person has to alter their mindset. An objection is easy to make. A solution is much more difficult. If a *"yes, but"* person cannot change their attitude, they are merely offering an objection for the wrong reasons, mainly due to ego. They are not going to help the culture, nor the process of idea creation.

Instead, I challenge my staff to find solutions, not objections, to how an idea could work. It is that possibility, that venture into the unknown, where people can create some of the most innovative marketing promotions ever witnessed. Because everybody loves a challenge where they can offer a solution and not feel that an objection is enough to roadblock the entire promotion altogether.

The majority of millennials that have worked for me tend to voice an opinion of wanting to be included in the process. They want to share the goals of the organization in a tied vision. This means greater flexibility in scheduling and tasks, along with recognition and feedback on their performance. These are not difficult demands to provide, nor are they extremely radical. Whether it is a generational clash or simply a personality conflict between two people of the same age, a minor league general manager needs to rise above and provide leadership. Not the type of leadership where people tend to pat themselves on the back for what they order others to do, but what they are willing to do in order to foster the culture that they want for their organization overall.

There is always that one young professional in the corner cubicle who is going to outwork their co-workers. And that young professional's mindset has the ability to either take them into a management role or cause them to not grow in their career. This is where a minor league general manager is required to shine, in their mentorship of those young professionals who have the potential to become a great manager themselves someday.

The trouble with the word "*talent*" is that it is often associated with "*under-achiever*" when the person has zero ambition or mentoring of their abilities. Too many people attempt to get by on talent alone, and end up wasting their lives not honing the skills that they are deficient in, which prevents them from becoming a well-rounded professional.

Everybody has weaknesses and flaws. It is whether they can overcome those trouble areas, complimenting the other skills to where they shine, that helps them showcase how great they truly can be in the field. It is no different for those players who are on the field than those professionals in the front office. A few people will turn into Hall of Famers, some will be good players, and others will have been distant memories of what they could have done, if only they had gotten everything together effectively.

The young professionals of today are experts at technology. They have grown up with technological advances unimagined by past generations. But where they sometimes need to hone their skills are with interpersonal efforts. Past generations developed the gift of gab, of engaging through networking and personal conversation in face-to-face interactions. They grew up as experts of conversation and being able to relate to strangers. This is harder for some young professionals to understand, which requires them to learn that skill much in the same way that older generations have to adapt to technological advances. It is about honing those deficiencies to become a well-rounded professional in possession of both technological and conversational skills.

Frankensteins

The Hartford Yard Goats pride ourselves as an organization on the great group of staff we have currently. It is the culture and the environment that we foster which separates us. We went through a few hard years of getting our ballpark open, and we're fortunate to have gone through that experience. But now that presents a greater challenge than ever before. Because we've started to hire several new people who didn't go through that experience the way that the older staff did.

This means that their perspective is different. They didn't experience the risks, the uncertainty, and highs of overcoming such a challenge. But that's where our culture saves us, because everyone on staff collectively comes together and helps those new people understand the same level of ownership required in order to keep the organization healthy and thriving. Despite everything that I have managed to list as reasons that someone may not want to work in the sports industry if they truly enjoy watching the game, I will say that there is something exciting about it that is unmatched in regular business.

When the team is at home, the players take the field for batting practice on an early spring afternoon, and the music wafts over the public address system into my office, I sense the energy. There is a hum that occurs as ballpark preparation begins. And a sense of something larger as the community gains momentum toward the gates opening that night. It cannot be replicated elsewhere other than the sports industry.

I love to stand near the gates and watch fans enter that evening. There are smiles all around. A look of wonderment on the faces of thousands of children who are watching the game of baseball, for their own enjoyment, and learning the game for the first, or the hundredth time, in a new way. That is what it's all about for me, and what keeps me as a minor league baseball general manager. Not the baseball, but the game itself and the experience that the fans have on the ideas that I helped create.

In life, there are always going to be plateaus. When you reach a plateau, there is a period of self-assessment and reflection. Hopefully, there is a high that comes with having achieved a sustained level of success that satisfies those seeking validation in what they are doing for a career. I've never been great at enjoying any plateau that I've experienced, to be honest. I'm more apt to look ahead to seek out the next goal, and begin to envision my route to achieving it.

Being content is about having the perspective of knowing that there are lessons to be learned along the way, and keep occurring as I grow as a general manager. That growth doesn't stop with age unless you want it to. And if you stop growing, your leadership as a general manager will suffer. Your staff will suffer because your management style will not adapt with the times. We are all *Frankensteins*, bits and pieces of experience and influence from those managers who have shaped our careers earlier. I am always in search of working on my own perspective, adapting my leadership style and becoming the best version of myself as a minor league general manager.

It is about being content about the journey, but not satisfied or complacent with the result. Always growing, listening and learning, with that high of 60, that low of 40, and that focus on perspective. That is my opinion on how to be the best minor league general manager for your staff, your culture and your organization during your tenure overseeing the team's front office.

Slow To Hire, Quick To Fire

Amy Venuto
Fmr. General Manager

About The Author

Amy Venuto worked for 15 years in minor league baseball, in positions ranging from account executive, director of sales, general manager and corporate executive. Her experience in minor league baseball includes starting an events department and serving as host president of an international youth tournament. She currently provides training and consulting. She now aids 40+ organizations with a clientele list that includes horse racing, auto racing, Minor League Baseball, Major League Baseball, collegiate properties, national associations, and startup tech companies. Proficient in sales, customer service, customer experience, and management development; Venuto provides systems and processes that enable her clients to achieve new heights.

Everything starts with who you hire. Finding the right employee is a critical function toward organizational success. If you have the right staff in place, you can attract and retain customers, naturally increasing revenues. Senior team leaders take shortcuts, settling on bad personnel simply to "*get a body*" on staff, and end up regretting their actions entirely. Hiring for "*just a body*" never works out for anybody in the long run.

First, you never want to hire the same type of employee over and over. You want diversity. You want diversity in terms of diverse backgrounds. You also want diversity in terms of personality. Additionally, too often general managers hire employees who are just like him or her. You want a lot of differing personalities. A variety of personalities on your staff foster a greater wealth of past experiences, which leads to better brainstorming, creativity, and a collective attitude that drives the staff forward to meet higher goals.

While you do not want to hire a staff who is just like you, you do want to hire people who believe in what you believe. So as a leader, first write down what you believe in. Know your core values and what is important to you. When you interview candidates, ask questions to dig into the prospective hire what he or she believes. The candidate's experience level is your base. What puts someone into the rare air is to hire those who believe what you believe. In fact, I would rather have less practical experience and more of a similar belief system. If you are good at training and providing training, you can hire someone who lacks some of the practical experience, provided he or she has those intangibles that are hard to train and he or she believes what you believe. This is just going to make your world easier.

Remember, having someone believe what you believe does not mean he or she has to be like you. A belief system that is similar can come in two very different personalities. The more you surround yourself with those who believe what you believe, the more you create a team of warriors who will fight the battles with you and charge ahead with you to meet the goals you want to exceed. You also need to know your core competencies that are important to each position. Before you hire a position, think of the core competencies that you believe are integral to that position. These are the traits that you would look for in a person to master this particular position. Identify these core competencies, and then use behavioral based questions to assess the candidate's strength.

For example, if you believe the position requires excellent oral communication skills, you might suggest that the candidate provide an example of when he or she had to deliver a speech in front of a large crowd, and how this turned out for him. You might additionally ask a question on when there was a time when the candidate had to convince a colleague that his or her concept was the right way to proceed, and how she won her colleague over to her idea. You might ask the candidate how he or she had to communicate a policy that was unpopular either to colleagues or to the customers verbally.

If the position requires initiative as a core competency, you can ask a question such as, "*Give me a time in your past - it can be work-related, athletic, academic, or social - when you had to take initiative. Give me the example, and how you really showed your initiative at this time.*" If the position requires strong customer orientation as a core competency, perhaps you can ask, "*Give me a time in your past where you dealt with an angry customer and what you did to rectify the situation.*" Some companies do personality tests. While I have never used these, I think it is a great idea to incorporate. It is not necessary, if you truly stick to hiring people who believe what you believe, and if you use questions to dive into appropriate core competency sufficiency.

Too many interviewers shorten the interview process. If building a company culture and building a terrific staff is a key to long-term success, interviews should take time, and you might need more than one interview to get to know him or her. I have never had an interview with even an entry-level candidate that I spent less than an hour in the face-to-face portion of the interview. Even with entry-level, we started with at least two separate phone interviews (*with two separate interviewers*) and the face to face interview at a minimum. My feeling is that if I am going to spend a lot of time with this person at work, I need to get to know him or her, and the longer I spend time in the interview, the more I will know if this is the right person. There have been times where the first 45 minutes of the interview went super, and then something happened in the last 15 minutes that threw us for a loop and we determined the person wasn't right for us.

And there is nothing wrong with determining the person is not the right fit. Sometimes it is best for the candidate too. You want a candidate who fits you and you fit them. We spend too much time at work not to have this happen.

A Three Part Interview Process

My suggestion is divide your interview into three parts. These three parts do not need to be equal to each other. *Part One*, you really scour the candidate's prior work background. Ask deeper questions, and keep it far from surface level. Ask for numbers anytime that you can. Look to see growth numbers - growth in survey results, growth in sales numbers. I am looking for percentage growth to show improvement. When your candidate answers, ask them for examples from their professional background. If the candidate keeps providing the same examples over the course of the interview, he or she is not experienced enough. One time, we hired a high level executive for one of our teams. This position was more than just sales, though it involved sales. There were at least four rounds of interviews for this candidate, and as the question kept coming up as to a story that showed his creativity in sales, he used the same example over and over. My *spidey senses* were telling me that this was a clear indication that he was not a very good revenue producer. We still hired him, and he was a brilliant executive, still making positive waves in this industry, though it was true - *sales was not his strong suit for us.*

Part Two of the interview is to share more information about your company. And yes, you need to sell them on your team and him or her wanting to be with your team. What can you provide to the person? What qualities does your company bring to help enhance his or her career? Tell them how wonderful your company is. Telling the candidate how wonderful your company is carries a positive effect on you too. I always found that my happiness in working with a company was so much stronger whenever I interviewed candidates, because as I was selling them, I was very aware of all of the great attributes of my company, too. Work takes a lot of time, and we want candidates who want to be at our company, too. My very first interview ever of a candidate, my boss stood over my shoulder and listened to me on the phone interview. My team, at the time, was middle of the road in attendance in the Pacific Coast League, though we had been doing 36 percent+ increases in paid attendance for the last few years. So I felt that any candidate would be lucky to work for us. I grilled him during the interview, and really did not sell my team much during the interview. At the end of the phone interview, my boss shared with me that I did not do a good job interviewing him. He said it is just as important to sell ourselves too. Needless to say, the candidate did not choose us. Oopsie.

Part Three is the part when you let the candidate ask his or her questions. This is so important, and you need to allot at least 15 percent of the interview time for this opportunity. It is important for the candidate, though it is important for you too. He or she must come prepared with questions. Her questions should show that she has done her research and knows about your company. She should not be looking for "*just a job.*" If there are not team-specific questions, either about your market, your team, and/or the personnel and ownership group, this person looks at you as "*just a job*" and not a place to grow her career. Stay away from this candidate. She needs to show you that she has done her prep work and homework for the interview. One time, one of my consulting teams was looking to hire a terrific position. This team called one of my other consulting teams who gave them a terrific candidate who had interned for them for several months. I adored this candidate, and the team she worked for was highly in favor of this person. In essence, this candidate had the position locked, sealed, and basically signed. When she got into the interview, the General Manager asked her why she wanted to work for his team, and she really didn't have any reasons of why she wanted to work there. She didn't get the position. To my knowledge, I am not even sure she is working in the industry.

Finally, extend the interview if you can. Above, there is a story for a high level executive who went through four rounds of interviews at least. This is important with high level executives. I have seen many high level executives "*fake*" (*not lie, though just expound*) his experiential level. The more time you spend with a candidate, the more you will recognize his or her tendencies that you might not see in a traditional interview. If you are interviewing in-season, and the person is a mid-manager to high level executive, invite the candidate to your game that night. See him in a more natural setting. How he acts in an environment that is not necessarily the traditional interview can open your eyes.

Several years ago, we were interviewing for an Assistant General Manager. We knew him through our annual conventions. He had talent, and was highly recommended. He aced the interviews during the day. He came to our game that night, and proceeded to have a few beers. Then he decided to go out with the staff after the game. While I was not there, I sure heard about it the next day. Apparently he partied a little too much, and was too friendly with the staff. Many staff members were already questioning his ability to lead, and he had not even been offered the position. It was not worth the effort to hire him, as he lost this opportunity to be a leader for our team on his own. He didn't get the job. He is probably a great person, and does still work in the industry. We just were able to see that he was not the right fit for us through those extra hours. It likely saved future headaches for him, our staff, and ourselves.

There are seemingly small indicators that I look for when I hire people. These are the "*out-of-the-box*" attributes that make a difference in a great hire. I love to hire people with hard work in their background. Perhaps he worked on a farm growing up, or he worked in construction when he was in high school. I love to hire these types for any position I have open, because his work ethic is already proven to be strong. If I find out the candidate worked hard in his or her past, this person receives bonus points for sure.

What To Look For

I love to hire people who worked in the restaurant industry. Many times, during an interview, I'll casually ask, "*by the way, did you ever work in a restaurant?*" If they answer no, I just move on. If she answers "*yes*", I will ask her to elaborate more. Again, this is bonus points. I love hiring people who worked in a restaurant. Restaurant work - whether as a busser, a dishwasher, a line cook, a bartender, or a server teaches three valuable lessons that apply to working in front office sports - you learn to serve others and have great customer service, you learn to work as a team to achieve, and you learn to meet small deadlines.

My daughter is going to get her masters degree in *Genetics*. She knows how strongly I feel about working in restaurants, that she spent last summer working in a laboratory studying topics in *Genetics* that I know nothing about, and still waiting tables at night. This is valuable experience for life. One of my clients - the Asheville Tourists - have a similar philosophy as I do on the value of past restaurant experience in a candidate. This team boasts an incredibly low turnover rate, and has set franchise records in attendance four years in a row. This growth is amazing, considering this team is playing in a park that is 94-years-old.

Another tip off I look for is the type of car that the candidate drives. Now clearly, if he rented a car, we cannot see this as an indicator. If he drives his own car, and is looking for an entry level position, the worse the car, the better the employee. You want non-entitled people working for you. And if *Mommy* and *Daddy* bought *Junior* a nice fancy car for *Graduation*, well, you have just hired *Entitled Junior*. This is not across the board a perfect assessment for a candidate, though I think we hit about 85 percent+ accuracy on this predictor. My staff used to love when I would interview an entry level candidate, as they would look for the car that the person drove up to the interview. They would then tell me what type of car the person was driving. We had a good idea at that point based on the car. Again, this is not a perfect predictor, though it has high results. Go ahead - ask your staff, your high achievers, what car he or she drove when she first started working for your team.

Ultimately, do not hire mediocrity. Do not just *"hire a body"* to fill space. Hire someone who you think can make a positive difference either on your team or in this industry five years down the road. Do not settle. Our mentality was that if we were not sure on a candidate, we did not offer the position. Did we miss out on some brilliant people because maybe we did not think he was excellent? Oh yes, for sure. I guarantee you that there is a man who works for one of my clients who has made such a terrific impact on his team for the last several years. I missed out on him, because while I was hiring for a position, I was also running an international, live televised event and the interview was a few days ahead of this event. I was so preoccupied with that event that I was unfocused on the interview, and therefore could not see how great this person was. I believe in this person so much, and he has become a friend. He teases me all of the time on missing out on him. And he is right. Sometimes you miss, and this is not the end of the world. If the person you missed is that good, he or she will end up at another team and be a terrific contributor to that team. Hopefully, you maintain the friendship.

I would not hire an executive recruiter for entry level or early management. This just does not seem to be worth the money. This is when you use your network. Know which teams have high expectations of seasonal interns. Know which teams teach their interns, so you are getting someone with a decent background. Call your friends in the industry, and ask them if they know of any former interns who are great and looking for positions. Even if you do not know other executives at a team that is excellent in the area that you are looking to hire for, reach out and call them. Finding quality hires, from teams that excel in that area, is always smart.

Look at the trends of those you hire from those teams. I used to hire many former Lakewood BlueClaws seasonal interns for entry level sales positions. They were accustomed to making lots of phone calls, so I did not have to overcome this barrier in teaching. The problem was that Lakewood would hire back these people after 1-2 years of working for us. In essence, I was training their staff, and having to rehire. I noticed this trend, and decided that unless it was an excellent candidate, it was not going to be worth hiring from them.

For upper level executives, I think it is a wise decision to hire an executive recruiter on a contingency basis. They have the connects to find talent and know how to find the *"diamonds."* There are so many quality candidates out there who are not going to respond to job postings. The best candidates are not necessarily currently looking, as they are too focused on their current position. The executive recruiter is going to find these *"diamonds"* and the good executive recruiters can really get an idea on where the candidate stands and how serious the candidate is, which can ultimately save you time. I have seen some excellent executive recruiters, and I have seen some that simply staff a body. They seem almost as adept at selling you on their services. Find out where the executive recruiter goes to find talent. Are they going to the same well over and over? And hire on a contingency basis. Even if you hire an executive recruiter, do not depend solely on this person. You should do your own search too.

Post listings anywhere you can. From what I hear, the job sites are not pulling the same candidate pool as they used to. You should diversify the places where you post your jobs, and who you incorporate for your search for a candidate. Consider contacting sports management professors both for entry level and executive level and see if they recommend anyone. Consider talent outside of just your sport. Consider collegiate, and Big Four, and all avenues.

Red Flags

In addition to some of the aforementioned *red flags* - sense of entitlement, not believing what you believe, not enough examples in work experience to show depth and dimension (*there are a lot of "fakers" out there*), not enough excellent personal examples on the intangibles (*the intangibles are the core competencies that you cannot teach, such as work ethic*), not being armed with quality questions for you; there are other red flags. Negativity is a huge *red flag*. I do not care if the candidate had the worst place ever where he last worked. If he is going to slam his former place of work in an interview with you, he will do the same to you. An interview is definitely not a place to be negative, and if you hire this negative interview-ee, you will do damage to your franchise. Another *red flag* is when a candidate does not dress up for the interview in a professional manner. It shows lack of respect.

You must check recommendations. I cannot share with you how much, especially for higher level executives, teams do not check recommendations. You should ask for at least three recommendations, and not hire someone unless two recommendations have checked out positively. The candidate can give you colleagues or other types of recommendations, though at least one of the checked out recommendations should come from a former supervisor. Even though a recommendation cannot legally say bad things about a former employee, you can easily tell if the recommender likes your candidate based on how much information the recommender gives. If the recommender is highly complimentary and almost gushes over your candidate, you are in good shape. Talk to the recommender yourself. I got duped once, and it was one of the worst hires I ever made.

We hired a Director of Sales and while he aced his interviews, during the recommendation process, one of his *"recommendations"* called and left me a message on my voicemail that was glowing on this candidate's behalf. I accepted it at face value, and hired him. This particular hire was not good. It took me less than two months to start thinking that this now employee could have easily just had one of his friends call me and leave this message. I had returned the call though never actually spoke with this person. *Hmmm.…*maybe I am wrong, though I quickly discovered a shady nature in this person. While not damaging to our team, his shady nature made me really think he got a friend to make that recommendation over voicemail. So I make it a point to only accept recommendations from those that were provided and that I called the recommendation directly.

I am blown away by how many teams and organizations do not promote from within, and instead look for the fancy new shiny person from the outside. Okay, if you truly do not have the talent, you should look from the outside. Challenge yourself to hire naturally curious staff members first and give these individuals the tools to broaden their interest in self-improvement and creativity. As they grow within their culture, they bring new ideas through their intellectual investment and curiosity. They will broaden your team.

Promote Over Recruit

There are several reasons to promote from within. Two really stand out for me. If you have a promote from within mentality, employees know that you will look for their growth and development. To me, if you give a staff member growth and development and if you are invested in their career outlook, they will be more loyal to you. Second, you know what you have in your company. Sure, someone can look bright and shiny to you from the outside, but you do not know them as well as you know your own staff members. So while you know the *"warts"* on your current staff member, who you might be considering for growth; that bright and shiny person from the outside might have bigger and uglier warts that are really hidden by that gilded sheen on the outside.

One of my teams does an amazing job with their seasonal intern program. They are three for three over the last two years in promoting from this seasonal intern program. Out of nine sales reps, three of their top five are from the seasonal intern program. Last time I spoke with them, I simply suggested that they should really not even look to the outside, they are having excellent success promoting from within. Hiring from the outside takes a lot more time, than to simply invest in developing your current staff with training, teaching, encouragement, and opportunity for growth. You have heard the phrase *slow to hire, quick to fire*. This is a good phrase to adhere to.

You might have also heard you are safe to fire if it is during a new employee's probationary period (*30 to 90 days, typically*). This latter part is no longer true. It used to be safe to terminate someone who is not working out well during the probationary period, and there would not be any legal actions on behalf of the employee. This is not true anymore. Even though this is no longer the case, I would still operate off of the phrase *slow to hire, quick to fire* as a base belief within your company.

Having an employee who is not doing well, is being mediocre, or being lazy, or bringing other poor attributes to your team only gives an excuse to your above average employees that it is okay to underachieve. Minimize and clear out your underachievers.

Will Versus Skill

There are ways to remove your underachievers without terminating. You can always reassign them into a different role - only do this though if they are hard workers and have a good attitude both. If the underachiever is not a hard worker or doesn't have a good attitude, find your underachiever a new team. Maybe your underachiever is a better fit for someone else. I have seen a few teams do this, and it is an art form to get this done. I would rather have a poor fit have a new start at a team that could be *their* fit any day any time, than have the underachiever linger at my team.

Sometimes termination is the only alternative. We had a question we were to ask, before determining whether or not we were going to fire someone. The question to ask is *Is it a Will or Skill issue?* You must ask yourself before terminating. If the employee does not have the skill, you are to provide them the skill before termination is an option. This could be through training or providing education opportunities or through assistance to get these skills. You cannot terminate someone if they have not been given the skills. This is why hiring or providing training is important so that you can ensure that this person has the skills. If it is a will issue, this means that the employee doesn't have the desire, showcase effort, or do the work necessary to fulfill the job expectations (*make sure you lay out job expectations upon the candidate being hired*).

First and foremost, know your state rules when it comes to terminating. States differ, and it is important that you have a grasp on what is okay and not okay, according to the state where you operate your organization. Early on, when you start to see that someone might not make it with your team, begin documenting any time this employee is making a mistake, not hitting his numbers or goals, or anytime that you had to have a conversation as to her inability to successfully fulfill her role. You do not need to show the employee your documentation. This is early in the process.

All you need to do is that every time there is a conversation where you need to address the employee's inaction, underachievement, and/or inability to fulfill his role, you need to have a word document on your computer where you document the date, time, and nature of the conversation that you had with this employee addressing her *issue/problem/underperformance*. In essence, you need a record that you have addressed your concerns as to this employee's ability to fulfill his job.

When you become more sure that you are going to have to make changes, and potentially have to terminate this employee, then you need to go through a period of corrective action and do a *Performance Improvement Plan* (PIP). This period of corrective action is at least going to take a few weeks, and probably even a month or more. To begin the termination process, and do the PIP, you need to meet with the employee and you need to address the behavior that needs to be corrected. You need to share with this employee what he or she has not done right over the past few weeks and why he needs to correct his behavior to move forward. Let him know that he is now in a position where he needs to meet the goals or perform his role as asked. Lay out in writing on a printed document what he will need to do and give him a deadline on when he needs to do this by (*date of improved performance*).

Have him sign the document so that you know he understands what he is to do. Verbally tell him that if he does not improve, and/or does not meet these performance metrics by the targeted date, that you could be having a different conversation that could even lead to termination. Ensure the employee that you are there for him, and that you will be of assistance to him as he should need. If he needs to ask you for help, you will certainly assist as you can. And you must be there for him if he does ask for help. You are supposed to give your best foot forward to help him through this. After all, you did hire him.

If you have never done a PIP before, I recommend doing some research on this subject and/or contacting an expert to ensure you do it in the appropriate manner

Sometime prior to the deadlines for these goals, you need to meet with the employee again and evaluate how he is doing and where he stands in relation to these performance metrics and the deadlines provided. You again need to give notice to the employee that if he does not hit these performance metrics that there could be more serious consequences, including termination. When the period of corrective action comes to a close, there is a slim possibility that you might have to do this again, and extend this out for a few more weeks. Clearly terminating takes time, so this is why it is important that as soon as you believe you might have issues that you start documenting behavior, as mentioned above.

It is important that an employee is never shocked by termination, and that you have given a heads up. I was once told that many times, upon the beginning of corrective action that the employee, upon given a PIP, will end up quitting, thereby saving you time and hassle. However this never happened under my watch, and if the employee did not hit his or her goals, we ended up terminating. It is never enjoyable, though you must remember and focus on the strength of your whole team. You cannot allow for underachievement. It will drag the achievers down to see an underachiever continue to have gainful employment.

Please note that other members of your team are going to need to hit their numbers too during this period of corrective action. You cannot measure one person's numbers and not look at the other members of your team too. One time, we had a *"casualty"* termination who was also let go even though we originally only had issues with a first employee. It was during corrective action of the first employee that the additional employee also was not performing. We ended up having to terminate two employees. Numbers and metrics are numbers and metrics. You do not get to keep someone longer, or at all, just because you like them more. All of this corrective action is unnecessary if the employee has done something unethical, whether this is harassment, retaliation, majorly violated a company policy or other such major offense. Additionally, make sure that when someone is terminated from your company, it is not an effect of retaliation. This is going to end up hurting you in the long run.

Most importantly, when terminating, save the dignity of the person who is being terminated. Do not discuss her corrective action period, PIP, or termination with anyone else on staff - especially her peers. You can and should discuss with your supervisor, and HR if you have HR, of course. When terminating, keep your conversation minimal, though be kind. You do not need to be sympathetic because she had a job to do, and did not accomplish it. Though, I highly recommend that you keep the conversation as short as possible; still be kind, and courteous.

Do this so that as few people as possible might see this termination occur. Respect her space here. You are changing someone's life. Ultimately, follow the Carnegie wisdom of *"let the other person save face."*[1] When you terminate, protect yourself and the company, and have another witness present during termination. Out of all of the teams and colleges that I work with, I have only had about five clients who have said that they focus on *Company Culture*. Perhaps there are a lot who think they focus on company culture, though few state it out loud. And I work with some of the best teams and colleges out there. So what this means to me is that while current upper level executives think that they strive for a great company culture, it does not mean that they are carrying this mission forward.

The first step towards developing a strong company culture is to state this mission out loud. Define key principles as to what your company culture should look like. Communicate this to everyone that you can. Let this permeate. And then follow your talk. No team or organization or department is perfect. Even those who verbally and actively carry out building a company culture have deficiencies. What I will share is the overall health of the organization, including revenue generation, is much better by those who verbally state and actively promote company culture.

Well...no one loves a quitter.

Three Motivational Options

Above, we focused on terminating an employee. Often times, both achieving and underachieving employees leave a company on their own accord. It is important to note that normally a departing employee is unhealthy for your company culture. When an employee chooses to quit, do not let them linger in an office for days on end. Even if an employee gives two weeks' notice, you do not have to accept that.

The options you have to weigh on when you let the employee leave are as follows: you can let them stay for the two weeks. I would only do this if you have a great relationship with the employee and you know that she will still do a good job for you during this time. It will help with the transition. Though, do not expect that she will give you the same standard effort, as she is excited about her new opportunity when she has one foot out of the door. *Option 2* is that you let the employee leave right away. You do not have to keep him for his whole two weeks. What you have to weigh here is how much burden your staff is undertaking in his absence versus whether he will be more of a distraction, either through current negative feelings towards your team and/or a distraction because everyone has to plan his going away party and has to hear about his new role during those two weeks. *Option 3* - you can send her home right away and pay her for the two weeks.

If you choose *Options 2 or 3*, check your state laws to see, just in case, if you are now putting yourself in a place for wrongful termination and/or unemployment claims. You should be fine since the employee quit, and it is just under two weeks. However, each state differs, and checking with your local attorney will help. An outgoing employee affects company culture. It is distracting, everyone wants to talk with this outgoing person all of a sudden (*because people love gossip and a goodbye story*), and you certainly cannot allow for them to take company property - including intellectual property. Allowing them more time to download files, while at your offices, is never a good idea.

Every time an employee left our old company, he or she would write a long email as to how he will miss everyone and how much he appreciated everyone and how much he learned from everyone. It was practically puke-worthy. And then everyone thinks this person should have a going-away party? Come on, how annoying! I have seen way too many teams keep an employee, who gave their two weeks' notice, and allow him to stay too long. Provided I am within state guidelines, I would do *Option 2* or *Option 3* all of the time. There is a possibility that if I do go with *Option 2 or 3*, that maybe other future employees might not give two weeks' notice, though frankly, if someone does not want to be at my team, I don't want them here anyhow. Everyone --- *even the top brass of your organization* --- is replaceable. And a fantastic employee would have people ready to take her job upon her departure. That is what true leadership is anyhow.

Staff Development

A great concrete foundation for creating company culture is to have a promote from within attitude. If your staff believes you will be looking out for their future, they will do anything for you. If they feel that you are invested in their growth, then they will go to battle with you. Develop your staff, and help them to grow. When I first started my business, I lost one of my biggest accounts over our differences in this philosophy. My client felt it was great to keep people at his team for a long time. He has excellent reasoning behind his philosophy, in that greater staff retention is going to lead to better results because the team knows each other more. Within his team, he has promoted a few select individuals.

I differ from him in that I think if you keep a person in the same role for longer than four years, he will get stale, and develop some saltiness and bitterness. I want the driven employee - the one who is going to challenge himself. I feel that if you have someone who is content with his role for 4+ years, then you have someone who is average. I want excellent. We had a philosophy at our former company that you could not get promoted unless you had someone ready to take on your role. This was wonderful because it meant that we had to train someone and develop someone on each of our teams to be ready to take our position so that we could get promoted. This led to excellent staff development and it aided in our top employees being excellent teachers, growers, developers, and delegators. To me, this is one of the reasons, when our company was in our *Golden Age*, that we were so strong. Everyone felt looked after, and we worked together.

One of my favorite people in this business is currently an Assistant General Manager for a Major League team. One day, I simply texted him, as part of a vent, the following question --- *"if communication is such a problem, why has no one fixed it yet?"* Within minutes, he responded, *"until upper managers and middle managers are less territorial and insecure, communication will always be a problem."* Well, if you do not promote and look out for your staff, the result will be territorial and insecurity.

As mentioned earlier, I like to promote from within because I would much rather take my chances on the people I know - for good and bad; rather than be fooled in an interview by a smooth talker from the outside. Plus whenever you hire from the outside, you are going to end up hearing all too often, "*well, back at (insert name of former team), we used to…*" While you definitely want to hire from outside periodically to get new creative ideas into your culture, I believe to create that base for company culture, build upon the concrete mentality of "*promote from within.*"

Gossip, In-Fighting & Cliques

Simply put, do not tolerate gossip, in-fighting, or cliques within your team. This is a work environment, and not middle school. Certainly, friendship groups will be fostered, though you should keep the environment as inclusive as possible. There is a phrase that I use a lot at work. "*Nip it in the bud.*" As soon as you start to be suspicious that individuals are being ganged up on, or that there is office gossip, address this as quickly and as confidentially as you can. You are going to likely have to address the "*gossipers*" and the person who is being gossiped about. Depending on the situation, you might not want to outwardly say that the gossip-ee is being gossiped about. Instead ask questions to make sure that his behavior is not necessarily producing unnecessary gossip. Help him out.

Foster a team atmosphere. Let your teammates know that varied and diverse personalities make the team stronger. Let your teammates know that they are part of a team within the department, and that department is a part of a larger unit - your team, and that team is part of a larger unit - the sports industry. We all work together to reach a goal. Let your teammates know that the ultimate focus should be on the customer.

Be absolutely strong about warding off cliques. Cliques are so middle school. Recently, I had a team where one person, who is in a small department, expressed that the office environment wasn't strong and that out of the three salespeople, one was on a totally different path, and it made it hard for the office dynamic to get along. I shared with this person who expressed this info that 2-to-1 is hardly a majority, and maybe in this case, the 2 are the wrong ones. I didn't know the entire circumstance, because I am only there a couple of days a year, and I like to believe the best in everyone. I suggested to this vocal person that he should be a leader and take the other party out to lunch or appetizers and openly discuss the issues at hand. Furthermore, this "*leader*" should anticipate hearing some feedback from the other party too.

I had a colleague for 12+ years that I really did not like, and he did not like me. However, not only did we co-exist and work together for all of those years, I think we hid our dislike of each other pretty well. We don't have to be friends at work. We need to respect each other, and we have to earn that respect from each other. This is what I focus on with my employees that they know that they are to act in a place of respect for each other.

How to help stem gossip is to have high expectations that first, all employees responsibly act with a strong representation of the company at all times. This alone will help minimize gossip by keeping gossip-able actions minimal. Second, stem the gossip by letting employees have funny opinions about other topics such as celebrity gossip, or which historical figure a person would like to have lunch with, or is golf a game or a sport. I consistently float aimless topics that can be discussed at work so that we talk about and ponder random-ness rather than focusing on inner-office gossip. While I truly do not take time to read celebrity gossip, I once read that it is good because it keeps the topic of conversation away from real-life gossip.

Snaking Sales

Many times, in-fighting in sales has to do with people feeling as if they got their accounts "*snaked*" from them. I have very little patience with people complaining about this.

First, this is one of the reasons you have a CRM to protect yourself from multiple people complaining about going after the same account. If you don't have CRM, then use call reports. You need a record of which sales rep contacted the prospect first. Again, this is just one use of call reports/CRM, though if a rep is too lazy to update his call reports or CRM, and the other rep does and there is a dual claim on the account, that account will go to the person who claimed them on CRM and/or call reports first. It is this simple.

Second, whenever I see more than one rep going after an account, that means I have an assertive outbound-focused sales staff. This is good. I used to coach softball, and every time there was a pop-up, and a little run-in because more than one fielder went after the ball, some idiot parent would yell, "*Talk, Girls*" in such a condescending manner. I would pull my players to the side and tell them that I would ten thousand times rather have a mixup running after the ball with more than one player, than to have three players not go after the ball and watch it drop between them. And then I would run through the process and teach who has priority. How does my softball coaching analogy apply here? I would ten thousand times prefer to have multiple reps go after accounts than have no one go after accounts. The process part is to make sure that once you start working on contacting an account, the rep needs to input this in CRM or on call reports to show a record of attempted contacts.

Third, I'm more worried about how it comes across to the customer. It can be handled professionally. When I was first an Account Executive, the sales staff that I worked with was real strong and assertive. We had crossover. If I called a prospect who mentioned that he was already working with one of my colleagues, I would simply respond, *"Oh that is great that you are working with (insert first name), he is awesome. If you need anything from any of us, simply let us know. You are in great hands with him."*

CRM Value

So in essence, having reps going after prospective accounts indicates an assertive sales staff. You just need to have a process for determining who gets the account, and this is where you should let CRM or call reports lead. Where crossover can be poorly done is when reps are calling on existing accounts. That is when it gets frustrating to the customer. There is a simple way to rectify this. Your Box Office manager can print out a list in alphabetical order of all of your accounts. Provide this hard copy print out list to each sales rep. Before a sales rep makes a call to a prospective lead, she can quickly glance at this list. If she sees that the prospective lead is currently a client, she does not call them. Oh, yes, there are people who will say that she can just look this up in CRM. Every time that a rep goes into CRM to look this up takes a few seconds. A quick glance at an alphabetical list of your team's current accounts, will save time and help your reps to be more familiar with your team's account base.

Two of my teams put a time limit on how long an account rep can hold onto a prospective account. This has worked so well with both teams. In fact, both teams saw record sales numbers that year. The base concept of this is that a rep has rights to pursue an account from the time he first called that account. There is a time limit on how long he has rights to pursue this account before there is a pitch (*whether by phone or by appointment*). Then once he pitches this prospective account, he has another length of time before that account says *yes*. By placing time limits on both the timeframe of when to make the pitch, and the timeframe to close that account, you are allowing more opportunities for a team to bring in more accounts, and eliminating the frustration. Nothing good comes from some rep who holds onto an account for 1.5 plus years and that account has not come in yet. That's just hoarding. This will frustrate your team. I like the idea of putting time limits, and allowing other reps to re-open conversations with prospective clients. If you truly have a sales staff that has diverse personalities, you never know which personality is going to be best suited for that prospective client.

Part of the reason I have little patience with those who complain about others "*snaking*" accounts from them, is that I always had a very positive attitude about what I could do in sales. That I control my future. When I was an Account Representative in Las Vegas, during my first year, my base salary was $16,000, and I was a single mother at the time, and the sole financial support for my daughter. And yes, we got commission, so every sale counted.

I was excellent at finding leads and setting appointments, and I sold. I was part of the outbound sales department. We did have an inside sales department. If that inside sales department sold a group of 20, that account belonged to inside sales. As an outbound sales rep, I was assertive, and there were times that I would set an appointment with a company, not knowing that that company had belonged to inside sales. Many times I sold this company into a new package that might entail four full season seats. This was a lot more money for our company. I had no idea that the account "*belonged to inside sales.*" No one told me. I was just doing my job bringing in customers.

So then my boss would call me into his office, and let me know that the origin of that account started with Inside Sales and that my sale (*both credit to my numbers and my commission*) had to go to Inside Sales. I remember responding calmly that if Inside Sales really had a relationship with that account, that Inside Sales would have upgraded them, since clearly the interest was there from that account. Still, rules were rules. And my positive attitude always said that if I am truly good at sales, I am better than losing an account here and there. I will make it up by selling more. Ultimately, the company and the customer were both benefiting. So if a single mom making a base salary of $16,000 had this attitude, my patience level for people complaining about losing accounts is very low. We are to truly think of the customer and company first before ourselves.

You need to motivate your staff on an individual basis. Everyone is motivated differently, and a key to management is learning how to motivate each employee individually and figuring out what makes each employee drive to the best of his or her ability. Sometimes it is as easy as simply making the ask. There are so many times that managers complain to me that an employee could do so much more. So I ask if that employee is meeting expectations and/or hitting her goal. When the manager says, "*yes, but…*" As in yes, she is hitting her goal though she could be doing so much more. My response will always be the same: if an employee is hitting her goal and/or meeting the expectations laid out for her and management wants more, then this is management's fault for not establishing higher goals.

Each year at the beginning of the year, you need to lay out goals - for sales and for non-sales roles. Too many times managers lay out goals that are soft. You should be growing your staff individually and your team collectively. To grow individuals and a team, you should be making goals and expectations stronger annually. They have more experience each year, so grow them each year. If they are hitting your goals and expectations, they are doing their jobs, even if you believe they have more to give.

Nip It In The Bud

Now, I love it when managers give stretch goals and reward their employees for hitting stretch goals. In this case, a manager would lay out the goal, and then provide a stretch goal. If the employee hits the stretch goal, he receives a higher bonus or commission.

Additionally, for that employee who is doing just barely enough, I will address that employee and "*nip it in the bud*" early. One time, one of my sales reps who had a lot of potential, simply "*checked the box*" all of the time. If the goal was 100 calls in a day, he turned in 100 every day. I spoke with him in my office, and I thanked him for hitting his daily expectations, though shared with him that when he does just the minimum every single day he is showing me that he is willing to just hit the base expectations.

That is fine, since he is meeting what I asked from him. I told him that I love to see those who do more, who have that extra fire, who go beyond the minimum, and I advised him that for future situations that wherever he works, if he does more and drives beyond the base expectations that that will always reflect more positively on him and help him with his growth long-term. It was that simple of a conversation and he responded to this message. I do not think anyone had ever taught him this. He became one of my stronger sales reps that year, and has continued to grow his career.

Another huge part of managing is to curb any behavior that is not conducive to a team. Sometimes you will have a sales rep who delivers sales and meets and exceeds numbers, though they are toxic. I have little patience for any toxic behavior. Toxic behavior is not necessarily unethical. If it is unethical, you need to remove this employee from your offices. If the toxic behavior is ethical, it still needs to be addressed, because it is not worth it for your office environment in the long run.

If, as a manager, you tolerate toxic behavior, for the sake of sales numbers, you are sending a terrible message to the rest of your staff. In fact, this is highly transactional. You have to believe that your team collectively is better than one individual who performs.

Toxic Behaviors

My very first year in management, I had a sales rep who everyone got along with, and he never did anything unethical, though everything he did was slightly shady. So I would get complaints, and address them, and then his colleagues who complained about him would never address it themselves, because they were pansies. So I looked like the bad guy over and over. Still, I knew what he was doing was not conducive to the staff makeup. Even though he brought in incredible numbers, I still sat down with him and addressed where he needed to improve. I did this with trying to appeal to his goals of what he wanted in his career. I shared with him that eventually he will want to grow into leadership and/or management. When you are in that role, you have to hold yourself to higher standards, and you are going to need to earn the respect of others, including those you manage in order to be effective. The behaviors he was exhibiting were not going to earn him this level of respect.

This is the key when you are dealing with toxic behaviors. It is hard to appeal to the *"nobler motives"* because this probably isn't important to the toxic employee, or they wouldn't be toxic. You have to put it in to terms of what's in it for him. Rarely does someone want to be a career Account Executive. Most want to grow into leadership or management. To be effective in management or leadership, you need to earn respect, and this is why cleansing them and getting them out of these toxic behaviors is going to be key to his future.

You must continue to teach and train, and develop your staff. This is becoming more the standard and expectation from employees. This does not mean you have to always hire training from the outside. Even if you do hire outside training, you need to still create internal sales training.

Creating internal sales training is integral to your managers having respect from their employees. When I see a team completely outsource the growth and development to an outside company, I cringe. You are taking away one of the biggest bonds that a manager can have with his or her staff. An employee is going to be incredibly loyal and driven for his supervisor if he feels that his supervisor can teach and grow him. So when you entirely outsource coaching, you are doing a disservice to your manager building that bond with his or her staff.

Training is my main source of income currently, and just as important as it is for me to provide training, I love it when a team asks me to train their managers so that they can continue teaching and growing their staff. Some level of teaching should be done at least once a week. This can be done in a sales meeting, or as a separate meeting, and really does not need to take a large investment of time. Perhaps 20 minutes a week. Perhaps it is constructive critique of a presentation (*do this in a one to one setting as much as possible*) by the in house manager.

Perhaps it is classroom style training to the team. If your managers feel as if they are not experts enough on a subject matter, send them to a class, or have them study, or contact an expert so they can grow in this area to deliver with conviction and strength. I love it when a team allows colleagues to teach colleagues, too, so this is a way to improve internal sales training. Take one of your sales leaders (*not the toxic one*) and have one of your reps who is excelling in a particular competency or area to teach her colleagues what she does, so she can help them grow in this area. This rewards outstanding efforts by one of your stars, and gives her or him validation for a job well done, in addition to fostering internal sales training.

Just as important as it is for you to manage your staff and work well with your colleagues, it is important to manage up to your supervisors. Communicate well with your supervisors. Be honest, forthright, very detail-oriented, and have great systems in place. Be able to predict your sales teams' trends and projections consistently weeks ahead. If you have a bad week, be able to point out to where you will be in three weeks from now. Most times, your upper level execs and supervisors want to be in the know. They do not like surprises - especially bad ones. Creating effective regular communication based on results and numbers, though also projections, is important.

A constant general manager complaint is that their owners do not really care, and do not really pay attention. That is the owner's right. Frankly, I do not think we understand enough how much investment an owner does put into his or her club. Still, even if you think the owner is not paying attention, you should provide him or her with regular updates, even if it is by email or written. The owner invested in and bankrolled the team. It is her money, and she has a right to know.

Communicate Above All Else

If you create a system of regular communication that you and your supervisors agree upon, it will help.

What I work to communicate to supervisors is what they want to know:

✓   If they want to know about weekly numbers, this is what I give them.

✓   If they want information on personnel, this is what to provide.

✓   I give them what they want, and I ask my supervisors how they want it delivered. I do it on their terms. Do they want the information electronically or verbally?

✓   If they want the information written, how many pages do they want the report in?

I work on their terms as they are my supervisor. Other than what they ask for, I do not give more, unless the extra information is important for the long-term viability of the team. For example, if there is a situation that arises that is potentially harmful to the club, yes I let my owners or supervisors know about this. Anything that could affect the team is important to communicate.

Additionally, I communicate really great news to the owners and supervisors too. For example, if a sales rep has far exceeded his goal, or if an employee went above and beyond on stadium operations, or if our team took on a big community initiative, I communicate great news. Owners and supervisors love to hear good news. Additionally, any time an owner or supervisor reaches out to an employee for outstanding achievement, this makes the employee feel great and motivates him to continue to succeed at a high level.

This regular communication is going to help keep the owners and supervisors from favoriting select staff members just because they are "*likeable*" --- especially those "*likeable*" ones who don't really get the job done, or just skate by. When management favors certain staff members who do not get their job done, you are creating an unhappy and unhealthy work environment. We all know that there are smooth talkers out there. Those who ride by on their personality. Those who are so loved because they project a certain image, never challenge the status quo (*also never making it better because they just go with the flow*), and they spend most of their time preening and getting their supervisors to love them. Oh, you can probably picture a current or former colleague right now who was this person. Personally, I find that owners and supervisors too often take the easy route and prefer the *"non-boat rockers"*, the ones who just conventionally float by. I always valued the boat rocker.

The boat rocker is going to challenge my team to get better. The boat rocker still has to play by the rules, and still manage herself to work as a teammate, and handle her emotions. Give me a boat rocker who plays by the rules, acts as a teammate should, and handles emotions, and you will have a team that will reach new strides and goals. However we are talking here about how to deal with the personality-laden, preener, who management loves though he or she does not get the job done. First, if you are good at establishing goals and metrics for performance, and regularly communicate this to your supervisors, you will help minimize this problem.

When an owner sees that the preener does not deliver, you will start to see a good owner not as impressed by this *"likeable"* underachiever. Regular communication, weekly goals, and performance metrics will make this much more manageable. An owner cares about his team's image in the community, the positive impact the team makes, customer retention, and of course revenue growth. If he knows the employees who are positively impacting this the most, your smart owner will gravitate to these individuals.

If you do provide the measurement and metrics, and your supervisor still favors the preener, please know that it normally works itself out. It is hard to hide behind preening for long. And if you are underappreciated for your efforts, know that there will be somewhere that will love and appreciate what you do. For those who cannot easily leave their current location, and feel under-appreciated as compared to the preener, your job is to be satisfied with what you do because you know you are delivering for your staff and for your customers.

True leadership is a thankless job. True leaders do not take credit when things go right, and take the blame when things go wrong. So true leaders are often going to feel underappreciated. You have to be knowledgeable and content with what you have done for the organization and for your staff, and rest your head each night knowing that you deliver positively. I highly recommend you keep track of your accomplishments weekly, and when you do have a review, you can point out all of the positives that you have contributed to your franchise, and let your owners and supervisors be aware of yours and your team's success.

Set Achievable Goals

A great franchise is going to have a core of anywhere between 2 to 5 goals that the entire team is committed to. You should communicate this to your entire staff, and everyone on the team needs to know the goals that the entire franchise is committing towards. These can change annually.

For example, when I was the host president of an international youth tournament, my team established the following three goals:

✓   We would increase attendance throughout the duration of the tournament with capacity crowds on the final two days of the Tournament.

✓   We would blend our local community into the fabric of this Tournament and create events and opportunities for the international and national teams to interact with our community.

✓   We would create a tournament that would be considered the best time of their lives thus far for our tournament participants.

These goals are established for everyone on staff, to our volunteers, and to our community leaders. Every time we had a staff meeting, we would reference these three goals and look at how we were doing on these three goals. We ran an incredibly successful tournament, and I believe having these base goals made a huge difference.

Each of your individual departments need to create their own set of goals too. Perhaps you copy one or more of your overall team goals, or maybe a department creates its own set of goals. I like for a department to have some autonomy and feel responsible for creating their own goals.

You need to set individual goals for everyone in your company. For the salespeople and those who do not sell, you need to set goals. Believe it or not, there are some teams that do not even set goals for their salespeople individually.

Let's start with sales. For each salesperson, you need to create individual sales goals. Start with what you feel the goal should be for the year. To set a good goal for a first year sales rep, be consistent with what you think is a challenging yet realistic goal for a first year. I was always good at measuring, so I had an idea of what a good sales goal was for a new sales rep on new sales. If they are inheriting renewal accounts, make a goal for where you want to see their renewal rate, and add the renewal rate to the new sales amount and there is your total individual goal for the year. For a returning sales rep, start here with renewal rate. Take their base of renewal accounts and multiply that by the renewal rate you want to see him achieve. Then add a new sales goal, and this is your individual goal for the year for that sales rep.

Each sales rep needs to have a new and renewal goal. Teams lump renewals and new into one lump sum. Of course, I want to see a rep hit the lump sum goal, so if they are higher in renewals, and hit the lump sum goal, that is fine. However, if you do not break it out into new and renewal, your sales rep will likely focus stronger on either new or renewal and ignore the other. I reward highest renewal rate and highest new sales on my staff.

What normally happens is if it is not broken into new and renewal, the sales rep will likely do more focus on renewals and ignore new. And then you will eventually have a mature sales rep who does not try to bring in new because he consistently inherits house accounts when others leave, and so while his sales numbers look great, he is bringing in peanuts when it comes to new sales. And your company feels committed to someone who is truly not growing your franchise. And if he is a preener, well you are now breeding a whole host of issues. Break your individual goals into new and renewal, so that you get each sales rep to focus on renewal and new. This makes for a solid franchise.

Goals should be challenging, yet realistic. If goals are not realistic, you are creating a feeling of inadequacy and hopelessness. If goals are not challenging, how do you expect your staff and team to grow and develop. So a rep's new sales goal does need to grow each year. If you've invested in developing her, she should get better, and help you to grow your franchise.

Staff members who are not in sales need goals too. Most teams do not do this. No wonder salespeople get bitter. In this case, the salesperson is measured, while the non-salesperson is not. Plus, the salesperson has to put themselves to the test of getting "*no*" daily, while the non-salesperson is not held accountable and gets by on being "*liked.*" This is a really big problem in the sports industry.

Accountability & Discipline

So set goals for your non-sales people too. Set goals that are measurable. Perhaps you tie these goals to survey results. Perhaps you tie these goals to measurables that one can see. These goals should always be tied to improving attendance (*notice, I did not say to revenue but to attendance*).

For all goals, it is ideal that while each person on staff has goals, maybe you give some guidelines for how to achieve those goals. For example, for sales, if you have a revenue goal to hit, give them some guidelines - does this also include x number of phone calls in a day, x number of appointments in a week, a certain renewal percentage by the end of November? For non-sales, provide similar guidelines to help achieve their goals.

Bottom line, I say to all staff members that as long as they hit their goal(s), I don't care how they get there, as long as it is ethical, doesn't hurt their personal brand, doesn't hurt the team's brand, and doesn't cost the company money. So if they can find a more efficient way to hit their goals without using the guidelines set, and it is ethical, keeps the brand intact, and does not cost additional monies, I am all for it. If, though, instead, they do not hit their goal and they are not hitting the guidelines presented, then this is a will issue, and we might have a larger problem with their results, performance, and effort.

Once an annual goal is set, you need to break these annual goals into monthly and weekly so you can see progress (*or lack thereof*) towards the overall goal. Evaluate this with your staff member regularly to make sure they are on track to their goal. I like for teams to play from ahead rather than trying to catch up on a goal. I always push a team to get out front early. It makes for a happier staff environment. I am completely upfront with my team that I push to get them ahead. Accountability and discipline is key. Discipline does not have to mean punishment. I look at discipline as structure. I believe most staff members thrive on structure. You need to reward your employees for a job well done. This is why I like guidelines in addition to goals. The more reasons that I can find to reward, the better for motivation and for staff happiness and success.

Guidelines, in addition to goals, help with the accountability side. As mentioned above, if a staff member does not achieve his or her goal, and is not achieving the guidelines set too, then we have a problem. You will have to hold this person accountable, even if you like them. You cannot let other staff members see that there is no accountability because either they will harbor resentment, or even worse, they will stop putting in the effort once they see there is no accountability.

One of my teams last year was so happy that they now had accountability in their office. Before, there was never any accountability. Guess what happened with no accountability? Their numbers were on a continuous downward spiral. My problem though, even after they established accountability, was that there were no accountability measures between lack of performance and effort and then termination. The first result on accountability should not be termination. Put in accountability measures leading up to termination such as a hard talk, or taking away internet, or taking away social time, or other such accountability measures before you have to get to the dreaded "*T*" word.

I love rewards. Though even without rewards, it is not as if your staff doesn't get something in return for their job performance. They do get paid. They earn their pay and they have to at least meet the guidelines for their goals and put in the effort. Address goals, rewards, and accountability as a group. Let your team know it is important to hit and achieve, and effort must be made and shown. Be clear with your team goals. Team goals should be publicly addressed, both when laid out ahead of time, and progress made as a team.

Individual goals should not be done publicly. That is one to one. Additionally, if there are individual accountability measures that need to be made, this needs to be done in private. I am a big believer in letting everyone save his or her dignity, even an underperforming employee. Make rewards public. Yes, there are some people who do not like public recognition.

Know who those people are, and do not be "*showing off*" in this case if they are embarrassed by public recognition. Somehow, even private recognition usually gets around the office. Reward on your individual employee's terms. Still, most employees do embrace public recognition. For those that like public recognition, then make their rewards public. When people see others receiving recognition or rewards, others strive harder to get the same treatment. Consistency in goal setting, goal evaluating, accountability and rewards will lead to a staff knowing what is expected of them, and a strong desire to achieve.

Service Clients
Like A Madman

Brent Conkel
Vice President
Iowa Cubs
Pacific Coast League, Triple–A Baseball

About The Author

Brent Conkel is in his 21st season in Minor League Baseball, all with the Triple–A Iowa Cubs. After holding numerous positions with the ball club, he is currently the VP of Premium Seating & Corporate Marketing. He holds a degree in Sport Management from Iowa State University. When he's not at the ballpark, you can find him spending time with his wife and 3 boys.

Sometimes pricing for the premium spaces is trial and error. But servicing an account can never be. You can do your research and figure out what you think the price should be based on comparable prices in the market and the other factors you are using to set the pricing. But it's the service that stands alone in whether people will look at the price at all. At the Iowa Cubs, we have had to adjust our pricing down in an area after sales weren't up to the level we were expecting.

Six years ago, our skybox rentals on Sundays were way down. We had quite a few open suites. We decided to actually lower the price from $550 per game to $350 per game. After we did this, our Sundays have become some of our busier days for suite rentals. Our Sunday rentals were packed, buying catering packages and extra tickets. And it allowed us to show the service that we could offer to each premium space. We have also increased pricing when we felt an area was selling well and we were missing on the extra revenue. We discovered that our *Budweiser Club* area pricing was less than the value we provided to our premium buyers.

My favorite premium space that we've ever created is called the *Budweiser Club*. This is an all you can *eat/drink* area down our leftfield line. It utilizes the top two rows of seven tables each in our Leftfield Picnic area, with a landing above that holds all of the *food/drinks*. We have four-top tables with four seats at each table. The cost for a table of four is $240 and it includes *food/drinks/beer* run from the time the gates open through the seventh inning. This area had always been a general admission area that didn't make us much revenue.

It was a trial for different ideas that we thought would work. Ultimately about 5-6 different things failed in that area. We tried this idea with one row of seven tables first. It went so well that we added a second row of tables to the area after two years. Now, entering our sixth season with the *Budweiser Club*, there is talk of adding more tables to meet demand. Last season we averaged nine tables per game.

Pricing premium higher than average bucket seats is one factor that clients have to accept. Once you get them to do that, making the entire buying process as smooth as possible for them goes a long way. If you can provide a high enough value included in the cost, people should be able to see that. When you can include items or experiences with the premium spaces that normal ticket buying customers don't get or have access to, that makes the premium buyer feel special and helps finish the deal. And hopefully it gets them to come back.

Another factor that helps get clients to buy premium is the fact that our team is very popular in the market. Clients who rent a skybox for 1-2 games know that they will have no problem getting their employees or hosted customers excited about coming to the game and will have a good turnout, making it worthwhile. People have positive feelings towards the Iowa Cubs, so this can help, provided we can keep that going.

Paint The Picture

Premium sales is sometimes about being persistent with the prospect who you think might be on the fence toward purchasing your product. If you can get them to come see the area, you have a better chance of getting them to buy. On some slow premium nights, we have tried inviting potential buyers to one of our premium areas for a game to give them a chance to experience it. This gives them a first-hand view of what that premium experience would be like. They can also socialize with other guests we invited and see who else is considering buying. We have gotten customers who have become multiple night skybox renters and even one who bought a full season suite the next year.

Storytelling can also be utilized in building a relationship with a potential premium buyer. It can help to tell a potential customer a certain scenario and how it worked well for a previous customer. Talking about our team or the Chicago Cubs can help as well, especially with the Cubs winning the World Series in 2016. Most of those players came through Des Moines, so it can be beneficial to talk about them as they came through to play for the Iowa Cubs before becoming legends of Wrigley Field. Prospects are not mutually exclusive to the idea of going up the ticket escalator from single game tickets to premium seating. I don't think all ticket customers are potential premium buyers. I've encountered some people who like to sit in the "*cheap seats*" over renting a suite or a premium seat. Those fans are still important in our general ticket sales and have value, but not as premium prospective buyers.

There are people who don't get premium areas who would rather sit in regular seating. For the most part, in my experiences these people are vocal about their thoughts on premium early on so I don't have to waste too much time on them. When you discuss the price with them up front, that usually will eliminate these people. There is somewhat of a mindset change when going from regular ticket sales to premium. You are dealing with customers on a different price level with higher expectations. This requires more attention to these potential premium customers and a higher level of service after the sale as well. You need to make sure they are getting at least what they expected, if not more. Higher attention to detail is required as well.

The best way to get referrals is to take great care of the premium ticket holders that we have. These people will share their positive experience with friends, who are typically potential premium ticket buyers as well. One example of this we have in our suites. Last year, we had three companies sharing a full season suite for the first time, each with one-third of the games. One of the partners decided not to renew their share. One of the remaining partners worked on their end to give us a name of a company that was interested in taking the open one-third. This company had been contacted by us previously, but it took a current suite holder who was a friend to sell the great experience in one of our suites. Now that suite has three partners who are friends and hopefully will be with us for the long term.

Most of our full season suite leases are on three year commitments. One of those three years has over half of the renewals, so that year is tougher than the other two. So far, we have done a good job of navigating through that process and keeping our renewals at a constant level, even in that more full renewal year. Our contracts with premium are typically pretty standard for all of our premium areas. We only have a handful of different premium options, so if we need to value add or negotiate a certain detail, we will do that and adjust the contract accordingly. We will value add to a contract if it will close the deal. We can add different value elements to increase what a premium experience is, such as extra skybox parking passes, promo items before they are given away, first pitches, chances to shoot the hot dog gun or participate in other on-field promotions. Our mascot "*Cubbie Bear*" can make appearances at their office, Cub Club memberships during games, among other things that are in our toolkit to sell to fans who purchase premium.

One example of a full season lease had us negotiating a renewal with one our suite holders. They are an Agriculture-based company, so they were looking for something to get better usage of their suite during the early season in mid-April, when most of their customers were still in the fields. I came up with an option to give them a "*suite bank*" of up to seven suites to use at later games from our nightly skybox rental inventory. This suite bank would build up as they had games not used in April for their own suite, not to exceed seven each season. They were very happy with this added value and renewed for this cycle. Tailor the product to fit the needs of the prospect with better service and you will win every time.

We do have different progressions in the premium field. With skybox suites as an example, we have nightly rentals ($550) to get someone started, 10 game skybox rentals (*10 percent discount off rental cost*), half-season leases (*35 games - $10,000*), up to full season suite leases (*70 games - $20,000*). Most of our full season suite leases are on three-year commitments. One of those three-years has over half of the renewals, so that year is tougher than the other two. So far, we have done a good job of navigating through that process and keeping our renewals at a constant level, even in that more full renewal year.

Utilize What You've Got

Premium spaces are always involved in our year-round sales initiatives. Knowing where we are on our suite lease renewal process. The usage of our ballpark for outside events has definitely led to sales in some of our premium seating. People that host their party, or even attend the event, get to see how well we can put on a show and how great of a facility it is. This has led to season ticket sales, skybox suite rentals and group outing purchases. We probably have 15-20 wedding receptions at the ballpark each year. We utilize the Cub Club Restaurant, LF suite area, along with the Veranda patio off of the Cub Club. And once or twice a year, we do have a wedding on the field in the offseason or when the team is on the road. We have the person who runs the Cub Club Restaurant that coordinates all of these during the offseason.

Over the last 20 years, I've learned quite a few lessons working in minor league baseball. Probably the biggest lesson is that even though we're a minor league baseball team, we're really in the entertainment industry. We don't have control over the players that we have on our team at any time, so we have to concentrate on the things we can control. Our mantra at the Iowa Cubs is "*Safe, Clean and Fun.*" We try to have promotions every night to bring people to the ballpark and help them enjoy a summer night out at the ballpark. If we do get a top prospect to come through or a rehab start by a big leaguer, it's just a bonus. It seems like if we have a bad team, it doesn't really hurt our attendance, but if we happen to have a good team, it could help us some.

My greatest mentor in Minor League Baseball has been Sam Bernabe. He's been with the Iowa Cubs for 35 seasons and has been the General Manager for the last 31 years. In 1999, my second season as an Iowa Cubs intern, I worked alongside Sam helping him with *tickets/contracts/promotions* for some of our larger accounts. And I've been working with him ever since. He leads our staff and provides direction to us, but allows us to do our jobs and give input on the direction of the organization. His door is always open and he's willing to help us out whenever we might need help on a sale or a new idea. He takes care of his staff by allowing us to do staff outings outside of games or even just taking the staff out for lunch.

My first experience in selling premium was in 2002 when I became the Director of Luxury Suites for the Iowa Cubs. Previous to this, I had worked primarily in group sales for four years. Selling premium can be a different animal than selling a block of reserved tickets. Especially with our full season suites or other premium areas, the commitment level of the buyer is much higher and will take more attention on our end to make the sale. My best premium customer is a life insurance company who has been a full season suite holder for three years now. Prior to becoming a full season suite holder, they would rent multiple skyboxes for a night each year. I approached them about the potential of buying a full season suite and they were somewhat interested initially. But after numerous conversations in person and on the phone, they ended up buying a full season suite for one season.

During the renewal process after that season, we tried connecting with them numerous times to discuss. We finally decided to take them a special gift, which was a 2016 Cubs World Series Champion[1] growler full of their favorite craft beer. The first time we tried this, the decision maker was not there, so we left the full growler for the office. When we tried to visit him again later with another full growler of beer, the decision maker is a huge Cubs fan so he was very excited with this gesture. They ended up renewing for another season. And after that second season, we renewed them for a two-year agreement.

As an organization, The Iowa Cubs go over our premium pricing yearly, usually get together as a sales staff or management staff late in the season to go over pricing for the following season. There are a few factors that we look at in determining pricing. We look at the current season's pricing and gauge our sales according to those prices. If things sold well and the demand was high, we would look at raising those prices for the following year. If something didn't sell very well, we would look at keeping those prices the same and possibly value adding to make more sales of that category. For some of our premium areas, we look at other premium options in the market to determine if we're competitive with them. Our main comparison is the arena in downtown Des Moines, which has G-League basketball, AHL hockey and indoor football, along with multiple concerts.

It's a pretty small group of people involved in creating a premium space for the Iowa Cubs. It could involve as little as 2-3 people, up to eight depending on the situation. Could possibly include ticket department, sales staff, management, ownership and myself. First, they have to know the pricing and details of the premium spaces and be confident in presenting it to a potential customer. They need to learn the premium areas and what makes people want to buy them. I like to bring along an intern or new sales person on a sales call or meeting. This is sort of a ride along program for premium sales. They get experience in the actual field and get to learn from my successes or failures.

Our best group experience in bringing in more customers is actually renting some of our nightly skybox suites on *Groupon*. I know this might sound counter intuitive to sell premium products at a discount, but it's been very successful for us. We do this for April games, which are typically more lightly attended because of the weather in Iowa. We have 45 suites in our ballpark, which is a very high number for a minor league stadium. We sell 27 of them corporately on a full season basis. This leaves us 18 skyboxes to rent out each night.

Those early games would be empty if we didn't use this option. We pick 10 dates in April or early May that we think might be slower and offer them on *Groupon*. These buyers might be paying a discount up front, but they do buy extra tickets and spend money on food/drinks when they are here in suites that might have been empty otherwise. Also, some of these buyers become repeat buyers later in the same season or the following season at full price. These buyers on *Groupon* are not our typical buyers, so it does expand our customer base for these rentals overall.

Pricing Right

Look, let's face facts, if you can sell, then you can sell. But in the world of premium, there are definitely people who can sell premium more effectively than others. It doesn't mean that you cannot sell at all, but premium is a complex animal of sales skills not reserved for everyone tasked with selling it. Some people are more comfortable in selling the higher level of tickets or packages. We have had a fair number of individual premium clients come from some of our companies who are sponsors. These individuals like to be associated with us since their company supports us as a partner. Also, we have had individuals who have used their company's suite and enjoyed it so much, that they end up renting a nightly suite from us later on.

I like to make sure that all potential clients have all of the pricing information up front when you start the initial conversations. That is a key component of selling that those in the premium world sometimes avoid. As if they are ashamed to mention the price they value their premium inventory at. If that's the case, you shouldn't be selling it all. Never be ashamed of what you are selling and the price that you are selling it. Let the customer decide if the value doesn't supersede the price of the product. The conversation on price is necessary, especially early on in premium with a prospect. That way any sticker shock either occurs or it does not, and you can continue speaking with the clients who are serious about buying. It eliminates those who merely want to tire-kick and aren't truly interested in becoming a premium seating customer.

I try to use many different cultivation tips when talking to prospects. In looking for new premium customers, I might use our suite rentals as a gauge to determine a list of potential full season suite options. If they rented multiple games, I can approach them about looking at a full season or even a half-season package. Another thing I've done is find out who has suites at other venues in our market. The lease holders that we don't have can be contacted to gauge their interest in our suites. They already have a suite somewhere, so you know they are premium buyers. Word of mouth from our current suite holders is another tip that we've used recently. Another tip is finding interest from a potential customer through someone on our sales staff. They discuss advertising with the customer and premium options come up and we do follow up on those leads in conjunction with our sales staff person.

The best premium space we created is our *Home Plate Club* seats. These are two rows of seats between the dugouts that we added 12 years ago. We felt that our ballpark needed more premium seating options and this was a perfect fit. There are 88 of these seats, which are closer to the catcher than the pitcher is. The seats are larger, padded and come with waiter service. These seats are sold as season tickets at double the price of our regular season tickets. We do have some of these available on a nightly basis and are always the first seats sold. Nightly they are also sold at double our next highest priced ticket.

We tried a family friendly section one season that was alcohol-free and kid friendly which eliminated things like swearing with new rules in place. This section was a smaller section of seats all the way down the leftfield line. The majority of nights we didn't sell many seats in this section. It could have been the fact that it was in the leftfield corner or the *"no drinking allowed"* policy, but it was not a successful space that season. Our stadium is pretty family-friendly everywhere, so people don't necessarily need to be confined to one location. Some things work for premium and others don't. Family friendly didn't work as a form of premium buying for the Iowa Cubs, but we learned from it and moved on.

Face-to-face interactions are very important in premium sales. If we can get a potential buyer to the ballpark to see the space in person, the possibility of a sale goes up exponentially. Being able to speak to them in person and show them how the suite or premium area will look is huge. This goes for a nightly skybox suite rental or a full season lease. Seeing the ballpark with the green grass and the sun shining (*fingers crossed*) and the ambiance of the stadium will typically sway them to buy.

At the Iowa Cubs, we "*stage*" a suite if a potential buyer is coming to look with the intent of buying. We'll have peanuts, popcorn, hot dogs, soda, and beer on hand in the suite, with the stadium PA and TVs on with past games. This gives them a real feel on what it would be like if they want that premium experience. We had a company who talked like they were interested for a couple years on a full season suite, but we couldn't get them to come out to the ballpark. After a few years, we were able to finally get them to come down to look at an open suite. We had it all staged up and we finally closed that deal. Who doesn't like to have a hot dog and a beer at the ballpark? It is the little things that sell your premium.

Pain Points

One thing that really changes the conversation is the catering issue with premium. It is another issue that prospective clients don't talk enough about, and end up feeling cheated by their sales representative when they get that first catering bill. Premium doesn't always come with food. The catering bill definitely factors in when a decision is made to buy premium. I think it is even more important on a renewal since they will have a track record on the amount spent in this area for a full season. For a new customer, you can estimate or show them what it could possibly cost for the catering, but until they actually use the suite or premium space, it's hard to completely convey this.

Each customer seems to have somewhat different thoughts, so it's hard to really know what they are using the premium space for until they get in and start using. The catering in the premium areas is higher than the general concessions in the stadium, so we have to be very sure that these people are getting value for the higher money they are spending on *food/drinks*. We work closely with Centerplate, our food subcontractor, to ensure the quality of the *food/drinks* is high and the service they receive from servers is top notch. Most people aren't going to have an issue with the catering costs as long as we provide high quality food in large enough quantities and the service they receive goes above and beyond.

Sometimes, there is a possibility of a corporate sale poaching a premium sale, or vice versa. This becomes a factor when a corporate client leaves as a sponsor only to fill a suite. We've had one of our partners who was a corporate partner for a few years, switch to a half-season suite last year. We aren't a large operation, so we don't necessarily care which way they go, as long as we make the sale on one side or the other. If the poaching creates an opening on the corporate marketing side or premium side, we will work to fill that spot with a new potential customer.

Believe it or not, parking is probably the biggest issue we deal with at our facility when it comes to how fans interact with our venue. And that in itself becomes a premium asset that can be leveraged to gain new clients. We're a downtown ballpark and probably have half of the parking that we should for a ballpark of our size. We do try to cater to our premium customers by reserving space in our main parking lot closest to the stadium. Our full season lease suite holders, nightly suite renters and Home Plate Club season ticket holders all get this premium "*Skybox Parking*" area to utilize with a parking pass. There are nights where even this lot fills up and we have to adjust to take care of these premium guests. If inventory is small, it's valued more and thus, premium assets are born. Think about that the next time you look at a small, empty space that everyone wants to fill. It could be your next premium area waiting to be created and sold.

Is Your Service Worth A Damn?

At the Iowa Cubs, we monitor usage of our premium areas by homestand. If we see that someone isn't using their suite for a few nights, we will reach out to make sure everything is ok and see if there's anything we can do to keep them engaged and using their tickets. We try to touch base before each homestand and remind them of promotions that we have upcoming for the next few games. Most of them appreciate this information as they are busy too and don't always have time to check our promo schedule. Also, if we happen to get a rehab appearance from the big leagues, we can let them know that too. We just want to find ways to stay in touch with them without always trying to sell them something. Hopefully this will increase usage rates.

We also invite all of our premium ticket holders to our holiday party at the Cub Club in the offseason, as well as our Ticket Pickup Party in the spring. Both of these are great ways to see these people face-to-face and host them with food/drinks at the ballpark. We also drop off gifts for them around the holiday season. The service and touch-points should never stop with clients, prospective or current.

Everyone is a potential referral or renewal, and if they cancel with you, it's because they didn't feel involved or connected enough to continue the relationship.

Our catering is an asset that we maximize to our full advantage, starting with The Cub Club Restaurant, which handles the catering for the restaurant and all off-season catering in the leftfield suites and other events in the ballpark. Centerplate focuses on all of our concessions and all *suite/premium* catering during games. Doesn't matter if they are a subcontractor or not, the fans don't care. They see Iowa Cubs in every component of the service, so it has to be the best in order to supersede their expectations. We work very closely with both to make sure that our customers are well taken care of. If we need to customize the catering to accommodate a certain customer, we are usually able to come up with something to go above what they're looking for.

As a sales staff, we utilize the Cub Club Restaurant to host potential customers or even current customers. Whether it's for breakfast or lunch, it's a great spot to meet at the ballpark and discuss what we have to offer. With the view from leftfield overlooking the ballpark, it goes a long way to help close the deal. Our GM always tells us, if you can get a potential customer to come down to the ballpark and see it in person, your chances for a sale go way up.

Some of our off-season events in the ballpark that are hosted by the Cub Club do drive people to buy tickets and premium spaces from us. A lot of the people who have their wedding or reception, office meeting or Christmas party at the ballpark probably aren't all baseball fans. This can create a new segment of fans or buyers for us. After their event, some of them say they really like how it went and want to come back for a game. We had a couple get married at the ballpark last year and enjoyed it so much that they are bringing their entire wedding party back this summer, renting multiple skyboxes for their group. We also have a handful of companies every year who decide to rent a skybox for their office after hosting an offsite meeting at the Cub Club in the offseason.

Our Cub Club Restaurant is open year around every day for breakfast and lunch. We cater numerous meetings, parties, receptions or other functions during the offseason and during the season when the team is on the road. It is set up right next to our leftfield suite area, which consists of 12 adjoining suites. We advertise the restaurant and our catering options on the Iowa Cubs and Cub Club website, Facebook and Twitter. We attend a handful of wedding shows in the area to showcase what we have to offer at the ballpark. Word of mouth is also a big way of people hearing about events at the ballpark. The Cub Club Restaurant was just named the Best View in Iowa for a restaurant by MSN.[2]

Price isn't as big of a factor as quality service. Price is only a barrier when no one considers your service worth a damn. Whatever you are selling, if people feel the service is beyond the measure of price, they will go with service. But you have to get there. And you have to continue to over-service the account to the point where price is never the question. Way too many people try to react to the price of premium. But the service is what supersedes price when it is done well, especially when selling premium seating in minor league baseball. Service the premium account and they never focus on the price for a minute.

Retention Means Reinvestment

Jeff Eiseman
President
Augusta GreenJackets / Boise Hawks
Agon Sports & Entertainment

About The Author

Jeff Eiseman and his partners formed Agon Sports & Entertainment, owning and operating two MiLB franchises, Augusta GreenJackets and Boise Hawks, as well as two iconic music venues. Eiseman oversees business operations for the GreenJackets and Hawks. Prior to Agon, Eiseman was Executive Vice President of Ripken Baseball for over a decade, running the Aberdeen IronBirds and Charlotte Stone Crabs. Along with his tenure at Mandalay Sports Entertainment, where he rose from an account executive to Executive Vice President of the Las Vegas 51s, Eiseman has had the honor of being recognized with numerous awards such as, Executive of the Year honors, Larry MacPhail Promotional Award, John H. Johnson President's Trophy, Bob Freitas Award for Outstanding Minor League Operations, Baltimore's "Top 40 under 40" by the Baltimore Business Journal.

10 percent.

Whenever I heard this percentage point, for years, I would cringe. It doesn't matter if it was a discount on food or the public approval rating for the U.S. Congress. When I heard 10 percent, I thought back to August 1997, in Las Vegas, where I entered my boss' office excited about what we had done for our minor league baseball team, only to discover that he was really worried about the retention of our minor league hockey team. And hearing that our season ticket holder retention was in the toilet at 10 percent turned my stomach quick. All of the energy that I had invested in feeling the excitement of selling a ton of season and group tickets for the baseball team was gone. And suddenly, I was hockey focused for all of the wrong reasons.

While this experience was more than 20 years ago, I remember it vividly. I never have thought of myself as bordering on the perfection of being a great ticket sales person. I do not profess that I have the greatest ticketing mind that ever graced the sports marketing landscape. But as a newbie, I thought I had most of the principles down, enough to avoid mistakes. And that is what created my blind spot with renewals, as well as an innovating tactic of coding our season ticket holders before C.R.M. systems existed. It is important to realize that we all screw up. But what we learn from those screw ups allow us to transform our business models into something better.

The Stars baseball season had been very successful and my staff was feeling great as a unit. The week prior to sitting in my boss' office, I had been sent to a sports marketing conference in St. Louis by my team to brag about what successes we'd had in baseball, and to see the next industry best practices were available to bring back to my club. Feeling secure and confident, the devastating news of the 10 percent renewal rate hit me hard. I was humbled instantly. Disgusted in myself that my hubris had allowed something so fundamental to occur. Despite a whole spring and summer over speculation about the Thunder's future on the ice, I didn't expect a 10 percent renewal figure. It forced the entire organization to work harder, smarter and still be forced to accept we could not fully recover our renewal income in one season. But we had to try.

My boss, Bob Murphy, was a great mentor to me back in 1997. He may have been one of the best supervisors that I ever had. I owe him a great deal of gratitude for not only providing me with opportunities, some of which I failed at, but also being my sports industry therapist and friend who guided my learning experience. Bob would eventually take over the sister baseball franchise known as the Dayton Dragons, a franchise that broke the record of 815 consecutive sellouts in 2011, and after 18 years in the Midwest League, had 1,242 games sold out by the end of 2017 with no signs of that streak stopping.[1]

Bob could have easily chewed me out in his office. I probably would have deserved it given the situation. But there is a reason that Bob was a successful mentor. Even when I screwed up, he was there for me. Which is why the number of 10 percent still causes me to shiver. With a different boss, who knows what would have happened to my baseball career? It makes me think of what happened back then, how I felt, and what I did to create a better ticket renewal system where that situation would never happen again. Neither under my watch, or the watch of the employees that I would supervise later in my career.

Keep in mind, my first day at the Las Vegas Thunder was July 31, 1995. Within a few hours of starting, I held stacks of photocopied renewal invoices, told to call accounts to gain renewals. No direction, formal training nor understanding of pricing. I was handed a sales brochure, couldn't name one player on the squad, and hadn't toured the arena to even familiarize myself with the seating or sightlines.

In August 1997, I was positioned into a dual Ticket Sales Director role for the Las Vegas Stars (*Triple-A baseball*) and the Las Vegas Thunder (*International Hockey League... i.e. minor league hockey*). One was a good baseball franchise, the other was a struggling hockey operation that was always rumored to end a sad death annually. Though the two franchises were independent of each other in many ways, especially in winning, they both shared a staff. This meant focusing on both clubs simultaneously, as opposed to having a dedicated staff for either club. In theory, this dual oversight method had more advantages than simply a cost-saving move. In reality, there were many more drawbacks, including which franchise earned more attention at the more opportune selling times. Generally, that meant the baseball team, because more people flocked to minor league baseball in Las Vegas than they did minor league hockey.

There were always pros and cons to dual oversight. I don't believe that it was performed perfectly back in the 1990s between the Stars and Thunder. We definitely tried every year to learn and improve our processes. The biggest challenge was understanding that one team in that duality requires flat-out much more attention. And by providing that total focus to that one team, you do it an opportunity expense to the other.

The 1990s Las Vegas Sports Scene

So, being called into my boss' office, I was excited about the baseball season and group sales efforts that my staff had made. We had been driving a ton of revenue, obliterating our sales goals for baseball, and ended up failing our minor league hockey team outright. Summer is a critical period for minor league hockey teams, but 1997 was unique in how the community viewed the Las Vegas Thunder franchise altogether: No one knew if the team would exist or fold by October. The local media had multiple stories of lease negotiation issues with the arena, using the terms *"going dark," "relocation,"* or *"fold."* None of this made renewing season tickets or creating group nights appealing to folks unsure that the Thunder would honor their investment for the 1997-98 season.

The city of Las Vegas was not a sports-centric town in 1997. At least not on the Major League level that it is experiencing with the NHL's Golden Knights, the incoming NFL Raiders, or the other teams *"prospecting"* relocation to that city. The trouble with Las Vegas is that a third of the population is always asleep, which makes it hard to sell to. Frankly, the sports landscape of Las Vegas was a far cry from what it has become 20 years later, or what it has the potential of becoming 20 years from now. The belief that Las Vegas would be home to two major sports properties had the potential to have someone committed to an asylum. It wasn't going to happen in my lifetime, not in yours either.

The mid-1990s of Las Vegas was essentially the wild west of minor league sports. Las Vegas has always been electric, but back then, mega casinos were opening every few months, with a new towering the cityscape down *The Strip*. Over 10,000 new residents were arriving in the Las Vegas Valley every month, making it the fastest growing city in the world. Conversely, the city also served as a massive graveyard of failed sports franchises. The Canadian Football League's Las Vegas Posse[2] had collapsed in 1994, coupled with an indoor soccer team and an Arena Football League franchise named the String[3] in 1995.

The only survivors of this wasteland of professional sports were the Las Vegas Stars baseball team and the Las Vegas Thunder hockey team. Both of these teams were purely supported by local residents. Despite all of the delusions that there is tourist support for professional sports in Las Vegas, I've never witnessed evidence of it personally. People do not travel to Las Vegas to be entertained by sports that they could experience in their home communities. Tourists fill up Las Vegas because there are cheap hotel rooms, gaming and world-class entertainment. Most professional teams in other cities could throw up a new videoboard and earn a spike in attendance. Las Vegas' gas stations have videoboards in each island pump, along with The Strip's exploding volcanoes, multi-million dollar water displays and a giant pirate ship. Adding a videoboard to the world capital of entertainment wouldn't even make a dent.

The framework of how Las Vegas felt about Major League Sports back in 1997 is a great time capsule. But as much as they weren't thinking about getting the National Hockey League to the area, they certainly weren't focused top of mind on minor league hockey. Especially the Las Vegas Thunder, rumored to be leaving the area even if no one had noticed. Granted, I believe that it's hard to generate a discussion around the coldest sport on earth even with die-hard season ticket holders when the temperature sits at 110 Fahrenheit. I get that. But I cannot undersell the actual support for The Thunder in the community at various times. They did bring people out. At least, at the start of their franchise run.

Long Live The Thunder... For A While

When the team launched as a new hockey franchise in 1993, they were very popular. Las Vegas is about the shiny new toy. They are all about bright lights on a big stage. The Thunder's first season drew over 8,000 fans per game. The first three seasons were fantastic, all above 7,000 fans per game. Quite respectable for a non-traditional hockey market. This was also a passionate fan base in a non-traditional hockey market.

The club was successful on the ice, players were accessible and supported by their base. One of my first renewal calls in 1995 as a new employee was to a Thunder season ticket holder. He screamed at me because the squad had traded away his favorite player, hated the direction of the team and he would not be returning for the 1995-96 season. I wrote down all of that irate season ticket holder's complaints about the Thunder, promising to get back to him with answers to alleviate his concerns. After hanging up with him, I told the Thunder Assistant General Manager, Clint Malarchuk, what had occurred. Malarchuk taught me how to not give up on a renewal. He came back to the sales area, called the season ticket holder back, answering his questions. Malarchuk handed the phone back to me and within a minute, the customer was reading off his credit card information, satisfied at the direction of the team.

And Las Vegas for that three-year period, was hockey-nuts for the Las Vegas Thunder. Hockey fans are a passionate bunch, with a great affinity for their team. What Malarchuk's actions revealed to me was that everyone on the team was in this together; from player operations to business operations. And you didn't give up a renewal if you could help it. That mentality served us well during the original three-years of sold-out situations for Thunder Hockey games. Then, the 1997-98 season changed everything in a negative light for the squad. The shine of the new toy wore off for the city. And each season after 1996, the average fan attendance started to dip.

A Tale of Two Fan Bases

This brings the conversation of 10 percent back up. That's all we had in season ticket holders who had renewed from the 1996-97 season into the 1997-98 season. That's not even close to being credible. That's damn near extinction. Sitting in my boss's office and hearing that 10 percent renewal number, I thought it was going to get fired. Our ownership and senior management were all aware of the challenges that the Thunder had found themselves in 1997, specifically due to the rumors of *"going dark"* or *"relocation."* It creates a scenario where the front office had to decide whether we should accept defeat and kill the franchise, or dig in to continue fighting. Luckily, my boss chose the latter, and continued to employ me as the Director of Ticket Sales with a mission to fix the 10 percent problem.

There was very little cross over between the Stars and the Thunder in terms of fan base. Some of them did share sponsors, but I wouldn't declare the two fan bases as absolute polar opposites of each other. The hockey base were transplants from Chicago or Detroit. But we also earned a lot of business from non-hockey fans who were transplants wanting a good time. One of our biggest hockey fans was a Wal-Mart district manager who had transplanted to Las Vegas but had never seen or watched a game. Within a few home dates, he purchased season tickets and wore a jersey every time we saw him.

The Stars fans were mostly older or young families from the Las Vegas community who had been there for generations, enjoying the slow game of baseball while drinking a beer. One night during the long baseball season, while standing in the club level corridor looking out at the parking lot, I witnessed two elderly season ticket holders walking to their car. Both were in their 80s, but able-bodied, and held a deep love for the game of baseball. A foul ball from inside the stadium came rocketing back into the parking lot, and on a bounce, whacked the husband in the back of the head. The wife, without skipping a beat, showed zero concern for her husband, chased that foul ball down, and almost became a widow in the process. The way she ran after that ball, I felt she could serve as a pinch runner for the Stars at some of our upcoming home contests.

There was always a fiduciary pressure on the Thunder that the Stars never experienced. The Thunder average single game ticket prices were much higher, as were the season ticket prices, and hockey was an expansive season of 6-7 months while baseball was only five months long. The renewal process was generally harder for those hockey fans as we were knee-deep into renewals at the start of the summer when the outside temperatures climbed and no one thought about cold weather in Las Vegas. I have zero doubt that baseball took a back seat to hockey in our ticketing department, but that baseball essentially subsidized some of the lost benefits.

What the public didn't digest about the Thunder Hockey team was that, despite how well it drew in attendance and how well supported it was locally, the arena lease was onerous and made for an untenable business model. While I've always viewed Las Vegas as a successful city for the National Hockey League, even back into the 1990s, I thought the area could support one major sports franchise that would rule the valley. That team would become the darling of the area, much in the same way that the NHL's Golden Knights have. However, my theory also felt concern at seeing that the first Major Sports Franchise to bring Las Vegas success would bring the attention of a second Major Sports Franchise, and potentially a third. As this will be the case with the National Football League's Raiders relocation, and a potential Major League Soccer franchise, I fear that in time, the situation will create two struggling franchises instead of one very successful one. The duality in the 1990s with the Stars and Thunder caused the same effect as I believe the Golden Knights and Raiders will. They may end up killing each other in the process, leading to one franchise discovering a 10 percent renewal factor.

The differences in the economics between minor league hockey and minor league baseball do not end there. For affiliated baseball, the key difference is that the team controls the venue; allowing outside event rentals, the choice between self-operate or contracted-out food and beverage business, as well as earned parking revenue and advertising from signage. In addition, baseball teams do not carry the weight of player payroll. Minor league hockey and other arena sports share no such luxuries as their baseball cousins. In most cases, they are merely a tenant in the building, compete for dates on the arena operator's calendar, having no control over pourage rights (*i.e. beer*), do not control the majority of arena signage thus competing with the arena itself for sponsorship cultivation. Arena sports are limited to small commission percentages on food and beverage from a contracted company that serves the arena as a whole, and see zero money in parking revenue. And minor league hockey teams typically assume player payroll costs.

From a revenue perspective, minor league hockey teams are generally restricted to income from dasher boards, in-ice advertising or courtside signage for sponsorship and their ticket sales. Arena operators then feel torn between having guaranteed tenants for their home schedule against missing out on key concerts or events which may be much more lucrative to book. In 1997, The Thunder were locked into the worse lease deal in the entire International Hockey League. Their lease was so heavily against the team that it rivaled what some NBA arenas offered. To make matters worse, the arena operators always wanted more concessions from the Thunder to host games. The arena itself was looking at a major renovation and didn't want a team taking up more than 40 dates annually during that period. The renegotiation tactic started to sour Thunder owners, who looked elsewhere in the city, discovering no better terms available. A few years prior to the lease's expiration, the situation became public.

Thunder-Stuck

Back in 1997, my boss mentioned the 10 percent of season ticket holders renewed number to me with concern. What was worse, as well as inexcusable, was that I frankly had zero idea that our renewal number was so poor. It hit me that I didn't have anything to compare or measure 10 percent renewals against. I also didn't know what the forecast of the season ticket renewal final numbers would be since the start of the Thunder hockey season was less than two months away. Remember my boss saying "*10 percent*" became psychologically scarring to me. The words punched me in the gut because they were so crazy low. I felt a responsibility as the Director of Ticket Sales that I had been oblivious this entire time to how small our season ticket holder retention for the Thunder Hockey team was. I was complacent in a fundamental job responsibility but could offer zero excuse.

In the sports industry, the word "*leadership*" is tossed around quite casually. The same with "*mentorship*." Often, it is used by those who want to receive praise for how they supervise, without any of the hard work of leading. The term "*servant leadership*" often results in a boss taking credit for stopping to pick up a piece of garbage at his facility, but forgetting that he also earns 20 times what his account representatives make in order to feel responsible for picking up that trash. Mentorship should go beyond the narrative of personal phrase for oneself. It should be how you impact younger professionals who you are guiding during times of crisis. My boss did that for me in 1997, showing me the true definition of a leader and mentor.

Any other boss would have fired me on the spot. They would have been upset with me, ranted and raved, and promoted someone else in my position. Teachable moments only occur when we allow there to be avenues to continue to instruct a person through an issue. Otherwise, they are simply punishments dealt out. And few people learn from those mistakes as feel imprisoned by those results. To my boss's credit in 1997, he was not upset with me. There was no level of disgust, no measure of disappointment in my lacking knowledge around what our Thunder Hockey renewal percentage was. Leadership is about making your subordinates feel like they are teammates with a common goal. My boss made me feel like we were in this together, and he ended up asking for my advice as well as assistance, on how we could turn this 10 percent renewal issue around prior to the 1997-98 Thunder Hockey season.

That left less than two months' time to correct the issue. It was a challenge, but myself as well as my staff didn't find ourselves starting at *ground zero*. As my boss had done with me, I did not turn on my staff. I did not blame them for the low renewal numbers. Instead, we focused on how to build each other up together. Keep in mind, this staff had done a fantastic job selling baseball season and group plans. This staff was hungry and had a great attitude. If I had chosen to kill that, by protecting my own bruised ego after being exposed for not knowing that 10 percent number, it would have been hypocritical. Worse, it would have been counterproductive.

Our staff had not ignored the Thunder Hockey season ticket renewal drive completely. We weren't having success at renewing it, but we still had some focus on trying to move tickets. A great deal of the baseball side's attention was paid because we were in the heart of the baseball season when that 10 percent season renewal number came to light for the Thunder Hockey team. It was a self-inflicted wound that I still admit to, openly, because it helps me understand more about how quickly the sales cycle can change from a positive to a negative within a few short weeks.

The Las Vegas Stars baseball team always possessed a niche that the franchise benefited from by being a long-standing member of the Las Vegas community. The Las Vegas Thunder hockey team was a phenomenon since its inception, games equaling true events. The timing couldn't have been better in the early 1990s, as the

NCAA had slapped sanctions on UNLV men's basketball[3], toppling the *"king of the city"* enough that the Thunder was essentially the only winter game in town.

Because of the duality of the situation, my Director of Ticket Sales role was overwhelming. I refuse to sugar-coat it. While most teams dealt with one seasonal sport with a 3-5 month period off, there was no off-time for my staff or me. There were always renewals and new business to attend to. My confidence was shaken by hearing that 10 percent number said aloud by my boss. I was concerned that absorbing, as well as articulating the gravity of the situation would be lost to my staff the time that the 10 percent figure left my mouth. How would I display any confidence that our renewals would end up in positive percentage? I had no idea where to begin with getting our staff to that goal.

A key issue with the lack of confidence concerned best practices for the sports industry in the 1990s. Organizational ticketing structure was not as refined as it is today. In the 1990s, a Director of Ticket Operations would send out renewal invoices for season tickets to account holders, with a postage indicia, then wait for the returned payment from the account holder. Then, the Director of Ticket Operations would post the payment, sending the required updated invoice(s) for whatever balances remained due. Not only was this an industry norm for decades prior, but it was also time consuming and difficult to gain traction on turn-around. Periodically, box office staff would reach out to those lapsed accounts, the account holders who had not responded yet by letter. Or they would ask one of the sales managers to do so, if a call from the sales manager being initiated would result in a better relationship between the account holder and the team. Again, very time consuming, and it bogged down the process overall.

The 1990s Sports Sales Floor

In the first half of the 1990s, that was standard operating procedure for any professional team that existed throughout the country. Most teams did not hire a dedicated ticket sales staff who focused specifically on selling and renewing season ticket accounts. Back then, there was zero specialization. You sold and you serviced. The front office sales floor was full of young professionals who wore many hats, they were sales and operations. This was a recipe to bog down the process even more. Everyone was working, but not as efficiently as you would have hoped. Specialization has its benefits.

There is a gamesmanship to how teams actually showcased high renewal rates from their season ticket holder base during the 1990s: *The bases were very small.*

The majority of minor league teams had season ticket bases made up mostly of those people with an absolute affinity for the product. They weren't actively sought out by the organization to buy the season tickets. Instead, they came to teams and demanded that they purchase the season tickets. Teams simply obliged. Season tickets were viewed by the team as an annuity made up of residential accounts. Each of the season ticket holders had a die-hard passion for the product. Sponsors owned season tickets automatically because they were baked into the team agreement. There wasn't any reason to concern yourself with a renewal rate with those factors involved. No team ever expected 100 percent renewals, with enough new people actively inquiring to offset what was lost, that you were close to a stable average of 90 percent on an annual basis. And yet, we were at a 10 percent renewal rate in August 1997, less than two months before the puck dropped on the Thunder's season.

Sometimes, you become a pioneer for managing to screw up a sure thing. The Las Vegas Thunder had that title in August 1997 by not having a stable season ticket renewal base. Instead, we were so far down that it was frightening. Apparently, we resembled a slot machine, where the gambler had pulled the handle too many times, and now was way down to their last $2 on the nickel slots after being up by $200. There are things you can choose to remember about the past. I can recall the glory days with the best of them. But I remember this scarring, *punch-to-the-gut* moment of a 10 percent renewal most of all. And that's why I'm harping on it continually now. Whatever sears into your brain, that's something that either makes you or breaks you. I decided to not let it do the latter, and instead sought to figure out a way to develop it into the former.

Previous to learning that we were doing horribly in the Thunder season ticket renewal campaign, I had felt confident in our sales floor innovations. We had been very active since 1995 toward trying to redevelop our ticket staff beyond what the team norms across the American professional sports landscape were. We had a dedicated Ticket Sales Director, a Ticket Operations staff, and a few dedicated ticket sales account executives making outbound sales calls. All shoved into a boiler room operation, with the majority of part-time staff being retirees who initiated a massive telemarketing campaign for group tickets and flex book prospecting. Essentially, we called half of Las Vegas within five months, then the other half, then would touch base with everyone again throughout the remaining part of the year. This was a numbers game, and something we got really good at.

Senior Sales Rep Fight Club

The first day that I took over our Direct Marketing department, I had my administrative assistant get into a shoving match with a 75-year-old man, over my promotion to a manager title. I had only been in the office three hours with the new job title, left for lunch, came back to a full mutiny. My only crime was that I was a 26-year-old man with no management experience who had been appointed to this department to manage grown men, who were almost three times my age. I actually begged my boss to demote me back to an account executive title, but he insisted that I keep working through all of this.

A specific difficulty of managing the retirees was that I had a hard time relating to them. I also knew that there were thousands of college graduates trying to get their foot in the door for a paid gig working in sports who would gladly lead a retiree staff with real-world sales experience if I was unwilling. I knew the guys on the floor could sell, but it was my job to win them over to the fact that I belonged on the floor with them. I bought *Dunn & Bradsheet* lists and got access to an excel file of single-game buyers to prospect flex plans to. While there were scripts and call sheets, the older guys had honed their skills over a lifetime of experience. I marveled at how they moved off of instinct on calls, while the new younger reps all followed the script. It showcased that experience beats youth every time when making a sale.

I've never subscribed to the 100 phone calls per day model as the holy writ: *If you can make 100 phone calls a day, that's great, but what is the result?*

Quality calls are always going to be the name of the game. Anyone in this business long enough hears the magic number of 100 calls per day, but to me, that's meaningless. I can make 100 calls, but if I don't reach people, or have calls returned, I have nothing to show for it. The 100 calls per day mistakes volume for result. The law of averages say that if you make 100 phone calls a day, you will have 15-20 conversations that could put you on the path toward a sale. Everything ultimately starts with phone calls, e-mails or texts, but it is all to get face-to-face meetings. I don't recommend making 100 phone calls per day as a habit, unless you want to finish last in your department. Selling should never be a victim to busy work, but a part of accomplishing the task of setting appointments with leaders. I have told my sales people in the past that if they make 15 calls, get 15 meetings with the right people, then want to screw off on Facebook all day, then have at it. I encourage them to make the most mundane part of their job as easy as possible.

Some of this comes down to preaching on how to ask for referrals. A lot of our training has always gone into it. If you ask for referrals, 90 percent of the time you get them, and 90 percent of those referred will take the appointment if done properly. If you go on 10 meetings per week, asking each for a referral, there's 30 or more business leaders to call on. Each time, you have their cell phone or direct line, and you're being referred by one of their more important clients that they personally spend money with.

I have always found that face-to-face beats phone calls any day of the week. If you are selling anything over $1,000, it is imperative to go meet with the people directly. Even more important than face-to-face is the follow-up, because it shows you have a plan to reconvene with people, and allows for you to show how to go the extra mile for your customer. Few of our industry sales people understand how to take advantage of working smarter, not harder. And some of them have come from my own staff. That's how you get into a 10 percent renewal hole. Because you don't try to do the little things to get referrals for new business and renewals on current business. Make no mistake about this. The lesson that I learned with the 1997-98 Thunder hockey team was that renewals mattered. Beyond all else, they were easy business. And instead, I hadn't focused on them at all. That's why a 10 percent shocker woke me up to how important renewals could be. They also helped provoke new business, a fact that few people tend to recognize. The less season tickets that you have available due to renewals, the more opportunities for new business to see that others have invested in the sports product, and so should they. The 1997-98 Thunder hockey debacle taught me never to ignore renewals again.

Group Sales?

Beyond season tickets, we didn't look down on group sales because we saw the value in them, but we may not have been smart enough to unlock the mysteries of group selling. We did have a senior executive upset with our progress on group sales for the Thunder at that time, feeling that the bar was set too low. We ended up hiring a group sales *wunderkind* who had been crushing it everywhere they had been, setting sales records and recommended by everyone in the business. This group salesperson was machine-like, heavy on the phone, no nonsense or slack off time, and was given latitude to do their job however they felt served best. At the end of the day, I found that while they were a fine hire, it was no different than having two group sales reps on staff, which didn't equal much of a dent in the revenue hole that the 10 percent renewal rate had given us at the Thunder.

Selling season tickets was more effective at generating revenue, which was why we invested a heavier amount of resources in that practice. It didn't mean we ignored or cared less for group sales, but it depends on how big the hole is that you have. What I have found is that adding more sales representatives at group sales does not equal more group selling. Sometimes two plus two does not equal four in group sales, because there are only so many groups out there to cultivate. The 1990s groups also did not offer as many options, especially due to technology, that are available to teams today. Venues have been designed now with groups specifically in mind, where in the 1990s, you did what you could with a cookie-cutter venue layout that didn't think of groups at all. There are some accounts that will simply die and need to be written off. However, the odds of success at renewing are always much better than that of seeking out new business.

This is a challenge that every general manager has to position themselves toward overcoming: *How does the team generate a greater chance of renewing business?*

This isn't a once a year challenge either. Consider it to be a continual obstacle that a general manager must overcome to improve their renewal opportunities. General managers of teams must be relentless at renewal business. It means asking the season ticket representatives to pull as hard as they can on the rope every day, week, month throughout the year to get those accounts to renew. While 80 percent is a good average, there should always be a mentality of trying to gain a higher renewal percentage. Let's see what it feels like to get 85 percent or 91 percent of accounts renewed.

Our account executives had been tasked with initially seeking out new business, renewing existing accounts whenever possible. But we did not make renewals our priority. Our staffing model and organizational philosophies for the front office sales floor evolved from 1995 to 1997. Except that we kept the duality roles, which bogged down responsibilities to where we were serving two masters in the Stars baseball team and the Thunder hockey team, instead of one. By 1997, we still had a dedicated Ticket Sales Director, who was managing anywhere from 10-12 full-time dedicated ticket sales account executives. In addition, we had a dedicated Ticket Operations Director, and a Ticket Operations Manager, who along with an in-house telemarketing boiler room setup, made a metric ton of outbound phone calls using a database leads system of individual buyers. We offered them smaller ticket packages and flex ticket plans, instead of trying to go for the massive commitment jugular of a season ticket.

Our 10-12 account executives had their roles split into season ticket representatives and group sales representatives. They didn't go full menu, sticking to what they did best, but we were top-heavy with 70 percent of them being season ticket representatives to 30 percent of them being group sales representatives. I realize that this generally bucks a conventional wisdom trend that most minor league teams follow today, whereas the majority of emphasis for team account representatives is to sell group tickets. Or they are almost absolutely group-focused with barely any season ticket sales coverage. Most clubs do not know how to obtain, nor cultivate new season ticket business. Investing in staff resources focused on new season ticket business is viewed as wasting resources.

Our innovative approach was the mirror opposite, but we had a difficult time finding the right people who could fit our season ticket sales culture. I always encourage season ticket representatives to make a ton of meaningful contact with their book of business. That doesn't mean simply having them call to say "*hi*," but also to share useful team news. Sometimes before the news media even has an opportunity to write about it.

In this age of digital, when a season ticket representative is allowed to spread the word first to those who invest in our product as account holders, it becomes impactful: *Why let every reader know the latest trade or coaching news before the general public gets to consume it?*

General managers should dole out all of this positive team news first to their season ticket representatives, allowing an engagement of multiple touch points with our account holders monthly, whether in-season or off-season. This avoids calling account holders only at times when the team is seeking payment or sell them on another product. Touch points are also personal seat visits in-season, and phone calls. Sometimes, e-mail and text, though those can be viewed as impersonal to older account holders.

Season ticket representatives should be put in a position of success, but so should the team's sales floor as a whole. Your staff should be seeking out report cards from their clients. Not simply earning praise. Learn what the team did that wasn't viewed as a positive in order to repair the issue for the following season. Earning complete praise is a waste. Your season ticket representatives should want to understand how their clients perceive their ticket usage. If that usage is falling down, or a pattern emerges that shows those clients are not attending as many games over the season, the season ticket representative needs to start engaging, offering solutions.

All of these negative signs of ticket usage are the easiest ways to see an account about to fall off the renewal cliff. If general managers monitor these types of data points, it is easy to determine with a high degree of accuracy which accounts are about to die or go dark. It is also easier to determine where the team's renewal rate should stand for the upcoming season long before the current season is finished. These problem accounts should also be flagged so that solutions can be put in place by the season ticket representative by the mid-point of the season, and to avoid a non-renewal to be passively shrugged off by the end of the season.

What is usually forgotten when setting up a sales culture is how sales representatives inherit their book of business on renewals through co-worker attrition. Someone leaves, the book of business goes to another person in the office to renew, and this practice leaves a lot to be desired. Teams suffer from the issue of distributive equality in how sales representatives are handed these accounts. This is not a practice that I subscribe to. I believe there should be a strategic approach toward any book of business distribution. A general manager's goal should be attaining the highest renewal percentage possible, without considering the feelings of those on the sales floor. Whether a new season ticket sales representative has sold prior, or demonstrated a skill set for successful relationship building, doesn't matter. Nor does the *"fairness"* of trying to give out plumb accounts that are a 100 percent renewal guarantee, or house accounts, in order to build up the confidence of a season ticket sales representative who is having a bad year. This is about those who drive the most sales getting the best opportunities to drive more business for the team.

New business is frankly more difficult to bring in as well as more expensive to cultivate. Too often, teams spend way too much time preaching about new business while forsaking the existing renewal business available. When a $2,000 renewal account refuses or does not return back calls, e-mails or letters, teams often give up on that account, writing it off to go after new business.

This begs the question of whether or not the team valued the existing season ticket holder's business in the first place: *Why don't teams focus on working harder for those account holders who they already know have purchased the product in the past?*

Especially when they know where the venue is and that they generally like us. Often, this common sense reasoning does not illustrate itself with front office sales floors. The account is simply considered canceled, and new business is sought out. When a team does this, they are harming revenue generation overall. The sales team is challenged to go out, bring in a new $2,000 account to replace the renewal that they lost, putting the profit margin at net zero.

Had the team managed to renew the account, or worked to see the account holder relationship rebuilt, they would have seen instant growth with a new sale, versus simply a replacement sale. There is a philosophy that we held to back in the 1990s. It is something that I still operate with today as my organizations go forward in selling sports. It *starts* with math, *ends* with belief.

Here is the example that I use for my baseball teams:

Assumption No. 1: A group of 250 tickets to one company at $7 per ticket will yield $1,750 in gross revenue.

Assumption No. 2: Four full season tickets will yield $500 each, consisting of 70 games = $2,000 in gross revenue, and 280 tickets cleared at $7.14 per ticket.

So, the challenge is to figure out which is easier to sell: *A group of 250 tickets, or four season ticket plans?*

This is where sports sales philosophy differs. The majority of clubs would disagree with my assessment in both *assumptions*. They would position the argument to say that, absolutely, it is easier to find a company or non-profit to purchase 250 group tickets, than it is to find a company willing to buy four full-season ticket plans. That is their belief system. They are welcome to it. However, my belief system differs. I say, go big or go home. Focus on the season seat plans. I am not against group ticket sales. But having a dedicated season seat representative who can set 8-12 outbound face-to-face meetings weekly with local business owners is worth it. This allows a cultivation of character, where the team's brand is showcased through a business program where the owner can actually generate revenue for their company by utilizing season tickets. It creates a clear desirability for the owner to earn a return on their nominal investment. This model has worked for decades, but it requires a stronger intestinal fortitude and dogged perseverance than most front offices are willing to undertake. Hence, the group ticket sales model gains privilege over its season ticket counterpart.

Staffing does become an issue when a front office decides to go with the season ticket over group ticket sales approach. It is a struggle and should not be viewed as an instant cure-all. The organization has to commit resources, as well as approach staffing with a different mentality. So many front offices tend to hire in bulk. They put inexperienced sales managers in charge, who in turn do not hire the best sales people. The law of averages yield out that if you do not know what you are looking for in terms of success and red flags during a hire, the less likely you will be to discover a diamond in the rough. Instead, you will find a bad, toxic employee who will not perform in the role.

I do not know which is a worse employee to hire. The person who performs who is a bad co-worker who makes everyone else in the front office feel miserable, or the person who is pretty nice, but still can't sell worth a damn. Both scenarios cause stress on your good employees who are working hard, thus causing an exodus to begin. Inexperienced managers only exacerbate the issue by not recognizing the change in office culture, therefore they do not respond to it quick enough to turn the negativity brewing around. Lessons have been learned over the years, one of the top teaching experiences for me has been that great salespeople do not always make great sales managers. It takes 2-3 years to get a sales manager to a level that a general manager can have real confidence in. Unfortunately, experienced senior ticket directors are in short supply, great demand, and right when they should be paying dividends to the team that cultivated their talent, they are recruited away for a more lucrative gig.

It does bother me that most teams do not have any clue on how to develop a sales manager. The majority of front offices use acquisition over development as their employee principle, recruiting away someone else's staff. Some of this comes from fear of a wrong sales manager being promoted internally, who ends up derailing your season or costing the general manager their job. That has to be taken into account when considering who will be reporting to this manager, what dynamic exists between the sales manager and staff, along with the risks felt if there is a negative fallout from this internal promotion. That's why most front offices hire away other team's staff, to avoid the risks by hiring what they consider an almost sure thing.

I view promoting sales managers akin to a "*Jedi Order*" relationship, where there is a teacher-student aspect, with the student eventually becoming a teacher in their own right to new students. You have to grow your sales manager, and they in turn have to do the same with those that they are training. The "*next in line*" should never be seen as a threat to the sales manager, but a confidant and trusted individual who displays leadership skills. They should be learning, growing, but with their own individual goals to build a successful team together. No one wants to be the understudy forever, and the young professionals of today have less patience. The hope is always that the "*next in line*" will be ready to assume the role and responsibilities if someone else transitions out. But that all comes down to whether you trained them correctly. Not just on their job, but also who they hire. If they are trained incorrectly, they will start hiring bad employees underneath them, which is both an opportunity and economic cost to the organization as a whole.

There are near worse case scenarios for the front office itself when considering how much a bad employee costs an organization when calculating out in a straight-forward manner:
Assumption No. 3: A new sales hire with benefits, payroll taxes, and on-board in-house training will cost an organization $30,000 fully-loaded.

Assumption No. 4: A new sales hire has worked for 90 days for a team. They have only shown one $2,000 sale. During this period of time, that sales hire has cost the organization over $7,500, thereby creating a cost of $5,500 that will never be made back from those lost 90 days.

Assumption No. 4 would be a painful experience to go through. However, you cannot expect to make a full return on employee investment in one year with the enormous weight of a failed hire. This will happen, but you can actually recoup your investment if you play the long-game. It requires turning that $2,000 sale into an annuity by season four. By then, that horrifically failed hire has gone long into the wind, but now, that season ticket has yielded a return of $500.

Despite taking a few years' time to generate, even some of the worst hires end up paying for themselves if they leave and you keep renewing whatever few clients that they managed to secure. The long-game play is that your team will develop a further relationship with the account holder after the horrible hire has been terminated or "*self-selected out,*" thereby renewing them over a period of years until it does become a sizeable return on investment. This also provides a chance for your team to show that business through your season ticket program that their investment will yield dividends long after that nightmare sales staff member is a faint memory.

The best way to avoid this scenario of picking up the pieces and trying for the long-game of a 3-4 year recovery return on your employee investment is to hire better employees from the start. This is not as easy as it sounds. It is harder, daily, as generational choices change, as do options. There are some people who won't work for a base plus commission salary anymore. Others who will do exactly that, as long as it comes with an inflated job title that would have taken someone else years to get promoted into. Even the most experienced recruiter cannot guarantee success on this front. It is all a crap-shoot with who you get and why.

Once you hire your sales representative, the task of on-boarding them properly begins. Proper training techniques, mechanisms of sales process and training are imperative to even the best new recruit's longevity with your organization. A lot of young professionals who are shining stars end up flaming out because the organization let them down by not on-boarding them properly. It is important to also clarify that I want to manage expectations of both them and you in this dynamic. They need to know where you stand, what you will tolerate in terms of sales and professionalism benchmarks, along with what is important compared to what isn't a big deal at all. You cannot expect sales to generate immediately from this new hire, but you should always expect them to do the little things that lead the prospect down the sales process. That is why on-boarding becomes so crucial for any organization moving forward with their new hiring.

Jokingly, I have referred to myself as the *"Ticket Doctor"* as I can instinctively diagnose where a season ticket sales hire was going wrong. In reality, it was more deductive reasoning that helped me make sound assessments of these employees. After a while, I built an illustrated checklist around learning where a season ticket sales person goes wrong and screws up their sales process altogether. A simple numbers game of developing enough sales calls, hitting the right appointments, and closing the prospect are all the entire formulaic background required for my checklist to work for any *"Ticket Doctor"* working for a team with a staff sales issue.

Eiseman "Ticket Doctor" Tool

Scenario No. 1: Rep has 10-12 meetings, but isn't earning a sale.

Question: *Does the rep meet with the decision-maker?*

- **Implementation:** Listen to the rep's sales presentation. Pay attention to their closing techniques. Listen for not only content, but delivery style.

Scenario No. 2: Rep is only earning 4-6 (or less) face-to-face meetings per week.

Question: *How many calls are they making per day?*

- **Immediate Assessment:** They are not making enough calls.

- **Implementation:** Have the rep make their calls during off-peak hours, such as early mornings, to reach decision-makers.

Scenario No. 3: Rep makes hundred-plus calls per day, but cannot earn face-to-face meetings with decision-makers.

- **Immediate Assessment:** Look at the call list that the rep is using. Has the list been over-cycled, do they have the proper type of businesses (focused on business to business, not retail or non-profit). Examine if a new list is needed, or should be purchased.

- **Secondary Assessment:** Diagnose if rep is having difficulty getting past gatekeeper or failing to speak effectively to a decision-maker.

- **Implementation:** Sit down with the rep, listen to their sales presentation, offer up solutions, and train on how they can improve their ability to get face-to-face appointments with decision-makers. Reward your rep when they are seeking referrals from your existing appointment base in order to encourage them to keep selling and prevent discouragement.

What A Rep Is Worth

Everything within earning a face-to-face appointment is about generating opportunity. The more opportunities to pitch a sales presentation to a decision-maker, the greater likelihood of success in selling the sports product. This is not a business to where you can gain 100 percent clearance of every face-to-face meeting you get with a decision-maker. Even if you are successful 10 percent of the time, there is some value in the volume of face-to-face meetings that you get. A season ticket representative earning 10 face-to-face meetings per week in a 35-week selling season generates 350 appointments. Figure that each close is worth four season tickets at $500 per seat, equaling $2,000 per close. At a 10 percent close rate, that's 35 closes per selling season, which generates $70,000 in new business per season.

The first year payoff of this calculation is straight-forward when hiring a $30,000 sales representative costing the team benefits, salary, commission and payroll taxes. The gross profit by having that sales rep generate $70,000 against their $30,000 salary means a $40,000 gross profit in new business. By renewing that $70,000 year one business in year two at an 80 percent rate, that same season ticket representative is retaining $56,000 of that business, while producing another $70,000 in new business. That combines for $126,000 in total business generated for the team in year two, with the employee earning an additional $10k in commissions, making their cost to the team only $40,000. This means that by year two, your total investment over two years of $70,000 in employee costs for a season ticket representative has yielded $196,000 (*counting new business and renewals*). That's a $126,000 gross profit, with a healthy 64 percent profit margin.

That is only in two years. Let's look at year three, where the sales rep produces another $70,000 in new business, renewing 80 percent of their book of business from the first two years of sales, which is $100,800 of that $126,000 available. That means they have generated $196,000 in renewals plus the $70,000 in new, year three business. This also assumes that the season ticket representative is getting no better or improving their skills during this three-year period either. At this time, they will cost $50,000 fully loaded (assuming a $10k commission improvement for renewals) by year three, equaling $146,000 in total gross cost to the team. In those three years, the team will have paid out $120,000 in salary, benefits, commissions and taxes for their sales representative. And that sales representative will have brought the team back $342,000 in new business over those three years, renewed that business at 80 percent annually. That earns the team a 65 percent profit margin by initiating the original team investment in a season ticket sales representative that only achieves a 10 percent closing average.

The problem of the 1990s or maybe the lesson of it, was that teams messed around with every type of commission plan. When I started in 1995, the team paid zero in renewal commissions. It was expected as part of our job. You found the time, you did the renewal, and then you hunted for new business, which was a 5 percent commission. Within a year or two, we focused on a 4 percent commission on new and renewal business. It also factored into who we hired. In 1996-97, we interviewed those who wanted to work in sports, but more sports marketing or public relations. In 20 years, the young professionals haven't changed much except that Gen-X hires were more amenable selling. Despite bitching, moaning and slacking a lot, they had an aptitude toward selling that was demonstrated in their acumen. I have had solid millennials hired onto my staff in the past decade. The biggest factor is that they often want their parents involved in the process. We had a few who brought their parents to the interview, asking them to sit in, which was a giant red flag that never allowed them past our interview process. There are a lot of young professionals now who have no real "*adulting*" skills when it comes to meeting in a professional setting. My impression with millennials is that they aren't motivated solely by money. They want recognition, opportunity for advancement. They will take less money to have a job they think will be more enjoyable even if it's not conducive to their personal style.

We have augmented our sales presentation over the decades to allow the young professional in front of us to find their voice. It works better than being scripted to a "*T*" but the whole industry has started to become more sophisticated, which helps with the overall process. With so many opportunities available in the industry today that were not there 10-20 years ago as new teams crop up out of nowhere, millennials see that there are always new sales positions available elsewhere. They seem to try to by-pass the internal promotion process for something that they think is more glamorous. By doing so, they have caused teams to react, by promoting people internally at a quicker pace to keep them, which means pushing up inexperienced sales managers who are not ready to supervise, but have the title to do so.

Unfortunately, supervisors below general managers do not view their tenure with a team as a part of ownership. Also, there isn't an initial feeling of accountability toward meeting the budget as well as the fiscal cost to the organization itself. Once sales managers are brought into the fold and upper management opens up the "*komodo,*" that ownership aspect begins as the general manager is provided with a world-view change. In order for a sales manager to feel like an owner or trusted member of management, they have to be taught what it is like to run a business. That means reading a balance sheet, understanding a profit & loss statement, as well as being engaged and involved in the budget process. This isn't about showing or exposing salaries, but everything else, allowing transparency to your sales managers. Too often, general managers make the mistake of bottlenecking information, controlling it and only allowing a select few to be privy to the real numbers. This is a recipe for disaster. You cannot expect sales managers to feel like a general manager, or feel some accountability to what they spend in hiring, if they do not understand the "*why*" or the impact on their department when concerning the fiscal bottom line of the organization.

None of the safeguards, nor renewal mentality, were in place in August 1997. Until I heard the 10 percent renewal number come from my boss, Bob Murphy, I hadn't created that type of system to ensure such a low renewal number. The genesis of how I've viewed renewals over the last twenty years is summed up in a panic mode of hearing the 10 percent number and responding to it with the old proverb: "*necessity is the mother of invention.*" Translated into my situation, it meant, my creative efforts were needed to solve the 10 percent renewal issue before I found myself unemployed or the team going belly-up with an empty arena midway through the 1997-98 Thunder hockey season.

Looking back at the main issue, I faced a dynamic problem that is common in the sports industry. There are always going to be points in selling sports where we are totally unprepared for the result. And mainly, that's on us, for sticking to the methods that used to work in the past. Clearly, those methods used in the 1980s were no longer relevant in the 1990s and needed to be updated.

The same can be said for 20 years later, which showcases that we must keep innovating, adapting and improving our methods in order to ensure that we are not swept under by a shocking issue such as a terrible renewal number that hits us shortly before the upcoming season. My challenge in August 1997 was that I had to get my hands figuratively around our current problem, but it did not stop there. I had to start learning how to project with confidence where our renewals would ultimately end up, not simply for this season, but for all seasons that followed.

Reworking The Renewal Process

My solution was not staring at an excel database of our customers in August 1997. Seeing hundreds of fields with customer names, addresses and phone numbers did not tell me a story. It gave me a headache and forced me to look away from the screen. I was forced to re-examine our entire sales method of how we looked at renewing accounts. Up until my near-nervous breakdown of hearing that 10 percent figure, our season ticket representatives were provided with photocopies of account invoices that they were told to renew. The invoices offered all of the pertinent information, and allowed for representatives to scribble notes all over the paper whenever they called or spoke to the client. Sometimes, these meetings generated 10 minutes or an hour worth of commitment from each representative. Although I was given *"data"* on all of these accounts from my representatives, it served more as white noise than actual productive data that I could glean in order to make a holistic decision on what we needed. The notes were long, sometimes incomprehensible, and felt as if they were pieces of a jumbled picture in a one-page snapshot.

My colleagues at other front offices shared the same issue: *It was something that they had no handle on either.*

I was stunned to talk to industry professionals, discovering that I had tapped into their worst fear. I was skeptical at first to broach the subject with my industry colleagues, figuring that I was an idiot for not managing renewals better. Turns out, the minor league professional sports model during the late 1990s to early 2000s had no way of fixing this issue. No one knew how to accurately project season ticket renewals in their current state. It was actually a simple fix, which meant that the solution was ignored as being too obvious. The solution to calculating a proper renewal percentage was, in fact, coding a letter or number to each renewal account. *Coding?* No, I am not referring to writing a computer program, nor am I suggesting that you have to create an algorithm. Simplistic coding merely offers a general manager the best way to look at every account in a holistic, global manner. Each letter and number offers up a category and key for the account it is assigned to. And it made the process easier to quantify when sorting through a massive excel file to break up accounts in a manner that allowed opportunities to see where we truly were with renewals so we could plan accordingly. Each code offered up such magic as *"will renew," "relocated out of town," "left voicemail/message,"* or even *"husband died, wife hates hockey."* I had absolutely zero resistance from the ticket representatives when implementing the coding system as it transformed our weekly one-on-ones into a more effective use of time.

The basic principle of the coding was to provide context, but also to avoid mindless hours wasted trying to renew accounts that were never going to buy again in the first place. Over the years, this system has evolved. The lettering system itself started off with *"A"* and ran through *"F,"* with each letter standing for its own category. Over time, my managers improved the redundancies, simplifying it with their own small innovations. Today, some of the letters in between A-F, such as *"C"* or *"D,"* have zero meaning with their assigned value in relevant coding combined in other letters.

A	CANCELLED/CANCELLING
A1	Died/Moved Out of State/Went of Business
A2	Doesn't Want to Spend/Have Money
A3	Time Issues/Schedule
A4	Team Management/Issues
A5	Didn't Use Tickets
A8	Sent In Cancellation Form
A9	Family Reasons
A10	New Management/Ownership Contact
A11	Bad Seats/Location/Fans/Ushers
F	RENEWING
F1	Paid In Full
F2	Renewed/Paid In Full
F3	Renewed/Made A Deposit/Payment
F4	Will Renew
F5	Should Renew
F6	Renewing/Upgrading
F7	Renewing/Downgrading
F8	Paid/Downgraded
F9	Renewing On Some Level/Talking To Others
F10	Paid/Upgraded

Coding jokes did spring out of this innovation: *"Did you hear about Bill Smith? He went A1 last week."* Code speak meant that he had passed away. The letter *"A"* represented *"cancelled"* or *"cancelling the number"* of season tickets. The number after the corresponding letter tells the story of why. For instance, *"A2"* meant that the person was cancelling their season tickets because *"didn't want to spend the money or didn't have the money to spend."* This allowed me enough context to understand the issue at hand. If I was asked by my boss, Bob Murphy, about how many accounts were not renewing at any point prior to the season, I could rattle off the number, providing him with a coherent answer on exactly why, as well as how much business, was at risk if we didn't find solutions.

B	LEFT MESSAGE(S)/NO ANSWER
B1	No Answer/Can't Get Ahold Of
B2	Left A Message On Voicemail
B3	Left Message With Family/Co-Worker
B4	Wrong Number/Phone Number Not In Service
B5	Left Message Via E-Mail
B6	No Longer Lives/Works There, New Contact
B7	Call Back
B8	Can't Find New Number
B9	Out of Town
B10	No Attempt Made

E	DECIDING
E1	Not Sure/Money Issues
E2	Not Sure/Time Issues
E3	May Downgrade
E4	Not Sure/Have To Talk It Over With Others
E5	Not Sure/Team Management/Performance/Personnel
E6	Not Sure/Family Reasons
E7	Not Sure/New Management/Ownership/Contact
E8	No Reason Given or Necessary
E9	Not Sure/Might Be Moving
E10	Not Sure/Hates The Seats

With the advent of deeper analytical customer relation manager (CRM) systems, coupled with sophisticated ticketing systems, the organizations that I've worked for have developed customized crystal reports that provide us with a breakdown of where each past season's accounts stand. It helps us gauge renewals in real time, not merely at a weekly interval when the Director of Ticket Sales has updated a spreadsheet after speaking with each representative. It also removes the anecdotal side of the sports sales, where *"everyone is having great calls"* yet no one is actually renewing. Now, a Director of Ticket Sales knows the reasons given in the conversation, and whether there is even a likelihood of renewing at all.

Coding these accounts created a simplification of the entire renewal process. General managers that have used this coding system have felt it is handy in strategizing what is required to win over some accounts deemed lost, as well as target a specific code to focus on. Each year, we will discover that a certain percentage won't renew because they did not use the tickets that they purchased (*A5*). By knowing this in the middle of the current season, there is little shock when they do not renew. This also puts the onus on ticket representatives to be hyper aware of ticket usage by their season ticket holders throughout the season, helping ensure that it is not news in the middle of a renewal campaign. By seeing this, our ticket representatives should be throwing themselves into action, making efforts to address the issue with their *A5* season ticket holders, showing them how to best utilize their season tickets, even if they cannot make it themselves to the games.

Sometimes, the customer will use this type of *A5* excuse as a reason to non-renew, and the coding system helps us verify against it. If a season ticket holder tells a representative that they did not renew because they didn't use the tickets, but the ticket system shows 70 percent of the game tickets were *"scanned in"* thus utilized, then it tells the team a different story. Utilization may not be the real issue at all. And that is when it becomes imperative that the ticket representative then reach back out to the account holder to dig down a little deeper, not accepting the non-renewal at face value.

The season ticket holder may have been providing those tickets to business clients, instead of using those tickets themselves. And the business clients may have provided the season ticket holder with zero feedback to whether to keep the tickets themselves. Internally, a general manager should be discussing and brainstorming with their ticket sales representative on ways to solve these type of issues. The questions should center around what our team can do to help our account holder receive feedback from their business clients using those tickets. It was also highly encouraged for our season ticket holders to develop more than one contact with our team. Nothing is static in our business, so it improved the odds of renewing those season ticket holders if they met as many of our staff members as possible.

Solutions may include seat visits to greet the client. Or placing the client on the videoboard strategically during one of the crowd shots, taking the still image, or having the client participate in half inning promotions. If the clients bring their children to games, it may require providing the kids with a unique experience such as running around the bases. These *"Kodak Moments"* should be captured by the team, e-mailed by the ticket representative to the account holder, so that the account holder has another personalized touch point with a prospective client thus providing a bonafide reason to call them. When an *A5* happens, it is important for the general manager and their staff to hedge on the likelihood of saving the account by ensuring drilling deeper down on issues, rather than letting it become a dead account that cannot be saved. This is about getting someone on a path toward non-renewal into a state of supporting the team for years to come.

Each code also offers up its own marketing solution, provided that a general manager is willing to put forth the time, energy and effort to solve the problem listed. The majority of professional sports teams discount the value of an existing season ticket holder. Under appreciated existing accounts are treated less important than new accounts. This is a result of the law of unintended consequences, where we have our season ticket account representatives spending a great deal of time prospecting, meeting and selling new business. Several clubs have generated a disparity in how they reward their ticket representatives, paying nothing in commission or less than nothing, when it comes to renewal business. Instead, teams focus all of the commission incentives toward new business. It does not take a rocket scientist or a ticket sales representative motivated by money to figure out whether seeking out new business will win over renewing business, when one has a commission benefit and the other clearly does not.

All accounts should be equal when it comes to rewarding behavior. Renewals should also be viewed as having potentially higher commissions earned by ticket representatives over new business, because the likelihood of renewing generating lifelong fans is so much easier and greater. However, my personal instinct is to make both renewal and new business sales identical. The goal is to instill an easier pathway for your ticket representatives to make money by taking care of existing business or finding the replacement new business through cultivation. New business is as equally important, not more or less, than existing business.

The in-season sales process for ticket representatives should be spent developing and cementing relationships. It is about delivering on promises, laying out foundations of growth. If you have a season ticket base that equates to $1,000,000, renewing at 80 percent, that leaves you with $200,000 in new business sold to get back to your previous year's benchmark. Many minor league front offices would see that $200,000 as a daunting number. To them, replacing $200,000 in season ticket revenue may not only be viewed as challenging, but also impossible to achieve. In most cases, I might agree with that assessment. That assumes that an average season ticket is $400, thus meaning that team would need to replace 500 full season tickets or equivalents via mini-packs, which is no small order.

Applying The Model

Many general managers do not want the financial responsibility, nor the headache, of season tickets. That's why the weight of their advanced sales goals are pushed onto group sales, with the season ticket portion of their budget reflecting minimal or flat increases. They view their season ticket base as a core that has stuck around forever and can be counted on renewing with minimal effort. This base was typically much larger in one point of time, but through attrition, only a hardcore base remains. This existing base, diminished from its largess of the past, generally renews now at a 90-95 percent range, and whatever doesn't renew is made up by the occasional call or walk-in buyer who replaces the 5-10 percent that left the year prior.

Senior management and ownership typically do not challenge this model or mindset by a general manager. It is viewed as a conservative method, as well as a general revenue model that clubs have operated under for years. It is accepted practice throughout minor league sports and I do not believe it will change despite my arguments printed in this text. However, my method of coding and renewal focus actually creates further ticket representative and general manager accountability. It requires dedicated people with the financial resources and a commitment toward managing the entire process.

The model that I put on myself as well as any team that I work with can generate $100,000 or more in new business annually in addition to growing a once-stagnant season ticket base. A team that has a $400,000 season ticket base should be expected to renew at 90 percent, leaving that the renewal base in season No. 1 at $360,000. The team should also anticipate a $100,000 to $150,000 increase in new business, taking the club from $400,000 to $460,000, or possibly, even $510,000, in a single year. Few teams can generate such increases of sales growth at a 20 percent clip. Not even teams that calculate out a 20 percent growth in group sales annually achieve what I am proposing in new and renewal season ticket business.

That $510,000 figure in year No. 1 becomes larger in year No. 2. A $459,000 renewal off of a $510,000 original base, adding $125,000 in new sales, brings the season ticket base to $584,000 by the end of the second year. In two off-seasons, the season ticket base has been increased by nearly 50 percent. Naturally, the ability to replace lost renewal dollars with new business becomes a zero-sum game, but that ultimately is a good problem to have. When that occurs, your group sales business can be ramped up to strike a diversified balance.

Looking back on the rumors we were going to move out of state, or threats in the media, my staff did what it could to build that 10 percent renewal base back up to a better number in 1997-98. The Thunder had transformed overnight from a dynamic success into a *lame duck* operation. No place to call home at the end of the arena lease, we were a man without a country. We started feeling the impact from the fans about two seasons prior to eventually folding. We all knew it was time, as did our fans, but we all went along with the idea of trying to make it work. Yet, we were rewarded with a thousand different papercuts.

Everything Ends Badly

Even in the 1998-99 season, which became the Thunder's final one before folding, we still tried too hard to generate interest in the club.[4] We were able to get new buyers interested in season tickets, but the renewal base was a fraction of itself from its heyday of 1994-96, and gaining new customers overall was absolutely challenging. When the ownership commitment vanishes, it doesn't take long for the staff or the fans to recognize that the end is near.

Even when it's not official or disclosed to staff. First comes the edict to curb spending, then game entertainment becomes *"value engineered,"* followed by staff reduction and the circling of the drain occurs. Mentally, this takes a toll on your staff, becoming harder to convince any front office member to have faith in the product. Instinctively, before we had reached the 1998-99 season to be formally told that this was the last run of the Thunder, we all knew the hockey team was about to fold.

The lesson that I learned from the 10 percent renewal shocker was that our organization was able to recover from it, as well as extend the life of the Thunder franchise by two years. But once we gave up our season ticket representatives' confidence as well as employment, nothing could be done to retain the base, even if the owners had decided to go two more seasons after that. Renewing season tickets is about building genuine relationships and staff confidence. You don't have to be a great salesperson to renew someone, but you do have to be attentive to your customer.

You have to reach out to them, build a relationship, and avoid only calling them for a payment. There's a price to be paid when you lose a sales representative that your account holders like. I've had folks decide to renew because of the relationship with their sales representative or decline renewing when their sales representative leaves.

Thinking about the lessons I learned since 1997, I don't cringe as often when I hear the 10 percent figure on anything. I remember what I accomplished when challenged, and why it speaks more of a positive opportunity rather than a dire negativity to overcome.

For What
It's Worth

Kyle Bostwick
Vice President
Vermont Lake Monsters
New York–Penn League, Short Season Class-A Baseball

About The Author

Kyle Bostwick has been a member of the Vermont Lake Monsters front office since 1994. Kyle started as an intern with the Vermont Expos, before being named General Manager in 1996. The New York–Penn League Executive of the Year in 1999, Kyle also served as General Manager of the Triple-A Ottawa Lynx from 2000–2007, before returning to the Vermont Lake Monsters in 2009.

When I first started in Minor League Baseball, you couldn't find a ball club that didn't focus a lot of their marketing and advertising energies into telling their fans that our game was affordable. It was, and there was reason to tell the world. You could go to a Minor League Baseball game for a fraction of what it cost to go to a Major League Baseball game and fans felt good about this experience. A funny thing has happened on the way to present day...our industry has continued to be affordable, but has also shown greater value.

Value is net result of allocation of resources and what is received in return. When looking to spend resources, such as money, there is an internal calculation that determines what the item, experience, etc...is worth....meaning, what are we willing to do or pay? These determinations can be based on many factors including market comparisons, past history, or even an *emotional trigger*. Whatever the determination is, if we feel that the resources we are asked to spend are less than what we feel it's worth, we typically move forward. Once completed, if the benefit is confirmed to be more than the resources spent, we have received value. Conversely, if the benefit is less, then we did not receive value for our resources. That is a long way of saying that if I saw value in something, then the benefit outweighed what it cost me in resources, regardless of the amount.

I really enjoy having a turkey sandwich for lunch. Over the years, I have had many combinations of turkey sandwiches, some good, some not so good, but the combination of these experiences has left me with the understanding that I enjoy having a turkey sandwich for lunch. The other day, I went to a lunch spot I hadn't been to before. There wasn't any particular reason I hadn't been, but I found myself in close enough proximity to the place to stop in. Nothing about the environment, or the first impressions, left me with anything memorable. Don't get me wrong, there wasn't anything that detracted from my initial observations, but nothing jumped out as making this place any more unique than the hundreds of lunch spots we have all been to. A quick peruse of the menu allowed me to see that there was a turkey sandwich being offered, and the description caught my eye.

This sandwich was created to bring a certain quality that one doesn't always see when ordering this lunchtime staple. Fresh made bread baked on site, turkey and bacon sourced from a local supplier with a reputation for high quality meats, fresh locally grown vegetables, Vermont made cheddar (*the best cheese in the country*), and homemade garlic mayo. Throw in a high-end pickle and kettle chips made from a low batch chip maker, and this sandwich had it all! All of this quality came with a price and the $17 price tag was certainly more than I normally pay for my turkey sandwich, but I am a connoisseur, a turkey sandwich aficionado, an expert in my own eyes, I had an obligation to try this sandwich! That sandwich didn't disappoint.

I left that establishment feeling good about my purchase, and while I had paid more than I normally would, I felt it was worth it, and I wouldn't have an issue buying the sandwich again. When I compare this experience to the $4.99 turkey sandwich I have had many times that didn't move me either way and was more or less just lunch, or the $9.99 turkey sandwich that I walked away from feeling "*ripped off*", I just felt better about lunch that day….I was shown better value in the $17 sandwich. How can this be the case? Everything we have ever learned tells us that, of course, the $4.99 sandwich is the best value, it costs less. The reason is what we use to establish and determine value. That $4.99 sandwich and that $17 sandwich were different, and I walked away feeling that the additional benefits I received (*ingredients, taste, etc…*) were worth more than the increase in price.

While we may not ever refer to it as value, there is no doubt that the feeling of value (*or lack of*) finds its way to be communicated. Many times when we share with folks a positive or negative experience, it is directly related to how we perceive the value we received. The higher on the spectrum of value or non-value, the more likely a person will share their feelings. "*Word of Mouth*" is just another way of saying that people are telling others they did or didn't receive value. I made the turkey sandwich purchase based on an internal, emotional curiosity. I will buy it again because I feel I received value. It seems like we are all busier now than we were 25 years ago. Everyone's schedule seems a bit fuller and time is an increasingly valuable commodity. I am not sure if each generation feels that way about their situation as compared to the generation before, but if it is widely believed by the masses, then it is true either way. For that reason, time has found its way into the value proposition as we market our ball clubs.

We understand that a fan attending a Vermont Lake Monsters game has many different choices and options when determining how to spend their resources … both money, and as we have established, time. Going to a Lake Monsters game continues to be an affordable evening, but as we have outlined in the turkey sandwich scenario, price is not all that matters when determining value.

Solid Value Sales

There is just so much more to a Minor League Baseball game than there was 25 years ago. Minor League Baseball continues to be a trailblazer with regards to our promotional events, offerings, in game entertainment, and customer service. The Lake Monsters, as a part of this amazing industry, have been able to grow and enhance our own fan experience, along with our colleagues, creating more value each season. Does it cost more to go to a Minor League Baseball game than it did 25 years ago? Of course, but when you factor in the better experiences, one would argue that our industry is showing more value also. You might want to say that we have added better ingredients to our industry sandwich, with the better experience benefits, greatly outweighing any marginal admission increase.

Each off-season, our team spends countless hours trying to bring better value to our fans. The baseline is a game without any special "*one-offs*". We dissect each component of our operation and make a determination if anything changes from the season before. Our giveaways are of better quality than they used to be. We understand that there is a direct relationship to how many tickets you sell to a giveaway night, and the quality of the giveaway item. Will this item be used once the event is over, or will it end up in the corner of a box somewhere? As we co-brand each of these giveaway items, we want them used, and they need to be of great quality. Over the years, we have found partners we can rely on to get us fair pricing, provide items of quality, and deliver what they say, when they say.

The relationship we have with our fans and our corporate partners depend on it, and sometimes it's not the best price wins. Unfortunately, we have used a company that has the cheapest price in the past, but when the item shows up and it is not a reflection of the relationship we want to have with our fans or the corporate partner, there is damage that is not easily repaired. We want the child to use the insulated lunch bag at school, or the pillowcase on their bed, or the baseball cap in the neighborhood. The result has been a corporate partner, seeing greater value in an item that is seen around town more often (*winter hat, replica jersey, t-shirt, etc.…*) and fans who look forward to and buy tickets in advance to these higher end premium giveaway nights.

The Vermont Lake Monsters play in the NY-PENN League, one of two short season leagues in MiLB. Our season begins in June and wraps up around Labor Day, right in the "*sweet spot*" of summer vacation. For that reason, we feel like any game has the ability to be well attended. By comparison, some of our colleagues who play long seasons in the Northeast, meaning their season starts in April, just don't have a fighting chance during some of those weeknights in late April when school is in session and its 34 degrees. Outside of rain, the weather shouldn't ever impact our attendance. For that reason, we are in constant collection mode when it comes to *Promotional Dates*. Ultimately, our goal is to create a calendar of 38 games, where if the weather is right, the dates have so much promotional power, that the sheer reputation or excitement of the event becomes an ally to our sales effort.

Minor League teams understand that a solid tickets sales effort is what makes or breaks our seasonal success, and this will never go away, it only makes it easier to fill the ballpark when a solid sales effort is complemented by fans buying tickets on their own accord. Our strategy is simple...continue to build on those days that are successful and add to them both days created by our internal "*think tanks*", or borrow an idea from another ball club and make it our own. Our $ 0.25 hot dog days, the post-game fireworks games, the baseball cap giveaways, and Halloween at the Ballpark are a few examples of these games we know will be successful if *Mother Nature* helps out. By continuing to show greater value on these games each year, and by adding events that we hope will be added to the list, we get closer to our goal of 38 "*home runs*".

Parking at Centennial Field is a challenge. There are less than 200 spots located on site and the nearest spots off-site are located about a tenth of a mile away. The bulk of our parking spaces can be found one mile (*yes, one mile*) away at the parking garage used by the University of Vermont for hockey and basketball games. Each night folks must deal with heavy traffic, and a series of parking options to get to the ballgame, but there are no other parking options available. If we allow the parking situation to "*be what it is*", our fans will not find much value in attending a game. If I were a young family and I had to park a mile away, I might do it...once. For that reason we shuttle our fans each night. We not only shuttle, but we use four buses, and they run all evening.

With a ballpark that holds over 3,000 people and parking for 150 vehicles, you can only imagine the need for multiple buses: *Would it be cheaper to only run two buses, of course, but at what point does the hassle of trying to get to your car at the end of the game or in the seventh inning prevent you from wanting to come to another game?*

We determine at what point, this shuttle bus is no longer a negative to the ballpark experience. We may be the only team in all of Minor League Baseball where parking is not a revenue stream but an expense. Parking costs our ball club over $50,000 a year. We factor in how the experience contributes to the overall value.

The Nuances of Value

Showing value is not a black and white action. It is not something that you can turn on and off, as many times, the determination of value may be decided as the sum of many parts. I shared earlier that I have had turkey sandwiches that I have not seen value in, yet the overall experience is one that is incredibly positive. If the "*bank*" of value you have created is large enough, it will be able to weather some negative hits, which is why the culture of showing value must be encouraged, and continually in practice. This is not a road the Lake Monsters front office can walk alone. The ballpark experience is only made possible with the help and assistance of the hundreds of game day staff that will encounter a fan during each season.

Thousands of fans will go to a Lake Monsters game and never have a direct interaction with a member of our Front Office. It is a scary feeling to know that the hard work we all do each season in preparation of summer, the countless community initiatives we participate in to foster goodwill and help make our communities better places, can all be nullified if someone representing the organization doesn't understand their role in creating this value.

Our pre-season training focuses as much on the nuances of their job, as the overall culture we are trying to create. We talk about this in an overall group, it is addressed as we break into smaller departments, and it is continually reinforced during the season. Because the front office can't be everywhere all the time, we identify folks that understand how important their actions are to the overall fan experience and we use their influence among their peers and co-workers to help continue the culture dialogue.

A few years ago, the Lake Monsters hosted their very first helicopter candy drop. The plan was for kids to be invited onto the field and hundreds of pounds of candy would be dropped and kids would be able to grab whatever they could. As the candy drop time approached, we had our participants waiting anxiously to see the helicopter and wait for the "*Mother Load*" of sweet candy to be dropped on the field. It was essential that each child knew that they had to stay on the warning track until we gave the signal, as the helicopter would need to immediately stop if any children were below.

Obviously it didn't work out that way. After prepping all of the kids and everyone seemingly on board, the helicopter approached. Just as it hovered and started to drop the initial part of the candy, the kids couldn't control themselves. They ran out onto the field and the helicopter needed to stop and depart, dropping only a fraction of what they were supposed to. With only a small amount of candy now on the field, it was a bit of chaos. The number of kids who didn't get candy was high, and you could see the frustration on the parent's faces. Thanks to the quick thinking of a staff member, the candy was retrieved from the helicopter, and quickly brought to the field exit. There, with the help of other staff members, crying kids were given candy, and crys turned to smiles. Taking it one step further, all remaining candy was brought into the stands and given to any kids missed.

Staff Buy-In

There is an area down the right field line that is perfect for people to watch the ballgame when not in their seats. We have an inflatable fun zone area, picnic tables, beer garden, facepainting, and a great vantage point of the action on the field. It has become an area for mom or dad to bring the child that just needs a break from sitting in the same area, to stretch their legs and just move around. In this area, we put one of our new ushers, who had expressed interest in working with the ballpark and was a very friendly person. As with any new hire, general rules of the ballpark, along with specific guidelines of their area of focus were shared.

The evening was going well until I received a complaint from a family that frequents the ballpark often. This family used the right field area for many of the reasons I described above. Their three-year-old boy needed to stretch his legs every now and then and sometimes would play in the gravel area where the picnic tables are located. This particular evening the boy was playing in the area and moving around amongst the picnic tables. From accounts shared later, this boy would be in the gravel with his truck, and maybe extend his play area to tables other than the ones his family was using. No one seemed to have an issue with this, but our new usher felt this child should not roam as much. After telling the child a few times not to stray towards others, the child continued to be a three-year-old and play in the dirt. As a foul ball later made its way into the area, the child in question got the ball, only to have it taken away by the usher as punishment for not listening.

After hearing the story, we discussed the issue with the usher in question, and realized she hadn't "bought in" and this wasn't for her: *Why did these folks handle these issues so differently?*

To get to a culture of value, it is first essential for those championing the cause to see value themselves: *We have established the importance of creating a culture of value, but what is in it for the gameday employee?*

Just like our decisions to spend money on turkey sandwiches, all of our staff, both full and part time, will weigh the benefit they receive as it compares to the time they allocate.

This analysis is different for all, but I can venture to guess that if they look back at their time at the ballpark, either by the game, or by the season, it will be imperative that they feel good about the organization they work for:

✓ Do they feel supported?

✓ Are they getting what they want out of the experience (*great part time job, career advancement, development of skills, opportunity to be promoted, etc…*)?

✓ Does the company's values reflect the ones they possess?

If we can get to that spot with our employees, we can then share the story of value.

If we haven't been able to connect with the employee on their needs, then the story of value is unheard.

If it's the ticket taker or the parking attendant or concession stand employee that doesn't "buy in" and foster the vision of your organization, or even the game day staff that is so rigid with the rules that common sense and situational awareness are not allowed to be used, these separate, unique interactions can be the single thing that no longer allows your fan to see value in your product.

✓ Does your usher understand that they have the ability to replace the slipped ice cream or dropped hot dog?

✓ Did your parking attendant understand, that while we don't have any parking spots left close to the doors, we will allow the person who has a bit of difficulty walking to be dropped off close?

✓ Do the ballplayers know that sharing that baseball deemed out of play by the umpire to a young fan can create a lifetime memory?

These may seem like common sense, but there are hundreds, if not thousands of times in our industry that these actions are not followed through on. Through the process of training, encouraging, and most importantly understanding why your staff sees value in sharing your vision, this continual culture of showing value can be achieved.

Impacting Factors

Sometimes an organization's biggest influencer on value is someone or something you can't control. A few years back, we secured the attendance of a former ballplayer at a Lake Monsters game to sign autographs and be available for our fan base. This ballplayer had played in Vermont years before and was a fan favorite by many. We were excited about this appearance and promoted his attendance as aggressively as any other promotion we had done. The morning of the event, pregame ticket sales were strong, promotion was plentiful, and the mood was excited...then the phone *rang*. The ballplayer called and said that he had to leave at 6 p.m. sharp. Our game was at 6 p.m., with gates opening at 5 p.m. There was no way we would be able to accommodate those folks who wanted an autograph, and would have expected the player to be there well into the game.

We were on the verge of impacting one of the factors in showing value...*their time*. Many of these folks would be in line prior to 5 p.m. in hopes of getting a chance to meet the ballplayer and get an autograph, and surely those arriving at gates open would be so deep into the lineup that their chances of meeting the ballplayer would be zero. We would have wasted their time, and while we could justify that their ticket purchase still shows great value based on what we provide each and every night, this "*sum of the parts*" would result in a negative for sure.

Our culture of showing value needed to be strong with all hands on deck. After deliberation, we decided to call in our ballpark staff early. If we were going to have a line up two hours before gates opening, then we needed to open earlier. These folks in line were not going to determine value whether they got to meet the ballplayer at 4 p.m. or 5:30 p.m., so we needed to get as many people through the line before 6 p.m. as possible.

That way, if the person showing up at 5 p.m. now is 100 people back, as opposed to 5:50 p.m., there is greater chance of an autograph. Because everyone understands the importance of continually showing value, our game day staff understood. Everyone was accommodating, we opened the gates hours earlier, and while we still had some folks who felt disappointed that our promotional appearance ended early, there is no doubt that hundreds of folks left that evening happier than what could have been.

Only Fans Can Forgive

Are you aware that some actions that show value to some folks, don't always show value to others? Unfortunately we are aware of this. One such example centers around a game in early July. The Lake Monsters were giving away a really neat performance t-shirt (*we have tried to make all of our giveaways items with high perceived value*), and we would be expecting a crowd to form hours in advance. The day before, the *National Weather Service* issued a severe thunderstorm warning for the afternoon before our giveaway. We knew that would be right around the time that folks would be in line, waiting for this really neat performance t-shirt. Thoughts of folks standing outside in the rain, with possible thunder was just not something we could do to our fans....we have a culture of showing value, and this sort of practice wouldn't fall in line with our principles. What we did next showed that one person's value proposition was another person's "*bait and switch*". We postponed the giveaway. We emailed everyone who had tickets to that game and told them that we would be playing the game (*the forecast was good for game time*) but the giveaway was moved to two weeks later.

As a way to show value to the folks that bought tickets ahead of time, we said any ticket for the postponed giveaway could be exchanged for the new date, whether we played the first night or not. We also took this message to social media, to our website, to the local media, to our email list and any other way we could get the word out.

This message was well received by many:

✓ *"Thanks for thinking of our safety, we will be there tonight and the next night."*

✓ *"This was the correct decision, thank you"*

However this message was also received as evil from just as many fans:

✓ *"You ruined our plans, we will never come back again."*

✓ *"I bought tickets to this game and you changed the plans...just old fashioned bait and switch".*

We also got a few expletive - laden rants that make you question why you do this (*for only a few seconds*). The point of this story is that creating value is not determined the same way by everyone. It will take a certain feel and understanding by you and your staff to develop this gut feel that works for your organization.

The risks associated with putting on an event that is so heavily influenced by the weather are high:

✓   A fear that any advance ticket holder has with an outdoor event, is how is the threat of weather handled?

✓   Am I risking my time and money by purchasing this ticket or has the organization developed a level of trust with me, that helps me determine good value?

I think that we all do a great job as an industry taking into account the fact that if folks feel like the weather can impact an event they have spent money on, with no acceptable method of remuneration, our pre-event sales would plummet.

Rain Checks

Our industry has accepted the policy of *Rain Checks*, allowing patrons to exchange an unused ticket for a rained out game for another game, the buyer feels they are given some level of protection if *Mother Nature* prevails to an extent. In some cases, our data has shown it may not be enough. Years of practice have shown us that ticket purchasers want two things when it comes to weather impacted ballgames....*transparency* and *consistency*. If the fan doesn't feel he/she is getting this, it will start to impact the value proposition negatively. Pre-sales are important to our ball club. A pre-bought ticket exponentially increases the chance of someone going to a ballgame as compared to a *"game time decision"*. Too many things can change a person's mind at the last minute if they plan on buying at the game, but a pre-bought ticket, increases the chance of attendance, even with inclement weather. For that reason, the value we must show to the person who already has the ticket is a big part of our rain-out policy.

We would see games that we knew would go on, but because the weather prognosticators had less than positive outlooks, not only would walk up purchases (*tickets bought at the time of gates opening*) but the folks that did buy their ticket in advance and show up, may be subject to a game that did not show great value. There were promotions that probably couldn't go on because of field impacts, maybe the inflatables were not up because of wind or weather and maybe some of the food carts were not in operation. There is not a doubt in our mind that we would not meet expectations and probably not showing great value. If the game went five innings then we would compound the issue by nullifying a *Rain Check*.

We had such a game and saw that we had an opportunity to show the value we need to show our fan base, each time they buy a ticket. The game went on that night, the rain fell and we delayed for a bit in the third inning. A quick look around the ballpark during that delay painted a picture of folks probably not thinking that this was their optimal ballpark experience.

We made a decision to honor each ticket that night as a *Rain Check*, whether we played an official game or not. We ended up playing a full nine innings that night, and many stayed. Some folks, mostly those with young kids, left a bit early, but the common belief that night is that we showed value to each and every one of those fans. What we lost in short term money, we gained in a belief system that they were not punished by buying a ticket in advance.

Engaging Partnerships

We also show value with our local business community and corporate supporters. It used to be different...call on the local business and see if they want to support the "*home team*" with season tickets, an outfield billboard, and maybe some group tickets. It was a one size fits all. Fortunately, this has all changed. Businesses don't have the luxury of supporting the home team and need to see this value in our relationships. By understanding that our ball clubs can be a part of many business solutions to include branding, retail activation, pre-paid entertainment, and community initiatives to name only a few, we create value for our partners.

There is no doubt that the reach and local impact that the ball club has in its community, can translate into an effective way for a local business to reach its potential audience. A local utility was looking for a way to change customer behavior. Many of their current customers were still receiving monthly bills through the mail. By switching these accounts to paperless billing, the end result would see thousands of dollars in savings each year by the utility. Using a night out with the Lake Monsters, this utility offered tickets and spending money to anyone who made the switch to paperless billing. The customer received a fantastic evening they saw great value in and the utility saw massive savings with the tremendous results of this campaign and the thousands of customers who now receive bills electronically. The utility used the ballpark as the driver of this campaign and the economic benefit far outweighed their cost of the tickets and spending money.

Sometimes these partnerships center on the parts of the business that can't be measured on an income statement. The ballpark in Vermont is a community gathering place during the summer. Folks from all walks of life can be found at a ballgame at least once each year, and because Vermont is such a small part of the world, both physically and demographically, you always run into people you know. This sort of *"familiar influence"* is a big part of the impact that Lake Monsters games can have on our community.

Recently, Vermont has seen more and more *"New Americans"* arrive in hopes of creating a better situation for their families. These folks are new to the United States, and unfamiliar with many of our customs and the ties that connect our community. This unfamiliarity has led to a real challenge of integration, and in some cases, we are seeing a night at the ballpark as helping to bring these folks closer. By partnering with some of our local businesses, many of these *"New American"* families are treated to a ballgame, with food and merchandise. The result has been the creation of common experience.

Understanding CPM

The kids are now a part of conversations at school or in the neighborhood about going to a ballgame. The parents are seen in a social situation with folks they may live near, but have never had the chance to get to know. By starting the process of going to a ballgame, we have seen the start of a routine. These families are now establishing themselves as parts of this ballpark community, and with it, a familiarity with others that they may not have had significant interaction with before.

The businesses that support this initiative have been thrilled with their ability to make such an impact on our community in ways they may not have been able to outside of the Lake Monsters:

✓   Does our partner need to see a proper cost per measurement (CPM)?

✓   Maybe they will judge success by the amount of people that come through their doors or visit their website?

✓   Maybe we have done such a great job showing value to our fans, that they want to do business with businesses who work with us?

The Lake Monsters have been a part of many successful branding campaigns, where an outfield billboard or video board messaging works in concert to an existing campaign outside the ballpark, or even a positive association with a company that does millions of dollars in sales worldwide, and almost zero locally. By continually putting this brand in front of our fans who see great value in our product, it creates a positive association that serves as a benefit when they are trying to recruit local talent to work at their business. Either way, by showing value to our corporate partners, in whatever way they determine a successful partnership, we create a relationship that has a greater chance of renewal, than one that is based merely on *"supporting the home team"*.

To show value in the previous examples, is to use value as a noun, but fans attending our ballgames can also use value as a verb. As we find ourselves spending more and more time burying our heads in our phones and participating in a digital world, the time we spend with people we care about becomes, you guessed it...more valuable. Ten years from now, a fan may not remember what they had for lunch one day (*maybe a turkey sandwich?*), but they remember having a hot dog with a sibling, or cheering a great play with Mom or Dad, or getting to know a co-worker a bit better than they had in the six months of sharing a cubicle wall, all while at a Lake Monsters game. They may not even remember what the final score was or who the Lake Monsters were playing, but these vivid memories of smiles at the ballpark will be with them forever. By creating an environment that promotes the creation of memories, our fans value their time with us, adding yet another benefit to the overall value proposition we hope to create.

Gone are the days of professional sports franchises looking around and determining competition by how many other teams play in your market. Competition today exists in the form of a hike in the mountains, going to a movie, eating at a restaurant, or just sitting on the back deck at home.

We understand that if someone chooses to go to the ballpark, we will be judged on how their resources were spent:

✓ Were we the affordable $4.99 turkey sandwich that was *"just lunch"* or was this evening out a great deal as the ticket price compares to the experience?

✓ Were the few hours they used at the ballpark a great use of their time, or could this precious commodity be better spent doing something else in the future?

Value The Experience

I started working in Minor League Baseball in 1994. From day one, I was drawn to the ability this industry has to create value through smiles, laughs, and lifetime memories. Our approach as an industry has changed with better practices, stronger understanding of what people want, and the ability to collaborate amongst ourselves.

I have exponentially grown personally and professionally over the years. The incredibly diverse nature of our business that sees us simultaneously have to become salesmen, food vendors, choreographers, security experts, human resource gurus, and event managers, to name only a few of the hats we wear, has given each of us professional experiences matched by few.

The lifetime friendships created with folks, I only see at baseball functions, but continue to talk to all year long, or the ballpark staff or season ticket holders who have spent countless hours at the ballpark with me are relationships I truly cherish. While I have missed out on many things like summertime barbeques with non-industry friends, worked longer hours than the norm, and probably missed out on a few hours of sleep here and there, but the takeaway is that without question, my involvement in this profession has given me great value.

"Free" Is The Foulest Word Of Them All

John Dittrich
Fmr. President

About The Author

John Dittrich has over 40 years of professional baseball experience at every level of the game, including a season in the Texas League office, 3 years in the National Association of Professional Baseball Leagues (MiLB) headquarters and 4 years in the front office of the Texas Rangers (MLB). General Manager at every level of the minor leagues (Independent – Rookie – Class A – Class AA – Class AAA). He has been named Executive of the Year seven times, by his peers in professional baseball.

As a frequent guest lecturer for sports management professors on university campuses, I deal with the misconception of why a free ticket is a *weapon of mass destruction*. My visits tend to be scheduled around a class project, which would bring me back to the same students several times during the semester. While it always has been a learning experience for the students, I've found the encounters to be enlightening as well. When you meet groups of people who have not become cynical about the sports industry or the world in general, you are encouraged. However, while thinking creatively and outside the box, many of those *"green"* students still offer up solutions where a free ticket to a sporting event is the encouragement to get customers to buy the same product later. Nothing could be further from the truth. Sometimes, being jaded from decades of experience in baseball has its benefits to the operator as well.

During my initial sessions with any sports management class, I ask the students to create their own marketing plan for a single baseball game. The goal is to inspire the public to purchase tickets for a minor league baseball game, where no one in the community recognizes any of the player names, where the level of play is subpar to that of the major league product, and where promotion drives attention to get people to the ballpark.

I do also add a *"catch"* to the project: **The plan cannot include free or discounted tickets.**

This is a stumper for the students. Everyone loves free tickets. Everyone loves a discount. The problem is that everyone isn't paying for the operation. Everyone doesn't understand the bottom line. And if you start giving it away for free, you never get anyone to value it, or pay for it ever. There is one *"F"* word in the vernacular of sports marketing that is more foul than the one that you are thinking exists: *FREE*. The other one is a sign of a poor vocabulary, but the word *"free"* is the sign of poor marketing prowess and should be avoided at all costs.

The majority of marketing textbooks disagree with my assessment on how horrible the word *"free"* is to a sports marketing product. Most marketing professors tend to focus on the idea that *"free"* is one of, if not the, most powerful words in the

English language for the world of marketing. The trouble with this mindset is that those writing those marketing textbooks have never put up their wallet against their ideas. Giving away other people's product without having skin in the game is exactly why "*free*" doesn't work. There are zero studies supporting free tickets either. Mainly because deep down, the marketing professor understands that their assertion of providing you a hamburger today for payment tomorrow doesn't work.

Free tickets in professional sports are a harmful marketing scheme that never delivers anything but decimated empty seats and a broken balance sheet. In over 40 years of accumulated professional files on working in the minor league baseball business, I have yet to encounter one sports marketing project performed by any of the university classes that I have guest lectured in, where despite the funny, creative and wildly imaginative promotional ideas that didn't center around the struggle of offering free or discounted tickets. If you have to give the product away in order to entice someone to attend, then the value really isn't there for them to show up in the first place. The struggle is that people tend not to push value over the idea that they can give away the product to generate attendance. And once you stay in that mindset, it is hard to get out of it entirely.

I have over 40 years of experience selling tickets in minor league baseball. I have seen the ways that minor league baseball has changed into more of a business and marketing structure, from the days when the promotion of the on-field product reigned supreme. My firm belief is that the marketing of "*free tickets*" is a death knell. I've never witnessed it be a successful mechanism for getting people to spend money later. It screams "*worthless product*" to our customers whenever it is used. When resorting to free tickets, you tell your fans that our product is so poor in value that we absolutely cannot sell tickets to it, and that they are foolish to spend a single dollar to buy anything at our games.

When you offer free or discounted tickets to attend a sporting event, it creates a consumer dilemma of whether it is worth your time to attend at all. When we value a tangible physical object that we see, touch and feel, we know that we can physically use it, as well as use it at different periods of time. Because when the free item is physical in nature, it's the time that shows most value. Time cannot be recovered, most of us place a great value on how our personal time is spent. A free or discounted ticket to an event negates understanding that our time is valued more than anything else. So fewer people actually redeem the free or discounted ticket, because why waste their valuable time on something that no one is willing to pay for.

In minor league baseball, we are working with a product that is less than a star system, meaning that we aren't selling tickets to see the best of the best, an entertainer that is well-known, or a sporting event that involves athletes at the top of their physical game. We are selling entertainment. Blocks of time where people aren't concerned with the scoreboard as much as the mascot races. Tickets are the initial fuel for getting our customers into a buying mood when they enter the ballpark.

We cannot sell food and beverage, merchandise or sponsorships without selling the ticket first. Free ticket redeemers, those who do attend without paying, often sit on their hands during the game, have no money in their wallets, and verbally diminish your product's value to others. They didn't pay, and tend to think that those who might pay are suckers for doing so. Every minor league baseball operator's mission should be to create value for their customer's time and money. Unleashing hundreds of thousands of tickets for free into a blanket community marketing effort kills that value proposition entirely.

Paper Hanging Legends

"*Paper hanging*" is not a new concept when showcasing how minor league baseball operators throw around free tickets in an area and kill the demand for that product entirely. Professionally, I never used ticket giveaways during my initiation into the business side of baseball. However, I learned the art of the free ticket, and truly how terrible it was, back in 1974, when I was a general manager in Alexandria, Louisiana to take over the Alexandria Aces. It was a nice market that had been steadily losing attendance and revenue over the previous decade. Seasons had gone by without anyone making a profit.

Paperhangers are a notorious bunch. Back in the 1950s and 1960s, Dick King was a legendary "*buyout*" guy who ran baseball clubs in Oklahoma City and Wichita, both with the team moniker "*Indians*."[1] He wallpapered the towns that his clubs were in with free tickets. King was a bitter man, who felt that his legacy in the industry was never respected. He had won some industry promotional awards in the minor leagues, even had a couple of shots at marketing for the Cleveland Indians and New York Yankees under general manager Gabe Paul. But King's methodology of paperhanging was to approach community businesses in multiple locations of high customer traffic, such as supermarket chains, convenience stores, fast food restaurants and offer them one or several "*buyout nights.*" The team would print off thousands of paper tickets, about 10-times beyond stadium capacity, and he would deliver them to the retailer to stuff every customer bag or leave stacks on the cashier counters for customers to help themselves to as many as they liked.

The Aces owner in 1974 was an absentee landlord who never came to the ballpark much and the only thing I can remember is that he owned race horses, including one called "*Hearts of Lettuce.*" The owner was about to give the whole baseball operation up when I arrived in 1974, and ended up doing so within the year out of obtuse frustration over the terrible on-field product, the dismal crowds in the stands, and the fact that Alexandria was a town too small for a Double-A franchise. Its ballpark was an old, run-down wooden structure not worthy of league standards called, Bringhurst Field. The locker rooms were actually industrial trailers, the front office a small "*tuff shed*" structure across the street from the ballpark in two tiny rooms. Alexandria had its general manager, Steve Chipp, depart the team a month prior to the season ending in 1974, because he was frustrated with attendance, homesick for San Diego and clearly out of his element. He didn't give away tickets so much as he just hated living in Alexandria. Texas League President Bobby Bragan sent me to Alexandria to complete the season as acting general manager at the fresh-out-of-college age of 23. At the time, I only had a faint idea of what the day-to-day duties of a minor league general manager were.

At the time, one of the few people who recognized Dick King as a great baseball promoter was the Texas League President Bobby Bragan. He sung King's praises about having massive standing room only crowds of more than 10,000 because King would distribute 100,000 free tickets into the community. A 10-percent redemption on free tickets is pretty standard. If you give out 50,000 tickets, only 5,000 or less will show up on that designated night because they have no other plans. It captured the attention and imagination of Bragan, who saw that Oklahoma City or Wichita was always one of the top attended teams in minor league baseball.

The standard math used for successful paperhanging, if it can be called that, is for the operator to give away about 5-to-10 times as many free tickets compared to stadium capacity in order to attract any significant attendance. This only helps support the image that the operation providing the free tickets is giving away a product with no value. If the customer takes a free ticket to an event, they are less compelled to attend. Conversely, if the ticket was paid for by their hard-earned cash, they are more certain to use it. And the free ticket philosophy is supported by more conjecture of a false narrative which says "*get them in the house, make your money off of hot dogs and beer and merchandise.*" With the free ticket redeemers who attend, it doesn't work that way.

Those that do come to the ballpark for free have no money. If they did, they would spend it on something other than your event, and would never have redeemed the ticket in the first place. Even if you pack the stands on a free ticket night, you gain less new fans than poor customers who won't spend on your ancillaries. They come to the event expecting other things to be free, then start to make a value judgment on what it cost them to attend and whether there is worth in paying for parking, buying food and beverage, or purchasing a hat before leaving for the night. The free ticket user is a cheap date consumer who is helping damage your customer base and revenue line with irreparable harm.

Trained Never To Buy

I've followed *paperhangers* several times in my career, tried to repair their damage done on the brand. In 1989-90, my first season taking over the minor league baseball operation was in Greensboro with the South Atlantic League, where a notorious paperhanger had been residing as general manager. Greensboro had led the league in "*announced*" attendance for several years, but their revenues were less than half that of what they should have been. Actual bodies in the ballpark were fewer on an annual basis.

The majority of telephone calls incoming to our Greensboro office were asking us when the next free night would be held, and at what store or location those free tickets could be scored from. The marketplace had been saturated and trained not to purchase tickets at all. The marketplace had decided to sit back, wait for the next free game. That type of damage could not be repaired in one season after a decade of abuse. Our first year in that marketplace was difficult mainly because so much of the product had been given away that the value of our tickets, signage and overall corporate sponsorship was diminished entirely.

When these situations occur, the new baseball operator taking over for the paperhanging regime has to overcome diminished value with the one tool they have: Wait out the customer base until it is ready to pay for that which it used to get for free. This means that you have to be prepared for a downturn in attendance as overall butts in seats will not be filling your ballpark on free nights. However, it does not mean that there will be a downturn in overall revenue. Those free people don't spend anyway. Per capita revenue for games where customers actually pay for tickets is much greater than those games where a lot of the attendees earned a free ticket. There is a difference of about two-times in food and beverage revenue alone, coupled with merchandise.

Paperhangers tend to negate this, to suggest that there need to be studies on why making people pay for tickets results in more spending elsewhere. Interestingly enough, they tend to also ignore any math. Call it the willful ignorance of *paperhanging* that they usually run a math deficit on their balance sheet and refuse to see why that is possible or happening.

Here is a simple table illustrating how a crowd of 3,000 full-paid admissions to a ballpark can generate a higher profit than a crowd of 1,500 full-paid admissions and 4,500 free admissions can:

REGULAR PRICE x 3,000 fans	REVENUE
3,000 Tickets Sold: $9.00 USD Avg	$27,000
Concessions Per Capita: $12 (55% Net)	$19,800
Merchandise Per Capita: $2 (50% Net)	$1,500
NET REVENUE GAIN	$48,300
FREE TICKETS x 6,000 fans	REVENUE
1,500 Tickets Sold: $9.00 USD Avg	$13,500
Free Tickets Given Out: 4,500	$ -----
Concessions Per Capita: $6 (55% Net)	$19,800
Merchandise Per Capita: $1 (50% Net)	$3,000
NET REVENUE GAIN	$36,300

From Alexandria to Amarillo

Our operation had applied for and were granted permission by the Texas League to move the Alexandria franchise to Amarillo, Texas for the 1976 season. It was a big year in the United States of America as it was the bi-centennial of our country. And a big year for us with the Amarillo Gold Sox. We were finally located in a market with a thriving business community and a ballpark that much more closely fit the definition of a class AA park at that time. Although Potter County Memorial Stadium is now obsolete, in 1976 it was considered a decent ballpark and Amarillo with a market of over a 200,000 population giving us a respectable number on which to build a fan base. Baseball had failed in Amarillo two years earlier, when the San Francisco Giants pulled out and hooked up with a new minor league owner in Lafayette, Louisana. So, we were looked upon with some skepticism when we arrived and announced that the "*Gold Sox*" were returning to the Texas Panhandle.

Our radio broadcaster in Amarillo was as much of a sales person as anyone. Because in baseball, everyone on staff has to sell. Current Seattle Mariners lead play-by-play announcer Rick Rizzs came into my office excited. He said that American National Bank wanted to buy out the ballpark for the July 4, 1976 game. He said they were willing to spend $3,000 but wanted at least 50,000 free tickets to give away. He further said that they wanted every fan who entered to get a free hot dog and a free soft drink. In addition they would be giving away a souvenir coin acknowledging America's bi-centennial.

The annual July Fourth fireworks were to be held in the 20,000 seat football stadium across the parking lot from our ballpark, so no fireworks were planned at the ballpark, but the timing of the game was to be such that the game would end before dark and fans could then move either to their cars in the lot or to the football stadium for the fireworks. Needless to say, we were eager to bring the bank aboard and at that time in history, $3,000 was a lot of money to us. We weren't landing the sponsorships we are able to get in these times. So, we took the deal and jumped on board with both feet.

As the season began we promoted the upcoming bi-centennial game in many ways. The bank bought media both print and broadcast to promote the night. We sent players to the bank every day to meet and greet customers and hand out tickets. When July Fourth finally came, we stayed up all night setting up temporary concession stands and stocking them to the hilt. We were unsure as to how many would come to our 6,500-seat ballpark but based on telephone activity and other hints, we felt it was going to be big. And it was.

By the time we squeezed the last fan into the gates with pretty large areas for standing room down both foul lines we moved 8,655 folks through the turnstiles. If I am not mistaken, that still stands as the largest crowd in Amarillo baseball history. Thanks to our soft drink sponsor, *Pepsi*, we were able to provide the free soft drinks without cost to the team and our only cost was the hot dogs, which ran about $0.30 cents with a bun.

You can do the math: *Yes, the hot dogs took most of the $3,000 sponsorship money.*

Of course the box office brought in a pittance as we were able to upgrade every box seat we had in the place for $1 and that may have amounted to about $500. Oh, and yes, the concessions deposit was well above an average day, something like $5,000 but well below the average per-capita. So, we had a glorious day. Set a record with the huge crowd. Won the game. And we nearly bankrupted the team because of it. Short-term thinking is what *paperhanging* is all about. It never factors in the long game at all.

Everyone left pretty happy and saw a fireworks show across the parking lot that cost us nothing. However, we didn't really profit financially. For the most part, early in our career we self-operated our concessions so we were our own concessionaire. We realized early that per-caps were going to be damaged by free or deeply discounted tickets, but the trade-off might be one of desperation. We may do a larger gross volume at the concessions even with a lower per-cap, that is if the ticket giveaway was successful in creating a significant impact on attendance.

It goes to the issue of long-term market damage more than the lowered per-caps. I really never had a lot of trouble with contractors and we have worked with concessionaires both large (*i.e. Levy*) and small local companies. If they are given a "*heads up*" about an upcoming game with free or deep discount tickets, they were usually prepared with extra staff and well aware that they would have a lower per-cap. They were just hopeful that the added volume of basic items like soft drinks, beer, hot dogs and popcorn would make up for the loss of per-caps. Again, we did very, very little of this in the latter days of our career and that is when we had more outside vendor contracts, so we really never had a lot of problems with this.

The Strikeout of Free

I've built a personal philosophy that I use on people advocating free ticket marketing. It's baseball terminology, but it works for me. Free tickets are nothing more than a strikeout, because of three factors. For *"Strike One,"* we find that both our full and partial season ticket holders who have doled out their hard-earned dollars to purchase tickets quickly learn that their money has been wasted because it is possible to attend a fair number of games without paying for tickets at all. This is particularly a killer for mini-plans or general admission book ticket sales. Why buy a ticket plan if you can just wait to find out when the free nights are held and attend those games?

A lot of operators will talk up the marketing of a *"theme night"* to drive attendance, such as *"1970's night"* or *"Halloween in May"* or *"Elvis Night."* These nights do not significantly impact attendance. What they do instead is send the message to your fans that the team is trying to make the experience fun and unique, where every night at the ballpark is different and special. Young promoters consider these nights as ways to attract fans. That's not what they are there for. Theme nights are used to keep the fans there once inside and get them to return again. But all of these theme nights avoid the destructive quality of free tickets on a marketplace's consumers. They add value of why you would invest time in attending, where free tickets do the opposite.

In Greensboro, consumers had been *trained* not to purchase tickets. The marketplace was saturated with free tickets. It *trained* our audiences to sit back and wait for the next free game, because only a sucker would pay for the experience. When we turned off the free ticket spout, the fans were upset and it took two years for them to realize that our operation was not going to cave in and provide free tickets again. In some marketplaces, the damage is done so effectively that people never spend with you after they've gotten it for free. That's why so many operations fold up their tent and move elsewhere.

That's the *"strike two"* of what happens in this philosophy. Single game fans who don't purchase larger ticket packages because they cannot afford it, stay away from our ballpark on paid ticket nights because they know they can attend enough games during the season for free. It's a value killer *"strike"* that presents the fans with the scenario that our tickets have zero value. The realization that we must give away tickets for free to draw a good crowd tells the consumer that they are a fool when they pay at all.

Things were never supposed to be this complicated for me professionally. I exited college with a journalism degree and the aspiration of becoming a play-by-play announcer. I pivoted toward a career in the front office, writing letters to the 24 Major League Baseball teams that existed in the 1970s. Being naive, I had zero idea how many applicants that I was competing with, along with how few opportunities existed. I heard from only a handful of teams, and all but two responses were form letters.

The Chicago White Sox' Roland Hemond was kind enough to meet with me in person. The Cincinnati Reds' Bob Howsam sent me a personal note suggesting that I seek employment in the minor leagues. Hemond agreed with Howsam that working in minor league baseball would be a great strategy for me. That's how I met my mentor Bragan, who was a former player and manager, who invited me to visit him if I were ever in Texas. I was living in Illinois at the time. Didn't matter. I was hooked. I drove all night from Illinois to Fort Worth, called Bragan to let him know that I was in the neighborhood, and to hold him to his promise to meet with me. Bragan invited me to his home where he was having a social gathering that evening. I arrived at his residence to witness Bragan on the bench of his piano, entertaining over 20 guests, gathered for Bragan's forty-second wedding anniversary. Bragan enjoyed touching the ivories, and I joined in the sing along, and it impressed him to have a young man willing to adapt to the surroundings. Enough that I earned an invitation to spend the night in his guest room. The next morning, he offered me a job as his assistant, beginning a life-long friendship with a sage mentor that lasted until the day he passed on January 21, 2010 at the age of 92.[2]

Bobby introduced me to Dick King, the man who had been such a huge proponent of buyout nights, famous for having as many buyout nights as possible in a season. Bragan didn't see the harm of what free tickets was doing to the marketplace. Bragan was a great baseball man and human being, but he had a blind spot for the business side of the sport. He loved seeing huge crowds, but never questioned revenue and *profit/loss* issues. Thus, Bragan's admiration with King meant believing that larger crowds would result in greater concessions sales and higher interest in the team, thus fans coming back and paying for tickets in the future. And in that case, Bragan was very misguided.

"*Strike three*" of my philosophy against free tickets concerns the impact on concession sales when you hold buy-out nights. I attended a promotional seminar once where the speaker was a notorious *paperhanger* who said that he wasn't in the baseball or ticket business, he was in the concessions business. Matter of fact, he isn't in business anymore. Because math disagrees with him. Per capita sales of food and beverage, as well as souvenirs and other ballpark revenues, are significantly lower when the patrons enter the facility using a free ticket. It seems that human nature, as well as demographics, play a role in this factor. When people come to the event on a free ticket, they appear to be focused on the cheapest possible night out and thus, tend to spend less at the concession stands as well. Some say that this is because folks who cannot afford a night at the ballpark are there on the free tickets and thus have less to spend. Both budget seekers and those with less disposable income are probably contributors.

Remember back to that 1976 July Fourth game in Amarillo, the one where the bank gave us a $3,000 sponsorship for free tickets, soda and hotdogs: *The cost of cleanup is figured in and the cost of goods and labor on the $5,000 bucks at the concessions were taken into consideration plus the $3,000 sponsorship being neutralized by the cost of the free hot dogs, we made about $2,000-2,500 bucks from a crowd of over 8,000 people.*

Keep in mind we are talking concession and ticket prices in place almost a half-century ago. So per-caps at concession stands were nothing close to those of today. When you cram 8,600 people into a 6,500-seat facility you cannot help but back up every facility in the place. You will have long lines at the concessions and bathrooms. This discourages purchasers who aren't interested in standing in a line for 2-3 innings.

Once fans realize that a baseball operation is desperate for their attendance, you end up getting less of it. Even when the ticket is free. It also makes your season and mini-season package holders angry, as they are paying for their seats, but discovering quickly that you are giving away tickets to everyone else. This is why it is better to focus on the creation of value beyond the ticket price, instead of merely seeing how many people can be handed a ticket for free. Value wins over time and everything else.

People Will Pay For Fun

When I learned more about my industry, I started focusing on building promotions that held value to them. So no one cared about the price of the ticket. Because the excitement was enough that they would be willing to pay for the opportunity to experience the product first-hand. Before each season, the board would be filled in with the schedule and then staff meetings would be held to suggest promotions which would fill in each date. I began to tell our staff that the words "*free*" and *"discount"* would be banned from all discussion. This made the project very difficult and that is instinctively where everyone goes when talking about ways to sell just about anything.

The most common strategy would involve filling every Saturday night with a promotional give-away item, provided by a sponsor of course. Items such as *Cap Night, Ball Night, Bat Night, Bobblehead Nights* etc. Then, Fridays would involve guest celebrities and other acts, such as *The Famous San Diego Chicken, Myron Noodleman, The Blues Brothers Act*, etc. Once teams realized that fireworks were a sure-fire draw, almost everyone went to *"Fireworks Fridays"* and scheduled the entertainers on Sundays. Then came the difficult part. That is trying to fill in the remaining weekday dates. Usually there were a few Holidays such as Memorial Day and July Fourth which would give you an easy promo and an opportunity to schedule another fireworks event. But most of the other weekdays ended up being pretty lame. The aforementioned *"theme nights"* fill it out.

As my career advanced and we became more aware of what works and what does not, we worked hard to train a solid group sales staff and worked hard within the business community to find companies and other organizations which would purchase blocks of tickets for their employees and families. We did use the dreaded *"discount"* for these group sales and the discount is deeper if the company will purchase the tickets for a weekday game. This would be the precursor of *"dynamic pricing"*. Eventually, the *"Spoelstra"* philosophy comes into play here. The strategy of creating sellouts for the weekends and other big dates causing a spillover of sales to the less attractive dates. We learned that we could create a *"tough ticket"* mentality if we could use the words *"sold out"* often enough. So eventually those planning meetings focused on identifying dates we could sell out. The more dates we could focus on this the better. Once the fans realize that they may not be able to get a ticket if they don't act quickly, you have the cycle working in your favor!

It took me a bit to learn that the *"F-word"* is a strikeout for us in the business of selling tickets. Again, this is particularly true for those of us who sell tickets to minor league or mid-major and below collegiate sports. We must understand that our product is the entertainment value we create. Most of our customer base is not attending because of our product's star power. We are not selling tickets to see current stars or even for sure future stars. We are not selling tickets to see LeBron James, or even the next LeBron James. Most of us won't be having a Heisman candidate to boast about. We won't be pushing the No. 1 baseball draft pick. And even if we have him, he won't be with us for long.

And, don't forget, our corporate sponsors also take note of what we are doing. If they see us pumping free tickets throughout the community, they will begin to question the value of their sponsorships. They will ask themselves if they are doing the right thing with their money. They will ask if they are getting the right kind of return on their investment. Of course, sponsors are looking for bodies in the stands, eyes on their signage, etc. But good marketers also know that the best kind of exposure is the kind that reaches the correct demographic. The demographic that sees value in the product and has disposable income as well.

One might ask: *"How, then, do we make our product have value without the benefit of star-power?"*

This is done in a wide variety of ways. It begins with the sales effort and the quality of that effort, from the person on the phone to the personal face-to-face. It involves a quality offer, a good presentation and a strong closing. That is followed by delivering the product. The customer must enjoy his or her experience in dealing with the organization. This includes everything from the initial sales experience to the contact on game days or fulfillment and delivery of product benefits. Good communications with the customer are a must! The icing on the cake is the ultimate delivery of a good entertainment product, this includes clean, attractive facilities, quality food and beverage offerings at reasonable prices, an exciting vibe in the facility, extras such as product giveaways and promotional entertainment during the event. It is difficult to specifically do a *"how to"* when it comes to creating *marketing/promotional* ideas that are unique. I was far from the most creative person in my industry. One of the best things about minor league baseball is that we are only competitors on the field and more like partners off it.

The ideas of one creative genius such as Mike Veeck can be copied. It is a form of flattery to see your promotional idea copied and we share ideas freely in our promotional seminars. In affiliated ball, you have to be slightly (*but not a lot*) more careful about your *"creativity"*. It is more important to affiliate farm directors and MLB teams that the players are never inconvenienced by promotions. For example, if something takes a little too long between innings, that will not sit well with your field manager and players as it can cause a problem with the pitcher warming up for the inning, etc. and also lengthens the overall game time. However, in independent ball, your manager is your employee, as are the players and they understand for the most part that it is important for them to go along with zany promotions in order to put fans in the stands. Most clubs conduct *"brainstorming"* sessions to develop ideas for promotions for the season. Promotions can be games and zany happenings that occur between innings during each game or they can be a game *"theme"* that is intended to both attract ticket sales and entertain folks at the game. I am not a big proponent of *"theme"* nights as I think they are generally ineffective in driving ticket sales. However, it is important to create a fun atmosphere at the ballpark and these nights do serve that purpose.

Embrace The Zany

A well-run brainstorming session for promotional ideas will occur in the fall, just after the season while the happenings, successes and failures of the previous season are still fresh in everyone's mind. The moderator, usually the General Manager, needs to make it comfortable for every member of the staff to toss out ideas without fear of rejection. It must be clear to everyone that no idea is too *"dumb"* or impossible. In order to come up with something new, everything must be on the table.

We've done many *"zany"* things over the years, but nothing on the level of Mike Veeck-led teams. One of the more memorable events for me was a *"Used Car Night"* we did in Amarillo when we gave away a *"junker"* every inning. We were able to purchase nine jalopies which did run but, but barely. We parked the cars in front of the stadium for several nights in advance to make it clear to folks that they were not great cars. Fans who thought they would like to win one of the cars were invited to put their name in a drawing. Thus, they saw what they were entering for. We drove a car out onto the field between each inning and brought three contestants down on the field. Each contestant was pre-drawn from the entry box and given a car key. One of the keys would start the car and that would be the winner of that car. The first time we tried this night in Amarillo, Texas it went well for a couple of innings and then, the third car we rolled out stalled in front of the visitor's dugout. It would not start and the visiting manager became very agitated. Finally, the players had to come out and help us push that car off the field! The managers weren't happy, but the fans thought it was hilarious.

On another used car night in Columbus, Georgia, our staff suggested we try a prank. After giving away three or four cars, one of the staff had managed to get their hands on the keys to our radio announcer's car. Lo and behold, while he is on the air, our broadcaster sees the outfield gates open and in comes his car as the next giveaway! We had arranged for three fans to go along with the prank with one of them winning the car and getting very excited. We told the fans that it was our broadcaster's car and that he had generously donated it to the contest. Needless to say, it was hilarious and later, when the fans were told the whole thing was a prank they also laughed and applauded.

Be A Creator of Value, Not Free

One of the more popular nights we were able to conduct for several years in Columbus was flying *Elvises*. Our operations director was a retired military skydiver and still involved in that "*hobby*." He was able to round up about four buddies to dress in *Elvis* costumes mimicking the event from the movie *Honeymoon in Vegas*.[3] They jumped before the game to deliver the game ball and then, after the game, they would do a "*night*" jump complete with holiday blinking lights on the *Elvis* costumes. During the game, we would play *Elvis* music at all opportunities and after the post-game jump, we would feature a performance by an *Elvis* impersonator, who also worked the crowd during the game. This was an example of a "*theme night*" that really worked because it was a lot of fun and as we repeated it every season fans began to look forward to that night. Even the entertainment editor of the local newspaper would cover it like one of the social events of the season.

One of the most zany "*in-game*" nightly promotions I can recall began as a one-time joke. One of our hard core season ticket holders came to my office one night with a big sombrero and a sarape. He asked if he could be introduced in the stands as "*Pancho Villa and his band of Thieves*". He said he would stand and wave the sombrero and his entire section had agreed to stand and be recognized as the "*band of thieves*". I could see the humor in it and in the '70's I didn't worry too much about political correctness so I agreed to the idea. It was so funny. Even the players came out of the dugouts to look into the stands and see what the commotion was all about. And it led to a nightly bit of humor. Every night after that, this same fan would be introduced as a different celebrity. He would often come with a prop to go along with the scheme and sometimes, he would just stand and wave. The regular fans understood the joke and started stopping at guest relations to offer ideas as to who should be the "*special guest*" that night.

Players and coaches came to my office to suggest ideas for our special guest each night. Both home and away teams. Fans who were not regulars would either ask him for his autograph if they believed he was that celebrity or they would come to the office and ask exactly where *Tommy Lasorda* or whomever it was, was sitting. Over the course of a couple of seasons, we had introduced him as a wide variety of famous people both dead and alive. Everyone from *President George Washington* to retired baseball superstars like *Mickey Mantle* or famous actors like *Charlton Heston*. It was a great running gag. All of these things create the value that our customers are looking for and, if delivered well, will keep them coming back for more.

What we must be in this level is a creator of value. We must convince our customer (*fan*) base that what we have to offer is worth something! We must make them feel that they have spent their money wisely and that it was a good decision. The game ticket is the engine that drives the value of a sports sponsorship. Without strong ticket sales, no sports or entertainment property can produce value for the operator or the sponsors. The value of the ticket is at the core of the overall value of the property. Free tickets have zero value. This is an absolute. Value is created by strong marketers who show every customer from a single game ticket buyer to a major corporate sponsor, that the product is worthy of the money they are spending.

Sell Events
Not Outings

Brad Taylor
Vice President / General Manager
MountainStar Sports Group / El Paso Chihuahas

Pacific Coast League, Triple-A Baseball

About The Author

Brad Taylor has served as General Manager & Vice President of MountainStar Sports Group and the El Paso Chihuahuas since their inception in 2013. Prior to that, he was GM then President of the Bowling Green Hot Rods from 2008–2013, served 9 years with the Trenton Thunder including COO/GM from 2006–2008, and had stints in Fayetteville, NC and Huntington, WV.

The focus on group sales is not about an outing. No one comes to an outing. They come to an event. That is what we sell. We talk about building an event, then ask how many people would benefit from attending that event in the community. It is a mindset change to get away from an outing for more group sales representatives. An event is so much larger than an outing ever could be, yet is not sold enough to group sales prospects.

When we train our group sales representatives, we don't define categories as much as teach them to draw the group sales circle around individuals that they meet. Everyone is a circle of influence to at least ten people that you do not know. Imagine the power of that; meeting all of the people around someone that you do not know. If you do it to 10 people, and they each have 10 people around them, chances are, 85 percent of them will be new acquaintances. That is how group sales prospecting is born.

I always look at myself as an example of a potential group lead. It is important to try to be insular, to imagine yourself in a similar opportunity as those you are attempting to prospect. If a group sales representative was to talk to me, they would find out that I work with a staff of 60 people in our front office. I also coach a youth league, serve as a board of director in six non-profits, which in turn opens up various circles of influence by simply chatting with me. Framing it that way, I can easily connect a group sales representative to eight different groups in my circle of influence without even trying.

Too many teams default on how to sell groups in the first place. They focus on lowest price, taking that low-hanging fruit. We encourage our account executives to try to supersize their groups whenever possible. Ask for ways to bring out hundreds of people, instead of dozens. Try to get that group coming to multiple games, not only one per season. Group sales are actually events in themselves for those attending. They aren't outings. They are *supposed* to be special. Companies, schools and other entities pay for that type of experience. But group sales take a lot of work and commitment in order to pull off, and a lot of teams treat it like order-taking, and often miss the potential to enlarge the crowd coming to their games.

Some of the missed opportunities in group sales are all around us. Non-profits, manufacturers and agriculture are a few areas that never have events built for their constituents to experience. Every team talks about improving the experience for the group leader, but I tend to believe focusing on the group sales leader in your own front office is another way to pay dividends. That means salary, commission and tiered bonus structures based on sales team achievement. We often hold fun contests with prizes, or provide time off or a nice meal to show our appreciation. Your best sales people are the ones you should be personally thanking the most, because they are the ones looking for the opportunities in the field that others are blind to.

Set Realistic Goals

Every September, we work individually with each account executive as they write their own business plan for the following season. This is where they look at setting achievable goals. We adjust those goals if they are lower than we think they should be, but there is always some leeway. More often than not, however, account executives often shoot higher than upper management does. That means working together to create a realistic "*bar*" to be set, and then, throughout the entire sales season, have the account executive refer back to their own business plan and path when setting a barometer for success. Our daily group sales report is e-mailed to me for review, along with our director of ticket sales and our account executives.

There is never a question of how we are pacing, because we are always keeping it top of mind. We also track our progress with a group sales board in the office, updated live each day. Along with our weekly ticket sales meetings, we manage to review all pacing of actual sales against projected goals and budget year round. The thing is, groups show up. Actual attendance from a group is higher than a normal ticket purchased, because no one in that group wants to miss their group's event. While season seats will always have some importance for base supporters, group sales is always an area of growth with unstoppable potential for new revenue streams and customers.

When I was at Trenton, New Jersey in 2000, I witnessed how our league partner the Reading Phillies built their ticket sales around their *mammoth* group sales efforts. They did calls, meetings and appearances all based around group ticket cultivation. They were fantastic at it and still are, building a culture around selling the group ticket. They prospected and built themes for groups to participate in, driving game attendance. Our own efforts in Trenton mirrored what the Reading Phillies were doing, and our group sales skyrocketed. Group sales is about wanting to know more about those prospects that you talk to. You have to learn how to ask for referrals, and draw those group sales circles around each person that you work with.

We are all linked by those multiple prospective groups through our personal and professional lives: *A great group sales representative knows how to tap into that information for each prospect, draw out the potential group contacts available, and connect the dots accordingly.*

Group sales should be fun, not monotonous, building relationships with like-minded people, making friends, asking for references. If you aren't doing that with each prospect, being genuinely curious about them, then you aren't cultivating group sales numbers effectively.

Form Leading Questions

A great leading question to generate group sales efforts is: *"Who else would like to have as much fun at the ballpark as you are?"*

This breaks barriers and gets your group sales buyers talking, allowing you to earn more business through their connections. All of this though, depends on the entire staff working as a team. The moment that your group sales effort becomes a silo, it harms the entire effort. I personally have an issue with one person being in charge of a theme night who refuses to let the other staff members help them.

When you "go it alone," you lose out on so much potential group sales buyers: *One person leading the effort is fine, but they should be enlisting the help of their fellow front office teammates.*

This should be a cooperative effort between members of the front office, where the leader of one theme night or group category can pay back the leader of another category by contributing to their event. Collaboration is a key part of sales.

Group sales efforts are also a form of living your brand: *It is everything to the growth and success of the franchise to gain total team buy-in for what you are doing.*

If your team doesn't buy-in, there is little that you can do to convey the right brand message to the community that you serve. You cannot sell a brand that your staff doesn't buy into either. From start to finish, living our brand is the whole reason for our success. We have fun with being The El Paso Chihuahuas. We put nachos in a dog bowl. We have a *Bark Brigade* for on-field promotions. The building in the outfield is the *Big Dog House* and has a *"wooftop"* deck on the top floor.

Pricing is less important for groups when moving the needle than the idea of experiential. That's why The Chihuahuas live the brand that we work for. We want groups to come out, see something unique, so that they come back. Because it is an event. Not simply an outing. We want the groups to get on the field, hold a big flag for the national anthem, create a tunnel for the team to run through, take the field with the team for pre-game. A group can have an exclusive post-game opportunity with the team, making them the only ones allowed to play catch on the field or run the bases. Groups care less about price as long as you can discover what their passion is. Sometimes, it's a passion project like supporting a charity, letting them table with information the night of that event, or supporting their cause overall.

Typically, it's the smaller groups that want the cheapest price available and are the most demanding of our staff: *That's why maximizing groups helps evade those issues.*

The differences, if there are any, between male and female group leaders are minimal or non-existent. I've never noticed a difference. Everyone wants less work to organize an event. And your team has to know that it is your job, not the group leader's, in order to make their event easier to manage. We look to build in-depth relationships, with more than one person, so a group opportunity never vanishes if the original point of contact leaves that company, non-profit or group.

It is also important to know who a secondary point of contact is for every group to keep them involved: *"Who is your backup in case you get sick or are unable to see this through? Who will we be working with next time for this event?"*

A Mega Offering

Too many teams attempt to force relationships through gifting models of giving things away. I disagree with that practice. You have to maintain value at all times. Once you've given it away for free or for a dollar, it is very hard to ever recapture the full value of what you believe that product is worth. Building relationships is a two-sided effort, you have to provide full value so that price isn't what any group wants to focus on. The best advice that I ever received was from the former owner and general manager of the Asheville Tourists, Ron McKee. *"Treat people like they are in your own living room as a guest."* You do that, you provide full value, and they aren't looking at what it costs them to receive that value or how to get it cheaper.

Over the past 18 years, another piece of sage advice from the Trenton Thunder co-owner, Joe Plumeri, has stayed with me. Keep what you got, get more out of them, and find new ones. He's a tremendous leader and motivator, along with being a former CEO of the Willis Group and Primerica Financial. I've used his advice at least once a week over the past 18 years since I heard it, and love to dole it out. Because it applies to sales as well as value.

This is where group sales combine all of that advice together into a mega offering of an event unlike anything that your customers have ever witnessed before or since.

Every market is different in how to engage on theme nights. Especially religious ones such as *Faith & Family*. During my time in Bowling Green, Kentucky, with the Hot Rods, the church nights were always huge and every church strived to participate. In other markets, I've experienced bigger churches seeking to have their own nights, without the other churches involved. We try and do both, where we can sell a group, build an event, and create an experience like no other. That's what group sales is all about.

Our Scout Nights are always interesting for us because we follow the game with an on-field sleepover: *It's actually an overnight "lets stay awake all night" event, but it provides the overall value point that I'm trying to make.*

Any time that you manage to exceed the idea that attending your game is simply a seat (*ticket*), by adding execution elements such as food, first pitches, parades and recognition pieces, you create intangible value that cannot be replicated. It is an event experience that supersedes any argument on price.

I encourage a team to live its brand by being present in the community it sells to. Team representatives should be going to youth league games, coach or sit on local boards of directors, go to schools, hospitals and volunteer their time. That's why the El Paso Chihuahuas have a "*Volunteer Pack*" where our staff and players are sponsored in their efforts to attend various community events and projects. Your community needs to be asked for feedback, so that you can use their ideas and give them a win out of the engagement opportunity you have with them.

Leverage Your Mascot

Sometimes, our group sales cultivation efforts are through more than a face-to-face with a representative. We utilize our mascot for over 500 non-game appearances annually, coordinated through our community relations department. I strongly encourage any team making this undertaking to have multiple mascot suits to prevent wear and tear issues. The goal is to be everywhere you can, and when we are there, we engage. The mascot is the brand ambassador for your team, the one member who most likely will never leave. Players and coaches will come or go. But the fans count on the mascot to always be there, present, to interact with.

Our mascot is a full-time, salaried employee who goes out on scheduled appearances daily. We also tie appearance opportunities to the group sales staff, so that they can tag along when appropriate to convert events into sales. The mascot creates warm, fun connection points with our community. It turns everyone into a kid having fun. When we go to school appearances, it's not the kids that hold us up from leaving for another event, it's the teachers who want pictures as well. This is why bringing group sales staff to mascot events is important. Our mascot actually has a revenue line that he is responsible for, including sponsored appearances and birthday parties.

When they are with a mascot at a school, youth league or business appearance, they can ask for the sale: *You brought us here. Have you thought about bringing your group out for an entire game for hours of fun?"*

A full-time mascot is critically important to these efforts: *It shows commitment from the team to the mascot's value as a community ambassador and creates consistency in its character.*

All of this comes back to the push for more group sales: *Now that we've been out to your place, how do we get you out to ours?*

This question isn't framed by a mascot that doesn't talk:

✓ It is by the group sales representative who is attending the event with them.

✓ It's about asking for the sale, not for an outing, but for an event. Something that they cannot experience anywhere else. Once you build that event, the group sales will follow.

Respect
The Process

Mike Birling
Vice President
Durham Bulls
International League, Triple-A Baseball

About The Author

Mike Birling is in his 21st year with Capitol Broadcasting Company, and is in his first year as Vice President – Baseball Operations. Previously, Birling served as the Bulls general manager from 2003 through 2017, and joined the franchise as assistant general manager at the conclusion of the 1998 season. Over the last four seasons alone, the organization has recorded its four highest single-season attendances, earned the John H. Johnson President's Award and hosted the 2014 Triple-A All-Star Game in addition to the 2015 and 2016 ACC Baseball Championships. Prior to joining the Bulls, Birling worked for the Wisconsin Timber Rattlers in the Single-A Midwest League from 1994 through 1998, serving his last three seasons as general manager. In 1998 he captured Midwest League Executive of the Year, and has earned the International League Executive of the Year award in both 2003 and 2015.

Over the past 24 years, I've worked in an industry so many people would do anything to get into, and I realize how fortunate I am to have that opportunity. When you hire a staff, whether it be game day or full-time, helping them understand how important professional sports teams are to the fabric of a community is imperative. Working in sports isn't for everybody, and that's a difficult conversation you must have sometimes with employees who just don't fit the mold. If you have the right hiring process in place, that conversation occurs less over time. I am a firm believer in process. You need a comprehensive plan going in to any hiring opportunity, whether it's a face-to-face interview for a full-time staff member or a game day worker job fair. The last thing you want is to have applicants at an interview or job fair see you are unorganized, as it reflects poorly on your organization. Just like the applicant should be putting their best foot forward, your organization should be putting its best foot forward.

When the Durham Bulls conduct a game day worker job fair, we set up stations so applicants are constantly busy and spend the least amount of time simply waiting for their name to be called. There are check-in stations, and applicants are then divided up by the department they are interested in working in. We then operate multiple interview stations where each interviewer checks off the basics for each applicant – can they work the days required, do they understand the time commitments and so on. Then our staff focuses on situational questions to see how this employee would handle customer service situations, both good and bad. Finally, we ask questions specific to each game day position to see if an applicant would fit well with that job title, those responsibilities, the manager and the team already in place.

Vetting so many applicants in such a short amount of time is a true challenge, but reliable, outgoing people are the best candidates we can train. We are in the entertainment business, and as our most customer-facing employees, our game day staff has to reflect that attitude.

After we've interviewed all candidates, all interviewers meet together a couple days later over lunch to hold a '*draft*' of all applicants. These discussions can get intense, as different departments can '*fight*' to get the best candidates on their team. We normally have upwards of 300 job candidates attend, thus it's important our hiring processes are efficient. We try not to complicate hiring our game day staff. If a candidate doesn't smile, or possesses negative body language, we can tell early on they're not right for our organization.

After they've been hired, we work quickly to get our game day staff invested in our fan experience through staff training. We train our staff all together over the importance of customer service, and go through the pillars of the Bulls' customer service model. When that is complete, we break up into individual departments so employees can be trained on their specific responsibilities. At Durham Bulls Athletic Park we're fortunate to host a lot of college games, so we have multiple opportunities to train our staff in a game situation before the Bulls' season begins.

The Nightmare Games

When the Bulls' 70-game home schedule begins on Opening Day, it's vital our staff is at peak performance for the first game and this is why it's helpful for our organization to re-hire as many past employees as we can. However, our training never stops, as every game day we host meetings to go over successes and failures from previous games, and how we can duplicate the good and correct the bad. We want our game day staff to feel empowered to make a fan's time at our stadium special, and hosting these daily meetings to go over expectations helps that process.

One asset that has helped me achieve success throughout my career has also proven to be a negative in certain situations – I take it personally when a fan says they didn't have a good time at the ballpark. That attitude continues to drive me to make our operation better, but when the DBAP welcomes over half a million people every year, those comments can wear you down over time. Through all the games I've worked in 24 years, there are two nights lodged in my memory that still give me nightmares – July 4, 2008 and April 3, 2014. Both nights went wrong for different reasons and for the most part were out of my control, but I still take those nights personally and use them to drive me to constantly improve our operation.

On July 4, 2008, there was a massive storm that blew through Durham and knocked out power for all in the area, which created chaos with a near record crowd in the ballpark. April 3, 2014 was the first game at the stadium after a $20 million renovation, and much of the construction wasn't completed until late the night before. The last-minute touches left our staff and stadium unprepared for a large Opening Day crowd, and we didn't hold up our end of the bargain for our fans. I've taken those two days very hard, and think about them often to use as motivation to always be better. Each fan who comes through our gates trusts us with their money and time to deliver an amazing experience, and when they enter the ballpark they deserve nothing less than a top-notch outing.

It's also worth remembering situations will occur that force you to change your plans, and it's important to contain your emotions when things happen beyond your control. We focus on putting systems in place and training our employees on a regular basis, so when a difficult situation arises, all parties are on the same page to ensure a smooth environment for our fans.

Your Mentors Matter

When you've been fortunate to work in this industry as long as I have you learn how to handle those difficult situations from those who have taught, trained and mentored you. Steve Malliet, Peter Anlyan and George Habel are three people who have enhanced both my life and my career. Steve was the person who gave me my first job in MiLB in 1994, Peter hired me as Assistant General Manager of the Bulls in late 1998, and George has been my boss for the last 17 years. Teachable moments are all around us, and to have mentors who are there to guide us in understanding those challenges makes all the difference.

There are many things I've learned from the mentors above, and the first one is never let anyone outwork you. My mentality has always been someone, somewhere is always working harder, so I always need to keep up with the best in the industry. Other important things I've learned throughout my career are sometimes you need to play for the tie, learn to delegate, never be afraid to take risks, and empower your staff while treating them well.

Over the years, I've learned to be very decisive. Sometimes those decisions have been right on and many other times they have been completely wrong, but you can't be afraid to make decisions. To me it's an important factor. Actually making a decision instead of being paralyzed by fear of making the wrong choice. If I make a wrong decision, I learn from it and move on. There must be trust when leading employees that your decisions will be executed throughout the organization to get the result you envisioned.

The philosophy of our organization is to never stop hiring good people. We always try to stack our lineup card with hard-working, passionate employees, which provides us flexibility to let folks go if they aren't the right fit or move on to bigger and better things. We've had former employees move on to other major sports leagues, including MLB, NBA and NASCAR. At the Durham Bulls, we aim to hire great people, give them the resources to be successful, and move on to bigger challenges after the Bulls.

Conversely, this line of work isn't for everyone and we have to identify when it's time to move on from them. In the moment it's difficult for both parties, but more often than not over time everyone realizes it was for the best. It hits home for our organization when this happens because in our business it's like losing a family member. We tend to put the blame on us because if we are training our staff the right way and setting the right expectations, our employees should be set up for success. For game day employees, we provide them a schedule at least one month out, and we want them to make plans based on our schedule. When issues such as sickness occur we ask them to be respectful of the Bulls organization and warn us so we can back-fill their positions as quickly as possible. If we notice a pattern of calling in sick or other attendance issues, we're forced to terminate their employment.

Safety Always

A good general manager understands what people are good at, what knowledge they may lack, and that is especially true of ballpark security. I leave the safety of our fans to the experts. Ballpark security is never something to cut corners on, and I recommend hiring outside companies who specialize in performing background checks and hiring uniformed officers to work security. At the Bulls, we brought in the head of security for Major League Baseball to see what our stadium and staff needed, and while we haven't been able to implement all of his suggestions, it has given us a framework of where we need to go moving forward.

Safety is one of the pillars of our organization. When fans come to a game at the DBAP they expect to arrive safely and enjoy the game with their friends or family without fear. Security isn't left to only our off-duty police officers or bag-check security staff – ballpark safety is the job of every single game day and full-time employee at the Durham Bulls. Game day employees and full-time employees are equipped with radios during games at the ballpark, and they are all trained that if they see something, they say something. They are expected to be in contact with the closest officer whenever they notice anything out of the ordinary taking place. We provide regular training exercises with the Durham Police Department, so they know what to expect if they are called to the stadium. I preach all the time you cannot be afraid to overstaff on uniformed security or bag check security. I know most teams try and keep payroll as efficient as possible, but the last thing we want is for our fans to not feel safe at the DBAP.

There are always instances where as an organization you have to choose between customer service and the safety of your fans. It's always a tough call, but I recommend erring on the side of safety. Many fans dislike having someone go through their belongings, and some fans think we only do it to stop them from bringing in outside food and drink. We make it a point that our security staff constantly reassures fans safety is of the utmost importance at our ballpark. It's extremely important we are consistent, open and honest with our fans. People who come to our games don't like to be surprised, so we do all we can to communicate with our fans what to expect on game days, from security information to promotional information to specialty food items. The first thing a fan experiences at the stadium is their entry, so it's imperative to get that experience right and inform them of the best guidelines to follow before arriving.

Unfortunately, in our sport inclement weather will always be a factor. Fans will never be happy with your weather policy, and you need to do all you can to remind them weather is beyond your control. We are very open about our decisions when fans become upset, and we explain in detail the reason we have certain rain policies. Further, we never treat all weather events the same. There are so many factors to take into account, such as what was the weather like all day long, how important is it we play that game from a team or attendance standpoint or how severe the weather was. Additionally, there's been times where even though we played an official game we've allowed fans to use their ticket as a *rain check*. We try to be flexible enough to make sure we meet their expectations and not lose business in the future.

Beyond weather the next fan experience issue is always parking. It's a big issue for us because we do not control any of it around the ballpark. When I talk to the folks who manage the local parking decks or lots, we convey to them they are the first touch point of our fans as they arrive at the ballpark. We don't want our fans to feel taken advantage of before they even walk through the gates. I remind them the costs of our tickets are very low, therefore they can't gouge a patron who wants to park as that is unacceptable. The difficult part is our fans feel it is our responsibility even if they aren't our employees. Fans don't care who is paying the parking attendants, they just want a problem fixed.

With that type of responsibility, we expect them to properly train their employees, have a smile on their face at all times, and remember their job is to make sure our fans arrive and leave as safely and efficiently as possible.

Transitioning back to personnel I feel one of the most important parts of being a general manager is developing your staff. It is one thing to know how to sell tickets, sponsorship and marketing, but the most important part is how you set-up your organization's employees, as well as the frontline ambassadors who are hired by third party vendors, into a model of success. Many times, it comes down to the self-awareness and willingness of the employee to adapt on whether they will be successful or not. It is my job as the general manager to give each employee the tools to do their job at the highest level. We offer many things to our employees, including an employee assistance program that is completely confidential. Over the years, I've also hired personal coaches for employees who may need to develop certain skills in order to be successful in this business.

"Million Dollar Arm, Five Cent Head"

At my age I tend to get frustrated by the questions I get asked from prospective employees wanting to get into sports. I get hundreds of resumes from folks who ask us about working with the players. Even the slightest bit of research into a MiLB team would show that we have little to nothing to do with the players or coaches. I once had a resume from someone who *quoted* me their little league stats. We also consistently get resumes from students just out of college asking for $50-$60k in salary with zero experience. My advice is please do your research, put the arrogance aside and show why you are different than the thousands of other people trying to get into sports.

Another question I get asked all the time is about the movie '*Bull Durham.*' We understand and appreciate the impact it has had not only on our franchise, but also on all of MiLB. During the 2018 season, we are celebrating the 30-year-anniversary of the film. It is such an important part of our history. The movie meant so much to our industry and was the catalyst to the massive success you see in MiLB today. I am still amazed how people from all around the world continue to purchase our merchandise. We have our own beer company called *Bull Durham Beer.* We have *Crash, Annie* and *Nuke* racers who entertain our fans at games. Each of these pieces keeps this classic movie alive.

Everyone who has watched the movie remembers the line "*hit the bull*". Our mascot, Wool E. Bull, is the face of our franchise and the biggest brand in the community. It isn't the players, the ownership or the front office that matters as much as Wool E. Bull. Every team must employ a full-time mascot. It should be the catalyst of your game presentation, your off-season community plan and every facet of your organization. It is very difficult for teams to stay relevant during the off-season, and your mascot is the key to that. Our mascot is involved in everything all year long. He goes out to schools, promotes anti-bullying campaigns, attends many charity events, and holiday parades. Anything that is happening, Wool E. is there.

Most of the events our mascot is invited to become *no-brainer* decisions to attend. But in today's climate, there are some times it requires us to take a step back, and make a difficult decision on whether to book the event appearance. We will always choose a charity function over a paid corporate function. We have to remember our mascot is an extension of the team, the owner, and the community. We don't allow the mascot to attend events that in any way could make us look bad. We are okay with sending our mascot to controversial events if we believe it is the right thing to do. But in the end, sports is a place where people try to get away from all the stressful things that happen day-to-day, and we focus on that.

Kid-Driven Business

An extension of your mascot should be a kids club. We must find ways to connect today's youth with the game of baseball. We all are stewards of this great game and it is our responsibility to connect kids to the game. I do believe the public is seeing through these clubs more and more, however. They know we are making an enticing offer to the kids so the parents will pay to attend with their child. I want parents to want to attend with the children because it will help bring much needed family time, not because they feel tricked into it by their kid getting a voucher. Our kids club isn't as large as other teams, but it does give us an avenue for a sponsor who wants to hit that demographic. Many teams offer a free kids club to grow their numbers as much as possible to attract a larger sponsor. We have tiered levels for our club.

We promote our kids club heavily on social media, utilize our Sunday games to push it in the ballpark, and allow any kids club members to move to the front of the line for the *"Kids Run The Bases"* promotion. While kids are running around on the field, we promote the kids club, letting fans know they can have their children move to the front of the line by joining up. We also hand out small kids club membership material to everyone in the run the bases line, as well as promote it through e-mail marketing.

We have seen a benefit in how we run our three annual kid camps through the same promotions as our kids club. The key is to be very honest about what the camp is, and what it is not. Our camps are meant to be fun, not teaching camps. If you are a kid on a travel ball team expecting to get one-on-one coaching from players, well, this isn't the place for you. We are very up-front about how our kids camps work. Our camp is meant to give children an opportunity to play on our field for three days and hang out with Triple-A baseball players. It is a combination of players providing basic instruction and playing games. The morning hours the kids go from station-to-station, everything from base running, hitting, fielding and throwing. In the afternoon, we have kids play games with our players pitching to them. We setup times over three days where kids can ask players any questions they would like, getting autographs. The key to running our camp is you must be detailed, organized and prove to the parents that the security of their child is a top priority. They are trusting you with their kid.

People are always amazed how year in and year out MiLB teams are so successful drawing fans to attend. Despite having Triple-A players, they aren't necessarily why fans come to the ballpark. MiLB is different from nearly all other sports. Most fans do not come because of the baseball. They come because of the experience and everything that comes with a MiLB game. That doesn't mean we shouldn't promote the baseball aspect, though.

A lot of our promotion of players comes during the game and on social media. We want our fans to get to know our players. If they feel closer to these players they are more apt to come to games. We will produce in-game videos that highlight certain team members and give fans a glimpse of who they are off the field. They are produced in-house at a high standard and our players love doing them. We also try to get our players out in the community as much as possible. We know it is hard with them only having one to two off days a month, but they understand the importance of it. Promoting rehab appearances of major league players is also tricky. It is really a matter of trying to learn as much as you possibly can about your fans, and the more you know about them the more you can target market. For instance we know our fans are NC State fans or UNC fans, so if we have a player on our team or a visiting team member who went to either of these schools we can target them with email blasts. Same thing with knowing who your fans favorite MLB team is. If we get a rehab from a visiting team we will send email blasts to local fans of that team. Rehab assignments from the Rays haven't led to much success for us because pretty much every star on the Rays came through Durham, so it hasn't been as exciting to our fans.

The PDC Won't Move The Needle

Speaking of the Rays, we have had an incredible partnership with them since we jumped to Triple-A in 1998.[1] Most of our fans don't really understand the relationship between a MiLB team and its Major League team, and what goes into a *Player Development Contract* (PDC). Every affiliated MiLB team has a two-year or four-year PDC with a Major League team, meaning the two teams will be linked for the duration of that contract. Most PDC's will not move the needle in terms of ticket sales or fan interest, unless the Major League team has a regional following. An affiliate of the Cubs, Yankees or Red Sox will see the ability to increase attendance, but the majority of affiliates won't.

The status of your PDC isn't what matters to most of your fans. What matters is the experience you provide on a nightly basis and what creative promotions you can come up with to attract fans. A very controversial move we made a decade ago was to eliminate the gate giveaways for the first '*X*' amount of fans, and I believe we are the only team to do this. We used to do it like every other sports team, but we grew tired of handing out giveaways and many people coming through the gates not even realizing there was a giveaway item for that night, and upsetting fans when we ran out.

I never liked the feeling of upsetting more people than we were taking care of, so we made the change to build momentum on our mini plans. We made the decision to reward fans who made a larger commitment (*eight games or more*) to us instead of rewarding fans who were able to get out of work before others. I believe this is a big reason we have more mini plan holders than any other MiLB team to my knowledge. Our fans are thankful they don't have to rush to the ballpark to get a giveaway because they know it's guaranteed.

This is one small example of the discussions we have as a staff on a regular basis. You will never figure it all out, and if you think you will you are fooling yourself. To me, what makes working in MiLB so much fun is figuring out the best way to please our incredible fans. It all goes back to that process, and understanding how to best utilize your comprehensive plan so your staff can feel empowered to provide an environment where your fans have the best experience. If you have a process, continue to fine tune it so you will have success whether you have your own movie or not.

Selling Baseball Isn't Enough

Josh Olerud

President
Scranton/Wilkes-Barre RailRiders
International League, Triple-A Baseball

About The Author

Josh Olerud has served as General Manager & President of the Scranton/ Wilkes-Barre RailRiders since 2016, having joined the club the previous year as its Chief Operating Officer. Olerud was named 2017 International League Executive of the Year. Olerud also served as the Potomac Nationals' Executive Vice President and General Manager (2010–15), earning the Minor League Executive of the Year Award by the Pitch and Hit Club of Chicago (2012) and the Calvin Falwell Executive of the Year Award (2013). A graduate of Minnesota State University at Mankato's sport management program, Olerud started in baseball with the Rockford Riverhawks of the Frontier League in 2004, serving 6 years as an executive with the independent franchise.

Everything about minor league baseball is about sales. No one gets away with not selling the product. And there is always enough inventory to sell, even when you put up the "*sold out*" sign in the ticket window. Every executive remembers their first big sale, and it's probably a story that they tell their younger executives when they are starting out as an example of what can happen with the right approach. It also sets the tone for this business; you will not survive if you cannot make a sale. Doesn't matter if your job title says promotions or social media or groundskeeper. If you can sell, you will survive and advance in your minor league baseball career.

Part of our culture is understanding that beyond the game itself, we don't sell baseball here. Selling the game is not enough. This provides a vehicle for ticket buyers, sponsors and community members to create lifelong memories at our facility. Whether it's the mascot races, the opportunity for kids to run out on the field, or stuff yourself silly with $20 *all-you-can-eat seats*, it comes down to understanding that selling baseball isn't enough. You have do more than that to get people from your community to come out. There are 4,000 baseball games and other events happening in your area during the summer. What makes your experience different is the amount of promotion behind it.

When hiring for our front office staff, I seek out diversity which helps create a vibrant culture. Generational varieties help create that culture organically along with other balances. The goal is to manage each employee to their traits, hopefully putting them in a place to succeed and grow as an executive. Generational gaps help me grow as a team president, because I find myself soaking up wisdom from the younger generational employees as I do with the generation older than mine. When you pass on sales knowledge, or experience, it helps encourage by example what is possible for someone to achieve. This creates a positive culture in the office, promoting reasonable expectations for new and old staff to adhere to.

Minor league baseball employees often struggle with knowing what they are selling. They forget that we aren't wholly associated with baseball. Beyond the child's game of a sport that has been around for over 150 years, we are selling to a ton of non-baseball ticket buyers. Not realizing this often creates a blind spot with employees that hurts the product we sell to fans, who received mixed messaging as a result. Thousands of fans enter our ballpark turnstiles based on the promotion or event, not the potential results that the game has on the league standings. Organizational culture is delivered through your brand promise to every fan. If the sales process is weighed down by *red-tape*, the concessions stand is devoid of mustard or onion bits, and the bathroom hasn't been cleared in two days, your fan's view point of your brand changes. All of these factor into team business. Same as they do when your promotions stink or don't routinely get carried out as they should.

The Art of Delegation

Whether your fan is attending for the millionth or first time to your venue, they are all touchpoints for major companies and organizations in your community. How they see your brand goes beyond the 40-person front office staff. Or the 80-person part-time game day workers. And all of it is as vital as any crazy promotion that you carry out. If the fireworks go off without a hitch, but your ushers are jerks, then your marketing stinks. Because the fan views every component of their experience as part of the promotion for that game night. And once you lose them, you'll never get them back. Ever.

All of this comes down to how you manage the organization, and how you delegate assignments. If you want your fingertips on everything, you end up not having enough time to ensure that the little things get done. Every person on your staff is frozen with the idea that you will micromanage them. Then, they wait until you sign off on everything from ordering, cleaning and even carrying out simple tasks. Delegating does not mean abdication, but it means empowering your staff to help ensure that the entire fan experience is something that is unrivaled in its delivery.

When I first became a general manager, it took me a while to convince myself to clean off my plate and allow others in the office to be more involved, to take ownership of the task that I didn't have to be directly involved with until after they got to a certain point in the process. It is natural to want to take on everything from the get-go, to make an impact instantaneously, but in reality you're slowing down the entire office process by not getting more people involved. I've been fortunate enough to work for a great GM and work with many of the industry's best. And collectively, they've been my mentors either directly or indirectly throughout my career.

Mike Babcock was the general manager who gave me a lot of early guidance on selling and how he ran his day-to-day operations with the Rockford Riverhawks. I still pick his brain from time-to-time when certain situations come about to see what his views are. The great thing about working in baseball so long as that you build up great relationships with other general managers in the leagues you've worked in. And usually, being the young guy, I always picked the brains of the GM's that have been doing it longer, who have had lots of success running teams. It's truly a fraternity in the baseball community. I continue to constantly ask our colleagues how they arrived at certain decisions, analytical questions, staffing, etc. I would consider most of the colleagues that I've worked with as mentors that I lean on from year-to-year to improve my acumen in this industry.

Manage What You Got

Those with the most experience set the tone of the office as well as your career. If they aren't selling, you won't sell as much. And if they are selling, you'll sell harder. It's that expectation that you receive from mentors and office leaders that allow you to either grow or become stagnant. It's also the dividing line to whether you learn from mistakes or become more creative when looking at different sales or promotional experiences.

My first big sponsorship sale was a scoreboard sign to a new bar and restaurant in Rockford, Illinois for the Rockford Riverhawks. I met with the owner multiple times to talk about the team, and all that was going on with the new stadium that was currently under construction down the road from his establishment. Finally, one day, the conversation shifted from small inventory to *"what is the newest addition to the ballpark that you are constructing."* I talked up the new high-definition scoreboard that we had purchased, watched his eyes light up, and got him to buy in. This is why storytelling of big sales is important, to provide examples of what is achievable. My conversation with the owner started off as a small sponsorship discussion, then ended up being a massive partnership because I chose to listen and ask questions. He did the same with me. And we changed the conversation to a big sale after building a solid foundation for a relationship.

What they don't tell you about selling in minor league baseball is that you are managing other people as much as you try to focus on your own sales goals. My first supervisor's role in baseball was as the Director of Promotions. It may not say sales in my title, but I was definitely selling what our product was to the local community. My main responsibilities were to manage the sponsorship inventory that ran on game day as well as the staff that it took to fulfill those sponsorship commitments. Planning the run of the show, fulfillment of inventory elements was fun as well as challenging, with the whole goal of keeping our fans entertained. However, I found quickly that managing staff and other game day personnel was a no man's land of duties. You're only as successful as the people you have working with you. It was beneficial for me to learn this early in my career, because it showed me the growing pains of management and allowed me to build from that experience for my later jobs supervising others.

Selling Rehab Starts

Promotions is about selling into the market what you've got to offer. Sometimes that's the creative side of having a theme night, or it's a rehab start. That last one is an exciting time that a lot of baseball operators don't focus on enough. When you are marketing a rehab start, you typically don't get much time to promote the rehabbing player as the club learns about their assignment to your roster in less than 48 hours. You have to get a buzz created through all of media available to your team. That means issuing a press release, social media promotion, e-blast, web post and direct client e-mails. Your press release then gets followed up by getting on radio, an interview with the local newspapers. Anything to get more attention. But the radio and newspaper aren't as powerful as they used to be. Your team has to possess a strong digital brand, enough that it's easy to change your message and highlight the rehabbing player who is coming to your city for only a few days on the schedule out of the blue.

I had the privilege of having Stephen Strasburg's first rehab start at the Potomac Nationals after his electric rookie season where he had filled visiting MLB stadiums one after another.[1] When we learned that Strasburg was coming to rehab at the Potomac Nationals, we sent out a press release that morning before his announced start. Sold tickets out to a standing room only capacity situation within 24 hours. The rehab start isn't going to be that situation with any average player coming down to a minor league club. However, if a team is lucky to have the right player rehabbing at the right time where player interest is at a fever-pitch, it can be a huge financial gain for the team, as well as a national platform to promote your brand.

I've seen promotions that didn't work, but that's part of the challenge of working in minor league sports. It's about putting on a quality, unique experience each and every night out. It's fun to brainstorm on how to bring ideas to life. Although I feel every promotion night we agree to do is going to be successful, there are a few promotions every year that under-achieve or don't perform to the level of what you expect. If we knew it was not going to deliver, we wouldn't put forth the effort of doing them. But you never know unless you try. And you are constantly testing out your audience on what they like and don't like.

One promotion that absolutely failed got a lot of hype in our front office, but didn't generate the interest at our gate, called "*Caturday Night Fever.*" A night filled with disco music, where fans could bring their cat to the game. We pumped out a lot of crazy cat themed videos, gave away "*disco cat*" shirts to fans as they entered the ballpark, but fans didn't bring a lot of cats. I think fans were intrigued and we did get some fans that dressed as cats, but it really didn't turn the gate like we thought it would. One bright side was that we did a cat donation, and there were fans who adopted cats that night at the ballpark.

The Potomac Nationals are only 17 miles from their parent club, The Washington Nationals. That makes marketing against a parent club to be a double-edged sword in most circumstances. The Potomac Nationals are in the Carolina League, and had a great opportunity to tap into a local market, drew them to Northern Virginia to watch highly-touted prospects in the Washington National's farm system, as well as rehab starts for Bryce Harper, Strasburg and Ryan Zimmerman.

The other side of that coin is how deadly being so close to the parent club was. If the Potomac Nationals were scheduled head-to-head with the Washington Nationals, sharing the same dates for home games, it hurt our draw from the bigger club's fan base. And our fan base usually decided to travel the short distance to watch the parent club play. The positives in these situations always out-weighed the bad, and both clubs worked hard to build the relationship together to ensure that both businesses thrived despite the short proximity.

Community Marketing

There are creative ways to promote a minor league team that the parent club doesn't have at their disposal. You can offer up new logos or name releases, even suggesting various potential name choices, and it builds interest with the fan base. These promotional components are exciting and transcending moments of your franchise. I've been part of name changes and logo changes for the express purpose of re-establishing the brand, giving it a fresh new look or a change of direction of what the team wants to represent, such as a player development contract affiliation change with a new parent club. It's about beginning a new chapter for the community that you serve.

At Scranton/Wilkes-Barre, we have multiple mascots that take on different roles to give the fans a ton of fun entertainment. Our main mascot is Champ, and he is active in pregame ceremonies, crowd visits, and on-field promotions. Champ is our biggest personality, and is one Railrider that fans can always count on being in the stadium. Mascots are the cornerstone of building a community feel for your team, both inside and outside the ballpark. Your mascot has to be anywhere and everywhere, documented with photographs and video for social media, to show that you care about the community that you are in.

There are also other ways to build presence in the community. At the Scranton/ Wilkes-Barre Railriders, we created *Railriders University*. A simple concept meant to grow our brand in the baseball community while helping youth baseball players learn from the best. These were things we were currently doing at the stadium throughout the summer and when we thought about what we could do with the facilities we have inside it made it an easy decision to create a year round program. We started with four cages and a weight room to do speed, quickness and agility. All training sessions were led by former Major League players and coaches along with several current minor league players from the area. It has exploded and is the place for players to train all year and has had a positive impact in the community for baseball and the RailRiders.

When we built Railriders University, we looked at what our assets were: instructors, our facility and all the local baseball relationships (*little league, high school and college*). After putting all of the assets on paper we created a model that gave group and team training times, dates, the instructors that would be involved, with web and social pages created to drive our target audience to. Our biggest draw to the youth athletes are *"Train Where the Yankees Train"* and *"Learn from the Pros"*, that marketing alone helped us establish PNC Field as a training facility. This off season we tied in Geisinger Health as our naming rights partner to the program and they have helped us host coaches clinics and arm care and safety seminars to add additional value to *RailRiders University*.

The only way to cater to the community is to increase the amount of family fun sports and entertainment offering that you have. We do very well with our family promotions and we put at least one specialty night on the calendar each month. The consistent top five nights for us are *Super Hero, Princess and Pirates, Little League, Military Night* and *Boy Scout Night*. We have also had great success with our *Man vs. Marathon Night, Lego Night, Fan Appreciation Night*, and *Pierogi Night*. We try to fit in several movies each season along with anything we feel is relevant that we can have fun with.

If you're doing a military appreciation night, it really comes down to forming partnerships with local military groups and agencies in your marketplace. Some markets are more prevalent than others, but one thing each community has in common is that we make an effort to show our thanks to the men and women who make this country into the great country that it is today. We have had success by dedicating a staff member to forming those relationships that continue to grow annually. We also have a military discount to select games, military appreciation nights and each night, we honor our *Home Town Heroes* by recognizing a special service man or woman in the audience. All of these collectively make our *Military Nights* great experiences at PNC Field.

Food is an integral part of the fan experience, if you have great food and beverage deals that run consistently throughout your season it can sway fans from coming on certain nights of the week. We utilize Monday – Thursday to do aggressive food and beverage discounts to drive early to mid-week games. Dollar hotdogs and *Thirsty Thursdays* still have a value for the minor league model. They provide a value night that fans really look forward to and it gives you an opportunity to get info and gain data from what is typically the casual fan. Our goal is to utilize the value nights to reach fans that are not ticket holders and convert them to more than a casual fan by educating them on all the other values our season ticket holders gain.

Nonetheless, minor league baseball prides itself on the three pillars: *Family, Affordable, and Entertainment. This staple still holds its own in most markets.*

Learn From Failures

There have been food promotions that have failed. In Scranton/Wilkes-Barre, we tried to do a Wednesday promotion that worked in previous ballparks that I've been involved in but failed in Scranton/Wilkes-Barre, called *"A Belly Buster."* It is an all-you-can eat promotion for an hour prior to the game, highlighting the food from a local restaurant. Good for the restaurant by getting their product to potential clients in a creative and fun way. For whatever reason, it never built the traction we thought it would and we discontinued *"A Belly Buster"* promotion in Scranton/Wilkes-Barre after a year.

Drink specialty nights are still huge draws to minor league parks. But, in this day and age, it is important to also educate your fans on how they can take advantage of your team's *"Drive Home Safe"* programs that most teams do offer. One of the promotional aspects is offering preferred pricing for Uber and local cab companies to your fans. Since Wilkes/Scranton-Barre is not in a downtown location where public transportation options are available, it is best to promote Uber or local cab companies to your fans to get them home safe.

Minor League Baseball is highly predicated on the entertainment aspect. I strongly believe most of the creative professional sports theme nights and giveaways come from minor league baseball and bleed into other professional sports industries. *Star Wars Night* has become a major staple in minor league baseball, in doing so it has created a model that you need to comply with and in return can do a great job giving the *Star Wars* fans an unbelievable night. We typically get *Lucas Films* approval for the jersey we wear on-field and put to auction. We also go through licensing on co-branded merchandise that is very popular within our team store.

Star Wars Nights have become staples to all of our minor league schedules and fans anticipate a jam packed night full of *Star Wars* fun. We traditionally get 15-20 characters to great fans at the gate, take photos and to be a part of a special pre-game ceremony. Giving away a *Star Wars* themed bobble head and jerseys that replicate a feature character from the movie provides additional fun for our fans to help round out the full on *Star Wars* experience. I believe that by adding a charitable organization to not only be the benefactor of the *Star Wars* jersey auction but to participate in all the events makes the night extra special. It all gets topped off with Fireworks and traditionally becomes one of the must-see games on our schedule each year.

Long Live Fireworks Nights

Fireworks set the minor league baseball experience apart from other sports. Especially resonating on the weekend games for a lot of cities. At Wilkes/Scranton-Barre, we have fireworks on Opening Day, Independence Day, the Last *Game of the Year*, and every Friday, and a few Saturdays each season. It is still a valued ticket that we can push groups toward, as well as provide incentive to generate great pre-sold and walk-up ticket sales numbers. It also helps maximize revenues by keeping fans in the seats for the entire game. I believe that fireworks nights have held their value as a draw over time strongly. In the future, I can see more teams turn to laser light shows that provide the same post game value.

Back in the 1990s and early 2000's, traveling acts were visible in the majority of minor league ballparks annually. But they tend to come and go in spurts of fan interest. Although traveling acts have a decent cost associated, they are very comparable to celebrity appearances and giveaways. We still do a traveling act each year, try to find the ones that our fans have never witnessed prior, to create that allure of a unique fan experience. One of the best traveling act promotions by far as a draw in the past few years for Scranton/Wilkes-Barre was David "*The Bullet*" Smith Jr., who is shot out of a cannon. It really helped us draw fans and keep them in the seats until well after the game had completed.

I think bobble heads are still a *magic bullet*, they definitely still make an impact to the attendance and are still highly collectable. I do believe that the allure to bobble heads are a strong name that is creative and different than the average bobble head. Prime examples would be creative names, how they are dressed and what they are doing. There is always a challenge to do a bobble head launch on an off-night effectively but if it's the right person and you put enough other promotional fun into the game, it has the potential to do well.

We will typically do a high profile bobble head early in the year that is tied into all of our mini plans and has the allure to draw strong presold and walk up. The past few years we did former players and had them sign autographs/bobble heads for the fans that night as well. These have been players we put into our *Bobble Head Hall of Fame* and unveil their 7-foot bobble head on-field that will stay in PNC Field for ever. I think all of those elements make it a night that can be successful in the early part of the schedule when you typically wouldn't do a bobble head.

Fireworks are still a part of the Minor League experience that resonate with weekend games for a lot of cities: *Yes. Of course. You will never not have fireworks nights. Fans love them.*

There is no promotion that I wouldn't do, it obviously has to be tasteful. The beauty of Minor League Baseball is the creativity, we aren't afraid to go outside the box and try something that is unique and one of a kind. Promotions is selling. So is social media. Same with getting on the phone and talking to someone about sponsorship or tickets for the first time. Minor league baseball never gets away from selling. In fact, it brings you closer to selling than any other industry possibly could. Because when you are pushing a fireworks night or a *Star Wars Night*, you are selling the product. And it's good for those in your office culture to hear as well as understand that. Minor league baseball is all about sales.

Final Comments

This collection of perspective chapters by industry professionals was first dreamed up in the summer of 2016, initiated in the fall of 2016, and completed by the start of summer 2018. It is a labor of love, time and effort by twenty-five people, each with better things to do than remember, compile, write, gain permissions, coordinate waivers, rate chapters, proofread, layout and publish a book for others to read. But it was well worth it.

The selection and order placement of each chapter was debated, agreed upon and set by Troy Kirby and Chris LaReau in an effort to have the ideas, strategy and knowledge complement each other. At no time were the strategies, concepts or opinions by any of the chapter contributors made to fit the world view of those editing this collection, even if the editors personally disagreed with their conclusions. Chris LaReau compiled all of the questions for each chapter.

About Troy Kirby

Troy Kirby has worked in the sports industry since 2003, with three athletic departments and several semi-professional soccer teams, including ownership in with the Lacey Pocket Gophers Football Club (2017 - Present). Kirby is a co-founder and two-time president of the National Association of Athletic Ticket Sales & Operations (NAATSO) an organization which oversees college athletic ticket professionals and the founder of The Sports Sales Boot Camp at The Association of Luxury Suite Directors, of which he is also a board member. Kirby's podcast, The Tao of Sports, is recognized as an industry leader for its category.

About Chris LaReau

Chris LaReau is a member of the University of Dayton Class of 2019. A native of Noblesville, Indiana, LaReau has gained valuable experience working in the Indianapolis sports scene, interning at Indianapolis Motor Speedway, Indiana University-Purdue University Indianapolis Athletics and Butler University Athletics. While at the University of Dayton, Chris has worked in ticketing, premium seating, and athletic communications for the Flyers. LaReau's passion for UD Athletics was further showcased as he took on the role of student section president, leading the school's largest student organization during the 2017-2018 athletic season. Following graduation, LaReau hopes to build upon these experiences by working full time in athletics.

EXTRA
INNINGS

3 Additional Chapters, Syllabuses,
Quizzes and Group Topics

SALES

THE

GM'S
HANDBOOK

EDITED BY TROY KIRBY & CHRIS LAREAU

THE GM'S HANDBOOK: EXTRA INNINGS

*Download 3 additional chapters by a MiLB Team President and 2
General Managers, academic quizzes, syllabuses and group topic discussion
questions in The GM's Handbook: Extra Innings.*

Download it for FREE in PDF or Amazon Kindle.

www.gmshandbook.com

CITATIONS

Discovering Your Baseball "Why" by Jenna Byrnes

1. Mackay, Harvey. "Why I Love Employees Who Ask 'Why'." Inc.com. March 30, 2012. Accessed June 18, 2018. https://www.inc.com/harvey-mackay/the-power-of-why.html.

2. Bennett, Shea. "Social Media Overload - How Much Information Do We Process Each Day? [INFOGRAPHIC]." Adweek. July 31, 2013. Accessed June 13, 2018. https://www.adweek.com/digital/social-media-overload/.

3. Maxwell, John C. The 21 Irrefutable Laws of Leadership: Follow Them and People Will Follow You. Nashville, TN: Thomas Nelson, 1998.

4. Angelo, Megan. "I Saw Sarah Silverman Last Night, And She Said This Thing I'll Never Forget." Glamour. September 13, 2012. Accessed June 13, 2018. https://www.glamour.com/story/i-saw-sarah-silverman-last-nig.

5. "Kris Kristofferson Quotes." BrainyQuote. Accessed June 13, 2018. https://www.brainyquote.com/quotes/kris_kristofferson_197369.

6. Patterson, Kerry, Joseph Grenny, Al Switzler, and Ron McMillan. Crucial Conversations: Tools For Talking When Stakes Are High. New York: McGraw-Hill, 2012.

Create Your Opportunities by Augusto "Cookie" Rojas

1. "Writing S.M.A.R.T. Goals." Hr.virginia.edu. Accessed June 18, 2018. http://www.hr.virginia.edu/uploads/documents/media/Writing_SMART_Goals.pdf.

2. Fischer, David. The 50 Coolest Jobs In Sports: Who's Got Them, What They Do, and How You Can Get One! Australia: Arco/Thomson Learning, 2001.

3. Jerry Maguire. Directed by Cameron Crowe. Performed by Tom Cruise and Cuba Gooding Jr. United States: TriStar Pictures, 1996. DVD.

4. "The Drowning Man." Truthbook.com. Accessed June 18, 2018. https://truthbook.com/stories/funny-god/the-drowning-man.

5. "King Cake." Wikipedia. Accessed June 18, 2018. https://en.wikipedia.org/wiki/King_cake.

6. "2017 Logomania - Finals Results." Baseball America. Accessed June 18,

2018. https://www.baseballamerica.com/stories/2017-logomania-finals-results/.

Passion Creates Brand Advocates by David Lorenz

1. "TinCaps Concessions Options." MiLB.com. Accessed June 18, 2018. https://www.milb.com/fort-wayne/ballpark/concessions-options.

2. "Parkview Field Ranked No. 1 Ballpark Experience in Minors." MiLB.com. Accessed June 18, 2018. https://www.milb.com/fort-wayne/news/parkview-field-ranked-no-1-ballpark-experience-in-minors/c-207549760.

3. Swindler, Andy. "Tuthill Corporation Exists to Wake the World | Mabbly." Science of Story. October 6, 2016. Accessed June 18, 2018. https://scienceofstory.org/tuthill-corporation-exists-wake-world/.

4. "107 Famous Quotes About Change in Life, Yourself and The World." Bright Drops. August 13, 2017. Accessed June 18, 2018. http://brightdrops.com/quotes-about-change.

5. Calkins, Matt. "Dick Enberg: Heartbroken Yet Happy." Sandiegouniontribune.com. September 26, 2014. Accessed June 18, 2018. http://www.sandiegouniontribune.com/sports/padres/sdut-dick-enberg-heartbroken-happy-padres-2014sep26-story.html.

Never Give Up On The Dream by Derek Franks

1. "San Francisco Giants World Series History: MLB Champions, Results, Stats." FOX Sports. Accessed June 18, 2018. https://www.foxsports.com/mlb/world-series-history?teamId=26.

2. Rovell, Darren. "Astros Affiliate Mulls Keeping Tacos Nickname After Large Early Fan Interest." ESPN. August 11, 2015. Accessed June 18, 2018. http://www.espn.com/mlb/story/_/id/13309077/fresno-grizzlies-specialty-rename-tacos-already-paying-off.

3. Yurong, Dale, and Tommy Tran. "Fresno Grizzlies Sign Deal with Astros, Cut Ties with Giants." ABC30 Fresno. September 18, 2014. Accessed June 18, 2018. http://abc30.com/sports/fresno-grizzlies-sign-deal-with-astros-cut-ties-with-giants/314399/.

4. Grizzlies, Fresno. "The Grizzlies Are National Champions." MiLB.com. September 22, 2015. Accessed June 18, 2018. https://www.milb.com/fresno/news/the-grizzlies-are-national-champions/c-151100670.

From Bottom to Top by C. Ryan Shelton

1. "DiSC Profile - What Is DiSC®? The DiSC Personality Profile Explained." DiSCProfile.com. Accessed June 18, 2018. https://www.discprofile.com/what-is-disc/overview/.

2. Spranger, Edward, and Paul John William Pigors. Types of Men: The Psychology and Ethics of Personality. Halle (Saale): M. Niemeyer, 1928.

Feeding Fan Ballpark Experiences by Joe Hudson

1. "The Original McDonald's: A Museum in San Bernardino." California Through My Lens. January 08, 2018. Accessed June 18, 2018. https://californiathroughmylens.com/original-mcdonalds-museum-san-bernardino.

Market Your Assets Off by Greg Coleman

1. "Promotional Seminar Awards." MiLB™ Promotional Seminar Awards. Accessed June 19, 2018. https://promo.milb.net/Awards.aspx.

2. Whitzman, April. "Team Ghost Riders." MLB.com. July 19, 2013. Accessed June 19, 2018. https://www.mlb.com/news/team-ghost-riders/c-54051730.

3. "MiLB Teams Take Eclipse 2017 in Perfect Stride." MiLB.com. August 21, 2017. Accessed June 19, 2018. https://www.milb.com/milb/news/minor-league-teams-take-eclipse-2017-in-perfect-stride/c-249772396.

4. McClure, Bruce. "When's the next US Total Solar Eclipse?" EarthSky. August 22, 2017. Accessed June 19, 2018. http://earthsky.org/astronomy-essentials/whens-the-next-total-solar-eclipse-in-the-us.

5. Williams, Alex. "How Fidget Spinners Became a Hula Hoop for Generation Z." The New York Times. May 06, 2017. Accessed June 19, 2018. https://www.nytimes.com/2017/05/06/style/fidget-spinners.html.

6. Report, Staff. "How Other Minor League Baseball Teams Were Named." KVIA. August 23, 2016. Accessed June 19, 2018. http://www.kvia.com/news/how-other-minor-league-baseball-teams-were-named/55529526.

7. Hill, Benjamin. "Hot Rods Claim Year's Best Promo." MiLB.com. October 14, 2009. Accessed June 19, 2018. https://www.milb.com/milb/news/hot-rods-claim-years-best-promo/c-7450724.

The Supervisor Grind Is Adapt Or Die by Michael Abramson

1. Abramson, Michael. "OUTSIDE LOOKING IN: A NON-BASEBALL GUY IN A BASEBALL WORLD." LinkedIn. June 21, 2017. Accessed June 18, 2018. https://www.linkedin.com/pulse/outside-looking-non-baseball-guy-baseball-world-michael-abramson/.

2. "Former Panthers Inducted into the Sac City Athletics Hall of Fame." Sacramento City College. Accessed June 18, 2018. http://sccpanthers.losrios.edu/sports/bsb/hall_of_fame.

Slow To Hire, Quick To Fire by Amy Venuto

1. Torre, John. "Dale Carnegie Principle #26-Let the Other Person Save Face." Dale Carnegie Training of Central & Southern New Jersey. July 27, 2011. Accessed June 18, 2018. http://www.dalecarnegiewaynj.com/2011/07/27/dale-carnegie-principle-26—let-the-other-person-save-face/.

Service Clients Like A Madman by Brent Conkel

1. Bastian, Jordan, and Carrie Muskat. "Chicago Cubs Win 2016 World Series." MLB.com. November 3, 2016. Accessed June 18, 2018. https://www.mlb.com/news/chicago-cubs-win-2016-world-series/c-207938228.

2. "Cub Club at Principal Park - Des Moines, IA." Yelp. April 14, 2016. Accessed June 18, 2018. https://www.yelp.com/biz/cub-club-at-principal-park-des-moines.

Retention Means Reinvestment by Jeff Eiseman

1. Spedden, Zach. "Dayton Dragons Maintain Long-Term Success." Ballpark Digest. May 31, 2018. Accessed June 19, 2018. https://ballparkdigest. com/2018/05/31/dayton-dragons-maintain-long-term-success/.

2. Lefko, Perry. "The Bizarre Story of the Las Vegas Posse and the CFL's Stint in Sin City." Sports.Vice.com. June 22, 2017. Accessed June 19, 2018. https:// sports.vice.com/en_ca/article/mbjyyn/the-bizarre-story-of-the-las-vegas-posse-and-the-cfls-stint-in-sin-city.

3. "Las Vegas Sting Archives • Fun While It Lasted." Fun While It Lasted. Accessed June 19, 2018. http://funwhileitlasted.net/tag/las-vegas-sting/.

4. Robbins, Danny. "NCAA Punishes UNLV : College Basketball: Sanctions in Daniels Case Will Limit Television Appearances, but Won't Keep Rebels out of Postseason Play." Los Angeles Times. November 10, 1993. Accessed June 19, 2018. http://articles.latimes.com/1993-11-10/sports/sp-55341_1_ basketball-program.

5. "Las Vegas Thunder, International Hockey League." Fun While It Lasted. December 06, 2017. Accessed June 19, 2018. http://funwhileitlasted. net/2013/11/30/1993-1999-las-vegas-thunder/.

"Free" Is The Foulest Word Of Them All by John Dittrich

1. Reports, Staff. "Former 89ers GM King Dies. Dick King: 1920-2007." NewsOK.com. January 24, 2007. Accessed June 19, 2018. https://newsok.com/ article/3002924/former-89ers-gm-king-diesbrspan-classhl2dick-king-1920-2007span.

2. Durrett, Richard. "'Mr. Baseball' Bragan Dies at 92." ESPN. January 22, 2010. Accessed June 19, 2018. http://www.espn.com/dallas/mlb/news/ story?id=4848392.

3. Honeymoon In Vegas. Directed by Andrew Bergman. By Andrew Bergman. Performed by James Caan, Nicolas Cage, and Sarah Jessica Parker. United States: Columbia Pictures, 1992. DVD.

Respect The Process by Mike Birling

"Tampa Bay Rays Minor League Affiliates." Baseball-Reference.com. Accessed June 18, 2018. https://www.baseball-reference.com/register/affiliate.cgi?id=TBD.

Selling Baseball Isn't Enough by Josh Olerud

1. Sheinin, Dave. "Stephen Strasburg Shines in Second Rehab Start." The Washington Post. August 12, 2011. Accessed June 18, 2018. https://www.washingtonpost.com/sports/nationals/stephen-strasburg-shines-in-second-rehab-start/2011/08/12/gIQAaWt9BJ_story.html?utm_term=.0a8e429c5bc4.

A

B

C

D

G

game 22, 24, 28, 29, 42, 50, 57-59, 61, 62, 65-67, 72-74, 77, 78, 80, 87, 90, 92, 93, 99, 108, 109, 119, 121, 125, 127-129, 131, 138-142, 144, 148, 153, 155, 156, 158, 163-165, 170-180, 182-188, 195, 196, 199-202, 205-209, 213, 220, 232, 246-255, 260, 262-269, 272, 274, 277, 284, 285, 287, 291-295, 297-303, 306-309, 311, 313-315, 317-322, 325, 326, 329, 330, 332-334, 336-341, 344-348, 350-352

gameday 23, 90, 92, 209, 296

gate 25, 28, 59, 62, 93, 94, 154, 165, 213, 246, 298, 300, 314, 320, 335, 337, 341, 348, 351

gate-keeper 67, 278

giveaway 73, 170, 171, 174, 177-179, 181-185, 187, 188, 293, 294, 299, 309, 314, 318-320, 341, 351

GM 35, 189, 255, 345, 346

goals 5, 17, 18, 20, 23, 24, 29, 32, 41, 43, 46, 47, 50-52, 54-59, 61, 63, 66, 69, 70, 76, 81, 84, 86, 88, 93, 109, 113, 118, 119, 123, 132, 133, 136, 152, 154, 155, 157, 161, 163, 164, 170, 188, 195, 198, 203, 206, 212, 214, 217, 226, 227, 231, 234-236, 238-243, 261, 266, 267, 273, 275, 285, 286, 294, 307, 326, 330, 344, 346, 347, 350, 358

gossip 85, 86, 90, 210, 211, 229, 231, 232

groups 16, 19, 23-27, 36, 42, 65, 67, 69, 71, 73-75, 79, 84, 88, 98, 105, 112, 120-122, 126-128, 131, 132, 136, 137, 139, 141, 145, 148, 151, 153, 154, 157, 160, 173-176, 179, 188, 195, 203, 213, 220, 231, 234, 243, 249-251, 255, 259, 261, 266, 268, 270-272, 274, 286, 287, 295, 301, 307, 318, 324-330, 349-351

H

hand-delivered 103

hand-written 93, 100, 102

I

K

kid 25, 33, 47, 57, 67, 72, 73, 75, 81, 118, 126, 131, 140, 141, 152, 161, 166, 173, 185, 252, 285, 295, 296, 301, 302, 330, 339, 340, 344

L

lapsed-agreement 109, 267

leading 3, 16-19, 22, 24, 26-31, 34-38, 41, 42, 49, 55, 69, 73, 74, 83, 86, 106, 112, 114, 115, 121, 136, 137, 139, 141, 144, 146, 148, 149, 194, 195, 197-199, 203, 212, 214, 217, 220, 230, 231, 236, 237, 239, 240, 243, 264-266, 269, 270, 275, 326-329, 335, 346, 354, 358

leads 32, 34, 88, 98, 138-140, 144, 145, 147, 161, 180, 203, 217, 234, 249, 252, 271

lease 132, 248, 249, 252-254, 261, 264, 265, 287

Leverage 74, 254, 330

listen 17, 29, 33, 46, 57, 65, 69, 70, 85, 97, 99, 101, 106, 111, 113, 115, 173, 193, 197-199, 201, 214, 219, 277, 278, 296, 346

luxury 200, 250, 264, 301, 354

M

mail 16, 62, 68, 89, 102, 301

manage 16-24, 33-36, 38, 42, 48, 61, 67, 85, 121, 132, 136, 145, 146, 149, 155, 166, 170, 194, 197, 202, 213, 235-237, 239, 268, 269, 271, 274, 276, 277, 281, 286, 320, 326, 328, 329, 337, 344-347

management 17-22, 24, 25, 34, 36, 37, 54, 61, 68, 69, 71, 89, 95, 121, 122, 136, 137,

P

Q

qualifies 178

quantify 206, 282

questioning 18, 19, 25, 27, 28, 32-35, 38-42, 46, 47, 50, 54, 55, 62, 63, 93, 96, 98, 101, 121, 153, 176-179, 199, 204, 217-220, 223, 225, 230, 231, 256, 262, 273, 277, 284, 296, 299, 304, 316, 319, 326, 327, 330, 333, 338, 340, 346, 354

R

rain 57, 170, 294, 299-301, 337

recommend 51, 91, 96, 103, 105, 106, 159, 223, 226, 227, 239, 269, 336, 337

recommendation 187, 220, 223, 224, 240, 270, 327

referrals 53, 54, 56, 108, 138, 162, 199, 248, 255, 270, 277, 278, 281, 327

relationships 24-26, 29, 30, 51, 55, 57, 61, 63, 64, 68, 73, 77, 80, 85, 87-89, 91-94, 96, 98-102, 104, 106, 108, 109, 114, 141, 165, 181, 182, 185, 187, 201, 204, 227, 229, 234, 247, 255, 267, 273-276, 279, 284, 286, 288, 293, 301, 303, 304, 321, 327, 328, 330, 341, 346, 348-350

relocated 18, 49, 75, 189, 282

relocation 31, 261, 263, 264

renewals 26, 30, 65, 76, 86, 89-93, 95-97, 99, 100, 102-105, 108, 109, 123, 132, 144, 240-242, 248-250, 253, 255, 259-268, 270, 271, 273, 274, 276, 278-288, 303

representation 65, 90, 110, 176, 182, 232, 283, 295, 348

representative 20, 24, 50, 53, 77, 88, 92, 98, 101-103, 108-110, 120, 126, 132, 135, 178, 203, 234, 253, 265, 271-274, 277-279, 281, 282, 284-286, 288, 325, 327, 329, 330

T